APOSTOLIC AND
POST-APOSTOLIC TIMES

BY

LEONHARD GOPPELT

TRANSLATED BY ROBERT A. GUELICH

BAKER BOOK HOUSE
Grand Rapids, Michigan

Baker Book House edition
issued under special arrangement
with Harper & Row, Publishers, Inc.

ISBN: 0-8010-3712-3

This book was first published in English by A. and C. Black Ltd., London in 1970. It is here reprinted by arrangement.

Translated from the German, *Die apostolische und nachapostolische Zeit*, by Leonhard Goppelt, being Section A of Vol. I of *Die Kirche in ihrer Geschichte: ein Handbuch*, edited by Kurt Dietrich Schmidt and Ernst Wolf (Vandenhoeck and Ruprecht, Göttingen and Zürich).

CONTENTS

AUTHOR'S FOREWORD

A HISTORY of the Apostolic Age recounts the whole development of the Church and her message in the New Testament times. This development is actually the emergence of the Church and her message from the witness to Jesus, the Crucified and Resurrected One, a witness which struggled with both Judaism and Hellenism from without as well as with Nomism and Gnosticism from within. The 'history of the Apostolic Age' is to the understanding of the New Testament what the 'history of Israel' is to the understanding of the Old Testament, for each presents the framework for all questions regarding the introduction, theology and exegesis of the Testaments.

The following portrayal of this period was originally written as the first, self-contained part of *Die Kirche in ihrer Geschichte, Ein Handbuch*, edited by K. D. Schmidt and E. Wolf. As a result the material had to be presented in a very condensed form. My goal has been twofold. First, I have sought to give information about the technical and extensive discussion of the various problems. Secondly, thirty years have elapsed since the last presentation in Germany of a history of the Apostolic Age, and these have been some of the most productive years in New Testament studies, so this is an attempt to fill this void by offering a new overall picture of the period under consideration.

I should like to acknowledge the work of Robert Guelich, who in 1964–67 completed his doctoral studies under me in Hamburg, for his work in translating this book into English. Because of the very condensed form of the material and the difficult German text, his work has demanded far more than that of the usual translation. It has involved not only expanding the text but also bringing together literature relevant to the English-speaking audience. As is always the case with books, several others have played an essential role in bringing this one to completion. I am deeply grateful to each one, in particular to Prof. G. E. Ladd of Fuller Theological Seminary of California, U.S.A., who kindly read through the majority of the translation and made numerous helpful suggestions for both the text and the literature, and to Mrs. R. Guelich for typing the manuscript.

It is my sincere desire that this book might also offer a picture of the fundamental development of the Church and her message to many of the English-speaking world, a picture which will help towards a better understanding of the New Testament.

Hamburg, Advent, 1967   L. G.

TRANSLATOR'S FOREWORD

THE so-called "Apostolic Age" is often approached in one of two ways. On the one hand is the more uncritical approach, which sees the developments within the emerging Church of the first century primarily through the eyes of the Book of Acts, using the New Testament epistles simply to supply the missing details. This view assumes that Acts was intended to be essentially a history of the early Church. On the other hand is the more critical approach, which first began to surface in the eighteenth century and which places the New Testament documents under the scrutiny of the historical-critical methodology. The result is a "history" of the Apostolic Age frequently colored by the dominant philosophical orientation of the "historian" and often at odds with the biblical witness. Since American evangelicals have tended to favor the former approach while much of German biblical scholarship imported to American soil has reflected the latter, American evangelicals have had considerable reserve towards biblical criticism in general and towards "German scholarship" in particular.

As a biblical scholar, Leonhard Goppelt (1911–1973) was neither radically critical nor uncritical in his approach to scripture. Rather his work stands in a long line of German scholarship that takes the biblical witness seriously while recognizing that this witness was placed in a given historical context. This approach to biblical studies sprang originally from the Great Awakening on the Continent. Its roots lay in the hermeneutical heritage of the Reformation (*sola scriptura, analogia fidei*); yet it was increasingly open to the contributions of the historical method during the past two centuries. This line of scholars has come to be associated with the term *Heilsgeschichte* ("redemptive history") and identified with names like von Hofmann, Beck, Zahn, Schlatter, Kittel, Schniewind and, most familiar to the American scene, Cullmann.

In Professor Goppelt's own words, the task of biblical studies is to "bring the principles of the historical-critical approach to scripture . . . into a critical dialogue with what the New Testament understands itself to be. The New Testament understands itself to be fundamentally . . . a witness to the God of the Old Testament whose redemptive,

fulfilling event has its center and focus in Jesus."[1] While recognizing
that God has uniquely and ultimately revealed himself through the
scriptures' witness to this redemptive event (*sola scriptura*), one must
also recognize that God has done so in and through historical contexts
(historical criticism). Professor Goppelt therefore uses historical
criticism in conjunction with a hermeneutic that takes seriously the
revelatory claim of the scriptures in order to ascertain the differences
between the New Testament message and that of its religious environment—whether Jewish, Greek or even the Gnostic or Early Catholic
tendencies within the early Church. The unique message of the New
Testament by comparison with its environment is a testimony to the
authenticity of the heart of its message. This message, given to and
developed by the apostles, is what Professor Goppelt has referred to as
the apostolic norm that is preserved in the canonical writings of the
New Testament in contrast to the other, noncanonical writings of
the early Church.

In his *Apostolic and Post-Apostolic Times* Leonhard Goppelt seeks
to define this apostolic witness, its beginnings and its emergence from
the Palestinian community. By noting the struggles of the Church
with Judaism both within and outside itself as well as its struggles
with Hellenistic influences in a Gentile world, he examines the apostolic
norm as it appears in the Church's interaction with legalistic Jewish-
Christianity, pre-Gnostic syncretism and incipient Early Catholicism.
Consequently the Apostolic Age is for Goppelt not merely the first
chapter of Church history, but the norm for all Church history.

The translator was privileged not only to have studied under Professor Goppelt but also to have had extensive help in translating this
work from Mrs. Dora Goppelt and Dr. Jurgen Roloff. Naturally the
translator accepts all responsibility for inadequacies in rendering such
a rich, compact treatise into English.

Easter, 1977   R. G.

---

[1] L. Goppelt, *Theologie des Neuen Testaments* (1975), i, 50.

ABBREVIATIONS

ARW   *Archiv für Religionswissenschaft.*
BZ   *Biblische Zeitschrift.*
EKL   *Evangelisches Kirchenlexikon.*
Ev-luthKZ   *Evangelisch-lutherische Kirchenzeitung.*
EMZ   *Evangelische Missionszeitschrift.*
Ev. Theol.   *Evangelische Theologie.*
Hennecke[2]   Hennecke, Edgar, *Neutestamentliche Apokryphen* ([2]1924).
Hennecke[3]   Hennecke, Edgar, *Neutestamentliche Apokryphen* (vol. I, 1959, vol. II, 1964), ed. by W. Schneemelcher. Cf. Eng. trans. ed. by R. McL. Wilson.
Hist. Jhrb.   *Historisches Jahrbuch der Görres-Gesellschaft.*
HNT   *Handbuch zum Neuen Testament,* bgr. von Hans Lietzmann, hrsg. von G. Bornkamm.
IDD   *Interpreter's Dictionary of the Bible.*
IntKZ   *Internationale kirchliche Zeitschrift.*
JBL.   *Journal of Biblical Literature.*
JTS   *Journal of Theological Studies.*
MünchThZ   *Münchner theologische Zeitschrift.*
Ned. Theol. Tijdschr. *Nederlands Theologisch Tijdschrift.*
NKZ   *Neue kirchliche Zeitschrift.*
Nov. Test.   *Novum Testamentum.*
NTD   *Das Neue Testament Deutsch,* ed. by P. Althaus and W. Friedrich.
NTS   *New Testament Studies.*
P.W.   Pauly-Wissowa, *Realencyclopädie der klassischen Altertumswissenschaft* (1893 ff.).
RAC   *Reallexikon für Antike und Christentum,* ed. by T. Klausner, (1941, 1950 ff.).
RSR   *Recherches de science religieuse.*

Rev. Bibl.	*Revue biblique.*
RE	*Realencyclopädie für protestantische Theologie und Kirche.*
RGG²	*Die Religion in Geschichte und Gegenwart* (2nd edition).
RGG³	*Die Religion in Geschichte und Gegenwart* (3rd edition).
RHPR	*Revue d'histoire et de philosophie religieuses.*
SAB	*Sitzungsberichte der Preussischen Akadamie der Wissenschaften zu Berlin.*
SAH	*Sitzungsberichte der Akadamie der Wissenschaften zu Heidelberg.*
S.–B.	H. L. Strack and P. Billerbeck, *Kommentar zum Neuen Testament aus Talmud und Midrasch* (1922–28).
Stud. Theol.	*Studia Theologica.*
ThLZ	*Theologische Literaturzeitschrift.*
ThR	*Theologische Rundschau.*
TriererThZ	*Trierer Theologische Zeistchrift.*
T.U.	*Texte und Untersuchungen zur Geschichte der altchristlichen Literatur.*
TWNT	*Theologische Wörterbuch zum Neuen Testament,* ed. by G. Kittel and G. Friedrich, (1933 ff.). Cf. Eng. trans. by G. Bromiley.
Vig. Christ.	*Vigilae Christianae.*
W. A.	M. Luther, *Werke: Kritische Gesamtausgabe,* Weimar (1833 ff.).
ZKG	*Zeitschrift für Kirchengeschichte.*
ZKTheol.	*Zeitschrift für katholische Theologie.*
ZNTW	*Zeitschrift für die neutestamentliche Wissenschaft und die Kunde der älteren Kirche.*
ZRG	*Zeitschrift für Religions–und Geistesgeschichte.*
ZThK	*Zeitschrift für Theologie und Kirche.*

INTRODUCTION[1]

THE history of Christianity in New Testament times is not the first chapter of church history but rather the setting of the stage for all church history. It is not the history of the Church as such but rather the history of the formation of the Church. Only towards the end of the first century did the fellowship comprised of Jesus' followers take on the form which it has maintained throughout the centuries. Only then did it become a separate entity apart from Jews and Gentiles, an entity within history composed of the eschatological People of God drawn from the peoples of the world.

The formation of the Church goes hand in hand with the formation of her message. In the period from the conclusion of Jesus' ministry to the end of the first century, the apostolic witness that has been authoritative in the Church throughout the centuries took on the form which found its expression in the New Testament canon. This was recognised therefore, as early as I Clement and Ignatius, to be a unique epoch. Eusebius called it the 'ἀποστολικοὶ χρόνου', the 'Apostolic Age'.[2] Consequently, since this period is bound up with both the introductory and the theological aspects of the New Testament studies, just as church history is entwined in Christianity's literary history and the history of dogma, it is the task of New Testament scholarship to depict the Apostolic Age.

In the history of New Testament scholarship the concern for an historical picture of early Christianity together with the various 'Lives' of Jesus gave rise to, and furthered, an historical investigation of the New Testament. Until the eighteenth century the earliest history of Christianity was recounted by lucidly paraphrasing the Acts of the Apostles and expanding it in light of the other documents of the New Testament and

---

[1] Literature on the history of the problem: E. v. Dobschütz, *Probleme des Apostolischen Zeitalters* (1904); J. Weiss, 'Das Problem der Entstehung des Christentums', *ARW* 16 (1913), 423–515; R. Bultmann, 'Die urchristliche Religion (1915–25)', *ARW* 24 (1926), 83–164; H. Windisch, 'Urchristentum', *ThR* 5 (1933), 186–200, 239–258, 289–301, 319–336; W. G. Kümmel, 'Das Urchristentum', *ThR* 14 (1942), 81–95, 155–173; *ThR* 17 (1948–49), 3–50, 103–142; *ThR* 18 (1950), 1–53; 'Judenchristentum', *RGG*³, iii, 967–972; *Das Neue Testament: Geschichte der Erforschung seiner Probleme* (1958), 596; L. Goppelt, *Jesus, Paul and Judaism*, 15–19 (Eng. trans. 1964 of *Christentum und Judentum* (1954), 1–15); H. Conzelmann, 'Heidenchristentum', *RGG*³, iii, 128–141.

[2] Eusebius, *H.E.* 3, 31, 6.

the early Church. In the eighteenth century, however, a new trend developed. Springing from diverse backgrounds in the Enlightenment, a desire to understand the earliest stage of Christianity in a purely historical perspective arose in German Protestantism.[3] This new development meant that the early period of Christianity would have to be reworked in terms of the historical methodology of 'criticism, analogy and correlation'.[4] It also meant that the period would be seen more or less consciously from a modern philosophical world-view rather than, as previously, from the point of view of the Church itself. This presupposed world-view is reflected especially in the scope and structure of the several studies.

F. C. Baur, conditioned by Hegelian philosophy, devised the first all-encompassing system according to these principles. He saw the decisive element to be the Idea which was embodied initially in Jesus and which then was further developed dialectally in the history of primitive Christianity (pp. 63, 147). This idealism of the 'Tübingen School'[5] was replaced in the second half of the nineteenth century by a positivism developed under the influence of neo-Kantianism by the school of A. Ritschl[6] (most notably represented by A. von Harnack).[7] Here 'religious personality' appeared as the decisive factor, as seen in Paul and John who stand in sharp relief against the background of the Christian community.[8]

Emerging around 1900 the history-of-religions school[9] stressed, in contrast to its predecessors, the religion and cult of the community. It sought to describe both the history and the theology of earliest Christianity together in a history of the religion of primitive Christianity. At this point, working within a world-view of a consistent historicism, the method became 'purely historical'. Nineteenth-century studies had relied especially upon the help of source criticism. This was now supplemented by a form-critical investigation and an historical analysis of the

[3] F. C. Baur, *Paulus der Apostel Jesu Christi* (1845), 1 ff.; *Das Christentum und die christliche Kirche der drei ersten Jahrhunderte* (1853, [2]1860), 1–22.

[4] E. Troeltsch, *Gesammelte Schriften* ([2]1922), ii, 734.

[5] Last of all, O. Pfleiderer, *Das Urchristentum* ([2]1902).

[6] A. Ritschl, *Die Entstehung der altkatholischen Kirche* ([2]1857).

[7] A. v. Harnack, *History of Dogma*, i, esp. 89 ff., 218 ff.

[8] A number of portrayals of this topic arose more or less independently of the history-of-religions school under the emblem of positivism: C. Weizsäcker, *The Apostolic Age of the Christian Church*, 1894–95 (Eng. trans. of *Das apostolische Zeitalter der christlichen Kirche*, [3]1902); E. v. Dobschütz, *Die urchristlichen Gemeinden* (1902); *Das apostolische Zeitalter* ([2]1917); R. Knopf, *Das nachapostolische Zeitalter* (1905); J. Weiss, *Earliest Christianity* (A.D. 30–150) (Eng. trans., 1937 of *Das Urchristentum* (1917)); H. Lietzmann, *The History of the Early Church*: vol. i, *The Beginnings of the Christian Church*, 1953 (Eng. trans. of *Geschichte der alten Kirche* (vol. i, 1932, [3]1953)). Completely independent of any 'school' is the work from the ancient historian, E. Meyer, *Ursprung und Anfänge des Christentums* (i, ii, 1921; iii, 1923).

[9] W. Bousset, *Kyrios Christos* (1913, [4]1935); in addition, cf. the works of W. Heitmüller, H. Weinel, P. Wernle and W. Wrede.

tradition behind these sources with a view to their *Sitz im Leben*. In addition, the religious environment of primitive Christianity, little regarded up to this point, was now brought fully into account according to the principle of 'analogy and correlation'. Nevertheless, the essence of the history of primitive Christianity was not grasped by this means since, in the final analysis, primitive Christianity claims to be without analogy. The picture of primitive Christianity is just as impossible to ascertain 'purely historically' as is the picture of Jesus. As Troeltsch himself has said, even 'purely historical' involves a 'complete world view'.

For this reason, and in keeping with the general upheaval in the history of thought after 1918, the scholars from a history-of-religions background not only exchanged their historicism for an understanding of history based on existential philosophy, but at the same time attempted theologically to open this philosophical framework to the revelatory claim of the New Testament documents. It was at this point that the course of scholarship pioneered by Rudolf Bultmann and Martin Dibelius first became prominent. As Bultmann explained, the history-of-religions school saw only the historical phenomena, which of necessity was mythological.[10] The essential element had to be extracted from this phenomenon through 'existential interpretation', i.e. theologically, through demythologization.[11] In other words the history of primitive Christianity is an offshoot of the respective Jewish or Hellenistic religious history; as to its essential content, however, it is both the history of the *kerygma* and of the Church. In line with this, Bultmann's *Theologie des Neuen Testaments* also includes the main outlines of the history of primitive Christianity.

Pursuing this method German scholarship, stemming from a 'purely historical' orientation, found itself close to a second line of thought which emerged from the Awakening. Having taken up the hermeneutical approach of the Reformation, this latter line of thought had also adapted itself more and more to the historical method in the course of the nineteenth and twentieth centuries. Nevertheless, even in this association it had attempted to remain as free as possible from any presupposed worldview. Thus during the nineteenth century, in order to prevent the history of primitive Christianity from being absorbed into history in general, it developed the concept of *Heilsgeschichte* which—while using temporally conditioned expressions—held fast the essential claim of the New Testament. This school of thought included J. C. K. von Hofmann, J. T. Beck, T. Zahn, A. Schlatter, G. Kittel and J. Schniewind. Schlatter's *Die*

[10] R. Bultmann, *Glauben und Verstehen*, i (³1958), 256 ff.
[11] *Ibid.*, p. 123; cf. *Kerygma and Myth*, ed. H. W. Bartsch, i, (Eng. trans., 1961), 17–44.

Geschichte der ersten Christenheit stands as the last complete portrayal of our subject from this point of view.[12]

For the Anglo-American investigation of this subject in the nineteenth century F. J. Foakes-Jackson and Kirsopp Lake's standard work on Acts offers a good survey.[13] At that time such studies were made independently of German scholarship, whereas today there is a mutual interchange. New Testament studies internationally have generally accepted the form of the historical method as well as the attempt to evaluate the New Testament writings as *kergyma*, i.e. God's proclamation to the Church during the first century. These common presuppositions within New Testament studies have made possible today an international and ecumenical conversation far beyond a mere exchange of detailed historical-philological research. The remaining differences in hermeneutical principles arise from the various ecclesiastical backgrounds of the respective scholars.[14]

A portrayal of the history of primitive Christianity is thus not simply dependent upon an evaluation of innumerable historical problems arising from the sources. Rather, more than any other portrayal of history, it depends upon the author's approach and existential involvement with the recorded events. Such history is truly scholarly only when it makes clear the historical uncertainties and the differences of approach, and not when it asserts that a single historical solution and one particular approach are the only 'scholarly' possibilities. Admittedly, such a procedure is possible only in light of one's own evaluation and approach. If there is neither exegesis nor portrayal of history apart from presuppositions, then we must make our presuppositions as clear as possible both to ourselves and to others. We cannot separate historical events and their meaning. We can however distinguish to a degree between event and interpretation, and thence between historical uncertainties and method of approach.

[12] A third approach, the historical-positive, whose roots stem from biblicism and pietism, has a limited representation on this topic in works like P. Neander, *Geschichte der Pflanzung und Leitung der christlichen Kirche durch die Apostel* (2 vols., 1832–33) or P. Feine, *Der Apostel Paulus* (1927).

[13] J. S. Foakes-Jackson and K. Lake, ed., *The Beginnings of Christianity*, Part I: *The Acts of the Apostles* (1920–33), i–v. A. C. McGiffert, *A History of Christianity in the Apostolic Age*, (1897, ⁵1951) which follows Harnack; B. H. Streeter, *The Rise of Christianity* (*The Cambridge Ancient History*, xi, 1936), which is similar to Lietzmann's portrayal; C. T. Craig, *The Beginning of Christianity* (1943); P. Carrington, *The Early Christian Church* (2 vols., 1957); G. B. Caird, *The Apostolic Age* (1955); F. Filson, *A New Testament History* (1965). In French: J. Lebreton and J. Zeiller, *Histoire de l'Eglise* (i, 1938); M. Goguel, *Jésus et les origines du Christianisme:* vol. i, *La naissance du Christianisme*, vol. ii, *L'Eglise primitive* (1946–47), *Jesus and the Origins of Christianity:* vol. i, *The Birth of Christianity* (1953), vol. ii, *The Primitive Church* (1964). In Dutch: J. H. Waszink, W. C. van Unnik, C. de Beus (ed.), *Het oudste Christendom en de antieke cultuur* (1951).

[14] L. Goppelt, 'Theological Bible Study', in *The Encyclopedia of the Lutheran Church*, ed. J. Bodensieck (1965), pp. 239–246.

Even after two hundred years of intensive study, the analysis of the sources which gave rise to the historical uncertainties has by no means been concluded. In general, any elucidation of the early history of Christianity stems solely from Christian sources, and the only writings available as primary sources from the period up to c. A.D. 125 are those which were accepted by the Early Catholic Church as 'orthodox'. These were essentially the books of the New Testament and the Apostolic Fathers. Later they were expanded by a fragmentary tradition which still needs fresh examination.

Three possible ways of helping to fill in the picture and to clarify it have been suggested. 1. One may attempt to deduce the various starting points within the primitive Church from an examination of its later development. Since the development did not take place uniformly, however, much more caution is required than has been practised in the past.[15] 2. A study of the environment from which the Church arose supplies not only the temporal framework but also the material from which the new movement gained its forms of expression. Nevertheless, when drawing conclusions one must remember that the early Church herself pointed to the great contrast separating her from her environment which disrupted any direct continuity. 3. The repeatedly disrupted stream of historical development running from Judaism and Hellenism through primitive Christianity to the Early Catholic Church does not appear in the primary sources merely in isolated instances, but as a recurrent strain throughout these sources. This is because the primary sources were not statements and reports temporally isolated, but rather expressions of tradition. In the Gospels we see today an expression of a history of tradition in which diverse situations within the Church were reflected, and we examine the Epistles for the early Church tradition which they have reworked. Such an analysis, however, still falls short of any widely acknowledged conclusions.

It has become increasingly evident today that the classical form-critical analysis of the Synoptic tradition related the pericopes too immediately to the situation within the Church. In so doing, both the meaning of the text and the situation of the earliest Church were misinterpreted. For example, the Sabbath controversies in Mark ii.23–iii.6 did not intend merely to justify the Sabbath practices of the Church[16]—the Palestinian Church kept the Sabbath commandment—but to explain in particular why and for what purpose Jesus died (Mark iii.6; cf. pp. 31 f.). The *kerygmatic* goal which determined the formation and the first collections of the pericopes still remains dominant in

---

[15] Cf. for example the extreme of H. Lietzmann, *Mass and the Lord's Supper* (1964).
[16] R. Bultmann, *History of the Synoptic Tradition* (1963), 12, 16 f., 48 f. (Eng. trans., of *Die Geschichte der synoptischen Tradition* ([2]1931), 9, 14 f., 49 f.).

the Gospels as we know them. Matthew's contradictory statements on missions (x.5 f.; xxviii.19 f.) strongly suggest that he understood Jesus' earthly ministry to have its own definite meaning in itself. Looking backwards in time, the Evangelist reflected upon a past self-disclosure of God (the Old Testament quotations), yet at the same time, by means of his redaction he *kerygmatically* interpreted it from a post-Easter point of view for the Christian Church (cf. §2, 2). He did not make an arbitrary selection but was conscious of his obligation to the tradition, and in precisely this way made it meaningful for the modern reader. When one ignores the first aspect in favour of the second, the inferences are improperly applied to the situation of the Church. For example, if one infers from passages such as Matt. xvii.24–27 that Matthew's congregation '. . . is still attached to Judaism and that it in no sense claims for itself exemption from the taxation of the Diaspora congregations',[17] one encounters a contradiction of the historical situation. At the time when this Gospel was written the Temple had already been destroyed and none of the subsequent taxes which replaced the Temple tax could have come into consideration here. If Mark xvi.7 is taken as an exhortation, originating from the days of the Jewish insurrection, to the Jerusalem congregation to move to Galilee in view of the expected parousia,[18] then it would contradict the exegetical findings concerning the actual historical situation. At the very beginning of the insurrection the Christians had to flee from the Jewish territory (cf. p. 61).

The methodological principle of classical form criticism that '. . . the congregation created the tradition found in the Gospels, and these give primary information about the circumstances which determined its life',[19] is in need of thorough revision.[20] If the Gospels are to be useful as trustworthy sources for the history of primitive Christianity, two things must be observed. First, the Gospel tradition as a reliable report of Jesus' earthly ministry intends primarily to say *who* the exalted Lord is, and then secondarily to indicate *what* the One who appeared in history and now appears as the exalted Lord has to say for the present congregation. Secondly, the situation of the Church must not be arbitrarily deduced from the individual pericopes, but must also be seen in contrast to the Gospel tradition with the help of other sources (cf. pp. 154 f.).

Thus we cannot uncritically accept the findings of the classical form-critical analysis of the New Testament writings. Rather we must seek

[17] G. Bornkamm, G. Barth, and H. J. Held, *Tradition and Interpretation in Matthew* (Eng. trans., 1963, of *Überlieferung und Auslegung im Matthäusevangelium* (1960), 17 f., 24, 36), pp. 19 f., 27, 39.
[18] W. Marxsen, *Der Evangelist Markus, Studien zur Redaktionsgeschichte des Evangeliums* (² 1959), 76 f.
[19] G. Iber, 'Zur Formgeschichte der Evangelien (Forschungsbericht)', *ThR* 24 (1957–58), 283–338, 320.
[20] Cf. H. Riesenfeld, *The Gospel Tradition and its Beginnings, A Study in the Limits of 'Formgeschichte'* (1957); Jürgen Roloff, *Das historische Motiv in den Jesuserzählungen der Evangelien* (Habilitationschrift, Hamburg 1967; to be published 1969).

critically to arrive at our own conclusions and in particular to determine what the sources, viewed in their totality, have to say about the situation of the Christian congregations. In this way the analysis of the history of tradition can offer reliable evidence for the *Sitz im Leben* of the Gospel tradition.

All this points towards our goal: our purpose is to outline the formation of the Church and her message, but we do not intend to depict the unfolding of her message and the development of her theology. Where the boundary lies between these will at times be a matter of individual judgment.

CHAPTER I

THE FOUNDING OF THE APOSTOLIC WITNESS
AND THE CHURCH THROUGH
EASTER AND PENTECOST

2. THE OUTSET AND THE VARIOUS INTERPRETATIONS OF IT

1. THE greatest historical puzzle of the Church's history is her origin. A few weeks after Jesus' death his disciples were proclaiming him to be the heavenly Messiah and were gathering together a messianic community.[1] Jesus himself, during the years of his earthly ministry, had neither made a public messianic claim nor had he attempted to gather together a separate community. How then did the disciples come to such an undertaking?

> For an ancient historian[2] the only actual analogy might be 'the work of Socrates and the formation of the Socratic Schools', but this analogy is just as remote as that of the Hellenistic cults with their deities[3] who die and return again to life. More recently, some scholars have pointed to the 'Teacher of Righteousness' and his meaning for the separatist Essene community,[4] but no one ever spoke of his resurrection and messianic role.[5] A much closer correspondence is to be found in the formation of the Baptist sect after the death of John the Baptist. This group honoured John as the messiah, although such honour was contrary to the intent of his work (cf. §12, n. 36). The conduct of Jesus' disciples after his death is therefore basically without analogy.

2. The New Testament documents offer a series of explanations for this transition from Jesus' earthly ministry to the development of the Church. According to the earliest Evangelist, Mark,[6] by proclaiming Jesus' messiahship in keeping with his instructions the disciples revealed the messianic

---

[1] W. G. Kümmel, 'Jesus und die Anfänge der Kirche', Studia Theologica, vii (1954), 1–27 (further literature); D. M. Stanley, 'Kingdom to Church', Theological Studies, xvi (1955), 1–29; see below note 20, §1, n. 1; §5, nn. 7, 11.

[2] E. Meyer, op. cit. (§1, n. 8), iii, 219.

[3] A. T. Nikolainen, Der Auferstehungsglaube in der Bibel und in ihrer Umwelt, i. (1944).

[4] A. Dupont-Sommer, The Essene Writings from Qumran (Eng. trans., 1961), 358–378.

[5] A. S. van der Woude, Die messianischen Vorstellungen der Gemeinde von Qumran (1957), 58, 186 f.; M. Burrows, More Light on the Dead Sea Scrolls (1958), 292–323; G. Jeremias, Der Lehrer der Gerechtigkeit (1963), 268–307.

[6] For literature on the Gospels see §17, n. 36, §18, n. 9 f.

8

secret with which they had been entrusted. Jesus, as Mark explained, was conscious of being the Son-of-Man Messiah who was establishing the present Reign of God through his work. However, Jesus had only revealed this secret to the inner circle of his disciples, and he had commanded them to remain silent until after his resurrection (Mark viii.30; ix.9). To the public he had hidden it under veiled speech (Mark iv.10–13), yet the resurrection was in no way the key which unlocked any sort of secret knowledge. For Mark, the disciples were not the 'knowing ones' in the sense of an esoteric group,[7] but rather they were the 'uncertain ones' who themselves did not understand the secret until the very end.[8] Their comprehension of the messianic secret was simply the last step along the road of faith to which Jesus had summoned all. (This is particularly true for a layer of tradition which, to a certain extent, may be perceived behind Mark.) It is not so amazing, therefore, that the disciples were all 'offended'—i.e. their faith was shaken—and 'scattered' when Jesus died on the cross after being sentenced by the religious authorities of Israel. It was through the resurrection that they were brought anew to faith and regathered (Mark xiv.27; xvi.7 f.).

Luke connects Jesus with the development of the Church from the point of view of redemptive history; his Gospel is continued by Acts, just as the second article of faith moves into the third. While the messianic secret recedes into the background, Jesus' earthly ministry becomes the paradigm for the Messianic Age of salvation (Luke iv.16–30), but, just as in Mark, the cross is only overcome for Luke by means of the appearance of the Risen One (Luke xxiv.21), in particular through the 'Gospel of the Forty Days'. The teaching of the Risen One enabled the disciples to understand his death in the context of the scriptures, in the same manner in which they later proclaimed it after Pentecost. He also made it clear to them that the promised Kingdom would come through their missionary efforts by the power of the Spirit—i.e. through the emergence of the Church (Luke xxiv.25 f., 44, 49; Acts i.2, 6 ff.).

By contrast, Matthew not only passes on the early Palestinian tradition in which Jesus directly sets forth the future establishment of the Church (Matt. xvi.17–19), but by means of his redaction he also makes the total scope of Jesus' earthly teaching become the word for the developing Church. Thus after Jesus had shown himself to the disciples as the Living One, it sufficed to leave them simply with the word, 'to teach all nations' (Matt. xxviii.16–20).

Finally, John's Gospel unfolds Jesus' word in terms of the christology

---

[7] E. Sjöberg, *Der verborgene Menschensohn in den Evangelien* (1955), 1–9, *contra* H. Braun, *Spätjüdisch-häretischer und frühchristlicher Radikalismus* (1957), ii, 21, n. 4.

[8] Mark iv.13; vi.52; viii.17 f., 21; ix.10 (all from his source!).

and ecclesiology current near the end of the first century, but stresses even more emphatically than the other Gospels that both the understanding of the appearance of Jesus and the corresponding witness in the world 'to gather his sheep' started with the appearance of the Exalted One at Easter (John xii.16, 20–24, 32, etc.).

According to the New Testament accounts, then, the proclamation of Jesus' Messiahship and the corresponding gathering of the messianic community after the conclusion of his ministry emerged from two starting points: Jesus' reference to this messianic proclamation as the goal of his ministry and the appearance of the Risen One. Both so complement each other that the one becomes understandable only in light of the other. Moreover, the indications given by Jesus during his earthly ministry only became fact through the first Easter, and the first Easter itself only became meaningful in view of the completed earthly ministry.

The New Testament accounts describe the two starting points quite differently, however, and in so doing they raise a twofold historical question. On the one hand, to what extent was Jesus' earthly ministry actually aimed at this gathering of a messianic community? On the other hand, what took place for the disciples at Easter to cause them to come forward as men set apart? These questions demand a critical analysis of the tradition behind the accounts and a coherent reconstruction of what happened. Unfortunately, such an analysis has become heavily weighted with the philosophical bias more or less continually applied by pure historical research extending from rationalism to the history-of-religions school. It is supposedly 'unscholarly' to trace a historical movement from a 'miracle', such as the appearance of one who had been raised from the dead.

3. Since F. C. Baur, the reconstruction of the events by means of the historical approach has usually taken the one indisputable fact of the Easter faith of the disciples as its point of departure. Scholars have attempted to explain the development moving from Jesus himself to the proclamation of him as Messiah as a history of the disciples' faith.[9] Wilhelm Bousset reconstructed this history psychologically from the impact of the personality of Jesus; Rudolf Bultmann reconstructed it *kerygmatically* from God's call to decision embodied in the appearance of Jesus.

[9] F. C. Baur, *Das Christentum und die christliche Kirche der ersten Jahrhunderte* (1853, [3]1863), 39, 'Either the faith in him had to be extinguished in his death, or this faith, if it was sufficiently firm and strong, of necessity had to break through the barrier of his death. . . . From the standpoint of history the necessary presupposition for all that which followed is not the facticity of the resurrection itself but rather the faith in it.' Similarly, H. Lietzmann, *History of the Early Church*, i, 61 f.

Bousset:[10] 'From the critical standpoint most are in agreement that here (with the Easter appearances) a purely spiritual event in the souls of the disciples is involved, and renounce any external miracle. . . . For a truly historical approach the experiences of visions must also be placed on a secondary level. The most important point . . . is that in the souls of the disciples the unshakable persuasion arose that Jesus . . . had become the transcendent Messiah. . . . Factors quite diversified in character have worked together to give shape to (this) persuasion. The motivating factor was . . . the immense and indestructible impression which the personality of Jesus left behind in the souls of the disciples.' Not to be forgotten is the fact that this persuasion was able to gain expression with the help of a ready-made messianic concept, the apocalyptic concept of the Son of Man who was to pass through suffering into glory.

Bultmann,[11] in contrast to this: 'The decision which Jesus' disciples had once made to affirm and accept his sending (as God's call to decision) by "following" him, had to be radically renewed in consequence of his crucifixion. . . . The Church had to rise above the horror of the Cross and did it in the Easter faith. . . . How the Easter faith arose . . . has been obscured in the tradition by legend and is not of basic importance.' Since 'Jesus' call to decision implies a christology', it is pertinent that this faith gained expression with the help of traditional messianic concepts. '. . . They understood Jesus as the one whom God by the resurrection (had) made Messiah, and . . . they awaited him as the coming Son of Man.'[12]

These and other attempts at reconstruction let the two starting points of the New Testament portrayals recede considerably behind the faith of the disciples. On the other hand, the fact that Jesus' earthly ministry pointed beyond itself is reduced either to the impression of the religious personality of Jesus or to the call to decision issued through him with its christological implications. The messianic secret acknowledged since Wrede[13] as the theory behind the earliest Gospel is thus eliminated from Jesus' earthly ministry. On the other hand, the Easter appearances also recede behind the Easter faith. This happens in a twofold manner:

a. The older historical reconstruction attempted to explain rationally the Easter experiences. Even in New Testament times the Jewish polemic used this means to make the empty tomb understandable: the disciples had stolen the body (Matt. xxviii.13 ff.) or the gardener had removed it.[14] Ancient criticism attributed the Easter appearances partly to a pathological disposition of the disciples and partly to a deceitful fabrication on their

[10] *Kyrios Christos* ([4]1935), 17 f.
[11] *Theology of the New Testament*, §7, 3.
[12] *Ibid.*, §7, 2.
[13] *The Messianic Secret* (Eng. trans. 1966 of *Das Messiasgeheimnis in den Evangelien* ([2]1913)); more recent literature, cf. E. Sjöberg, *op. cit.* (n. 7 above).
[14] Tert., *De Spect.* 30, cf. John xx.15.

part.[15] Modern criticism in its initial phase during the period of rationalism explained the Easter-stories either as a fraud by the disciples or in terms of the trance theory.[16] In the second half of the nineteenth cen.ury the psychological explanation prevailed most generally in critical studies:[17] the disciples returned to Galilee; there they regained their senses and began to reflect. The appearances were '. . . . not, as it then seemed (to the disciples) the cause but rather the effect of their faith'.[18] Since one could think of the resurrection only in terms of actual physical resuscitation, the legend of the empty tomb came into being.

This reconstruction, nevertheless, starts with two assumptions which are not historically justifiable. First of all, the various New Testament accounts are unanimous on one point, that the disciples failed and were incapable of finding any disposition within themselves to overcome the cross by means of an Easter faith.[19] Secondly, if the Easter faith had brought about the appearances, why then did they cease in such a short time, even though the Easter faith and early enthusiasm remained?

b. Thus it began to appear more appropriate to forgo any explanation. F. C. Baur and others felt that the Easter appearances could not be considered as history, and Bultmann added that they were theologically irrelevant. They were thought to be relevant only to maintain the historical fact of the disciples' Easter faith and to understand it both as the response to Jesus' earthly ministry and as the starting point for all that was to come (cf. p. 11).

4. This restraint leaves open what by nature of the matter cannot be left open. Certainly, the history-conscious theology of today must take into consideration the history of the disciples' faith and the influences of their environment far more than the New Testament accounts did, but one must not allow the self-attestation of the Risen One, which came first in these accounts, to be placed as a secondary event. Our entire understanding of primitive Christianity is decided by whether we agree with the New Testament, and permit this order to remain. By this basic decision three other questions are determined: a. the form of the earliest proclamation; b. the interrelation between the Church and Jesus' earthly ministry; and c. the character of the Church's development.

---

[15] Celsus, c. 178, according to Origen, *Contra Celsum*, iii, 55; cf. P. de Labriolle, *La Réaction paienne, Études sur la polémique antichrétienne du Ier an VIe siècle* (1934). For further lit. cf. Goppelt, *Christentum und Judentum*, p. 280.

[16] A. Schweitzer, *The Quest for the Historical Jesus* (Eng. trans. of *Geschichte der Leben-Jesu-Forschung*, ²1933, 21, 43, 47, 54 f.), 21, 43, 47, 54 f.

[17] J. Weiss, *Earliest Christianity*, i, 26 ff.; E. Meyer, *op. cit.* (§1, n. 8), iii, 214 ff.

[18] J. Weiss, *Earliest Christianity*, i, 30.

[19] The Johannine accounts about the 'beloved disciple' at the cross and the empty tomb relates how the true disciple should accept these events, not how a historical figure accepted them.

a. According to the New Testament accounts the earliest proclamation never said: 'Jesus has risen'[20]—an unhistorical abstraction—but rather: 'He was raised (on the third day in accordance with the scriptures) and he appeared to Cephas (then to the Twelve)' (I Cor. xv.3-5; Luke xxiv.34). Thus the character of the earliest proclamation was not merely the confession of the Church's Easter faith but was a witness to the basis of faith. Obviously, this was not a report of 'historical' events but a witness of faith to a revelation which by its very nature was bound to faith. This revelation addressed itself in a unique and exclusive manner to the authorized witnesses of the earthly ministry since, from this point on, the Risen One revealed himself only through their witness to him as the Living One (John xv.26 f.; Acts v.32; cf. pp. 153 f.). This is the sense in which the earliest proclamation is the apostolic witness. Understood as witness in this way, the earliest proclamation sets forth the Risen One. When, however, it is construed as merely an expression of the Church's Easter faith, the Risen One is either subdued or completely replaced by it (cf. pp. 36 ff.).

b. The earliest proclamation declared that the participation of the Risen One in the founding of the Church was the purpose of Jesus' earthly ministry. The Gospels arising from the Easter witness depict Jesus' temporal ministry as directed towards this end; more precisely, the statements about the messianic secret expressly direct Jesus' work on earth toward this goal. Thus we are faced with the question: was Jesus' earthly ministry actually directed toward this end, that is the hidden resurrection and the hidden gathering of the redeemed community through the Risen One? Did Jesus intend the Church?

Without question, Jesus' earthly ministry started with the announcement of the coming of God's Reign—the New World described in the Beatitudes—and the corresponding radical demand for repentance. However, Jesus not only demanded repentance, but also effected it in that he conferred his help to the helpless and his fellowship to the 'sinners'. The faith which Jesus effected in this manner is the essential enactment of repentance. When he grants to men his helping fellowship and effects faith, the prodigal son returns to his father's house (Luke xv) and the Beatitude of the poor (Luke vi.20) is fulfilled. He who has faith, that is he who in view of the ministry of Jesus *in actu* yields to God, has a place in the Kingdom, since his relationship to God has been restored even if the physical restoration of creation has not yet taken place. Thus to the outward appearance, Jesus' ministry resembled that of a prophet or rabbi; for those who knew the secret of his teaching (i.e. for those of faith)

---

[20] Christological formulae such as Rom. i.3 f.; x.9; I Thess. iv.14 are all responses to the *kerygma* (cf. §6, 4c).

however, his message and work were eschatological fulfilment. Jesus not only made such a claim when confronted by the disciples of John the Baptist (Matt. xi.2–6) but he also revealed this to his disciples. He explained to them through the parables of the Kingdom of God how God's reign was then dawning in his work, contrary to the letter of prophecy (Matt. xiii). Is it not reasonable then that he should have disclosed to his closest followers the secret of his person and the purpose of his ministry, as the predictions of his suffering and Peter's confession recount in spite of their subsequent, reworked form (cf. p. 40)?[21]

One only took part in this fulfilment, this salvation, as long as one had fellowship with the person of Jesus (Matt. xi.6).[22] Consequently, during Jesus' days on earth, he could not, as did the Essenes and Pharisees, gather a separate community to be the holy remnant which would live in accordance with his teaching. Instead, he could only gather about himself a circle of disciples out of which his representatives to Israel would arise and which would foreshadow the redeemed community, the new twelve-tribe nation (cf. below, pp. 28 f.).[23] This is indicated by the choice of twelve for his closest followers. The redeemed community could only be gathered when Jesus, as he announced at the Last Supper, no longer offered himself to his own through the sharing of a communal table, but later, when as the Risen One he offered himself in a new kind of fellowship—even before the marriage feast of the Lamb.[24] The essential question is thus not how far Jesus went to prepare his disciples for the development of the redeemed community after his suffering and death,[25]

[21] Cf. L. Goppelt, 'Der verborgene Messias', in *Der historische Jesus und der kerygmatische Christus*, ed. by H. Rüstow and K. Matthiae ([2]1961), 371–384.

[22] The Beautitude on the poor was fulfilled initially by those who followed Jesus or who permitted him to help them, not those who accepted his word as the message from God.

[23] W. G. Kümmel, *Kirchenbegriff und Geschichtsbewusstsein* (1943), 31 ff., correctly rejects the viewpoint that the calling of the Twelve and the institution of the eucharist were acts which founded the Church. However, he does not emphasize enough the fact that these have a demonstrable character which points to the establishment of the eschatological, redemptive community after the completion of Jesus' earthly ministry. Kümmel's thesis in 'Jesus und die Anfänge der Kirche', *Stud. Theol.* vii (1954), 27, deserves complete agreement: 'It is the person of Jesus as the hidden Messiah-man and as the Risen One which is the historical root of the Church, not the teaching of Jesus.'

[24] L. Goppelt, *TWNT* vi, 141 f.

[25] Only one passage, Matt. xvi.17–19 (cf. Matt. xviii.17), of all four Gospels speaks explicitly about the establishment of the 'Church' after the completion of Jesus' earthly ministry. In so doing it is set off from the rest of Jesus' *logia* which merely hint at such a designation by applying the terminology belonging to the people of God to the disciples (Mark iii.35; xiv.27; Luke xii.32). Perhaps the saying in Matt. xvi was formulated in the Palestinian Church from elements of tradition which stem in part from Jesus (see E. Stauffer, 'Zur Vor- und Frühgeschichte des Primatus Petri', *ZKG* 62 (1943–44), 3 ff. cf. O. Cullman, *Peter: Disciple—Apostle—Martyr*, 161–217 (Eng. trans., 1953, of *Petrus, Jünger—Apostel—Märtyrer*, 1952, [2]1960, 78–243).

but what was the aim of his ministry. The goal of his earthly ministry was not, as was the case for John the Baptist, merely a movement of repentance in view of the imminent establishment of the Kingdom in power by means of the judgment of the world; rather it was the gathering of the redeemed community through a faith which, in view of his completed early ministry, would yield to the God of Israel (cf. below, pp. 19 f.).

Since the disciples to whom Jesus had revealed the messianic secret accepted it by faith alone, it is perfectly understandable that they should become confused about Jesus after his rejection by Israel's authorities. This follows in spite of their confessions of his messiahship and in spite of his predictions of his own suffering, both of which were originally much more obscure than in the present portrayals of the Evangelists. They were first led into renewed faith by means of his appearance at Easter, a faith which also understood from a new standpoint what had previously transpired. The oldest christological formulae through which this understanding expressed itself confirm this reconstruction of the relationship between Jesus' earthly ministry and the development of the Church (cf. p. 40).

c. If, in keeping with this, the ministry of Jesus as the hidden Messiah and as the Risen One came first, and if the faith of the disciples followed in sequence in the initial development of the Church, then we have an indication as to the nature of the entire history of primitive Christianity. It suggests that this history is definitely to be understood as the response to that which was and had been ordained by God, and only secondly as a product of the faith and thought of the disciples under the influence of their environment.

Thus to answer the question about the starting point of primitive Christianity is to clarify the competing points of view. We cannot eliminate one to the advantage of another. We must recognize the revelatory aspect of the New Testament just as much as the historical, but we must allot to each its due place and in this way produce a relationship of tension.

Let us now take a closer look at the decisive starting point for the history of primitive Christianity.

3. THE FIRST EASTER[1]

1. According to the New Testament accounts no one saw the actual

[1] *TWNT*, i, 368 ff.; ii, 332 ff.; E. Hirsch, *Die Auferstehungsgeschichten und der christliche Glaube* (1940); P. Althaus, *Die Wahrheit des kirchlichen Osterglaubens* ([2]1941); W. Michaelis, *Die Erscheinungen des Auferstandenen* (1944); A. M. Ramsey, *The Resurrection of Christ* ([2]1946); W. Künneth, *The Theology of the Resurrection* (Eng.

resurrection,[2] which corresponds to the very nature of the event. Jesus did not return to this world (as Lazarus did, according to John xi), but entered into the New World of God; he is its first-fruits.[3] When the disciples spoke of the resurrection, they spoke of an event which, in keeping with the common Jewish conception, introduced the future Aeon,[4] and so they spoke of an eschatological event. They did not actually see it with their eyes but rather bore witness to it, since the Risen One had appeared to them.

The Easter message was not established by the finding of the empty tomb, neither in the early *kerygma* of I Cor. xv.3 f., nor in the missionary sermons of Acts. This does not stamp the narrative of the empty tomb as a legend,[5] in fact it corresponds to the narrative, since, according to its original formulation, the finding of the empty tomb did not bring the Easter faith into being.[6] The account is meant merely to be a preparation for the appearances. This is the *kerygmatic* meaning which one hears in the angel's words of Mark xvi.6 f. The empty tomb is the final sign of Jesus' earthly ministry—a sign in the Johannine sense—which first received its interpretation through the appearances of the Risen One.

---

trans. 1965 of *Theologie der Auferstehung*, [4]1951); H. v. Campenhausen, *Der Ablauf der Osterereignisse und das leere Grab (S.A.H.*, 1952); K. H. Rengstorf, *Die Auferstehung Jesu* ([4]1960); C. H. Dodd, 'The Appearances of the Risen Christ' in *Studies in the Gospels* (ed. D. E. Nineham, *in mem.* R. H. Lightfoot, 1955), 9–35; H. Grass, *Ostergeschehen und Osterberichte* (1956); W. Nauck, '*Die Bedeutung des leeren Grabes für den Glauben an den Auferstandenen*', *ZNTW* 47 (1956), 243–267; G. Koch, *Die Auferstehung Jesu Christi* (1959); B. Klappert, *Diskussion um Kreuz und Auferstehung* (1967).

[2] By contrast, The Gospel of Peter (Hennecke[3]i. p. 186) and The Gospel according to the Hebrews (Hennecke[3]i. p. 165). Matt. xxviii.2–4 borders on this.

[3] I Cor. xv.20; Col. i.18.

[4] S.-B., iii, 827 ff.; iv, 971 ff.

[5] On the basis of a historical reconstruction of the Easter event, it has been concluded that the narrative is a legend (cf. pp. 11 f.). However, this conclusion is not supported by an examination of the history of tradition, as Nauck, *op. cit.*, has shown. Rather the contrary is the more probable. The account of Mark xvi.1–8 par. (!) John xx.1–10 is doubtless a very old and reliable tradition. In favour of its authenticity are: (1) the formula of I Cor. xv.3 ff. with the emphatic 'he was buried' presupposes a knowledge about Jesus' tomb (cf. Acts ii.29), and that could only be a knowledge of the empty tomb. (2) The finding of the empty tomb on Easter morning is the only reasonable explanation for the ancient *kerygma* of the resurrection on the third day (I Cor. xv.4). (3) It is remarkable that the Jewish polemic also tried to explain the fact of the empty tomb quite early rather than to reject the narrative as simply a lie (cf. p. 11). Perhaps one could actually point to an empty tomb in Jerusalem. (4) Archaeological discoveries correspond with this (J. Jeremias, *Heiligengräber in Jesu Umwelt*, 1958, 144 f.). On the contrary, there is little of relevance in the Διάταγμα Καίσαρος of Nazareth (J. Irmscher, *ZNTW*, 42, 1949, 172–184) and even less from the Holy Shroud of Turin (*ThLZ*, 81 (1956), 105 f.).

[6] Mark xvi.8; Luke xxiv.9–11, 22–24. Only John xx.8 speaks of the 'other disciple': '. . . and he saw and believed . . .' (not: 'and he was convinced'), cf. §2, n. 20.

The statements of the Gospels about the course of the Easter appearances diverge, above all, in their locale. This is not surprising in view of the redactional character of the Synoptic framework. We must, as in other cases, disregard this divergence and attend to the content of the pericopes. In so doing we discover the following course of events: according to the Marcan tradition,[7] which Luke xxiv.6 later changed, the first appearances took place in Galilee. The first appearance was to Peter,[8] after he and his companions had apparently returned again to their occupation at sea.[9] In contrast, at the time of the appearances in Jerusalem the disciples were together again, even if behind closed doors.[10] Since the earliest history of the Church is closely linked with Jerusalem, the appearances would not have been transferred later to Galilee. The disciples had apparently dispersed and returned to their homeland of Galilee and perhaps also to Judea. Because of the appearances, which possibly occurred simultaneously here and there, they then gathered together again at the next feast, the feast of Pentecost in Jerusalem. Here the appearances came to an end (cf. §4, 2). In any case, the appearances continued for a brief time only, and they remained confined to the circle of disciples of the earthly ministry.

In comparison with these particulars of the Gospels, the *paradosis* of Paul in I Cor. xv.3b–8[11] raises two questions: First of all, why are the Evangelists silent about such an impressive event as the appearance before 'more than 500 disciples at once'? Is this appearance identical with the event of Pentecost in Acts ii?[12] This suggestion lacks a sufficient basis. A more probable explanation would be that the later emphasis on the apostles (evident in Luke) overshadowed an ancient Galilean tradition (which had come down to Paul). Secondly, how can Paul associate his Damascus experience with the Easter appearances as being of the same nature? In so doing, does he not betray a conception of the nature of the appearances essentially different from that of the Evangelists, especially Luke?

2. It has been maintained that for Paul, the appearances were essentially the revelations of the Risen One and the Exalted Lord from heaven;[13]

---

[7] Mark xvi.7 par. Matt.; cf. xiv.28.

[8] I Cor. xv.5; Luke xxiv.34; cf. John xxi.15 ff.

[9] John xxi.1–14; cf. Luke v.1–11; Mark vi.48 par.

[10] Luke xxiv. 36–53; Acts i.3–14; John xx. 19–29.

[11] Paul passed the confession of I Cor. xv.3b–8 c. A.D. 50 on to his church in Corinth as a fixed tradition (I Cor. xv.1 ff.). The heart of the formula which he himself had received, included above all vv. 3b–5 (so Kümmel, *Kirchenbegriff*, 2 ff.). In keeping with its Semitic form it originated in the Palestinian Church (J. Jeremias, *Eucharistic Words*, 187 f. B. Klappert, Zur Frage des semitischen oder griechischen Urtextes von 1. Kor. xv, 3–5, *NTS*. 13 (1967), 168–173).

[12] Initially in E. v. Dobschütz, *Ostern und Pfingsten* (1903). Cf discussion in Grass *op. cit.* (n.1), 99, n. 4.

[13] E. Hirsch, *op. cit.* (n. 1), 4–8.

for Luke, on the other hand, they were the encounters with the One who still lingered briefly on earth in a transfigured body and who became exalted only through the ascension. This second conception is found in early Christian statements like, for example, the unauthentic conclusion to Mark (xvi.19) and in the *Epistula Apostolorum*,[14] but it is not present in Acts i.

The 'ascension' in Acts i.9[15] concludes not a period of forty days in which the Risen One had shared life together with his disciples, but only one of his appearances. The occurrence, according to the explanation of the angels (Acts i.10 f.), was to make it known that the disciples would no longer see him until the parousia. The ascension is therefore basically the symbolic conclusion of one appearance which stood for the end of the Easter appearances. There is not one word about the exaltation in the entire ascension narrative. The exaltation coincided for Luke, just as it did for Paul, with the resurrection.[16] For both men the appearances were revelations from the New World of God, and for Paul they were essentially concluded, even if not in such a schematic way.[17]

The appearances were actually revelations in the narrow sense of the word. This is evident in the term with which all the New Testament accounts describe the appearances: ὤφθη is a term used in the Old Testament to express the perception of a revelation and not the establishment of a fact through evidence.[18] It is not to be translated 'He was seen', but

---

[14] Ed. by C. Schmidt, *Gespräche Jesu mit seinen Jüngern nach der Auferstehung* (*T.U.* 43, 1919), 38 ff.

[15] Contrary to the hypothesis that the ascension narrative was first inserted into Acts i by a second hand, H. Conzelmann, *Die Apostelgeschichte* (1963), 23. Literature on the ascension: V. Larranaga, S.J., *L'Ascension de Notre Seigneur dans le Nouveau Testament* (1938); P. Benoit, 'L'Ascension', *Rev. Bib.*, lvi (1949), 162–203; P. A. van Stempvoort, 'The Interpretation of the Ascension in Luke and Acts', *NTS*, 5 (1958), 30–42.

[16] Acts ii.32 f.; v.30 f.; xiii.31 ff. Luke tends to represent the Easter appearances as encounters with One who comes and goes. In keeping with this, he portrays the parting through the ascension as a departure into the heavenly world. Nevertheless, he does not simply pass on his own conception, but rather he bears witness to that which was transmitted to him by theologically interpreting it. He accentuated *kerygmatically* among other things the end of the appearances: Luke xxiv.51 (*v. 1.*) '. . . He parted from them . . . ,' Acts i.3, 11, 22: '. . . Until the day when he was taken up from us (into heaven)'. Along with this, he permits the original interpretation of the resurrection as exaltation (Acts ii.32 f.; v.30 f.; xiii.33) and the uniqueness of the Damascus experience to remain and does not place the latter in the same category with the Christ-visions (§10, 2). Consequently, this *kerygmatic* representation is not to be reduced to the Lucan conceptions which occasionally shine through and then placed along a fixed schema of conceptions.

[17] I Cor. xv.8; 'Last of all . . . he appeared also to me', wrote Paul twenty years later!

[18] *TWNT*, v, 359; cf. Gal. i.16.

'He appeared'. Thus H. Grass[19] felt that he had retained the essence by explaining that the Easter appearances were 'objective visions' through which God revealed to the disciples that Jesus had arisen, but this reduction ignores the vital point of difference. Even Paul differentiated between the Easter appearances and the visions of Christ which had been abundantly granted to him and to others.[20] In the visions the Exalted One disclosed himself through the Spirit; at Easter he appeared bodily, i.e. in person.[21] The disciples did not receive information about him, but actually encountered him personally.

The encounters, in keeping with their nature, were confined to the circle of disciples of the earthly ministry. Paul called himself τὸ ἔκτρωμα (I Cor. xv.8), the single exception. He is this exception in terms of time and person, but not as regards the character of the revelation. He also became a 'believer' and not a 'knower' through the experience. The Easter appearances concluded the gracious revelation during the days on earth, a revelation which brought men to faith. They were not judgment for the unbelieving as would be the revelation of power at the parousia. Jesus' public preaching on repentance spoke of the parousia of the Son of Man; for the disciples to whom the messianic secret had been disclosed, his instruction spoke of the resurrection of the Son of Man. It was for these disciples that the appearances were intended.

Such an intention corresponds to their content. The disciples had forsaken him and had given up; he came and through forgiveness reestablished fellowship with them.[22] The first appearance came to the very one who had denied him. In that he offered himself anew to the disciples for fellowship as the Living One, he brought to them conclusively and to all men God's salvation. He brought them into faith in that all the faith displayed on their part during the earthly ministry attained its goal, faith in the God who had raised him and exalted him to be the Messiah.

At the same time this conclusion meant a new beginning. The Evangelists unanimously and independently of one another recount that the Risen One renewed the apostolate.[23] The commission reads differently

---

[19] Grass, op. cit. (n. 1), 246 ff.   [20] I Cor. xv.8; cf. II Cor. xii.2 ff.

[21] The materializing of the bodily aspect which occurs later in levels of the tradition and which makes a recognition through sense perception possible (Luke xxiv. 39 (contra I Cor. xv.20); Luke xxiv.42 f.; Acts x.41; John xx.20, 25, 27) contradicts the essence of the appearances. The One who appears is first recognized by his speaking and his actions (Matt. xxviii.17 ff.; Luke xxiv.16 ff.; Acts ix.4 f.). The statements about the bodily aspect attempt to bear witness in their contradictory manner to something which is no longer understandable in earthly terms.

[22] When he broke the bread for them once again in the manner of the father of a household, he intended to announce the renewal of their fellowship (Luke xxiv.30, 41–43; Acts. i.4; x.41; John xxi.13).

[23] Matt. xxviii.19; Luke xxiv.47; Acts i.1; John xx.21; xxi.15 ff.

in each passage; it has been formulated from the evidence of the fulfilment and of the later conceptions about the apostles, but there can be no doubt about a commissioning as such (cf. p. 180). Already in I Cor. xv.7 this commissioning is accepted as common tradition of the Church: 'Then (he appeared) to all the apostles.'

Apostles were the Easter witnesses who had received a special commission. The apostle according to the Hebraic root of the term is the representative of his superior.[24] As Jesus' representatives the apostles were to continue his 'service' to the surrounding world and to the brethren. The apostle is, as in the later terminology, called to be a missionary witness before the world[25] and to be a pastor among the brethren.[26] Men such as Peter actually attended to both tasks from the very beginning.

As well as the commission, each was given the promise of either Jesus' continuing transcendent presence[27] or the corresponding presence of the Spirit.[28] This promise has also been formulated from the evidence of the fulfilment, but without the promise how could the work of the Spirit have become intelligible to the disciples as the work of the Exalted One?

Thus the Easter appearances established the apostolate and the apostolic witness, but it was only after the Spirit gave birth to this witness that the band of disciples, reunited because of the appearances, became the 'Church' in the essential meaning of the term.

4. THE COMING OF THE SPIRIT[1]

1. The transition between the coming of the Exalted One in the Easter appearances and his working through the Spirit was probably much smoother than it now appears in Acts. According to John xx.22 the Spirit was imparted earlier during an Easter appearance. While the fourth Evangelist has compressed here,[2] as he often does, two separate but homogeneous elements, Luke does just the opposite by schematically

---

[24] *TWNT*, i, 413 ff.
[25] Matt. xxviii.19; Luke xxiv.47; Acts i.8; John xx.21.
[26] John xx.22; xxi.15 ff.
[27] Only in Matthew (xxviii.20; cf. xviii.20).
[28] Luke xxiv.49; Acts i.7 f.; cf. John xx.22 (see below, §4, n. 2).
[1] N. Adler, *Das erste christliche Pfingstfest* (1938); E. Lohse, 'Die Bedeutung des Pfingstberichtes im Rahmen des lukanischen Geschichtswerk', *Ev. Theol.*, 13 (1953), 422–436; *TWNT*, vi, 49 ff. (further literature there); E. Schweizer, *TWNT*, vi, 408 f.; G. Kretschmar, 'Himmelfahrt und Pfingsten', *ZKG* 65 (1954), 209–253; B. Reicke, *Glaube und Leben in der Urgemeinde. Bemerkungen zu Apg. 1–7* (1957), 27–37.
[2] John xx.19–23 describes the fulfilment of John xiv.16–24. For further discussion, E. Hoskyns, *The Fourth Gospel* (1947), 546 f.; *TWNT*, vi, 440 f.

recounting overlapping events in terms of epochs of redemptive history,[3] but in so doing maintains to a great extent the correct historical situation. 2. How is the historical course of events to be understood? The Easter appearances lasted for only a short time. Doubtless the Palestinian Church and not, as has occasionally been supposed,[4] the Hellenistic Church first experienced the work of the Spirit. That the experience of the Spirit began in Jerusalem with the unique event after the Passover on the first Pentecost is suggested by the following.[5] Contrary to Acts i the disciples had returned to Galilee. Yet after a brief time they moved back to Jerusalem (cf. p. 17). The majority of them, at any rate the influential ones, moved permanently from Galilee to Jerusalem. It was there that Paul, three years after his conversion, quite logically sought Peter and the rest of the apostles (Gal i.17 f.). Just what caused the disciples to leave their homes in Galilee and to move to Jerusalem is seen in the tradition of the Palestinian Church. For this tradition which has found its written expression in Matthew and Revelation, Jerusalem is the city which kills the Promised One and his witnesses.[6] At the same time it is 'the Holy City' and 'the Beloved City'[7] where the redemptive consummation will start and the redeemed community be gathered.[8] This corresponds to the Old Testament belief.[9] As soon as the disciples became certain of Jesus' resurrection and his exaltation as the Messianic Ruler, they 'had' to move to Jerusalem (cf. §6, 2).[10]

The Feast of Pentecost, the second of three yearly pilgrimage feasts, gave them occasion to come to Jerusalem. As a thanksgiving feast it concluded the fifty days of the grain harvest which began the day after the Passover with the Feast of Unleavened Bread.[11] In some circles this feast had been given a certain significance by relating it to the promised Salvation of God as the day of the renewal of the covenant.[12] This and other meanings[13] played a very minor role for the disciples. The decisive fact was that their expectations of Jerusalem was fulfilled and enhanced

---

[3] L. Goppelt, *Christentum und Judentum*, 228, n. 7.
[4] *TWNT*, vi, 401, n. 457, and 402 n. 462.
[5] E. Lohse, *op. cit.* (n. 1), and G. Kretschmar, *op. cit.* (n. 1).
[6] Matt. xxiii.32 (M); Rev. xi.8.
[7] Limited almost exclusively to the NT (*TWNT*, vi, 530).
[8] Matt. xxi.5 (M); Rev. xx.9; xxi.9 ff.
[9] Since Isa. ii.2 ff.; cf. *TWNT*, vi, 523 ff.
[10] The Qumran Sect separated itself in the end times—*prior* to the imminent end—from Israel's masses and withdrew into the wilderness. In so doing they fulfilled Isa. xl.3 (I QS viii.13 f.). They expected after the final battle with the Sons of Darkness (I QM xii.13 ff.) the fulfilment of the promises of salvation for Jerusalem (Isa. lx ff.).
[11] *TWNT*, vi, 47.
[12] Jubilees vi.17–21 (*TWNT*, vi, 48).
[13] It first became a memorial day for the giving of the Law at Sinai after A.D. 70 (*TWNT*, vi, 47 f.).

by the final appearances of the Risen One and by the experience of the Spirit at Pentecost.

In this way Jerusalem became the centre of the emerging redeemed community—even for the disciples who lived farther out in the towns of Judea and Galilee (Acts ix.31; Gal. i.22). There was no 'Galilean Church' which developed its own tradition different from that of Jerusalem.[14]

3. What was the nature of the occurrence at Pentecost? The narrative in Acts ii.1–13 has been extensively reworked by both the tradition and Luke.[15] At the heart of it is an account of ecstatic speech on the disciples' part, the earliest form of the primitive Christian gift of tongues. This speech, which was often the first effect of the Spirit,[16] was interpreted here and elsewhere as adoration and praise to God.[17] In this interpretation the original meaning of the event becomes evident at Pentecost: through the Spirit the disciples became a fellowship offering its adoration to God. This is the redeemed community of the end times,[18] and indeed all the disciples, not merely the apostles, were seized by the ecstatic speech (Acts ii.1 f.).

> The reworking of the account in Acts ii interpreted the event in this way, but too much so for the following historical development. It emphasized that a large number comprised of Jews and proselytes from the Diaspora (ii.5, 11) as representatives of the nations became witnesses to these events, and it understood the ecstatic speech as praise to God (not as a missionary address). This picture is reminiscent of the pilgrimage of the nations to Zion, but Luke was not depicting the fulfilment of this eschatological prophecy so much as the fulfilment, through his symbolic synopsis, of the history of missions, the development of the universal Church. Acts ii systematically summarizes at the very outset the content of Acts just as the Nazareth pericope in Luke iv summarizes in a similar fashion the content of Luke's Gospel. Thus the event in question is interpreted both by subsequent events and by the former prophecy of the Scriptures and Jesus' promise of the Spirit.

[14] Contra E. Lohmeyer, Galiläa und Jerusalem (1936); Gottesknecht und Davidsohn (1945); R. H. Lightfoot, Locality and Doctrine in the Gospels (1938); see for discussion, E. Johnson, 'Jesus and the First-Century Galilee' (in mem. E. Lohmeyer, 1951), 73–88; R. Bultmann, Theology of the New Testament, §7, 5.

[15] The accompanying appearances in Acts ii.2 f. are essentially pictures of the nature of the Spirit's working. Acts ii.9–11 is an Antiochian list of nations (Reiche, op. cit. (n. 1), 34 ff.). It places the speech at Pentecost in an obscure relationship to the languages of the nations.

[16] Acts x.46 (x.47; xi.17 reference to Pentecost as being comparable?) and xix.6. Consequently, Acts ii.4 is probably to be translated: '. . . And [they] began to speak in other tongues' (not, according to ii.11, in 'other languages'), i.e. with a new language which was in keeping with the age of salvation (cf. Mark xvi.17, with 'new tongues'). On Glossolalia in general, cf. I Cor. xiv and TWNT, i, 721–726.

[17] Acts ii.11; I Cor. xiv.2, 14 ff.

[18] Rev. iv.10 f.; v.8–14; xv.2–4 and its background.

This is an indication of how the meaning of these events was directly revealed to those taking part. In the Jewish world, according to rabbinic teaching, the Spirit had become extinct with the last of the writing prophets,[19] so that the apocalyptists who belonged to these circles concealed their beliefs concerning the Spirit under pseudonymous authorships. Among the Zealots, on the other hand, prophets did appear, and among the Essenes every member of the community—especially the Teacher of Righteousness—was considered to have the gift of the Spirit. Prophecy was considered first and foremost to be the work of the Spirit, a belief in keeping with the Torah (especially in Qumran), but ecstasy in such a context was quite sporadic.[20] The Nebiim belonged to the misty past,[21] and the pneumatic ecstasy of the Hellenistic world[22] lay far beyond the horizon of the first disciples.

The further experiences of the Spirit in the Palestinian Church might well correspond basically to the accounts of Acts, which are entirely free from the Spirit-problem of the Hellenistic churches and Paul's pneumatology.[23] In contrast with the experiences of 'spiritual men' in Corinth (I Cor. xiv), the ecstatic speech in Acts was an unusual occurrence which only occasionally accompanied the initial reception of the Spirit.[24] In general, the Spirit was received as a power as well as a liberation to a speech and action freed from self-centredness.[25] In other words, it was the gift of power and freedom for exactly that which Jesus had commanded in his eschatological summons to repentance and which he had granted through his fellowship. Therefore the disciples, having been prepared by means of both the Old Testament prophecy and Jesus' promise of the Spirit,[26] saw in this liberating power the work of the Exalted One through the Spirit of the end times.

The meaning of the Pentecost events was disclosed to those who took part in such an experience; the ecstatic praise was the product of the Spirit of the end times which as the gift of the Exalted One would make them into the redeemed community of the end times.

4. Luke arranges what the coming of the Spirit meant for the develop-

---

[19] W. Bousset, Die Religion des Judentums, 394–399; TWNT, vi, 382 ff., 813–828. For Qumran: I Qp Hab 7 : 5; I QS 9 : 3–5; I QH. 16; 18. F. Nötscher, 'Geist und Geister in den Texten von Qumran', Mélanges A. Robert (1957), 305–315.

[20] Eth. Enoch lxxi.11; Josephus, B.J. 6, 299 f.

[21] Num. xi.25 ff.; I Sam. x.5 ff.; xix.20 ff.; cf. Isa. xxviii.10.

[22] TWNT, i, 722 f.

[23] TWNT, vi, 402, 413.

[24] See n. 16.

[25] On the difference between the appearances of the working of the Spirit in the Palestinian Church and that in the Hellenistic Church, see below, pp. 99 f.

[26] Only Mark xiii.11 during the earthly ministry (see TWNT, vi, 400), corresponding to this is Acts iv.8, 31; vii.55; cf. §3 n. 26 f.

ment of the Church in a similar historical manner. Out of the circle of disciples awaiting their Master behind closed doors Acts ii lets develop, almost in one day, a fellowship through which the Exalted One by means of the Spirit effected missionary proclamation and baptism (ii.14, 38), instruction, breaking of bread, solidarity, and prayer (ii.42). This fellowship, especially since it included representatives of the nations, was the Church.

What Luke condenses into one day, several historical portrayals have seen as a development in Hellenistic Christianity stretching over more than a decade (cf. pp. 62 f.). Rather than recognizing a miraculous gift and instructions from above, these historical representations view the development as having been greatly influenced by the disciples' environment and as having been the product of their faith and thought.

In this respect Acts ii also previews the Church's development, in a systematic summary, but at crucial points comes much closer to the actual course of events than do some of the historical reconstructions of the development. The work of the Spirit was not a phenomenon developing out of a long history of similar conceptions, but a unique reality in redemptive history. The work of the Spirit, moreover, meant that out of the circle of disciples who were waiting and listening for their Master the eschatological, redeemed community developed which then proclaimed the Master himself as the Promised One. It meant that the 'sacramental' encounter with the Exalted One developed from the personal encounter with the Master—even though all this was at first realized and practised step by step and only later theologically interpreted. Pentecost meant the essential founding of the Church and the release of the apostolic witnesses established through Easter.

We shall now attempt to see how the Church and the apostolic witness appeared at the beginning and how they gained form initially in the context of the Jewish community.

CHAPTER II

THE CHURCH AND THE APOSTOLIC WORD WITHIN ISRAEL (THE PALESTINIAN CHURCH)[1]

A word about the sources. Although Jewish sources offer exhaustive and informative material concerning the environment in which the Church arose and lived during the first decades,[2] these sources provide practically no direct information about the development of the Church. The Jewish historian of that epoch, Josephus, ignored her just as he had Jesus.[3] Apart from a few isolated traditions of the ancient Church we are therefore dependent upon the New Testament writings, the portrayal of Acts,[4] information and tradition in the Pauline Epistles, traditions in Revelation, and the Didache. Above all, the Synoptic tradition, especially Matthew,[5] reflects the life and teaching of the Palestinian Church. Nevertheless, what one may extract from the Matthean source is so debatable that it is the most uncertain factor in the reconstruction of the history of the Palestinian Church.[6]

5. THE APPEARANCE AND SELF-UNDERSTANDING OF THE FIRST CONGREGATION[7]

1. The traditional picture of the first congregation which the Church

[1] Literature: The pertinent chapters of the histories of primitive Christianity, New Testament theologies, and commentaries on Acts. K. Pieper, *Die Kirche Palästinas bis zum Jahre 135* (1938); H.-J. Schoeps, *Urgemeinde, Judenchristentum, Gnosis* (1956).
[2] Literature: the histories of the New Testament times (H. Preisker, W. Foerster, B. Reicke and F. Filson), as well as the standard works on Judaism of those times by E. Schürer, W. Bousset, A. Schlatter, G. F. Moore, J. Bonsirven, S.J.; J. Jeremias, *Jerusalem zur Zeit Jesu* ([3]1962); K. Schubert, *Die Religion des nachbiblischen Judentums* (1955).
[3] Cf. Goppelt, *Christentum und Judentum*, 156, nn. 4, 5.
[4] The latest commentaries on Acts: E. Haenchen (*Meyer Kommentar*, [14]1965), A. Wikenhauser (*Regensburger NT*, [3]1956), B. Reicke, *Glaube und Leben in der Urgemeinde. Bemerkungen zur Apg. 1–7* (1957); C. S. C. Williams, *A Commentary on the Acts of the Apostles* (1957), a summary of the Anglo-Saxon research; H. Conzelmann (*HNT*, 1963); G. Stählin (*NTD*, 1962); a survey of the research on Acts: E. Grässer, 'Die Apg. in der Forschung der Gegenwart', *ThR* 26 (1960), 93–167.
[5] A. Schlatter, *Die Kirche des Matthäus* (1929); G. D. Kilpatrick, *The Origins of the Gospel according to St. Matthew* ([2]1950), 100–137; cf. §17, n. 36.
[6] V. Taylor's commentary on Mark ([2]1966) continues the analysis beyond R. Bultmann and M. Dibelius but not yet to its completion.
[7] Literature: K. Holl, 'Der Kirchenbegriff des Paulus in seinem Verhältnis zu dem der Urgemeinde', *Gesammelte Aufsätze* (1928), ii, 44–67; O. Michel, *Das Zeugnis des Neuen Testaments von der Gemeinde* (1941); N. A. Dahl, *Das Volk Gottes* (1941); W. G. Kümmel, *Kirchenbegriff und Geschichtsbewusstsein in der Urgemeinde und bei*

has taught originates from the redaction and summary accounts in Acts.[8] In contrast to this, von Dobschütz explained in his popularly formulated lectures of 1904[9] that for nearly 100 years a different interpretation resulting from the historical approach had prevailed. According to this reconstruction, Jesus' disciples in Jerusalem had not really constituted a church among the Jews since Pentecost, but were a messianic conventicle of Jews who were recruiting as quietly as possible fellow Jews through propaganda for their separate faith. This idea had in fact been supported by the nineteenth-century critical studies.[10] After 1900 a truly historical approach went beyond this and discovered, after combining in 1918 with a theological approach, the 'church-consciousness' of primitive Christianity in a new way.[11] Through the historical method we have learned to distinguish the appearance of faith from the self-understanding of faith and thus to focus on faith as such.

2. Acts also states quite clearly that, seen from a historical standpoint, Jesus' disciples represented in the eyes of their Jewish environment a αἵρεσις, i.e. a religious party within the Jewish nation,[12] as did the Pharisees[13] and Essenes.[14] Jesus had been outlawed as a Jew because he raised the question of the validity of the Law and the Temple.[15] His disciples, however, were faithful at first in their observance of both, as Acts unobtrusively recounts (cf. pp. 30 f.), so that their special teaching and customs offered no occasion for them not to be considered as Jews. Indeed, they had not separated themselves publicly nearly as much as had the Essenes. Only after A.D. 70 did the requirements for membership in Judaism become more stringent.

This leaves us then with the question: Did Jesus' disciples understand themselves to be a separate Jewish movement? At first impression this appears to have been the case since they applied to themselves by and large the same designations as the Essenes and the Pharisees. Like the

---

Jesus (1943); A. Oepke, Das neue Gottesvolk (1950); A. Fridrichsen, 'Messias und Kirche' und 'Die Neutestamentliche Gemeinde' in G. Aulén, Ein Buch von der Kirche (1951), 29–50; 51–72.

[8] Acts ii.43–47; iv.32–37; v.12–16. On the history of research, see Foakes-Jackson and Lake's The Beginnings, v, 392–402; Haenchen, op. cit. (n. 4), 155 ff.

[9] E. v. Dobschütz, Probleme des Apostolischen Zeitalters (1904), 28.

[10] H. J. Holtzmann, Lehrbuch der neutestamentlichen Theologie (²1911), i, 421.

[11] Report on the course of this research: O. Linton, Das Problem der Urkirche in der neueren Forschung (1932) and W. Kümmel, Kirchenbegriff, 1 f.

[12] Acts xxiv.5, 14; xxviii.22. Cf. TWNT, v, 95, on the designation, 'the way', which also appears.

[13] Acts xv.5; xxvi.5; Vita Josephi, 12.

[14] Josephus, B.J. 2, 8, 7.

[15] Mark iii.6 par.; see L. Goppelt, Jesus, Paul and Judaism (1964), 82 ff. (Eng. trans. of Christentum und Judentum, 59 ff.).

Essenes, they called themselves 'the Holy Ones',[16] 'God's Chosen Ones',[17] and 'the Congregation of God',[18] although they most probably did not use 'the Poor'.[19] With these designations the Essenes wanted to identify themselves as the true Israel of the approaching end times, which was to inherit the salvation promised to Israel at the coming consummation. In so doing they denied the remaining Jews the attribute of being the people of God.[20] The Pharisees also called themselves 'the Holy Ones', and claimed thereby to be the true Israel, the holy remnant, although not as exclusively as did the Essenes.[21]

Did the fellowship of Jesus' disciples claim to be the true Israel in a similar fashion? They have often been understood in this way.[22] In fact however, they meant something entirely different with these designations than did the Essenes and Pharisees. This is evident from their usage of the designation ἐκκλησία (Church) and especially from their overall conduct (cf. pp. 23 ff.).

Following that fundamental word (Matt. xvi.17–19) which had been formulated in Jerusalem (cf. §2, note 23) they called themselves 'Congregation of Jesus' and not as the Essenes 'Congregation of God'. They are 'Congregation', people of God,[20] since Jesus had accepted them into his Messianic Reign and in so doing into God's Reign. The first part of the saying (verse 18) speaks of the Congregation (Church) of Jesus; the second part (verse 19) speaks of the Kingdom of God. According to verse 18, Peter is the foundation stone upon which the Congregation (Church) of Jesus as the Temple of the end times will be built. He is so designated because he was the first to confess Jesus as the Christ. According to verse 19 he is simultaneously the trustee (not the door-keeper) of the Kingdom of God because the entrance to, or

[16] This is to be concluded from Rom. xv.25 f., 31; I Cor. xvi.1; II Cor. viii.4; ix.1, 12; Acts ix.13, 32, 41; xxvi.10.

[17] This is to be concluded from Mark xiii.20, 22, 27 (cf. Kümmel, *Kirchenbegriff*, 18 f.). Corresponds with I QS i.4; viii.6; ix.15; I QH xv.23.

[18] Matt. xvi.18 corresponding to I QM iv.10; CD vii.17.

[19] *Contra* K. Holl, *op. cit.* (n. 7), Lietzmann, *A History of the Early Church*, 63, and *TWNT*, vi, 909.

[20] K. Schubert, *The Dead Sea Community* (Eng. trans. 1959 of *Die Gemeinde vom Toten Meer*, 1958, 73 ff.), 80 ff.

[21] J. Jeremias, 'Der Gedanke des "Heiligen Restes" im Spätjudentum und in der Verkündigung Jesu', *ZNTW*, 42 (1949), 184 ff.

[22] R. Bultmann, *Theology of the New Testament* ([2]1959), 37, 'This Congregation . . . is the vestibule, so to say, of God's Reign that is shortly to appear;' cf. further pp. 43 f., 53 f., and the foreword to the third German edition. Cf. Dahl, *op. cit.* (n. 7), 181 f., in contrast to the Pharisees and others, '. . . the certainty of being the True Israel was founded (for them) through the new relationship before God brought through Jesus'. W. G. Kümmel, *Kirchenbegriff*, 18 ff., 62: 'The chosen people of the end of days who could count on acceptance into God's Reign' (p. 22) and who '. . . [lived] in the age of salvation which had begun but had not yet reached its consummation' (p. 18).

[23] *TWNT*, iii, 530 f.

exclusion from, the Kingdom is based upon his report to Jesus as the Christ. The Congregation (Church) of Jesus is not identical to the Kingdom of God. The Kingdom of God, the redemptive Reign of God of the end times, is completed and represented through Jesus the Christ, and not through his Congregation (Church). The latter, like Peter, has an active part in the Reign only through her witness, but all who confess Jesus as the Christ, and only these, are taken into the Kingdom of God;[24] they are the redeemed community of the end times.

Thus Jesus' disciples did not consider themselves, as did the Essenes and Pharisees, to be the *True* Israel who were soon to inherit God's salvation. Rather they considered themselves to be the *New* Israel upon whom God's salvation had already dawned, even though the word 'new' was not expressed at first. Unlike the others they did not disparage the Jewish nation outside their own fellowship, but addressed it as a whole, just and unjust alike, and emphasized its being the people of the promise.[25] In contrast to the other groups they did not exhort their fellow Jews to a better practice of the Law, but standing beyond the eschatological rift arising out of the rejection of Jesus and his resurrection, they summoned all Jews to the fulfilment of the promise.

3. This self-understanding actually blossomed in the earliest period of the Church. The account of Peter's confession corresponds to a short-lived early stage in the leadership of the Church; yet, at the same time, it further confirms this self-understanding. It was not a later idealistic picture but a hardly emphasized element of the oldest tradition from the Palestinian Church which took for granted that Peter together with the Twelve represented and directed during the initial years in Jerusalem the 'Congregation of Jesus', the entire body of the eschatological people of God, as far as it reached at that time. The heart of the earliest *kerygma* (I Cor. xv.5) named Peter and the Twelve at the head of the list as the witnesses to the resurrection. Moreover, when Paul three years after his conversion, between A.D. 35 and 40, sought contact with the Church in Jerusalem, he made contact with Peter (Gal. i.18). This state is also reflected in the tradition behind the narratives about Peter in Acts (Acts i–vi; x f.; xii) (cf. §21, 3).

The Twelve[26] were doubtless called by Jesus himself since no one

---

[24] L. Goppelt, 'Reich Gottes', *EKL*, differently, W. G. Kümmel, *Kirchenbegriff*, 22 and different again O. Cullmann, *Königsherrschaft Christi und Kirche im Neuen Testament* ([3]1950).

[25] Acts iii.25 and throughout the Synoptic tradition (Luke xix.9).

[26] Literature: K. H. Rengstorf, *TWNT*, ii, 321–328; J. Munck, 'Paul, the Apostles and the Twelve', *Stud. Theol.*, iii (1950), 96–110; V. Taylor, *Mark* ([2]1966), 619–627; v. Campenhausen, *Kirchliches Amt und geistliche Vollmacht in den ersten drei Jahrhunderten* (1953); G. Klein, *Die zwölf Apostel* (1961); J. Roloff, *Apostolat-Verkündigung-Kirche* (1596).

would have invented the story that the one who 'betrayed' him was 'one of the Twelve' (Mark xiv.10). By means of the number twelve, Jesus most probably intended on the one hand to give expression to his claim to Israel as a whole, since the Jews still occasionally called themselves the nation of twelve tribes in view of their election to salvation (Acts xxvi.7), and on the other to make reference to the (new) twelve tribes whose restoration was expected at the end times.[27] When the Twelve led and represented in Jerusalem the Congregation (Church) of Jesus, they declared that the new twelve tribes had come into existence and that they were summoning all Israel to them. Perhaps the obscure word in Matt. xix.28 intended to distinguish them in this manner as the witnesses of the Son of Man and Judge of the World to the new as well as to the old twelve tribes.[28]

Peter, however, was not only first among the others, but he was also ahead of them. The Risen One had appeared to him before he had to them, and the various *logia* about Peter were characteristic of him personally. He really was what his older Aramaic surname Cephas (= Peter) meant, 'the Rock', in the sense of Matt. xvi.18.[29] His 'primacy' was his precedence in being the first to be called as a witness, and because of its nature, a temporary position in the Church's initial period. We shall see how he worked together with the Twelve both within the Church and in the mission beyond the Church.

By the year A.D. 44 when the circle of the Twelve had disintegrated through the death of James, the Son of Zebedee, and through Peter's flight and separation from Jerusalem, the first form of Church leadership had become out of date because of external and internal changes.[30]

---

[27] Rev. xxi.12–14. Similarities with Qumran make it probable now that Palestinian tradition has had its effect here in Revelation. In the Qumran community a 'Council' consisted of '12 men and three priests' (probably inclusive), and it quite probably guided the entire group. This council is called the 'foundation' of the community, 'precious cornerstone' and 'tried wall' (I QS viii.5–10 cf. Matt. xvi.18; Gal. ii.9; I Tim. iii.15; Rev. xxi.14). The terminology of the constitutional forms in the earliest Church are also echoed in Rev. iii.12 (Gal. ii.9 'the pillars') and possibly in Rev. iv.10 (the twenty-four elders on the thrones—Matt. xix.28, the twelve apostles).

[28] Cf. Taylor, *Mark*, 622 f.

[29] Literature: E. Stauffer, 'Zur Vor- und Frühgeschichte des Primatus Petri', *ZKG* 62 (1943-44), 3–34; O. Cullmann, *Peter: Disciple—Apostle—Martyr*, 29–37 (as in §1, n. 25, German, 30–39); G. Schulze-Kadelbach, 'Die Stellung des Petrus in der Urchristenheit', *ThLZ*, 81 (1956), 1–14.

[30] Acts xii. According to the *Kerygma Petri* in Clem. Alex. *Strom.*, 6, 43, the Twelve remained in Jerusalem for twelve years at Jesus' command, and then they moved as missionaries into all the world. According to Harnack, *The Mission and Expansion of Christianity*, i, 44 (Eng. trans. 1908 of *Die Mission und Ausbreitung des Christentums*, i, 49), ancient tradition has been preserved here. Peter (cf. p. 106) contradicts the assumption that the Twelve had limited their mission to Israel and only became Gentile missionaries in view of the post-Pauline Church (Matt. xxviii.18–20; Acts

Paul's report of his visit to Jerusalem for the Apostolic Council (Gal. ii.1 ff.) shows a new form of the Church leadership becoming prominent. At this time the 'Church' for the Palestinian Christians was represented by the 'Three Pillars' (in the Temple of God).[31] Among these James was now the foremost man in Jerusalem. Peter represented the mission to Israel just as Paul represented the mission to the Gentiles. John comes into consideration if and when the tradition in the Johannine writings is to be connected with him (cf. pp. 128 f.).

Thus the leadership of the Congregation (Church) of Jesus in the initial period was amazingly varied, and yet it was always an expression of its true nature (cf. §7, 5).

4. The self-understanding of the Church which developed was not contradicted by her keeping of the Law and Temple observances, and in fact these supported just such a self-understanding and even to a certain degree expanded one further aspect of it. The keeping of the Law assumed by Acts[32] becomes even more puzzling in view of the Synoptic tradition which came itself from the first congregation. In this tradition Jesus both annulled the Law through his conduct and words and yet simultaneously admonished men to keep the Law to the very last letter (cf. §8, 1).

> Some have attempted to explain this juxtaposition which is particularly striking in Matthew's Gospel[33] by means of a genetic succession. It is to be supposed that the Church had initially assumed a freer attitude of mind toward the cultic and ritual ordinances. Later a certain regressive development set in as a result of the impression made by the founding of the Gentile Church, the reactions of the Jews, and the influence of James, the Lord's brother, in Palestine. Thus Jesus' critical statements about the Law were supposedly retained at first in the Palestinian Church, and furthermore, the Sabbath controversies or the controversies over things clean and unclean were actually fabricated to justify the Church's practice. Later, however, such words as Matt. v.17–19 were put into Jesus' mouth in order to justify the the new course, different as it was to that of the Gentile Church.[34]
>
> This genetic explanation fits neither the sense of the pericopes nor the historical situation. Certainly in Palestine restriction did set in later, but a liberal practice like that described had never preceded it. As soon as Stephen

---

i.8; I Clem. xlii.2 f.), J. Munck, *Paul and the Salvation of Mankind* (Eng. trans. 1959 of *Paulus und die Heilsgeschichte*, 1954, 275), 208.

[31] C. K. Barrett, 'Paul and the "Pillar" Apostles', in *Studia Paulina* (ed. J. N. Sevenster and W. C. van Unnik in hon. J. de Zwaan, 1953), 1–19; cf. n. 27.

[32] Acts x.14 is supported by Gal. ii.12; Acts ii.46; iii.1 ff.; v.12, 20 f., 42; xxi.26; cf. Matt. v.23 (cf. pp. 23 f., 54 f.).

[33] Matt. v.17–19; xxiii.1 ff., 23; Matt. v.21 ff.; xv.17 ff., etc.

[34] Bultmann, *Theology of the New Testament*, §8, 2; and *History of the Synoptic Tradition, in loco.*

dared speak of the temporary nature of the Temple, he met the same fate as Jesus, although Peter and the other representatives of the Church were never indicted in this way. The Cornelius story and the incident in Antioch assume that the men of the earliest Church strictly followed the Mosaic Law until their encounter with the Gentile Christians (§8, 4).

Why then did this Church make Jesus' critical statements about the Law a part of its tradition? In so doing it did not intend to justify its practice but to bear witness to and to explain Jesus' earthly ministry (cf. §6, 3): Jesus was condemned by the representatives of Israel because, for example, he broke the Sabbath in this manner (Mark iii.6). The disciples bore witness to this, but they did not infer from it that they were to give up the Sabbath nor to break it in similar fashion. In fact Jesus had not annulled the Sabbath Law; his breaking of the Sabbath Law was meant rather to be a demonstration of total obedience which transcended the Law. The words of Matt. v.17 f. are basically no less those of Jesus than are the following Antitheses in the Sermon on the Mount. These words about the Law's continuing validity prevent Jesus' demands from being 'enthusiastically' (in its technical meaning) understood as a new Law. From the point of view of content, not of history, Jesus' demands always stand in antithesis to the Law which, according to Matt. v.18, remains valid 'until heaven and earth pass away'—and until it be invalidated through the eschatological fulfilment. For Jesus the Law's validity and invalidity belonged inseparably together, and the first witnesses had correctly grasped this fact, so that, a conditional adherence to the Law was possible in the Church if one lived solely by repentance, i.e. if one no longer concealed oneself before God by means of the Law but rather surrendered oneself totally to that fellowship with God effected through Jesus.[35]

In the initial years the disciples apparently gave themselves entirely to that which was new. While so doing, they thoughtlessly permitted the old to remain. Through their witness they summoned Israel to repentance solely in the light of Jesus' cross and resurrection, and ignored at first Jesus' demand for repentance from legalism. They were primarily concerned in their own conduct to give a good account of the whole faith and the (whole) love. In so doing they kept the Law—though not the Pharasaic ordinances[36]—without reflecting upon it. When the problem became acute through Stephen and the Gentile Christians, the main

---

[35] Cf. L. Goppelt, Jesus, Paul and Judaism, 1964, 59–65 (Eng. trans. of Christentum und Judentum, 45–49).

[36] Jesus had expressly rejected these as ordinances of men, Mark vii.9–13. Matt. xxiii.3 can only be understood as a kerygmatic overstatement, since even the Judaizers did not follow the Scribes.

body of the Palestinian Christians followed the rule set down in the particular tradition of Matthew's Gospel (xxiii.23). 'These ought you to have done, without neglecting the others.' In this way they made an effort to have a 'righteousness' which exceeded that of the Pharisees (v.20). They were conscious of being bound to the Mosaic ordinances, as we saw in the Cornelius story and in the incident at Antioch, and they did not observe these only from the standpoint of Matt. xvii.26 f.: 'The sons are free. However, not to give offence to them ...' (cf. §8, 2 ff.; §11, 1).

In so doing were they disobedient to Jesus? To a certain degree Jesus' affirmation of the Law demanded this conduct of them. It demanded that his Church in Jerusalem and also in Antioch and Rome should live in accordance with the social orders of this world and bring salvation by means of her message to those who believed. In the world of the Church, the Mosaic Law was both a social regimen and the law of the land. Should Jesus' pronouncement have been a new Law, then his Church would have been forced either as the Zealots to revolt, as the Pharisees to reform, or as the Essenes to move into the wilderness. Jesus' affirmation of the Law obliged his Church, as Paul makes clear in Rom. xiii, to live according to the social orders of this world, but according to Jesus' pronouncement, she must so live in this world that she bears witness to the New World which has dawned for her with Jesus' resurrection, and this meant tension and conflict in relation to every worldly order and especially in relation to the Mosaic Law (cf. §12, 3).

The Mosaic Law was not only the social order of the earliest Church's environment, but also the redemptive order of the Sinaitic Covenant, so that the time had to come when Stephen would have to bring forward the side of the message critical of the Law at the point when his audience wanted to evade his message with the help of the old order ordained by God. Similarly, the time had to come when Peter would have to abandon the commandment concerning clean and unclean in order to remain obedient to Jesus' instructions of salvation for all by means of faith alone. The time also came when James, the Lord's brother, was killed by the High Priest's executioner in the Temple where he prayed daily for the conversion of Israel. He died because he remained to the end a witness of Jesus in spite of his obligation—indeed too strong an obligation —to the Law and to the people under the Law (cf. p. 60).

The later Palestinian Church, particularly after the year A.D. 70, avoided more and more this attitude of tension with the Law, so that its message became blunted and it became what it had not been at the beginning, a Jewish αἵρεσις (cf. §5, 2). It became the prototype of the Christian who breaks off the sharp edge of the message for the sake of his obligation to the world. At the beginning, its conduct with reference to the Law had been an undecided feature of her understanding of faith; in the later period, it brought about a complete breakdown in her faith.

With this breakdown the Palestinian Church surrendered the basis which had united the earliest Church in all its diversities and modifications up to and beyond A.D. 70 in its attitude to the Law. It was this basis which had caused all the leading men from Paul to James unanimously to reject Judaism. From the start, the Congregation (Church) of Jesus no longer expected her salvation by fulfilling the Law but by the grace of the Son of Man who would then 'confess' those who had 'confessed' him here (Matt. x.32 f. par.; cf. Acts xv.11). The Jewish groups used the practice of the Law as the dividing line; the Congregation (Church) of Jesus used only the confession of Jesus as the Bringer of Salvation who simultaneously confirmed and annulled the Law.

This self-understanding stood behind the work of the Church in the world as well as her inner life. We turn now to a discussion of both of these aspects.

6. THE MISSION, MESSAGE AND BAPTISM

1. According to Acts, from the earliest beginnings the Church's missionary work was the most important expression of life in the Congregation (Church) of Jesus,[1] but is this impression only received because Luke wanted to portray the basic missionary character of the Church's development, if not to relate an actual history of missions? Or was the missionary intent actually the most characteristic trait of this αἳρεσις?

Special movements had developed in Judaism not only in order to practise a particular religious point of view but also to represent this point of view to the rest of the nation. In addition, the eschatological claim by the Essenes, Zealots, and Pharisees led to an energetic recruiting of members. The Essenes, by means of a most complicated initiation procedure, established a close-knit order which, without any 'mission', was to attract the 'Sons of Light' solely by means of its existence.[2] The Zealots dragged the nation into insurrections through prophetic agitation.[3] The Pharisees finally succeeded in making the entire nation, to a

---

[1] Literature: H. Schlier, 'Die Entscheidung für die Heidenmission in der Urchristenheit', in Die Zeit der Kirche (²1958), 90–107; L. Aalen, Die Begriffe 'Licht' und 'Finsternis' im Alten Testament, im Spätjudentum und im Rabbinismus (1951); J. Jeremias, Jesus' Promise to the Nations (Eng. trans. 1958, of Jesu Verheissung für die Völker, 1956, 64), 76, for further literature. D. J. Bosch, Die Heidenmission in der Zukunftsschau Jesu (1959); F. Hahn, Mission in the New Testament (Eng. trans. 1965, of Das Verständnis der Mission im Neuen Testament, 1963).

[2] K. Schubert, The Dead Sea Community (Eng. trans. 1959, of Die Gemeinde vom Toten Meer, 1958, 42 ff.), 43 ff.

[3] Josephus, B.J. 2, 14–17.

greater or lesser degree, submissive to their programme after they had taken over the political leadership in A.D. 70. They accomplished this feat both by a persistent exhortation for repentance and by social pressure.

Jesus' disciples took an entirely different way. While the Essenes, having given up the masses of Israel as apostate, retreated into the wilderness to await their hour, the disciples came from Galilee to Jerusalem. They came neither as the Zealots in order to set the nation alight with messianic insurrection, nor as the Pharisees to wrestle doggedly for the religious and political leadership. They came instead, ignoring these struggles which arose from the Law, to place before all Israel a unique message. Their representatives spoke neither as prophets nor as experts of the Torah but as 'apostles'. Their recruiting alone earned the name 'mission' (cf. pp. 20, 82).

2. How was this carried out? The New Testament texts offer quite diverse answers to this question. Acts has the missionary efforts of 'the apostles' limited at first exclusively to Jerusalem (Acts i.4; viii.1). Here the Lucan redaction has the apostles publicly preaching the message of Jesus and the Church growing by leaps and bounds through mass conversions,[4] but this picture is corrected in the more specific account of Acts iii f. Here, Peter and John are quite unknown to the city as representatives of this message (iii.3 f.; iv.13), and their attempt to preach to a gathering attracted by a miracle ends with their arrest (iv.1 f.). In fact therefore, the missionary effort took place with much more restraint than the Lucan redaction depicts. It conducted instruction in small groups and by personal contact, but after a while, no doubt their claim became generally known to the city, which one could cross in less than thirty minutes.

Nevertheless, did the main part of the mission actually concentrate on Jerusalem in the initial years as Acts depicts? Would the disciples have brought over the accounts of their commission into the Synoptic tradition (Mark vi.7–11 par. Luke; Luke x.3–12 Q; Matt. x.5–16) if they had never acted in keeping with the accounts? Weizsäcker has suggested that the apostles, contrary to Acts, had from the very beginning moved two by two through the villages of Galilee and Judea, although Paul (cf. p. 28) confirms that between the years of A.D. 35 and 40 the leading men were still to be found in Jerusalem.

The Galilean disciples would not have moved to Jerusalem if they had not expected that the salvation for all Israel would dawn through their witness (cf. §4, 2) there, where all Israel, including those from the Dias-

---

[4] Acts ii.6, 41; 3,000 baptized; iv.4; 5,000 disciples; iv.33; v.12–16, 28; '. . . You have filled Jerusalem with your teaching. . . .'

pora, gathered together especially at the feasts.[5] This expectation probably included the concept of the eschatological pilgrimage of the nations to Zion which Jesus had adapted in a unique manner. By means of a centripedal movement beginning with, and moving beyond, a converted Israel, the nations of the world were also to have a share in the salvation of the end times. When the disciples worshipped and taught in the Temple, they did so not only in view of their ties to a cult which for them was already invalidated, and not only for the sake of missionary tactics, but also in view of the probable expectation that the consummation would dawn in and through the Temple by means of a total renewal of worship (cf. §7, 6; §8, 1).[6]

Luke no longer saw this eschatological background to the disciples' conduct, but explained it in terms of missionary history by means of his concept of mission centres. Historically, however, he had correctly maintained that the leading men, above all the Twelve, in the initial years had carried out their mission basically in Jerusalem.

Perhaps people other than the apostles had moved earlier two by two over the roads of Palestine. At any rate, the itinerant mission began when Jerusalem failed to fulfil the expectation. It began for Peter, at the very latest, when he had to flee Jerusalem in the year A.D. 44 (cf. §8, 5). According to I Cor. ix.5 he was already in the fifties engaged in his mission as an apostle. In this second stage of the mission the picture of the itinerant apostle, from the accounts of the sending of the disciples, came to life again. It was still alive in the Syro-Palestinian tradition of the Did. xi.3–6 (cf. §8, 4).

The apostles, who were synonymous with the Twelve, and other men, like Stephen and Philip (vi.8; viii) who were later designated as evangelists (xxi.8), appear in Acts as representatives of the mission, but the most extensive expansion took place through the anonymous members of the Church, through the Hellenists who fled Jerusalem (viii.4; xi.19 ff.). The fragmentary and outline statements correspond essentially with the historical events. The mission was initially carried out by the apostles whom Jesus himself had commissioned and whose number certainly exceeded the Twelve. Soon after, it was also being carried out by itinerant missionaries who had been commissioned by the Spirit or the Church and who were also called apostles in Palestine, while in the Pauline area

---

[5] Matt. viii.11 par. Luke (in keeping with Isa. xlix.12; xxv.6); cf. Isa. ii.2 f. (par. Micah iv.1 f.); xlv.20, 22 ff.; lv.5; lvi.7; lx et al.; cf. J. Jeremias, *Jesus' Promise to the Nations* (1958), 55 ff.; cf. n. 6 and §8, n. 1.

[6] Mark xi.17 (= Isa. lvi.7 '. . . My house shall be called a house of prayer for all peoples'); Mark xiv.58 par. (the new Temple); Matt. xvi.18 (Peter, the foundation stone of the new house of God), et al.

the designation 'evangelist' later emerged for them.[7] Nevertheless, the rapid and broad expansion which Acts assumes and Paul supports[8] could only have been possible if every baptized member had become a missionary witness wherever he was. Only in this way can one explain the fact that already at the time of Paul's conversion believers were to be found in remote Damascus (Acts ix.1) as well as in Galilee and Judea (Acts ix.31). This missionary activity lacked organization; the nature of the force of the message dictated this work. While the Essenes had been instructed to love all who shared their convictions and to hate everyone else,[9] the Gospel urged the believers out of love to seek and to save the lost. For this reason the mission also went beyond the boundaries of Israel (cf. §9, 1).

3. What was the content of the missionary *kerygma* which the disciples placed before Israel after Pentecost? Acts recounts in chapters ii–v four of Peter's missionary sermons.

As we can see from their style, their usage of the LXX, etc., they take their literary form from Luke. The writer of history in those days was not expected to reproduce the content of the speeches of his principal character, but to compose them himself in order clearly to convey the situation. Did Luke operate according to this rule? This has often been suggested,[10] but we can see from his Gospel that basically he did not intend to be a writer of history so much as an evangelist. He did not even think about putting speeches which he had composed into Jesus' mouth. On the contrary he sought, for example in Luke iv. 16–30, merely to reproduce the tradition. In the same way, Luke did not intend in Acts to record past history in chronological terms nor to create a story for the edification of his congregation, but to bear witness before the Church to the events which founded it. For him the apostolic word was definitely part of these events. There are actually several indications that traditional elements underlay the speeches of Acts so that, apart from Acts v.29–32, Semitisms and a theology foreign to Luke often

---

[7] Luke does not call the seventy in Luke x.1 apostles. They are a symbolic reference to the Gentile nations without any historical significance. Perhaps the missionary discourse in Q (Luke x) was not originally connected with the circle of the Twelve.

[8] Gal. i.22 f.; I Thess. i.14; II Cor. xi.32 f.

[9] I QS i.9 f.; ix.21 f.; x.19–21.

[10] M. Dibelius (see *Studies in the Acts of the Apostles*, Eng. trans., 1956) 'Die Reden der Apg. und die antike Geschichtsschreibung', *Aufsätze zur Apostelgeschichte* (1951), 120–162, and yet: they contain '. . . without doubt sermon material of the Church from the early period . . .' (p. 158). The classical examination of this problem goes beyond Dibelius: C. H. Dodd, *The Apostolic Preaching and its Developments* (1951). We follow him considerably in the subsequent discussion. *Contra* E. Haenchen, *Apostelgeschichte* (*Meyer Kommentar* [10]1956), 152 and U. Wilckens, *Die Missionsreden der Apostelgeschichte* (1961), 188: the sermon outline which lies at the heart of the missionary speeches in the first part of Acts is '. . . an essential element of Lucan theology'.

occur in Peter's sermons.[11] These sermons are different from Stephen's speech in Acts vii and from James's speech in Acts xv.[12] It is quite possible, according to the present state of the critical analysis of the tradition, that Peter's sermons in Acts ii–v, being based on tradition, reproduce correctly the outlines of the earliest apostolic *kerygma*.

This is supported by their content. Since they all have the same outline, one can place the four sermons side by side in a synopsis. After an introduction follows:

Chapter	ii	iii	iv	v	I Cor. xv
1. The central proclamation: You put Jesus to death, God however has raised him and (by so doing) exalted him to be the Christ.	22–24	13–15	11	30 f.	3 f.
2. Scriptural evidence for both:	25–31	18	11	—	'in accordance with the Scriptures'
3. Reference to the witnesses:	32–36	15b–16	—	32	5 ff.
4. Call to repentance and offer of salvation	38 f.	19	12	31b	—

This outline is further supported as early tradition in that it agrees to a surprising extent with the *kerygma* in I Cor. xv.3 ff. We have before us, therefore, the earliest outline of the apostolic *kerygma*. Doubtless a fifth element must be added which appeared in the very earliest form of these sermons, namely Acts iii.19 f. The call to repentance is strengthened here by the reference to the imminent consummation through the parousia of Jesus the Messiah. Originally, this reference was probably stressed much more than it is now in Acts, but without doubt the witness to Jesus' resurrection and not the announcement of the imminent parousia had been the focal point. Expectation of the end was widespread in the world in which the Church existed, but the Easter witness was unique. Dodd was probably correct in thinking that the Church looked upon the resurrection, the parousia, and the gathering of the redeemed community in the intervening period as a single eschatological event.[13]

4. Let us attempt to analyse briefly this earliest preaching by the Church in order to get a better look at the elements which shaped it (cf. §2, 4 a).

a. From the beginning, the central theme was no longer 'Jesus' Gospel'

[11] Dodd, *op. cit.*, 27; F. J. Foakes-Jackson and K. Lake, *Beginnings*, ii, 44–65.
[12] B. Reicke, *Glaube und Leben der Urgemeinde* (1957), 39.
[13] Dodd, *op. cit.*, p. 33.

(of the coming Kingdom) (cf. Matt. iv.17; x.7), but the 'Gospel of (about) Jesus the Christ'.[14] This change was not, as Harnack thought, a crucial defection from Jesus,[15] but the unveiling of the mystery of the Kingdom of God which Jesus had disclosed to his disciples (cf. §2, 4b). The message of the Kingdom had now become the message of (about) Jesus, since the Kingdom comes through his works.[16]

b. This message was proclaimed as the witness, as a very contingent witness, of the Easter witnesses. Since the second century, men have attempted to make this witness credible either by interpreting it as an expression of general truths, by using proof texts from scripture, or by referring to the miracles which often accompanied the witness.[17] According to Acts, even the first preaching was accompanied by miracles.[18] This is basically supported by Paul (II Cor. xii.12; Rom. xv.19). For Paul and Acts, however, the miracles were only signs which referred to the redemptive event and its proclamation (Acts iii.11 ff.). According to both,[19] the witness of the disciples was substantiated only by means of the witness of the Spirit, in whom the Witnessed One himself worked. Through the witness of the Spirit it became kerygma, that is a compelling and self-authenticating address from God. The first witnesses only attempted to explain the message in terms of Jesus' earthly ministry and the scriptures, and to reveal it to the understanding of faith. This two-fold explanation became the beginning of Christian theology. It developed as follows:

c. Already in I Cor. xv.3 Jesus' death was (catechetically) interpreted by the words 'for us' which were a product of Jesus' earthly ministry. This reference to the redemptive significance of his death is missing in the sermons in Acts—probably in view of their missionary character. In place of this and in contrast to I Cor. xv, one is referred back to the course of Jesus' earthly ministry. In Acts ii.22 and iii.22 the reference is quite brief, while in x.37 ff. it is so detailed that one can see here the starting point for the outline of Mark's Gospel.[20] This outline emerges as soon as the apostolic Easter kerygma is expanded and explained by Jesus'

---

[14] A. v. Harnack, What is Christianity? (Eng. trans. of Das Wesen des Christentums, 1950 r.p.), 103, 124 f.

[15] Ibid., 108, 'Not the Son, the father alone belongs to the Gospel as Jesus proclaimed it'.

[16] Luke correctly explains it so in Acts i.3–8; xxviii.23, 31.

[17] On the latter, Justin, Apol., II, 6; Irenaeus, Haer. II, 31, 2 f.; cf. A. v. Harnack, The Mission and Expansion of Christianity, i, 101–146 (= Die Mission und Ausbreitung des Christentums, i, 129–170).

[18] Acts ii.43; iii.1 ff.; iv.30; v.12–16; vi.8 (Stephen); ix.32–43; xiv.3, 8 ff. (Paul and Barnabas); xx.10 (Paul), etc.

[19] Acts v.32; II Cor. iii.3 et al.

[20] Taylor, Mark, 106; (cf. §19, 4a).

earthly ministry, so that the Easter witness led even in the missionary sermon to a building of the Synoptic tradition (cf. §7, 1; 19, 3). Every pericope has been formulated in terms of the Easter witness as well as for it. However, the reverse is also true, that the Easter witness would have remained unintelligible and empty had it not been explained and expanded by Jesus' earthly ministry.

This entire witness to Jesus received its interpretation first when it was seen in the light of the scriptures—i.e. the Old Testament. This was necessary for the sake of the people in Jerusalem, because they could only accept such a message as far as they could incorporate that which was 'new' into their faith in the God of the Covenant. It was also necessary for the sake of the message itself since the meaning of Jesus' appearance could only be understood in terms of the scriptures. This message alone made clear that the eschatological, redemptive act of the one true God, whom the scriptures had borne witness to be the God of the Covenant, had taken place in Jesus (Acts iii.18; II Cor. i.20). The myths, among which were even some Jewish messianic speculations, were able to supply means of expression for the faith, but they were not a help in making the faith understandable, since these myths were not recognized to be God's witness, nor were they.[21]

Unlike Justin, who attempted to construct a scriptural proof in his *Dialogue with Trypho the Jew*,[22] the first disciples knew that it was impossible to prove Jesus' Messiahship from the scriptures, although they could understand it through faith. Jesus was a Messiah in a completely different manner from what one would have expected from the words of prophecy. The disciples had confessed him as the Christ without demonstrable proofs, since they recognized in faith that his work was the work of the God of the Covenant and since they had found through him the eschatological fellowship with God which had been promised for the time of salvation. This confession of faith now required conscientious rescrutiny. Consequently, the attention of the disciples shifted from the incarnation of Jesus back to the scriptures, and after gaining support from this source they turned again to the present (cf. II Cor. iii.12-18).

The Jewish exegesis had already made various use of this procedure. In I QpHab the present was interpreted as fulfilled prophecy in this way,

---

[21] The history-of-religions school has basically removed the difference between a *heilsgeschichtlich* interpretation in terms of the scriptures and mythical modes of expression, since they have ignored the judgement of faith which differentiates between scripture and myth. In so doing they call into question a central claim of the entire New Testament. E. Käsemann, 'Zum Thema der urchristlichen Apokalyptik', *Exegetische Versuche und Besinnungen* ii (1964), 105-131; L. Goppelt, 'Apokalyptik und Typologie bei Paulus', *TLZ* 89 (1964), 321-344.

[22] L. Goppelt, *Christentum und Judentum*, 192 ff.

and the Qumran Community had compiled for themselves messianic *testimonia*.[23] Most important of all, Jesus himself had already placed his appearance in the light of the scriptures as a guide for the disciples. Every pericope in the Synoptic tradition reveals to us how the first disciples compared Jesus' appearance with the scriptures. This is seen more from their allusions to the Old Testament than from direct quotations from it, but by their allusions they in fact carried out a basic theological task in in formulating the pericopes.[24] The scriptural quotations in Peter's sermons of Acts may well have been put together for the first time by Luke, but from the first the preaching was certainly supported by references to the scriptures. In this way the disciples gained their understanding of Jesus' appearance; simultaneously they gained a new understanding of the scriptures (cf. §9, 2b).

Thus the earliest christological confessions arose out of the Easter *kerygma*, deriving both from Jesus' earthly ministry and from the scriptures. It was confessed and proclaimed: Jesus, the Risen One, will soon appear as the Son of Man and Judge of the World and bring about the consummation.[25] At the same time it was asserted: God has exalted him already through the resurrection to be the heavenly Messianic King.[26] This in no way says that he had not already been the Messiah.[27] We are not to understand these formulae of the earliest Church in ontological terms. They simply express a calling to a work, and the exaltation of Jesus to be 'the Son of God in power . . . by his resurrection' (Rom. i.3 f.) does not exclude, but rather includes, the fact that he had worked before as the concealed Messiah on earth and that he was called to this work, as recounted later in the Synoptic tradition, at the baptism in the river Jordan (cf. p. 13).

Consequently, the christological formulae were open for the statements about Jesus' relationship to the cosmos, his mediating role in creation, etc., which became necessary in the Hellenistic Church. The formula about the exaltation of Jesus to be 'the Son of God in power . . . by his resurrection' first became a theory of 'adoptionist Christology'[28] when

[23] H. Bardtke, *Die Handschriftenfunde am Toten Meer* (1958), ii, 298 ff.; F. F. Bruce, *Biblical Exegesis and the Qumran Texts* (1960), O. Betz, *Offenbarung und Schriftforschung in der Qumransekte* (1960).

[24] L. Goppelt, *Typos* (1966 r.p.), 70 ff.

[25] Acts iii.19 f. and the Synoptic sayings about the future coming of the Son of Man.

[26] Acts ii.36; iii.13; xiii.33; Rom. i.3 f. (a formula from the Palestinian Church, so E. Schweizer, *Erniedriegung und Erhöhung bei Jesus und seinen Nachfolgern*, 1955, 55 f. (cf. Eng. trans. *Lordship and Discipleship*, 1960).

[27] E. Schweizer, *ibid.*, 86, correctly opposes the history-of-religions school and its offshoots which speak about an adoptionistic Christology of the earliest Church.

[28] L. Goppelt, *Christentum und Judentum*, 167 f.; H.-J. Schoeps, *Theologie und Geschichte des Judentums* (1949), 71–78.

the later Jewish Christianity rejected this extension of christology. This took place towards the end rather than at the beginning of the history of the Palestinian Church.

5. From the very beginning the goal of the missionary sermon was baptism.[29] Without doubt, from the earliest period baptism was generally practised in the Congregation (Church) of Jesus as a rite of acceptance and initiation,[30] and it was most certainly related to the baptism by John. Jesus had recognized only John's baptism as God's ordinance (Mark xi.30 par.), not the washings of the Pharisees and Essenes, and he had submitted to it (Mark i.9 ff. par.). This was the actual establishment of Christian baptism. According to an element of the tradition which has been obscured by the practice of the Church (Matt. xxviii.19), the Risen One had commanded the practice of baptism.[31] This command to baptize would resemble in character the command to repeat the Lord's Supper. Its transmission is uncertain, but without it the general practice of baptism from the very beginning would be most difficult to understand.

Acts introduced baptism at the end of the sermon on Pentecost with the following interpretation: 'Repent, and be baptized every one of you in the name of Jesus Christ for the forgiveness of your sins; and you shall receive the gift of the Holy Spirit' (Acts ii.38). This sentence was formulated by Luke, but it certainly contains early tradition. Baptism by John was a baptism of repentance for the forgiveness of sins, and it has been suggested that the baptism of the earliest Church was nothing more than this;[32] the invocation of Jesus' name and the promise of the Spirit would then represent later additions. This is out of the question, however,[33] since during the earthly ministry repentance and forgiveness were already mediated to the disciples through Jesus. The disciples, therefore, could hardly have permitted to follow the preaching of the Risen One a

---

[29] Literature: *TWNT*, i, 527–544; K. Barth, *Teaching of the Church Regarding Baptism* (Eng. trans., 1954, of *Die Kirchliche Lehre von der Taufe*, [4]1953); H. Schlier, 'Zur kirchlichen Lehre von der Taufe', *ThLZ*, 72 (1947), 321–336 (and in *Die Zeit der Kirche*, [2]1958, 107–129); O. Cullmann, *Baptism in the New Testament* (Eng. trans. 1951 of *Die Tauflehre des Neuen Testaments*, [2]1958); W. F. Flemington, *The New Testament Doctrine of Baptism* (1948); J. Jeremias, *Infant Baptism in the First Four Centuries* (Eng. trans. 1960, of *Die Kindertaufe in den ersten vier Jahrhunderten*, 1958); N. A. Dahl, 'The Origin of Baptism', *Norsk Teologisk Tidsskrift* 56 (*Festschrift* for Mowinkel, 1955), 36–52. G. R. Beasly-Murray, *Baptism in the New Testament*, 1962; G. Delling, *Die Taufe im Neuen Testament*, 1963.

[30] In Rom. vi.1 ff., Paul takes for granted that all have been baptized in the Church of Rome, although he was not familiar with it. So Acts ii.38; viii.12, 16; ix.18; x.47 ff., etc.

[31] Cf. Mark xvi.16 (secondary ending); Acts i.5 (?); John iii.5.

[32] Recently by Bultmann, *Theology of the New Testament*, §6, 3 and §13, 1; cf. Lietzmann, *History of the Early Church:* vol. i, 63 f.

[33] On Acts xviii.24 and xix.1 ff., see §12, n. 36.

baptism which had no more meaning than John's baptism. They invoked Jesus' name at healings and thus all the more over the baptismal act (not over the water or the one being baptized). This took place either with the formula 'into the name' (εἰς τὸ ὄνομα), i.e. baptism dedicates the one being baptized to Jesus, or less often with the formula 'in the name' (ἐν (ἐπὶ) τῷ ὀνόματι), i.e. in baptism Jesus comes to work in the life of the one being baptized.[34] Both formulae state that baptism effects what it effects, repentance and forgiveness, because Jesus places the one being baptized in relationship to himself. To be placed in relationship with the exalted Jesus, however, always means by the nature of the event to be surrendered to the work of the Spirit, so that of necessity the promise of the Spirit belonged from the beginning with baptism. Thus baptism was a baptism of repentance for the forgiveness of sins which was performed under the invocation of Jesus' name and which was bound up with the promise and the experience of the work of the Spirit.[35] Baptism was given to the Church in this form; we must fundamentally differentiate what was given from its theological interpretation.

In the first period, baptism was granted to everyone who desired it after hearing the missionary sermon. We first hear in the post-Pauline period about a catechumen circle or a probation time comparable, for example, to that developed by the Qumran group.[36] We will discuss below the performance of baptism in our portrayal of the Christian worship service (cf. §22, 3). At this point, we simply want to make clear that the message of the preaching was physically and personally appropriated by means of baptism. In view of this, it becomes evident that the disciples did not intend to be a movement or a fellowship with a particular religious cause but rather the eschatological people of God in an historical form: not Christianity but Church.[37]

7. THE INNER LIFE OF THE CHURCH

The community of the baptized '... devoted themselves (as though held by a magnet) to the apostles' teaching and fellowship, to the breaking of bread and the prayers' (Acts ii.42). What this sentence enumerates are the basic elements of the Church's life, especially of their worship service which was the celebration of the sacramental meal. Consequently, the whole life of the Church, which the sentence actually intends to describe, is set forth in the worshipping assembly, and conversely the Church's

---

[34] TWNT, v, 274 f.
[35] TWNT, iv, 410 ff.
[36] See n. 2 (I QS vi.13–23; CD xv.7–11 cf. vi.10; xv.5 f.).
[37] Contra A. v. Harnack, History of Dogma, ii, 18 ff.

life itself is designated as a service of worship.[1] This becomes clear when we examine the parts individually.

1. The role of teaching in the Church[2] must be seen in terms of the background of teaching in the Church's Jewish environment.

The life of the Church's environment was governed according to the principle of Judaism by the teaching of the scribes.[3] The public listened to the official scribes who were predominantly the Pharisees; groups such as the Essenes listened to their own teachers of the Law. Teaching always meant the authoritative application of the scriptures to life, especially the Law, in keeping with the tradition (and, for Qumran, with inspiration). The scribe imparted his teaching as oral tradition through didactic conversations with his students, and he made religious and legal decisions in the synagogue and Sanhedrin according to it. His teaching also influenced the teaching by the laity, especially the sermon in the synagogue worship service which could be delivered by any adult Israelite chosen by the synagogue's leader (Luke iv.16 ff.; Acts xiii.14 ff.).[4] Besides this, as illustrated by the liturgy of the Feast of the Passover, the head of each household was obliged to teach his dependents,[5] while youths from the age of six were instructed to read and write from the Torah by the men of the synagogues in elementary schools attached to the synagogues.[6] The sectarians submitted their members to their own intensive teaching.[7] The Pharisees attempted in this way to dominate the public teaching, the Essenes withdrew their members from it.

Since Jesus' teaching and that of the scribes were mutually exclusive, those baptized followed their own chosen teaching, that of the apostles, but unlike the Essenes, they took part not only in the Temple worship but also in the life of the synagogue in the hope that the synagogue would open its doors to the new teaching. In following the teaching of the apostles rather than that of the scribes, which was the authority for all the separate Jewish movements, they declared that the Torah had been superseded through its fulfilment in Jesus. Whereas the scribes of all the

---

[1] P.-H. Menoud exegetes the verse in this way in his work *La vie de l'Église naissante* (1952).

[2] 'Teaching of the apostles' in Acts ii.42 means primarily 'teaching' and not, as in Did. Inscr., 'doctrine'. However, the teaching is also modified as to its content by means of the attribute in the genitive: It was important in that they '. . . [were] from the beginning . . . eyewitnesses and ministers of the word . . . ,' which they passed on as tradition (Luke i.1-4). Literature: *TWNT*, ii, 138-168; P. Carrington, *The Primitive Christian Catechism* (1940); F. Filson, 'The Christian Preacher in the First Century', *JBL*, 60 (1941), 317-328.

[3] E. Schürer, *A History of the Jewish People in the Time of Jesus Christ*, Div. II, vol. i, 306-379 (Eng. trans. 1886 of *Geschichte des jüdischen Volkes im Zeitalter Jesu Christi*); S.-B. i, 79 ff. 691 ff.; ii, 647-661; J. Jeremias, *Jerusalem zur Zeit Jesu*, ³1962, 127-132, 265-278, 286-291.

[4] S.-B., iv, 171 f.; *TWNT*, ii, 141 f.   [5] S.-B., iii, 664; iv, 67 ff.
[6] S.-B., iii, 664 f.; iv, 149; *TWNT*, v, 646.   [7] I QS vi.6-8; I QSa i.4-9.

various movements represented the Torah, the apostles represented a person, Jesus.

The form of the apostles' teaching was Old Testament-Jewish; it was not socratic in the Greek sense. They, like Jesus (Matt. v.2; Mark viii.31), set forth authoritatively God's will and plan for the particular situation with the help of the scriptures,[8] although they no longer developed their teaching according to the guidance of the tradition of the Torah but, as we have already seen in their missionary discourses, in terms of the Easter *kerygma*. Consequently, their teaching was basically a sermon, aiming at a submissive and loyal belief in the doctrine of Easter.[9]

The content of the teaching develops from this starting point. On the one hand, the Easter *kerygma* gained significance in view of Jesus' earthly ministry. Just as the Synoptic tradition resulted from the missionary preaching and teaching in the form of Mark's Gospel, so the tradition from the teaching within the Church resulted in the 'sayings source' (Q) and in Matthew's Gospel.[10] On the other hand, after the Easter *kerygma* had gained its significance in view of Jesus' earthly ministry, it was unfolded through teaching in christological and soteriological statements, in ethical instructions and in other forms of instruction which are met later in the especially impressive form of I Corinthians or Hebrews. Even from this teaching, as we shall see, a tradition arose. Teaching of the Old Testament-Jewish type always aimed at further transmission of fixed formulation (cf. §19, 3).

Just as the Church followed the Jewish *form* of teaching, so she followed the Jewish custom in carrying out the teaching, so that the teaching was doubtless given at the sacramental meal.[11] The father of a Christian household definitely taught as much as his Jewish counterpart, and it may even be that there developed in primitive Christianity a special instruction for the youths like that among the Essenes, and a theological schooling similar to that of the scribes.[12] Although Jesus forbade his disciples to become teachers similar in kind to the scribes (Matt. xxiii.8 ff.), would not his teaching in the circle of his disciples, which appeared

[8] *TWNT*, ii, 140 (line 21).
[9] Therefore the terms 'proclamation' and 'teaching' often overlap in the New Testament usage.
[10] According to H. E. Tödt, *The Son of Man in the Synoptic Tradition* (Eng. trans. 1965, of *Der Menschensohn in der synoptischen Überlieferung*, 1959, 215–231), 235–253, the Q tradition originated in a Church different from that of the Mk-tradition. In reality, Q is the latter's catechetical complement. Cf. J. Schniewind, 'Zur Synoptiker Exegese', *ThR* 2 (1930), 129–189, see n. 14 for a different evaluation.
[11] Acts xx.7. As at the Passover, S.-B., iv, 67 ff. and perhaps at the communal meals of Qumran.
[12] Josephus, *B.J.* ii; 120; I QSa i.6–8. Naturally this would have been necessary with the practice of infant baptism.

outwardly to be identical to that of a scribe in the midst of his students, have given rise to a Christian scribal teaching of corresponding form (Matt. xiii.52)? Both Matthew's Gospel and the Johannine writings appear to presuppose just such 'schools'.[13] At any rate, from the earliest period the Gospel tradition as well as the 'catechetical' tradition of primitive Christianity was less homiletical than catechetic in nature because of the role of teaching in the Church (cf. §21, 5d).[14]

Furthermore, it is significant in understanding the nature of the Church that, at the same time as this teaching, a new voice of prophecy[15] arose in her midst. This prophecy spoke independently of the scriptures and of the developing tradition, but like the teaching was influenced mainly by the Easter witness. 'The testimony of (about) Jesus is the spirit of prophecy' (Rev. xix.10). According to the New Testament, this principle from the most outstanding document of primitive Christian prophecy was valid for the Church in general.[16] The earliest prophecy of the Palestinian Church may be echoed in some of the sayings of Revelation and may have entered the Synoptic tradition in certain sayings as words of Jesus. From the start, though, the words of the Exalted One through the Spirit were fundamentally differentiated from the words of the Jesus of history during his life on earth just as clearly as they were later in Paul (cf. §21, 5c).

2. According to Acts ii.42, the teaching was combined with the 'breaking of the bread'.[17] A breaking of bread in the Jerusalem Church is briefly mentioned elsewhere only in Acts ii.46: '. . . and breaking bread in their homes (i.e. in groups which were gathered in the individual homes) they partook of food with glad and generous hearts'. According to this verse, the breaking of bread designated a meal. It is also mentioned as parallel to the attendance at the Temple observances, and so had the character of a worship service. After giving thanks the Jewish father began the dinner with the 'breaking of the bread'. Here in Acts, the phrase has become a fixed designation in the Church's language for a sacramental meal. How are we to understand this meal?

[13] K. Stendahl, *The School of St. Matthew and its Use of the Old Testament* (1954); §17, 3.

[14] Cf. Bultmann, *A History of the Synoptic Tradition*, 61; V. Taylor, *The Formation of the Gospel Tradition* (²1935, r.p. 1964); B. Gerhardson, *Tradition and Transmission in the Early Christianity*, 1964.

[15] *TWNT*, vi, 849–857; cf. Matt. vii.22; x.41; xxiii.34; Acts ii.17; xi.28; x.32; xxi.9.

[16] I Cor. xii.3; I John iv.2 f.

[17] Literature: *TWNT*, iii, 729, 737; vi, 142; E. Lohmeyer, 'Das Abendmahl in der Urgemeinde', *JBL*, 56 (1937), 217–252; E. Schweizer, 'Das Abendmahl, eine Vergegenwärtigung des Todes Jesu oder ein eschatologisches Freudenmahl?' *ThZ* 2 (1946), 81–101; B. Reicke, *Diakonie, Festfreude und Zelos* (1951); P.-H. Menoud, 'Les Actes des Apôtres et l'Eucharistie', *Rev. hist. et phil.*, 33 (1953), 21–36; cf. n. 18.

Later, according to Acts xx.7, the Hellenistic Church designated by 'the breaking of bread' the same celebration which Paul in I Cor. xi.20 ff. called the Lord's Supper. It involved a regular meal which, similar to the Jewish sacral meals,[18] was combined with teaching, praying and liturgy, but culminated in the sacramental eating and drinking which the liturgical formula in I Cor. xi.23 ff., the so-called words of institution, describes. Every part of this meal points to Palestinian tradition, even the words of institution and its earliest interpretation in I Cor. x.16 which was a formula of the Church's tradition.

Nevertheless, Hans Lietzmann and other scholars[19] have had misgivings about tracing it back to the breaking of bread in the earliest Church. According to Lietzmann, the Lord's Supper proclaimed (in keeping with Paul's interpretation in I Cor. xi.26) the Lord's death, whereas according to Acts ii.46 the meal of the earliest Church was celebrated 'with gladness' (over the salvation of the end of time) and was thus an eschatological meal of rejoicing. The prayers at the meal in Did. 9 f. presuppose a meal of rejoicing without any relationship to the words of institution. From this Lietzmann concluded that the earliest Church's celebration of the meal in the form of a worship service was a different type of meal than the Lord's Supper of the Hellenistic Church. It did not reflect the (supposed) institution on the night of the betrayal but continued the table-fellowship of the earthly ministry. The Church considered the Risen One to be invisibly present in their midst, just as the Emmaus disciples had experienced him in a visionary manner. This concept of the meal continued to exist in the prayers of the meal in Did. 9 f. and in the liturgical tradition attached to it. The sacramental Lord's Supper and the corresponding words of institution arose for the first time in the Hellenistic Church (perhaps on the basis of Jesus' words of farewell).

It has become clear, however, that the prayers of the meal in Did. 9 f. refer to the regular meal which preceded the sacramental eating and drinking. The liturgical formulae at the end of Did. 10 form a transition to the latter, so that, in the terminology of the end of the second century, the prayers are not eucharistic but *agape* prayers.[20] At the same time the conviction that the words of institution are historical in their nucleus has

---

[18] The Passover (S.-B., iv, 56–74; TWNT, iii, 732 f.) and the Essene meal (I QS vi.1–6; I QSa ii.17–22; Josephus, B.J., 2, 8, 5).

[19] *Messe und Herrenmahl* (1926), 250–255; Bultman follows him in *Theology of the New Testament*, §6, 4; §8, 3; in a different way cf. K. G. Kuhn, 'The Lord's Supper and the Communal Meal at Qumran', in *The Scrolls and the New Testament*, ed. K. Stendahl (1957, Brit. ed., 1958), 65–93 (= 'Uber den ursprünglichen Sinn des Abendmahls und sein Verhältnis zu den Gemeinschaftsmahlen der Sektenschrift', *Ev. Theol.*, 10, 1950–51, 508–527): The accounts of the institution are *logia* which were first taken over by the Hellenistic Church. Contrary to this, E. G. Gaugler, *Das Abendmahl im Neuen Testament* (1943), 34 f.

[20] Cf. §22, n. 42.

prevailed more and more in critical studies.[21] In that case, Jesus told his disciples at the Last Supper how the table-fellowship of the earthly ministry was to be continued after his death. He would no longer offer his fellowship to them through a common eating from the same bread but through a new eating and drinking which one might call 'sacramental'.[22] This promise corresponds to the manner in which the Exalted One actually worked after Pentecost; he was, as the Palestinian tradition (Matt. xviii.20; xxviii.20; Rev. iii.20; I Cor. xvi.22) emphasized much more emphatically than Paul or John, present among them in a divine manner.[23] Indeed, his presence was always so strong that he became operative in them through his Spirit or with them through his name. Thus they could not have resumed that special physical fellowship which the table-fellowship had once meant, by considering him to be present among them as before, but the fellowship was resumed in that they permitted him to become operative among them in keeping with his institution. Consequently, they combined with the regular meal an eating and drinking according to the words of institution. Such an eating and drinking was certainly unique in the Jewish world[24]—as unique as all that which was central in the earliest Church and which had been given through the first Easter. As with many other questions, because of the paucity of tradition we can no longer determine whether this special eating and drinking was combined daily with the regular meals. In Jerusalem, these regular meals together received through the 'sharing of common goods' a particular emphasis (Acts vi.1 f.) which they did not have in the outlying regions. In all probability the sacramental meal in Jerusalem also differed in many other ways from that in Antioch and Corinth, but the institution by Jesus was just as much the basis for the meal in the Gentile Church as in Jerusalem (cf. §22, 5).

3. Like the celebration of the meal, the Christian's prayer[25] in many ways follows the Jewish custom; yet it is new in its starting point. The two most important new starting points are evident in the formulae taken over by the Hellenistic Church in their original Aramaic form.

[21] J. Jeremias, The Eucharistic Words of Jesus: K. G. Kuhn, op. cit.; E. Schweizer, 'Abendmahl', RGG³.

[22] L. Goppelt, TWNT, vi, 141 f.

[23] He is at the right hand of God! Acts vii.56; Matt. xxii.43 f.; xxvi.64, etc., in keeping with Psa. cx.1.

[24] The concept of the sacramental communio is foreign to both Judaism and the Essenes. Consequently, whoever takes the principle of analogy found in the history-of-religions school as being the final measuring rod must either interpret the accounts of institution as symbolic, contrary to their own words, or make them cultic legends of the sacramental meals in the Hellenistic Church.

[25] Literature: TWNT, ii, 774 ff. (older literature), 801 ff.; E. v. d. Goltz, Das Gebet in der ältesten Christenheit (1901); J. Jeremias, 'Das Gebetsleben Jesu', ZNTW, 25 (1926), 123–140.

According to Rom. viii.15 and Gal. iv.6, when the Spirit impels Christians to appeal to God in a way that goes beyond their conscious understanding with the address, 'Abba, Father!', he bears witness in a most elementary manner to their being children of God. This was Jesus' unique address in prayer (Mark xiv.36 par.). The Jewish world knew this only as the most intimate address of the small child to his father. Jews were not familiar with this formula as the form of an address in prayer.[26] In this address a child-like relationship to God is evident which corresponds to the awareness of God which only Jesus could have, and which was mediated only through him.

Perhaps originally the Lord's Prayer began with this address (cf. Luke xi.2). At any rate, the Lord's Prayer was intended as the paradigm for a prayer of this type (Matt. vi.9), and was most probably given as a prayer formula which was to replace the Eighteen Benedictions.[27] Although it is basically in direct antithesis to this particular Jewish prayer, it follows its form and content. Just as the Eighteen Benedictions were prayed three times a day by the pious individuals and regularly in the synagogue worship service by the congregation, so the use of the Lord's Prayer might have been accepted quite early as a corresponding custom for Christian prayer. When Did. 8:2 f. orders the Christians to pray the Lord's Prayer three times daily instead of the corresponding Jewish prayers, it is without doubt a legalistic hardening which is frequently evident in the Didache but which was quite remote from Matt. vi.9 and Luke xi.2.[28]

The Church not only appealed to God in a new way but also to the exalted Christ. The Hellenistic Church also retained this second starting point in its original Aramaic form. We find among other formulae of the eucharistic liturgy in I Cor. xvi.22 and Did. 10:6 the prayer: *Maran-atha*. This can mean: 'Our Lord is coming', or, probably the more original in view of the earliest Greek translation in Rev. xxii.20, 'Come, our Lord!'[29] With this appeal at the breaking of bread the earliest Church implored (precisely according to the words of institution) the present and future coming of their Lord. The formula and the eucharistic words comprise the earliest pieces of the primitive Christian liturgy that we know.

Beside these independent, newly constructed formulae, parts of the Jewish liturgy were naturally taken over, for example the 'Amen' with

---

[26] *TWNT*, v, 984 f.; J. Jeremias, *Abba* (1966), in spite of Braun, *op. cit.* (§2, n. 7), ii, 128.

[27] S.–B., iv, 208–249; K. G. Kuhn, *Achtzehngebet und Vaterunser und der Reim* (1950).

[28] The prayer in Acts iv.24–30, which could be early tradition, is reminiscent of the Lord's Prayer.

[29] *TWNT*, iv, 470–475.

which the congregation appropriated for themselves the prayer of the leaders (I Cor. xiv.16) or the doxology with which it concluded the Lord's Prayer (Did. 8:2; Matt. vi.13 variant reading).[30] Just as teaching combined with prophecy, so prayer in the set formulae combined with the spontaneous prayer of the Spirit. Did. 10:7. 'But suffer the prophets to hold eucharist [to give thanks] as they will' (cf. I Cor. xiv.13 ff.) (cf. §22, 6b).

4. Fellowship appears in Acts ii.42 as well as the teaching of the apostles, the breaking of bread and the prayers. If it is only the worship service which is here being described, 'fellowship' could mean the collection (Rom. xv.26) or the sharing in the distribution of offerings (I Cor. x.16; Acts vi.1 f.), but, in fact, fellowship is the more inclusive, divinely ordained bond between the members of the Church which makes the Church a living fellowship (Gal. ii.9 f.; I John i.3, 6 f.).

This bond found a special expression in the earliest Church in the fact that, as Luke stated with an ancient Greek catchword, they had 'all things in common (κοινά)' (Acts ii.44; iv.32). The summary accounts leave the impression that a type of 'communism based on love' had been dominant in the earliest Church at Jerusalem (Acts ii.44 f.; iv.32, 34 f.), but this portrayal is corrected by the more specific accounts (Acts iv.36 f.; v.1–11), according to which the members of the congregation had made their possessions, including the necessities of life, available to the leadership of the Church in order that the latter might distribute them to those in need. This was not the case for every member[31] but it did involve the great majority of them—otherwise Ananias would not have feigned his offering. This did not take place on one occasion at the time of entrance into the congregation but more probably in a progressive manner according to the particular need.

When we examine the essence of this practice more closely in terms of similar practices, it reminds us first of all of the Essenes' sharing of common goods.[32] However, the early Church's practice differs fundamentally from that of the Essenes, for among the Essenes everyone was obliged on the occasion of his final acceptance into the group to transfer

---

[30] p. Berak 9, 14c, 10 Bar: In the sanctuary one did not respond with 'amen'. What did one say? 'Praise be the name of his glorious reign for ever and ever' (cf. S.–B., i, 423 f.). Thus, according to Cullmann, the addition of the doxology to the celebration of the meal was brought about through the use of the Lord's Prayer, *Early Christian Worship* (Eng. trans. 1953, of *Urchristentum und Gottesdienst*, ³1956, 16), 12 f.

[31] Otherwise Barnabas would not have been singled out in Acts iv.36 f., cf. Acts xii.12.

[32] Josephus, *B.J.*, 2, 8, 3 f.; *Antiq.* 18, 1, 5; Philo, *Quod omnis prob.*, *CW* vi, §75 ff.; I QS i.11–13; v.2 f.; vi.18–23; *CD* xvi; cf. Haenchen, *Apostelgeschichte*; H. Braun, *Spätjüdisch-häretischer und frühchristlicher Radikalismus* (1957), i, 162.

his possessions and also his income to the order for a common distribution. In the earliest Church the offering of one's belongings was absolutely voluntary (Acts v.4). Consequently no one could consider it to be a collective economy which centrally administered the regular income, and the practice in the earliest Church appears more to be a radical extension of the care for the poor which the official Pharisaic Judaism organized with the help of generously given alms.[33] In the earliest Church though, alms were not given with an ulterior motive, even the belongings necessary for life being offered out of an uncalculating love (Matt. vi.31 ff.).

The reason behind this particular practice becomes clearer when we note that it remained confined to the first period of the Jerusalem Church in spite of the fact that much was done in (early) Christianity through brotherly love.[34] Here in Jerusalem it was conditioned by a special situation: a great part of the Church had left both possessions and possibilities for income with their home in Galilee, and these and other members of the Church could only live in Jerusalem where there was already a great number dependent on aid[35] from the sacrifice by others of the necessities of life on their behalf (Mark x.28 ff. par.).[36] The moving to Jerusalem brought about a close daily fellowship necessitating a central distribution of the goods through the leadership of the Church, and it also declared the readiness to put everything in order in view of the imminent consummation. Since it remained a matter of personal, voluntary decision about one's possessions, unlike Qumran, it becomes evident that the Church did not act out of an enthusiasm arising from an expectation of the imminent end, but acted in their particular situation out of obedience to Jesus' words. Their realistic fellowship of love is therefore not a pattern to be imitated but more an illuminating witness for all ages of their faith. It is not surprising that at just such a central and vital matter problems of organization and structure of the Church should arise (Acts v.1–11; vi.1–6).

5. From the very beginning, we can observe in the organization of the Church, as in the service of worship, the same characteristic tension between historical forms and pneumatic freedom. The Church conducted herself as a living organism in keeping with the constitutional forms

[33] S.–B., ii, 643 ff.; Haenchen, op. cit., 218 f.; H. Bolkestein, Wohltätigkeit und Armenpflege im vorchristlichen Altertum (1939).

[34] Gal. vi.2–10; I Thess. iv.9–12; II Thess. iii.12 f.

[35] J. Jeremias, Jerusalem zur Zeit Jesu (³1962), 127–155.

[36] The Gentile Christians' collection for Jerusalem was conditioned primarily by the needs of many Christians in Jerusalem for support and not by the impoverishment of the Church on the basis of the initial 'common goods' policy. Neither was it conditioned by Jerusalem's claims, which, e.g. would be comparable to the Temple tax (§20, 4).

which she had taken over in an attitude of uninhibited independence from the Jewish tradition, yet she never made these forms into a constitution. This is still reflected in the accounts of Acts. In contrast to the *Manual of Discipline* from Qumran, we find in Acts, as in the entire New Testament, no trace of a Church constitution, although there are numerous legal and constitutional terms[37] which we meet again and again in the Qumran texts but which were completely foreign to Luke.

In the first years, the Church was represented and directed by Peter and the Twelve (cf. §§5, 3). Even before the Apostolic Council, these were replaced in the leadership of the Church [among Israel] by the 'Three Pillars' (Gal. ii.9) and in the local church of Jerusalem by James, the Lord's brother (Acts xii.17; Gal. i.19; ii.9, 12), with whom appeared a council of elders (Acts xxi.18).

Nevertheless, the entire congregation had always taken part in the regulation of congregational matters. The whole body of disciples had gathered (Acts vi.2, 5) for the appointment of the Seven. They also gathered for the discussion with Paul and Barnabas at the Apostolic Council (Acts vi.2, 5; xv.12, cf. 30) so that the Decree was agreed upon by 'the apostles and the elders with the whole church' (Acts xv.22). This is a Lucan formulation, but even according to Gal. ii.2, Paul had met with 'the pillars' in the presence of the congregation: 'I went up . . . and laid before them [the congregation] the gospel . . . but privately before them who were of repute.' Thus the entire congregation took part in all matters, and any one could speak out in the meeting of the congregation (Gal. ii.5). We never hear that a minority was overruled; all decisions are made with an apparent unanimity in that each one finally agreed with the majority vote either by silence or acclamation (Gal. ii.5, 7, 9; Acts vi.5; xi.18; xv.7, 12, 25).

Since I QS has presented us with a similar constitutional procedure, we can better understand the Lucan account. There we also find that there was an organizational structure, indeed a very rigid hierarchy, but that all the important questions were brought before the entire community. In the community assembly each could speak in turn according to his rank (I QS vi.8–11), but the decision was made neither by an individual, a group nor a majority, but by the entire company which listened to every one and which was, nevertheless, more than the sum of the individuals.

---

[37] B. Reicke, 'The Constitution of the Primitive Church in the Light of Jewish Documents', *The Scrolls and the New Testament*, ed. K. Stendahl (1957, Brit. ed., 1958), 143–156; S. E. Johnson, 'The Dead Sea Manual of Discipline and the Jerusalem Church of Acts', *The Scrolls and the New Testament* (as above), 129–142. W. Nauck, 'Probleme des frühchristlichen Amtsverständnisses', *ZNTW*, 48 (1957), 200–220: e.g. the terms τόπος, Acts i.25, and κλῆρος, Acts i.17; I Pet. v.3.

We cannot describe this constitutional procedure with the Greek categories familiar to us. It was neither monarchic, oligarchic nor democratic. It corresponded in part to the ancient concept of the community and in part to the conception, which was current in primitive Christianity as in the Essene community, that a Spirit rules over every individual. Thus it was not an idealized fantasy when Acts in a portrayal of the Apostolic Council reported after 'much questioning' a 'keeping silence and listening' and a 'coming to one accord' (Acts xv.7, 12, 25), nor simply an empty phrase which introduced the conclusion: 'For it seemed good to the Holy Spirit and to us. . . .' (Acts xv.28).

Just as the constitutional forms of primitive Christianity become clearer through the similarities in the Essene organization, so do the principles peculiar to primitive Christianity become clearer through the differences.

> The division of the Qumran community is determined by three principles which overlap one another. First, the community was (as the true Israel) divided according to birth into priests, Levites (elders), and 'the many' (I QS i.18 f., 21 f.; ii.19; vi.8; I QM xiii.1; cf. *TWNT*, vi, 660). In other words, it used the traditional division of Israel (Ezra ii.2–42). Secondly, within these groups the individual was rated 'according to his understanding and his works with regard to the Law' (I QS v.20–25; vi.13–23). This was the principle of Judaism which had become more and more predominant since Ezra. Everything had to be measured in terms of the Law. In addition to these is a third principle which mentions an order 'according to the Spirit' or 'the Spirits' (I QS v.24; ii.20, cf. vi.17; ix.14). Within the Church the charismatic order corresponded to this third principle much less than did the Gnostic order. We find the first principle only in the later Palestinian Church's esteem for the Lord's relatives (cf. p. 121). The second appears in a modified form when a member is examined to see if he is capable of teaching and whether or not he has proven himself faithful.

The principle which determined a man's position in the Church was his call by Jesus. It is not mere coincidence that the series of men who stood at the head of the Church in the first period happen to correspond to the list of witnesses to the resurrection in I Cor. xv.5 ff. All of the men who came into prominence later in the Church were authorized through the Spirit of the Exalted One (Acts vi.3, 8, 10; vii.55; viii.29, 39; xxi.8 f.), so that all work in the Church can only be a serving (Mark x.43 par.), while in Qumran the rule held, '. . . They may all obey each other, the lower (obeying) the higher' (I QS v.23; cf. §21, 1).

Since the Church was determined by faith in the visibly crucified and unseen resurrected Lord, her constitution was never fixed and uniform to the degree of that in the separate Essene community for example. On the other hand, the faith protected the historical forms of the organization from being dissolved by an enthusiastic perfectionism (cf. §20, 4; §21, 3).

6. The same thing holds true for their ways of life and their thought. The account of the conflict between the Hellenists and the Hebrews in Jerusalem (Acts vi.1–6) demonstrates this, giving us the first glimpse into the sociological and theological structure of the Church and introducing us to the forces which would carry it further.

What lies hidden behind the names 'Hellenists' and 'Hebrews'? Both conveyed a particular type within the earliest Church; they were only used here in the primitive Christian literature for the members of the Church. The previously unrecorded term 'Hellenists', according to its etymology, must have referred to the members of the Church whose native tongue was Greek. This would then be the Christians from the Diaspora synagogue(s) of Jerusalem (Acts vi.9).[38] The Hebrews, accordingly, were those whose native tongue was Aramaic. The terms emerged when the Hellenists became more prominent in the life of the Church. They most probably established their own house-congregations in which they made use of the Greek language, the LXX, and the traditions related to it as they once did in the Diaspora synagogue. Thus the Gospel had probably already been carried over from Aramaic into Greek in the earliest Church of Jerusalem, not in an academic fashion but in the vigorous everyday life of a bilingual Church. Just as the Hellenists with Greek as a native language were conversant in Aramaic, so the reverse was true since many Palestinian disciples could speak Greek.

Nevertheless, something more than simply a new language appeared with the Hellenists; we also find a new theological element. This becomes clear when we realize, as has been noted for some time, that the seven 'overseers' of the 'daily ministration' came from the circle of the Hellenists; they all have Greek names and one of them was a proselyte. Stephen, intentionally named first, came into conflict with the members of the Diaspora synagogue who had previously been his companions (Acts vi.5, 8 f.). It is evident from Stephen's address that he represented the Gospel differently from the men around the Twelve. While the latter were tolerated in Jerusalem as long as they did not disturb the public order, Stephen was driven out of the Jewish community. In the persecution which followed, all those who shared his viewpoint had to leave Jerusalem permanently. These were, as far as they were named, all Hellenists (Acts viii.4 f., xi.19 f.). Stephen thus represents the theological intention of the Hellenists who carried the Gospel beyond the boundaries of Israel to Samaria and among the Gentiles.

[38] *TWNT*, ii, 508 f.; Munck, *Paul and the Salvation of Mankind* (as in §5, n. 30), 218–220.

Actually, the statements with which they had accused Stephen (Acts vi.14) explain, as does his speech on his own behalf (Acts vii),[39] this radical development. Stephen differed from the Twelve in his attitude towards the Temple but not, as Paul did later, in his attitude towards the Law. For both Stephen and the Twelve the Temple was no longer the present means of grace, but unlike the Twelve, Stephen could no longer await the eschatological consummation of salvation in the Temple. In his statements about the Temple one sees the tradition which had been stressed since Deutero-Isaiah in view of the Diaspora situation, that God's redemptive presence was no longer bound to the sanctuary in Jerusalem.[40] Stephen followed this line of thought to its conclusion, not because he was moved by the liberalism[41] appearing on the outer perimeter of Diaspora Judaism—this liberalism was quite remote from such a 'Zionist' as Stephen—but because he was influenced by that obscure teaching of Jesus about the end of the Temple which the Palestinian disciples had conveyed but not actually put into practice (Acts vi.14; cf. Mark xiv.58 par. Matt.; John ii.19). Stephen brought this into the open, as did Jesus, when the members of the Diaspora synagogue attempted to avoid his missionary summons to repentance by their appeal to the Temple. As soon as this teaching was established, every reason to concentrate the movement on Jerusalem vanished (cf. §6, 2).

These observations appear to force us to the conclusion about the account in Acts vi which has often been drawn in critical studies:[42] It was not an organizational oversight but rather theological differences which led to the conflict between the Hellenists and the Hebrews. The Seven were in reality the leaders of the Hellenists just as the Twelve were of the Hebrews. It is unthinkable that the Seven would ever have obtained an office in the Church as a whole under these conditions,

[39] Stephen's speech must involve tradition in view of its unusual theology. Munck, op. cit., 221, n. 1, and 222, n. 1; B. Reicke, Glaube und Leben der Urgemeinde (1957), 131–136.

[40] O. Cullmann, 'L'opposition contre le temple de Jérusalem', NTS, 5 (1958–59), 158–172, finds in the attitude towards the Temple such a strong similarity between the Essenes, Hellenists and John's Gospel that he supposes the Hellenists to have been influenced by the traditions of heterodox Judaism, and they in turn are to have been the source of the Johannine tradition. We would prefer to distance the Hellenists more from the Essenes who continued to ascribe an eschatological meaning to the Temple and also from John's Gospel (cf. pp. 130 f.).

[41] More recently, W. Grundmann, 'Das Problem des hellenistischen Christentums innerhalb der Jerusalemer Urgemeinde', ZNTW, 38 (1939), 45–73; Haenchen, Apostelgeschichte, pp. 222 ff.; by contrast, B. Reicke, Glaube und Leben der Urgemeinde (1957). The most recent comprehensive discussion of the question about Stephen and the Hellenists, M. Simon, St. Stephen and the Hellenists in the Primitive Church (1958); cf. §8, 3.

[42] More recently, Grundmann and Haenchen, see n. 41.

so the accounts of Acts are an abortive attempt by Luke to harmonize them.[43]

Primitive Christianity thought differently. According to Paul's Epistles, representatives of the diverse theological viewpoints ranging from Paul to Peter and to James associated with one another as members of the one redeemed community. If, as is implied, the Hebrews and the Hellenists did not stand against each other like two Jewish movements (αἵρεσις) but rather lived together as two very different brothers, it becomes clear that the *ecclesia* of Jesus in Jerusalem included not only people from the most diverse movements in Palestinian Judaism, as did the group of Twelve disciples during the earthly ministry, but soon even former Diaspora Jews and proselytes, though not yet any of the uncircumcised. The background of these people was, as it were, transformed, because of their conversion, not simply erased. In this way the Gospel was expressed quite early with conceptual, linguistic and theological variety. It is significant that the separation of these various groups from one another in the earliest Church of Jerusalem did not result from forces within the Church but from without, through her diversified relationship with Judaism. For this reason the circle around Stephen (cf. §8, 4), and later the one around Peter, were forced to leave the city so that finally James, the Lord's brother, came to dominate the church in Jerusalem.

Consequently, what Acts vi recounts is on the whole quite possible, even if it was not historically the most decisive factor. An inner conflict might have arisen over the central distribution of material provisions, and resolved by the device, often proven effective, of pressing leading representatives of the complaining group into service for the whole body. Although Stephen and Philip appear elsewhere as missionaries, this does not exclude their working also within the Church, but in terms of primitive Christian practices it includes this. Luke does not intend to indicate that the Seven were subordinated to the Twelve just as the deacons were later to the bishops. He does not designate them as deacons, and he reports the origin of Church offices neither here nor elsewhere. Furthermore, the Seven might well have been originally representatives of the house-congregation of the Hellenists. The number Seven recalls the seven elders of the synagogue congregation.[44] The Hellenists would then have established in the *ecclesia* a type of synagogue congregation just as the Diaspora Jews did within the Jewish community. Whereas the Twelve were representatives of the eschatological nation of

---

[43] Haenchen, *Apostelgeschichte*, 246: 'One does not hand over the daily support of his own group to the leaders of another (who have in addition a different task)'. Who is the 'one' who thinks in this manner?

[44] S.-B., ii, 641; Josephus, *Antiq.* 4, 8, 14, 38.

twelve tribes, the prominence of the Seven indicates that the Church would come to the consummation not immediately, but by a development in history.

8. THE PRIMITIVE CHURCH AND ISRAEL

1. In Jerusalem, as in the whole of Palestine, the disciples had conformed to the life of the Jewish community. They lived in accordance with the Law and limited their mission to Israel. This limitation of the mission raises the same question as their life in accordance with the Law (pp. 30 ff.): in so doing were they doing justice to Jesus' intent? They appear to have been acting in keeping with the instruction found in Matthew's special source: 'Go nowhere among the Gentiles and enter no town of the Samaritans: but go rather to the lost sheep of the house of Israel' (Matt. x.5; cf. xv.24). It has often been conjectured that the leading circles of the Palestinian Church had developed this saying prophetically at the time when the Hellenists carried the Gospel to Samaria and Antioch.[1] The Judaizers themselves, though, had never opposed the Gentile mission in this fashion, but only opposed baptism without circumcision. Even the Palestinian Pharisees zealously recruited proselytes at that time (cf. p. 82). The logion actually corresponds to the course of Jesus' earthly ministry, since he had basically limited his work to Israel. The disciples as well as the Evangelist had preserved the saying as an explanation of his earthly ministry, but according to Matthew's Gospel the saying was superseded after Easter by the Great Commission of Matt. xxviii.19 f. (cf. John xii.20–24) which was universal in scope. Nevertheless, the conduct of the disciples after Easter rules out the possibility that they had received the Great Commission in this form. The versions of the missionary commission at Easter as we possess them were formulated in view of the universal character of the later itinerant mission (cf. pp. 19 f., 115). Originally, the disciples had thought it necessary to move to Jerusalem and to persevere there (cf. §6, 2; cf. Acts i.8; viii.1). They had understood Jesus' reference to the nations' participation in the salvation which he had brought (Matt. viii.11 f.) too much in the sense of the Old Testament prophecies of the pilgrimage of the nations to Zion. Easter had initially brought about a *theologia gloriae*.[2]

[1] E.g. Bultmann, *History of Synoptic Tradition*, 155, in contrast, J. Jeremias, *Jesus' Promise for the Nations* (as in §6, n. 1), 19 ff.; 25.

[2] Jesus did not expect, as Jeremias supposes, *ibid.* 70, that the nations would be included 'as God's eschatological act of power, as the great final manifestation of God's grace', that e.g. they would be gathered by means of the angels (so Jeremias, *SNTS*, iii (1952), 25 ff.), since he included the nations finally in that he declared his death 'for all', i.e. for all, even the nations of the world (Mark xiv.24 cf. x.45). In all his encounters with Gentiles it is expressly stated that their faith has saved them (Matt. viii.10 par.; Luke xv.28).

Israel's opposition to the Gospel demonstrated to the disciples for the first time that the dawning of a universal salvation would not come as one might have expected from a literal understanding of the Old Testament prophecies. It was not to come through a swift conversion of Israel as a whole. Acts, however, has preserved neither such an expectation nor its disappointment (cf. §6, 2). It praises the rapid growth of the Church but paints the picture as though it were perfectly natural for the masses of Israel as well as the Jewish officials to have been unresponsive to the Gospel. This is the viewpoint of the second generation, but for Paul this fact, inevitable in terms of the history-of-religions, was an insoluble puzzle (Rom. ix–xi); and James, the Lord's brother, did not want to accept it even up to his dying day.

2. Thus the initial history of the Church and her message resulted from Israel's attitude toward her. Luke characterizes the first stage in the accounts of Acts iv and v. The Sanhedrin did not take action against the Church as such but merely against the public missionary preaching. The measures were initiated by the Sadducees (Acts iv.1; v.17) who saw in every messianic movement an endangering of their own existence (their disappearance after A.D. 70 substantiates this fear). They wanted to kill the apostles after they had disobeyed the prohibition against preaching (Acts v.33), but the speaker for the Pharisees, Rabbi Gamaliel the Elder, rejected this act of violence contrary to the Law, and his point of view prevailed.

How could the Pharisees who are pictured in the Synoptic tradition as bitter opponents of Jesus, have interceded for his Church? Since F. C. Baur, historical criticism has declared this to be inconceivable and thus the portrayal of Acts to be unhistorical,[3] but the accounts do characterize correctly the general situation in spite of several historical inconsistencies. As long as the disciples kept the Law, the Pharisees considered it improper to suppress them by force solely because of their fanatical concepts. This is substantiated by Josephus's account, reliable at this point, of the execution of James, the Lord's brother (cf. §8, 5).

The conduct of the disciples in the country's synagogues (x.17 f.; xxiii.34) reflected in Matthew's tradition also takes for granted that basically they were tolerated within the synagogues, although they were known to be Jesus' disciples. They were closely observed and were called to give an account from time to time when they had transgressed the Law.

3. Things had to change after Stephen[4] declared the Temple and the accompanying ceremonial Law to be fundamentally transitory (Acts

[3] Haenchen, *Apostelgeschichte*, 212 ff.

[4] W. Foerster, 'Stephanus und die Urgemeinde', *In Dienst unter dem Wort* (*Festgabe* for Schreiner, 1953), 9–30.

vi.14; cf. p. 54). He, like Jesus, was unanimously condemned by the Sanhedrin on the basis of his statements. After his execution a general persecution of the Church followed (Acts viii.1-3). If such attacks against the Temple were to arise from the faith of this group, then it, like Jesus, must be eradicated from the Jewish community.

4. Acts does not clearly relate the effect of the persecution. According to Acts viii.1, only the Twelve were to have remained in Jerusalem while the rest of the Church fled, but those named in the following chapters as the ones who fled are all Hellenists (Acts viii.4 f.; xi.19 f.). This does not mean that the persecution was directed solely against the Hellenists, while the Twelve along with the Hebrews remained unmolested.[5] All were affected,[6] but only those sharing Stephen's viewpoint had any cause to escape the clutches of the Sanhedrin permanently. Those standing true to the Law could continue to live, after a brief time, undisturbed in Jerusalem.

Thus the Jewish reaction caused the 'Congregation of Jesus' to break up externally in two directions. They did not divide because of theological schools of thought but because of a previously latent aspect of Jesus' proclamation which could not permit the Church to remain permanently within the Jewish community if the Jewish community persisted in its previous pattern. The members of the Church who shared Stephen's viewpoint went first into the Diaspora—they were mostly Hellenists, and they carried with them the message into the Diaspora synagogues and soon thereafter to the Gentiles (Acts xi.19 ff.). Because of this, they were forced out of the synagogues completely. Thus the Gentile mission in the sense of Matt. xxviii.19 came about, not through any systematic instruction by Jesus and not through epoch-making decisions by a congregation or a leading man, but, as it were, through the content of the message itself and its rejection by the representatives of Israel. The real problem for Jerusalem was not the Gentile mission but Gentile Christianity and its relationship to the Law (cf. §9, 1 f.).

The part of the Church which remained behind in Jerusalem consciously repressed this side of Jesus' preaching and from then on kept the Law scrupulously in order to be able to live and work further among Israel, but various problems related to this initial question in the Church's teaching arose in the following period even among those who had

---

[5] Numerous scholars from F. C. Baur, *Das Christentum und die christliche Kirche der drei ersten Jahrhunderte* ([2]1860), 39, to Lietzmann, *History of the Early Church*, i, 71. By contrast, J. Munck, *Paul and the Salvation of Mankind* (as in §5, n. 30), 224 f.

[6] Neither does Paul say that he persecuted only one group in the Church. It is incorrect to conclude from Gal i.22 that his participation in this persecution as well as his presence in Jerusalem prior to his conversion are legends (so most recently, Haenchen, *Apostelgeschichte*, p. 257, see below, §10, 2).

remained behind. This becomes evident in their conflicts with the Gentile Church (cf. pp. 75 ff.).

5. Let us first of all pursue the external route of the Palestinian Church to its temporary end. She was able to live within the Jewish community, disliked but basically tolerated, until the beginning of the Jewish insurrection. This was possible because of her loyalty to the Law and also to a great extent because of the Roman administration. The act of violence against Stephen was possible only because Pontius Pilate had to favour the Jews after his protector, the anti-Semitic Sejanus, had been overthrown in Rome in A.D. 31.[7] After Pilate's dismissal in A.D. 36, the procurators no longer permitted any such irregular acts.

Just how little Judaism had become reconciled to the existence of the Congregation of Jesus in their midst became evident when Herod Agrippa I extended his rule in the years 41–44 over the whole of Palestine, thus bringing Jerusalem under his administration. He had James, the son of Zebedee, executed (Acts xii.1 f.).[8] Peter, whom he then had arrested, escaped from him (Acts xii.3 ff.). The Pharisees, whose favour Herod cultivated[9] as even the Jewish accounts relate, were happy to see the long-awaited condemnation of these fanatics.

After the sudden, unexpected death of this ruler,[10] Jerusalem as well as all Palestine was governed directly by Roman procurators. Under the first three (44–52), peaceful relationships prevailed in the land. The strong warning of Emperor Claudius in the year 41 to the Jews of Alexandria[11] to keep peace with the Greeks also subdued the forces of the Zealots in the mother country. In the decade of the fifties, by contrast, the Zealot movement intensified. Their hatred was directed against every Jew who had contact with Greeks and Romans and who departed from the Law. This pressure may have been one of the contributing factors for the intervention at that time (cf. pp. 79 f.) in the affairs of the Gentile Church by certain circles from the Palestinian Church, who strictly observed the Law. When Paul, probably around A.D. 58, made his last visit to Jerusalem, James asked him to give evidence of his loyalty to the Law out of consideration for those '. . . zealous for the Law' (Acts xxi.20). This clarifies the situation in one stroke. James speaks of the men within the Church who were 'zealous for the Law', but he

---

[7] E. Stauffer, *Jerusalem und Rom* (1957), 17 f.; Reicke, *Glaube und Leben der Urgemeinde*, 171 ff. traces this to the benevolence of Vitellius who was the legate of Syria from A.D. 35.

[8] Gal. ii.9 excluded the possibility that on this occasion Mark x.39 was also fulfilled for his brother, John (M. Goguel, *Birth of Christianity* (as in §1, n. 13), i, 107 f. *et al.*).

[9] E. Schürer, III⁴, 553–562.

[10] Acts xii.21 ff. in agreement with Josephus, *Antiq.* 19, 8.

[11] S. Lösch, *Epistula Claudiana* (1930).

probably had in mind even more so those among the Jews—if indeed this was not originally what was meant. The oath of the forty *Sicarii* not to eat again until they had murdered Paul illustrates their fanaticism (Acts xxiii.12–15). In this atmosphere, the continuous persecution of individual members of the Church was intensified as Paul had already mentioned in I Thess. ii.14–16 (A.D. 51–53).

By contrast, James, the Lord's brother, was the victim not of the Jew's fervour for the Law but rather of the ancient mistrust of the Sadducees. When the governor Festus, known from Paul's trial, died prematurely in A.D. 62 and his successor Albinus had not yet arrived, the high priest, Annas the Younger, made use of a turbulent interregnum in order to put James and others objectionable to him on trial, although the Pharisees and the people condemned this action against such a man who had strictly observed the Law.[12] The fact that the Church of Palestine, in spite of all her concessions to Judaism, had not become basically a separate Jewish movement, is demonstrated by what happened soon after in the year A.D. 66 when the Jewish insurrection broke out. While all of the Jewish groups, even the Essenes,[13] permitted themselves to be drawn into the war that was ultimately messianic in nature against Rome, the Christians did not take part. As a result they were killed as traitors throughout the whole of Palestine by the insurrectionists. The Jerusalem Church fled to Pella in the land of Trans-Jordan, but many entered the service of the Gentile Church which had arisen in the meanwhile.[14] This was the temporary end of the Church among Israel (cf. §16, 3). Let us now turn to the development of the Gentile Church and her relationship to this Palestinian Church.

[12] Josephus, *Antiq.* 20, 9, 1. According to the tradition of Hegesippius in Eusebius, *H.E.* 2, 23, 11–18, James was thrown from the pinnacle of the Temple shortly before the beginning of the Jewish insurrection 'by the Pharisees and Scribes'. This is a legend, but it may well be accurate when it is reported here that James, who was also called 'the Just' by the Jews, prayed daily in the Temple for Israel '. . . so that his knees swelled like those of a camel'.

[13] Josephus, *B.J.*, 2, 8, 10 and the discoveries of the Qumran excavations.

[14] Eusebius, *H.E.*, 3, 5, 2 f. *et al.* in Schoeps, *Theologie und Geschichte des Judentums* (1949), 264–269. The persecution of the Christians for taking part, which is to be concluded from all appearances here, is expressly attested for the Bar Kochbar Insurrection (J. P. Migne, *Patrologia Latina* xxxi, 1093; Justin, *Apol.* i, 31, 5 f.).

CHAPTER III

THE DEVELOPMENT OF THE CHURCH CONSISTING OF JEWS AND GENTILES AND A GOSPEL FREE FROM THE LAW

9. THE ORIGIN OF HELLENISTIC GENTILE CHRISTIANITY AND ITS PROBLEMS[1]

1. As well as the Church in Israel whose path we have pursued up to this point, a Church arose remarkably early outside the Jewish nation, a Church which no longer kept the Mosaic Law. Just as the former emerged from Jerusalem so the latter emerged from Antioch on the Orontes, at one time the capital city of the Seleucid Kingdom. This magnificent Hellenistic city had approximately 300,000 inhabitants, 30,000 of whom were Jews.[2] It was here, according to Acts xi.19–21, that several of the Hellenists who had fled from Jerusalem turned directly to the Gentiles with the Gospel and brought them to faith (cf. §8, 4). They baptized the believing Gentiles without circumcising them and were able to live together with them by ignoring the objectionable regulations of the Law. While the disciples in Damascus at the time of Paul's conversion, which took place approximately during this same period, still lived within the synagogue, an independent congregation emerged alongside the synagogues in Antioch. This group had set aside the Mosaic Law in the manner indicated by the Synoptic tradition. They kept the central commandments which they understood anew in faith (Mark x.18 f.; xii.28 ff.), but neglected the Mosaic ordinances contrary to Matt. xxiii.23. All the accounts about the beginnings in Antioch appear to assume this to be the road they had taken (Gal. ii.3 ff., 11 ff.; Acts xv.1, 5). The believers not only surrendered their membership in the synagogue but also the accompanying legal rights. Nevertheless, the atmosphere of a large town seems to have permitted this small group to develop undisturbed in its first decades. At any rate we do not hear of conflicts with the

---

[1] Literature: Harnack, *The Mission and Expansion of Christianity*, 44–72; K. S. Latourette, *A History of the Expansion of Christianity* (1937), vi; H. Schlier, 'Die Entscheidung für die Heidenmission in der Urchristenheit', in *Die Zeit der Kirche* (²1958), 90–107; R. Liechtenhan, *Die urchristliche Mission* (1946); F. Hahn, *Mission in the New Testament* (as in §6, n. 1).

[2] V. Schultze, *Altchristliche Städte und Landschaften*: vol. iii, *Antiochien* (1930); G. Downey, *Ancient Antioch*, 1963.

synagogues or the city officials. Soon they were recognized by those from the outside as a fellowship related to Judaism but nonetheless independent from it, so that the name arose for them (Acts xi.26), possibly even by A.D. 40, by which the new fellowship generally came to be known twenty years later in the capital city of the world: 'Christians'. While the name was only used in the first century by those outside the fellowship (Acts xxvi.28; I Peter iv.16), it became a self-designation for the first time at the beginning of the second century with Ignatius of Antioch.[3]

Scarcely ten years after this beginning in Antioch, Claudius banished the Jews from Rome in A.D. 49, since they '. . . constantly made disturbances at the instigation of Chrestus. . . .'[4] Unknown Christians, brought perhaps by the heavy international traffic of those days from Antioch to Rome, had apparently preached the Gospel in the synagogues. Indeed, they had preached it in a form which led to a split in the synagogue. The Epistle to the Romans assumes the same congregational situation as in Antioch.[5] The event in Antioch was thus a second beginning in the setting of the stage for church history. What had taken place in Antioch and perhaps had begun even prior to this in the Palestinian-Phoenician coastal cities (Acts viii.40; ix. 32 ff.; x f.; xxi.3, 7; xxvii.3) was shortly repeated in the same or similar way in some of the other cities of Syria and Cilicia (Gal. i.21; Acts xv.23), and even in Rome before Paul first went to Corinth.

2. The problems which this second beginning involved were only gradually recognized. Beginning in the second century, the Church has only been interested through the the centuries in the relationship between the apostolic authorities, namely between Paul and the Twelve.[6] The heretical Jewish Christianity of the second century appealed to Peter and James against Paul and the Gentile Church free from the Law;[7] conversely, the Gnostic Marcion played Paul off against the earliest apostles. The developing Catholic Church connected Paul with the Twelve as a unit and placed him below Peter; the Reformation, on the other hand, favoured Paul and emphasized his individuality. From the eighteenth century, modern historical studies have attempted for the first time to

---

[3] Harnack, *The Mission and Expansion of Christianity*, 411 ff. (Ger. i, 424 ff.).

[4] Suetonius, *Vita Claudii*, 25; this edict was issued in A.D. 49, according to Orosius, vii, 6, 15. That corresponds with Acts xviii.2.

[5] K. H. Schelkle, 'Römische Kirche im Römerbrief', *ZKTheol.*, 81 (1959), 393–404.

[6] J. Wagemann, *Die Stellung des Apostels Paulus neben den Zwölf in den ersten zwei Jahrhunderten* (1926); K. Holl, 'Der Streit zwischen Petrus und Paulus zu Antiochien in seiner Bedeutung für Luthers innere Entwicklung', *Gesammelte Aufsätze* (1928), iii, 134–146; J.–L. Leuba, *Institution und Ereignis* (1957), 78 ff.

[7] Schoeps, *Theologie und Geschichte des Judenchristentums* (1949), 118–135.

gain a total picture of the situation. According to F. C. Baur,[8] the earliest apostles clung to the outward appearance of Jesus, the Jewish Messiah, while Paul grasped the idea hidden beneath this external appearance. Consequently, primitive Christianity split into the antithesis between the particularistic Judaism of the earliest apostles and the universalism of Paul free from the Law. A reconciling synthesis, to which the portrayal of Acts contributed by obscuring the points of contrast, set in for the first time at the beginning of the second century.

In contrast to this critical reconstruction which attributes the historical viewpoint of heretical Jewish Christianity to the Pauline period, the school of Albrecht Ritschl[9] emphasized correctly that one must differentiate between the earliest apostles and the Judaizers (Acts xv.1, 5; Galatians) as well as between Paul and Gentile Christianity, which arose independently of him and which was historically tangible for the first time in I Clement. The history-of-religions school went beyond these approaches, which had only seen a development of thought and theology, and focused its attention on the religious experiences of the congregations and their religious activities conditioned by the religious currents of the times. This school's portrayal of primitive Christianity no longer turned immediately to Paul after describing the earliest church in Jerusalem,[10] but placed Hellenistic Christianity, which as we have seen, arose before Paul and was to a great extent independent of him, alongside the Palestinian Christianity. The picture of this Hellenistic Christianity was reconstructed from materials found in Acts, in the Pauline Epistles, and in the later early Christian literature which were thought to preserve source material reflecting in general the Christianity between Antioch and Rome.[11] In this manner, Bultmann's *Theologie des Neuen Testaments* presents for the first time the total picture of the *kerygma* of the Hellenistic Church.[12]

[8] *Paulus* (1845), 1 ff.; F. C. Bauer, *Das Christentum und die christliche Kirche der drei ersten Jahrhunderte*, i, 1–22.

[9] A. Ritschl, *Die Entstehung der altkatholischen Kirche* ([2]1847); A. v. Harnack, *History of Dogma*, i, 86 ff., 218–222 (Ger. i, 99 ff., 239–243).

[10] W. Heitmüller's thesis in *ZNTW*, 13 (1912), 330, 'Paul is not only separated from Jesus by the primitive Church but also by another element. The development followed: Jesus—primitive Church—Hellenistic Christianity—Paul'. Recently an attempt has been made to differentiate in the development of the tradition a further level, that of Hellenistic Jewish Christianity (cf. F. Hahn, *Christologische Hoheitstitel* ([2]1966), 11 f.). To be sure, Hellenistic Jewish Christianity was a mediating element between the Aramaic speaking Jewish Christianity of Palestine and Hellenistic Gentile Christianity. Nevertheless, it is often impossible to grasp this second element in the development of the primitive Christian tradition. Indeed, apart from Jerusalem and Egypt, there were hardly any purely Jewish-Christian congregations to be found. In all these a Gentile-Christian element soon became active.

[11] Initially by W. Bousset, *Kyrios Christos* (1913), 92 ff.

[12] *Theology of the New Testament*, §§9–15, cf. 'Die Bedeutung des geschichtlichen Jesus für die Theologie des Paulus', in *Glauben und Verstehen* ([3]1958), i, 188 f.

This appears to substantiate to a remarkable extent the antithetical viewpoint which has lingered on since Baur in a branch of German scholarship: The Hellenistic *kerygma* differs in its entirety from the Palestinian, whereas according to Acts there was never any other difference between Jewish and Gentile Christians than the observance of the ceremonial laws. According to this view, there arose in the Hellenistic Church a christology entirely different from that in the Palestinian[13] as well as different conceptions of the Spirit, the Church, her offices and rites. For example, christology is no longer developed in terms of the Old Testament, Jewish messianism but from the Hellenistic mythology of the redeemer, and baptism and the eucharist become sacramental under the influence of the Hellenistic mystery religions.[14] Men such as Paul and John came from this Hellenistic Christianity and had the function of interpreting these mythical conceptions by means of a critical theology with the intention of disclosing the actual heart of the message (demythologizing). Even this approach has subsequently proved itself to be one-sided.[15]

A picture which corresponds to the actual situation can only result when we correctly relate the various approaches to one another and clearly differentiate between them in their details, just as the progressive development of scholarship has demanded.

a. From a history-of-religions point of view, the step from Jerusalem to Antioch led Christianity from the cultural sphere of Palestinian Judaism into that of Hellenism. The message was not merely taken over into a different language but was also received and transmitted further through different ideologies and thought-forms.[16] To just what extent the message could be Hellenized by such a process is demonstrated by the conceptions of the Spirit and sacraments, bodily existence and the resurrection, against which Paul spoke in I Corinthians (cf. §13, 2). Such a Hellenization by no means set in everywhere between Antioch and Rome, otherwise Paul would also have attacked it in his other Epistles. The history-of-religions school overestimated the influence on Christianity of the cultural spheres

---

[13] Cf. Bousset's derivation of the *kurios*-predication which Bultmann took over in *Theology of the New Testament*, §12, 2. In the meantime, this has been disproven by W. Förster, *TWNT*, iii, 1093 f.; E. Schweizer, *Erniedrigung und Erhöhung*, 93 ff. (as in §6, n. 26); O. Cullmann, *The Christology of the New Testament* (1959) (Eng. trans. of *Die Christologie des Neuen Testaments*, 1957, 209 ff.); Hahn, *Christologische Hoheitstitel* (²1964), 81–95.

[14] Cf. p. 46, and Bultmann, *Theology of the New Testament*, §6, 3 f.; 8, 3; 13, 2.

[15] See n. 13 and works like A. M. Hunter, *Introducing New Testament Theology* (1957).

[16] T. Boman, *Das hebräische Denken im Vergleich mit dem griechischen* (³1959); D. G. Dix, *Jew and Greek* (1953); E. Schweizer, *Erniedrigung und Erhöhung*, 118–121 (as in §6, n. 26); *TWNT*, vi, 413 f.

of both Judaism and Hellenism. We now see that both spheres had extensively penetrated one another precisely in the geographical areas where the churches arose. In spite of all the protection against it, elements of a Hellenistic ideology had penetrated Palestinian Judaism. Most important is the fact that the 'Hellenists' had been included in the earliest Church in Jerusalem and had already carried over the message in to Greek (cf. §7, 6). Outside Palestine, moreover, churches arose in all important centres within the milieu of Diaspora Judaism, so that in the liturgical materials of the New Testament, for example, we meet exclusively Semitic rather than Greek style and forms.

In addition, it is becoming more and more evident that primitive Christianity did not simply take over the Jewish and Hellenistic terms, but reworked them and filled them with new content. Like every creative movement, they constructed to a certain extent their own language by coining words and thus developed their own Christian terminology (pp. 157 f.). In a similar fashion, concepts and traditions were refashioned into a distinctive Christian tradition, such as the tables of duties found in Stoicism and Hellenistic Judaism which we now find in the Christian tables of household duties.[17] Faith developed a christology which used the various conceptions found at hand as aids and means of expression, but this faith did not simply clothe Jesus in an unreflected manner as a figure of his times with the ready-made garments of mythology.

It is not surprising, therefore, that a stream of independent Christian tradition, accompanied by an intensive exchange of personnel, bound together the churches inside and outside Palestine. For example, in I Corinthians Paul referred to the central traditions of the Church's teaching against the acute Hellenization of Christianity. For the most part these traditions originate from Jerusalem rather than from Antioch as was first thought immediately after the discovery of 'Hellenistic Christianity'.[18]

Even beyond the influence of the environment and the anonymous tradition of the Church we should not underestimate the authority of those called as servants of the Word and the churches' common confession of faith, especially since the churches lived by the principle of separating themselves from the unconscious influences of the 'former man' by means of a conscious decision of faith. Accordingly, we can only speak

[17] D. Schroeder, 'Die Haustafeln des Neuen Testaments' (unpubl. diss., Hamburg, 1959).
[18] Thus the tradition in I Cor. xi.23 ff. and xv.3 ff. do not come from Antioch as Heitmüller, ZNTW 13 (1912), 324 f., 331 f., et al. thought. Rather, as Jeremias, Eucharistic Words of Jesus, 101 ff., 187 ff. (Ger. 95 ff., 179 ff.) has shown, they come from the Palestinian Church, even though I Cor. xi.23–25 may possibly be the Antiochian formulation of the eucharistic tradition.

of Palestinian and Hellenistic Christianity in order to characterize the spheres in which a given congregation lived and which predominantly determined the means of expression and the thought patterns.

b. Moreover, we can only appreciate the step from Jerusalem to Antioch when, with the early Christians, we view it theologically. It then means not only the transition from one culture into another, which has often taken place in the course of church history, but the very first departure from the sphere of the ancient nation of the Covenant. In Antioch, the Gospel not only had to be proclaimed under altered presuppositions and ideologies but, most important, under different conditions of redemptive history. It had to be expressed not only for Hellenistic men but for Gentiles. For Paul 'the Greeks' were the 'Gentile nations'. This meant that before preaching the kerygma, 'Jesus is the Christ', which had sufficed for Israel, the message had to add 'God is One', He to whom the Old Testament bears witness (I Cor. viii.6). The Law of the Old Testament could not, however, be imposed on those who were converted to the God of the Old Testament and to Jesus his appointed Saviour. Thus a unique theological task came about: the kerygma about Jesus, the Promised One of Israel, which was the Gospel of Jerusalem and which had left the question of the Mosaic Law open, now had to be developed into a Gospel free from the Law for both the Jews and the Gentiles. This Gospel had to unite the message of Jesus and the Old Testament into a consistent unity. A message similar in kind had arisen in Antioch of its own accord, but there the Christians had detached themselves from the Law for a reason just as obscure as that which had caused the Jewish believers in Jerusalem to continue to observe it. Both Churches could only protect themselves from foundering in syncretism on the one hand and Judaism on the other by means of the theological development of the Gospel. Through this means they could become united with one another in a new fellowship, the Church.

While many took part in carrying out this task, one was uniquely conscious of being called to it, Paul, the apostle of Jesus to the Gentiles. He emphatically referred Hellenized Christianity in Corinth, which was sinking into syncretism, to the Old Testament history of redemption (I Cor. x.1 ff.) and to the tradition of Jesus who had appeared in history (I Cor. xv.1 ff.). Paul also decisively rejected any obligation to the Law on the part of those who believed (Gal. ii.21). In the light of this his position becomes clear to us, a position which was unclear even for Acts and thus all the more so for subsequent generations. He did not create and influence, as the head of a theological school, a universalist Christianity (F. C. Baur); nor did he stand above the popular Gentile Christianity as a great, prominent theologian (Harnack); nor did he as a leading theologian critically interpret the mythical Hellenistic Christianity (Bultmann). Paul was, at least according to his own picture of himself, the apostle to the Gentile Church. That is, on the basis of the revelation of Christ, comparable only to the Easter experiences (cf. p. 72) and thus establishing a new beginning, he had given the Gospel for Jew and Greek its fundamental character. Entirely on the basis of this Gospel he had created the fundamental structure of the Gentile Church. In this way, he entered the scene of the Roman Church which had arisen completely independent of him by setting forth in his Epistle to the Romans the guide lines of this Gospel (Rom. i.16 as the theme of the letter) after finishing his work in the East. Furthermore, he was recognized as apostle in this sense by the Church between Antioch and Rome. His Epistles were already authoritative witnesses to Christ for I Clement (c. 96, in Rome) and Ignatius (c. 110, in Antioch). This would have been possible only if they had in the meantime been preserved as such. It was not his theological influence which was so decisive—this was surprisingly small—but both his claim that his Gospel stood as the apostolic norm for the Gentile Church, and the general recognition of this claim in principle.

The attempt to reconstruct a sketch of the *kerygma* prevalent in Hellenistic Christianity, which by the nature of the case remains a hypothetical abstraction, is therefore irrelevant. It is more appropriate to point out the *kerygma* of Paul which was recognized by Hellenistic Christianity as authoritative. Nevertheless, in so doing one must differentiate between that which he considered to be valid tradition of the Church and that which was his own theological explication and his own urgent message. In this way one will not focus attention on Paul as a personality but rather on Paul the apostle of the Church which arose before as well as with him. (We shall have to leave the actual execution of this task to New Testament theology.)

c. At this point we meet the problem of the relationship between this apostle, whose calling stood apart from all previous continuity, and the apostles in Jerusalem. Ever since the second century this problem has received much discussion in the Church, yet it has never been more acute than it was in its own day. Furthermore, since the Church as a whole was always involved, this problem is only one section of the larger question concerning what attitudes the Church in Palestine, initially represented by the Twelve, and the churches outside Palestine, which arose almost entirely without the former's assistance, had displayed towards one another. The Gentile Church was represented by Antioch and theologically by Paul; but Antioch was never a metropolis comparable to Jerusalem, and Paul never exercised a representative leadership comparable to the

Twelve or the 'Three Pillars'. Consequently, the Hellenistic churches never established a unity in the same sense as did those of Palestine.

From this examination of the relevant historical and theological problems, we gain an understanding for the point of view from which the New Testament records, i.e. Acts and Paul, depict the events. We understand that they emphasize primarily the way to the 'Gentiles' or, as they put it, the way to the 'Greeks'. Consequently, it concerned the Law and thus simultaneously the *koinonia* of Jesus' *ecclesia*. Acts represents this fellowship as a continuous development with Jerusalem as the point of departure, while Paul points out his personal struggles on behalf of this fellowship. Historically, we may consider them as two movements which merged into each other. Jerusalem had sought for contact with the churches outside Palestine in the very same areas where Paul was working, and men like Barnabas and Silas were sent from Jerusalem to the churches, becoming Gentile missionaries in Antioch. Paul, who was made a fellow worker of Barnabas on his first missionary journey, chose Silas for the second journey as his companion. On the third missionary journey, Paul worked for the first time exclusively with men who had been converted under his ministry. Thus to a remarkable extent the Gentile mission actually arose, even though indirectly, from a movement of those in Jerusalem toward the Gentile Church. Paul, on the other hand, not only emphasized his own independence and individuality (Gal. i.1, 11 f.; II Cor. iii.2 f.) but, as we have just seen, also considered it important to work together with men from the earliest Church in carrying out his mission, since the earliest church represented the tradition of Jesus' earthly ministry. Paul strove most energetically for the *koinonia* of the Gentile Church with Jerusalem and the earliest apostles (Gal. ii.1, 9; I Cor. xv.11; Rom. xv.27 and 31), a concern which remained with him to the end. The entire Gentile Church did the same and not merely her Jewish Christian members. Let us now pursue these two movements, since the later fortunes of the Church depend above all on how each comes to relate to the other.

10. JERUSALEM AND THE DEVELOPING GENTILE CHRISTIANITY (PAUL) UNTIL THE APOSTOLIC COUNCIL

1. The movement emerging from Jerusalem is to be found essentially in the accounts of Acts. These accounts view the events from the Jerusalem standpoint in keeping with Acts' own intention as well as that of the Palestinian tradition which it reworked. The accounts in Acts viii–xi do not merely intend to relate how the message spread as in Acts i.8 and how the Gentile mission arose, but to record in particular how the earliest

Church was led to a recognition of the developing Gentile Christianity. The accounts are therefore arranged in an ascending order more on the basis of content than chronology. After the conversion of the Samaritans, who were already circumcised, there follows the conversion of the Ethiopian Eunuch who could not be circumcised and thus could not be accepted into Israel (Acts viii.36; Deut. xxiii.1), of Cornelius an un-circumcised 'God fearer', and finally of the Gentiles in Antioch.[1] They all came to faith, and on the basis of their faith the missionary had to grant them participation in the eschatological salvation just as Jesus once had done for the Centurion and the Syro-Phoenician woman (Matt. viii.10; xv.28). They were accepted by means of baptism as members into the redeemed community, without circumcision and without subjection to the Law.

The Jerusalem community could not ignore this growth of the Church which was accomplished without her assistance. They sent out representatives to both Samaria and Antioch (Acts viii.14; xi.22), which they knew to be their duty simply on the basis of the *koinonia* which they experienced among their members in their own unique manner (cf. §7, 4). They therefore investigated to see if churches had really arisen in Samaria and Antioch, and they had to recognize this to be a fact in both cases. The earliest Church was not brought to this conclusion primarily through theological reflection but through obedient submission to the redemptive working of God which had imparted faith and the Spirit without circumcision (Acts x.46 f.; cf. viii.15–18).[2] Those sent from the Christians in Jerusalem sought and experienced the fellowship of the one Church of Jesus—as representatives of the Church's original base, furthermore, and not as official emissaries nor as visitors from another local congregation. Christian Jerusalem did not intend in this way to achieve a supremacy as had Jewish Jerusalem.[3] They did intend to incorporate the believers in Samaria and Antioch into the Church whose foundation was Peter, whose foundation stones were the Twelve and whose pillars were the three 'men of repute', but they did not intend to subject them to the organizational leadership of the Twelve nor to the 'Three Pillars'. Precisely because the representatives of Jerusalem, in spite of the contrast in the various ways of life, produced a church fellowship on the basis of faith alone which transcended the national antagonisms that separated

---

[1] When Zahn, *Die Apostelgeschichte des Lucas* (1919–21), 367, and P. Gaechter, S.J., who follows him in *ZKTheol.* (1948), 12, explain that the Hellenists were to have dared the Gentile mission in Antioch (Acts xi.19 ff.) for the first time on the basis of Acts x.1–11, 18, then they miss the intention of Acts entirely.

[2] Discussion in N. Adler, *Taufe und Handauflegung* (1951) and Haenchen, *Apostelgeschichte*, 263–266. For solution, see *TWNT*, vi, 412.

[3] Of recent, Hahn, *op. cit.* (§9, n. 13), 266.

Jew and Samaritan and reached over the barriers set by the Mosaic Law, they confessed that they also stood solely on faith. Thus no authoritarian instructions but only a summons to obedience in faith was possible from them, but it is true that the representatives did not differentiate as clearly as did Paul between the commitment to the tradition stemming from Jerusalem and the personal authority of the men of Jerusalem (p. 175). In view of our examination so far, Luke has correctly related in substance the guide lines of the movement from the Jerusalem Church. His limitations first become evident in his portrayal of the problems.

Luke brings into the open the questions regarding the Law, which had made themselves felt to the Jewish Christians in this development, in the Cornelius story. First, Peter was shown that the observance of the Laws pertaining to things clean and unclean was no longer to hinder him from going to the Gentiles with the Gospel (Acts x.15, 34 ff.; cf. xi.3) because God had cleansed the hearts of the Gentiles through faith (Acts xv.9). Thus Jesus' word in Mark vii.15 became real to this extent. When, consequently, the uncircumcised received the Spirit through 'hearing' his sermon 'in faith' (Gal. iii.2), he was not able to refuse them baptism (Acts x.47). The second question concerning the extent of the Law's claim on the Gentiles was only briefly touched upon in the Cornelius story (Acts xi.17 f.). It was handled in detail at the Apostolic Council where it was agreed that they should not be circumcised, but by observing the Decree of the Apostolic Council, the Hellenistic Christians were to make it easier to live together with the Jewish Christians (Acts xv.18 ff.). In both cases Luke writes as though the solutions initiated on these occasions were complete and final, whereas in reality they were disputed for a long time. He remains silent about the incident in Antioch (Gal. ii) where the first question came into bold relief, and he is also silent about the Judaizers in Galatia. These later events do not invalidate what Luke reported about Cornelius and the Apostolic Council, but they do show us that the decisions were more temporary and incomplete in character than Luke's schematic, summary account would indicate.

The baptism of Cornelius was certainly no 'harmless' episode[4] for the strict observers of the Law in the earliest Church. Initially, it was an offence to them, which later through Peter's explanation became a divine sign with far-reaching implications. Luke has probably given the event too much weight, but also according to Gal. ii.8 f. the decisive factor in the attitude of Jerusalem towards Gentile Christianity was what 'God had done.' Coupled with this was a basic theological clarification of the question of table-fellowship from the standpoint of the heart of the

---

[4] M. Dibelius, *Studies in the Acts of the Apostles* (as in §6, n. 10); cf. Goppelt, *Jesus, Paul and Judaism*, 115, n. 5 (*Christentum und Judentum*, 84, n. 4).

Gospel, as Gal. ii.2 stresses and as Gal. ii.14 ff. clearly reveals. Paul was the one designated to fulfil this necessary task. Acts recounts Paul's marvellous call between the redemptive acts just discussed without pointing out its intrinsic meaning for these events. Before looking more closely at the Apostolic Council let us trace Paul's path and with it the particular development of Gentile Christianity up to this turning point.

2. Paul[5] was already uniquely prepared in background and education for the ministry which he was to carry out in the Church. He was born at the turn of the century in the Hellenistic city of Tarsus in Cilicia[6] (Acts xxi.39; xxii.3; cf. ix.11; Gal. i.21). As well as his Jewish name, Saul, he bore from childhood the surname Paul (Acts xvi.37; xxii.28; xxv.10 ff.). Such a surname was an expression of an inherited Roman citizenship. As a son of a very devout Jewish family,[7] he did not attend a Hellenistic school but was instructed from the time he was six years old in the Torah, which he read in the form of the LXX. Life in the Hellenistic city familiarized him with the Cynic-Stoic peripatetic philosophers who held their discourses on the street corners. The coins found in Tarsus depicting the immolation of the god Sandan must have passed through his hands[8] so that the conception of deities dying and coming again to life would have been familiar to him. These cults, which portrayed the cycle of nature, had spread through the Near East, but Paul met the idea of imitating this mysterious destiny of the deities only through aphorisms; the idea had developed during the Hellenistic period from the earlier conceptions of the dying and rising deities. Most important, he was a Hillelite through his studies of scribal tradition under Rabbi Gamaliel

---

[5] Literature on Pauline Studies: A. Schweitzer, *Paul and His Interpreters* (Eng. trans. 1912) of *Geschichte der Paulinischen Forschung von der Reformation bis auf die Gegenwart*, 1911); R. Bultmann, 'Zur Geschichte der Paulusforschung', *ThR* 1 (1929), 26–59; 6 (1934), 229–246; 8 (1936), 1–22. Comprehensive biographical portrayals: in the histories of primitive Christianity; K. Pieper, *Paulus, seine missionarische Persönlichkeit und Wirksamkeit* (1929); W. v. Loewenich, *Paul, His Life and Work* (Eng. trans. 1960, of *Paulus*, 1940); A. D. Nock, *St. Paul* (1938); J. Holzner, *Paulus* (1937, 1947); *Rings um Paulus. Blicke in die Umwelt und innere Welt des Apostels* (1947); W. L. Knox, *St. Paul and the Church of Jerusalem* (1930); *St. Paul and the Church of the Gentiles* (1939); M. Dibelius–W. G. Kümmel, *Paul* (Eng. trans. of *Paulus*, 1951); G. Ricciotti, *Paul the Apostle* (1953); A. C. Purdy, 'Paul', *IDB* 1962, iii, 681–704. Pauline theology: Bultmann, *Theology of the New Testament*, §16–40; W. D. Davies, *Paul and Rabbinic Judaism* (²1955); *Studia Paulina*, ed. J. N. Sevenster and W. C. van Unnik (*in hon.* J. de Zwaan, 1953); J. Munck, *Paul and the Salvation of Mankind*; H. J. Schoeps, Paul, *The Theology of the Apostle in the Light of Jewish Religious History* (Eng. trans. 1961, of *Paulus, Die Theologie des Apostels im Lichte der jüdischen Religionsgeschichte*, 1959); R. Longenecker, *Paul, Apostle of Liberty* (1964); B. Rigaux, *Paulus und seine Briefe: Der Stand der Forschung* (1964).

[6] H. Böhlig, *Die Geisteskultur von Tarsos im augusteischen Zeitalter* (1913); A. Steinmann, *Zum Werdegang des Paulus: Die Jugendzeit in Tarsos* (1928).

[7] In Phil. iii.5 f. he emphasizes the proper character of his circumcision.

[8] Böhlig, *op. cit.* (n. 6), 23 f.

the Elder in Jerusalem (Acts xxii.3; cf. xxvi.5; Gal. i.14; Phil. v.3). Whether he was ordained as a rabbi or not is uncertain, since this would only be possible from his fortieth year on. As a student of a rabbi he learned, as was the custom, a handicraft; he became a tentmaker (Acts xviii.3).[9] Thus Paul's background combined in an unusual way the elements of the Hellenistic world, the Jewish Diaspora and the Pharisaic rabbinism, although we cannot determine to what extent he had assimilated, before the revolutionary change which took place in his life, the Hellenistic and Jewish concepts evident in his Epistles.[10]

Scholars have frequently attempted to explain the Damascus experience[11] like the first Easter as the result of a psychic development which was perhaps occasioned by a pathological disposition, but Rom. vii.7-25 is not to be understood autobiographically. Paul, the Pharisee, did not suffer under the burden of the Law as did the monk Luther, and still less did he suffer from any doubts whether Jesus might actually be the Messiah. The secondary phrase in Acts xxvi.14 does not speak of a thorn in the heart. According to his own unequivocal testimony, it was not a tormented man who was consoled on the road to Damascus, but a self-righteous man whose confidence was shattered (Phil. iii.6). The experience was not the final external expression of an inner development, but an unintentional break with his entire past as the result of an intrusion from without, by means of a self-disclosure of the Risen Jesus. In Acts this event stands out as prominently as does the figure of Paul himself (ix; xxii; xxvi), but Luke did not have a suitable designation for either, since he had set an absolute temporal limit on the Easter appearances and had limited the apostolate to the Twelve. Paul himself, on the other hand, placed the event in absolute direct continuity with the Easter appearances. In light of this event he was conscious of being called not only to faith but also to the apostolate, in spite of the fact that he was also conscious

[9] Cf. Haenchen, *Apostelgeschichte*, 475 f. It is very questionable (cf. G. Delling, *Paulus' Stellung zu Frau und Ehe* (1931), 86–91) that Paul had married as a Rabbi so that in I Cor. vii.7 he spoke as a widower (J. Jeremias, 'Nochmals: War Paulus Witwer', *ZNTW*, 28 (1929), 321 ff.).

[10] Cf. E. Lohmeyer, *Grundlagen paulinischer Theologie* (1929); W. D. Davies, *Paul and Rabbinic Judaism* (²1955); Dibelius-Kümmel, *Paul* (as in n. 5, Ger. 31 ff.; Schoeps, *Paul, The Theology of the Apostle in the Light of Jewish Religious History* (as in n. 5, Ger. 1–42), 13–50.

[11] W. G. Kümmel, *Römer 7 und die Bekehrung des Paulus* (1929); O. Kietzig, *Die Bekehrung des Paulus* (1932); E. Pfaff, *Die Bekehrung des heiligen Paulus in der Exegese des 20. Jahrhunderts* (1942); A. Wikenhauser, 'Die Wirkung der Christophanie vor Damaskus auf Paulus und seine Begleiter nach den Berichten der Apostelgeschichte', *Biblica* 33 (1952), 313–323; E. Benz, *Paulus als Visionär* (Monograph, Mainz, 1952), 79–123; H. G. Wood, 'The Conversion of St. Paul', *NTS*, 1 (1954–55), 276–282; U. Wilckens, 'Die Bekehrung des Paulus als religionsgeschichtliches Problem', *ZThK* 56 (1959), 273–293.

of the exceptional circumstances of his calling (I Cor. ix.1–6; xv.5–11; Gal. i.1, 12–16).

Paul recognized his pre-Christian past[12] to have been characterized by two things: he was zealous for the Law, and the persecutor of the Church (Gal. i.13 f.), the latter obviously springing from the former. He was possibly introduced in the Diaspora synagogues of Jerusalem to the message about Jesus in the form which Stephen and the Hellenists had represented. Thus, prior to his conversion, and all the more afterwards, he would have seen the way of salvation according to the Law to be mutually exclusive to faith in the crucified Christ. After all, it was his zeal for the Law that had made him a persecutor of the Church. The knowledge of this irreconcilable difference between the Law and the way of faith moulded his faith, his work, and his theology.

The individual character of Paul's calling set him apart for a unique service which disrupted the previous continuity, although he permitted himself to be placed in the line of the tradition stemming from Jerusalem. After his conversion he first worked for three years in the kingdom of Nabataeans,[13] then, in a fourteen-day visit to Jerusalem, sought the fellowship of Peter, who represented both the Church he had persecuted as well as the tradition from Jesus' earthly ministry. In the following fourteen years he stayed away from Jerusalem in Syria and Cilicia.[14] After a period in his native land, the duration of which is no longer determinable, Barnabas sent for him to come to Antioch, the original base of Gentile Christianity. Together with this apostle from Jerusalem (I Cor. ix.6) he was sent out on the so-called first missionary journey. In his own Epistles Paul stresses both his individuality based on the special nature of the calling and also his solidarity with Jerusalem (pp. 175 f.).

In all probability he had already done missionary work before coming to Antioch in both Arabia and his native land. It was apparently primarily his work in the Diaspora synagogues which had led to sharp, intense conflicts with the Jews. Since he was to have been arrested, obviously at the instigation of the Jews, he had to flee from Damascus (II Cor. xi.32 f.;

---

[12] Gal. i.13 f.; I Cor. xv.9; Phil. iii.6; I Tim. i.13. His persecution of the Church in Jerusalem (Acts vii.58; viii.1, 3; ix.1) is not contradicted by Gal. i.22 (*contra* Heitmüller, *ZNTW* 13 (1912), 327, *et al.*).

[13] Gal. i.15–24; II Cor. xi.32 f.; Acts ix.10–30; xi.25–30; xii.24 f.; 13 f.; see H. Schlier, *Der Brief an die Galater* (*Meyer Kommentar*, [10]1949), 66–78, for a synopsis and evaluation.

[14] On the journey reported in Acts xi.27–30; xii.24 f. in contrast to Gal. ii.1, see J. Jeremias, 'Sabbathjahr und neutestamentliche Chronologie', *ZNTW*, 27 (1928), 98–103; Haenchen, *Apostelgeschichte, in loco*; S. Giet, 'Les trois premiers Voyages de S. Paul à Jerusalem', *Rech. Sciences Rel.* 41 (1953), 321–347; J. Dupont, 'La Mission de Paul "à Jerusalem" (Acts xii.25),' *Nov. Test.*, 1 (1956), 275–303; R. W. Funk, 'The Enigma of the Famine Visit', *JBL*, 75 (1956).

cf. Acts ix.23 ff.). In the same context he remarked (II Cor. xi.24) that he had five times suffered the severe synagogue penalty of forty stripes at the hands of the Jews. This must have taken place before the beginning of his work in Antioch, because after this time he no longer appeared before the courts of the synagogues. If as a missionary he lived solely from the donations of his churches and by the work of his own hands, then it might mean he had broken with his own family whose acquisition of Roman citizenship betrays their prosperity. In any case, after Paul had taken up his missionary work from Antioch, he alienated himself from the synagogues forever after a short and sharp dispute. How did this come about?

Paul was conscious of being called as apostle for the Gentile world, but he began his proclamation in the Diaspora synagogues and maintained this procedure in spite of the repeated conflicts.[15] He was conscious of being obliged to pursue this method because of redemptive history (Rom. i.14, 16), and at the same time he viewed it as a practical necessity since the Diaspora synagogues provided a bridge to the Gentiles (p. 82) in that 'missionary age of the Jewish religion'.

In view of this situation one has, to a limited extent, an explanation of why Paul's work always led quickly to a break with the Jews, whereas the men of Jerusalem were able to work for decades among Israel. Paul's initial missionary *kerygma* was probably not very different from that of Jerusalem, and the example in Acts xiii. 16–41 could well be accurate, but when the God-fearers and Gentiles who were present asked about the way of salvation, Paul could only answer them as he did the Philippian jailer: faith alone, without circumcision. This type of proclamation had far-reaching results. It denied any basis for the further existence of a synagogue which made salvation in both time and eternity dependent on obedience to the Law. If, then, the synagogue did not want to renounce itself, it had to drive Paul out under violent protest,[16] although with him they drove out not only several of their own best members but also many God-fearers and the Gentiles in general who were seeking a universal salvation. While these turned to the Church, the synagogue remained isolated and robbed of its religious value, so the synagogue persecuted Paul with bitter hatred (I Thess. ii.14 ff.; Acts xxi. 28). Here begins the great turning point in the history of Judaism. From the Israel who had brought witness to the Gentile world of God's salavation now developed the post-Christian Judaism which closed itself off from those outside. Even more important was the effect of what was taking place on the

---

[15] Acts xiii.34; xiv.1; xvi.13; xviii.2, 10, 17; xviii.4, 19, 26; xix.8.
[16] That stands behind the action of the Synagogues in Acts xiii.45 ff.; xiv.2; xvii.5; xix.9, but it is no longer clear in Acts itself.

development of the Church. A new unity between the Old Testament and the message of Jesus developed in Paul's preaching to the Gentiles which grew out of the mission in the Diaspora synagogue. It was a Gospel for Jews and Gentiles whose main outline Paul laid before the Church of Rome at the end of his work in the East in the Epistle to the Romans. Everywhere Paul presented this Gospel, the congregation of Jewish and Gentile believers withdrew from the synagogues and lived 'apart from the Law' because of their faith in Christ (Rom. iii.21).

3. This Gospel free from the Law which Paul defended but which had not been sufficiently explained to believers in Antioch became the centre of attention when—perhaps occasioned by the news of the disputes in the Diaspora synagogue—men of the earliest Church in Antioch demanded circumcision of the Gentile Christians as a sign of the subjection to the Mosaic Law[17] necessary for salvation. They wanted, as Gal. ii.14 has put it with the formula current in the Hellenistic world, to force the Gentile Christians, ἰουδαΐζειν, i.e. to live according to Jewish customs. Christians who demanded this from their brethren were therefore designated, even in the second century, as 'Judaizers'.[18] According to Acts xv.1–5 and Gal. ii.4, the appearance of Judaizers in Antioch was the cause of the Apostolic Council.[19] Apparently the Judaizers in Antioch, as later in Galatia, appealed to the men 'who were apostles before Paul' (Gal. i.17), and to the earliest Church which lived for all practical purposes according to the Law. Barnabas and Paul therefore travelled to Jerusalem at the appointment of the Church in Antioch (Acts xv.2; cf. Gal. ii.1). They were not seeking any sort of authoritative instruction on the part of those 'of repute' (Gal. ii.2, 6)[20] nor a vote of confidence from the majority of the Church there, but the *koinonia* resulting from the confession of the one Gospel. Without this *koinonia* Paul would have 'run in vain', since a discrepancy between his Gospel and that of the earliest apostles would not only have been an offence to the churches but to him personally. The

---

[17] Cf. Josephus, *Antiq.* 20, 2, 4: When King Irates of Adiabene became a God-fearer, a Palestinian Jew demanded him to be circumcised, whereas the Hellenistic-Jewish missionary had expressly exempted him from it.

[18] Ignatius, *Magn.* viii.1; x.3; *Phild.* vi.1.

[19] The discussion centres primarily around the evaluation of the accounts in Acts xv (cf. xi.27–30) and Gal. ii. While Acts xv is merely a literary product according to Dibelius (*Studies in the Acts of the Apostles*, Ger. 84–90) and Haenchen (*Apostelgeschichte*, 401–419—further literature given here), in spite of its redactional form it contains concepts foreign to Luke from the earliest Church according to Munck (*Paul and the Salvation of Mankind*, 233 ff., cf. 123–131). According to O. Linton ('The Third Aspect', *Stud. Theol.*, iii (1949), 79–95), Acts xv contains an aspect which coincides its several points with that presupposed by the Judaizers in Gal. i f. and thus involved ancient sources.

[20] W. Foerster, 'Die δοκοῦντες in Gal. 2', *ZNTW*, 36 (1937), 286–292, *TWNT*, ii. 236; C. K. Barrett, 'Paul and the "Pillar" Apostles', *Studia Paulina* (as in §5, n. 31).

koinonia itself was only realizable through a mutual hearing of God's word. This is the context in which the portrayals in Acts and Galatians recount the course of the debates (cf. §7, 5).

The principals involved were all men addressed according to the usage of that time by the title 'apostle'. Paul and Barnabas were on one side, with the 'Three Pillars' on the other. To this extent it was an Apostolic Council, but at the same time the entire congregation took part.[21] After much dissension (Acts xv.7; Gal. ii.5), two factors helped them reach an agreement. On the one hand, Paul and Barnabas (Gal. ii.7-9; Acts xv.12), and thus in all probability Peter too (Acts xv.7-9), gave witness to what had taken place through them among the uncircumcised. On the other hand, the Gospel was theologically explained with special reference to the question at hand. This took place according to Gal. ii.2, 6 through Paul and according to Acts xv.10 f., 13-21, through Peter and James. In fact both were necessary, and the decision in Acts xv corresponds so closely to the ancient theology of the earliest Church that it must be based upon tradition. James spoke about the addition to the new Israel of the Gentiles who were seeking the Lord, and Peter stated that the Jewish Christians, even though they lived according to the Law, based their hope for salvation on faith; Jesus himself had based his disciples from the very beginning on faith alone, so they could not now deny salvation to the uncircumcised who believed.

A Gospel free from the Law was now recognized. This was the decisive result according to both reports (Gal. ii.6; Acts xv.28). More specifically, in Gal. ii.9 f., the result was an agreement among the apostles. It did not mean a division of the work according to geography[22] or personnel[23] but basically a mutual recognition of each other's missionary work (Gal. ii.7). According to Acts, a decree was agreed upon in Jerusalem for the churches in Syria and Cilicia, the so-called Apostolic Decree, but this formula placed by Luke in Acts xv also settled a question which first came into prominence for the Palestinian Church through the incident in Antioch and which was a result of the decision at the Apostolic Council; so the Decree was probably first enacted after the Council.[24] Regardless of these

[21] Gal. ii.2 Paul laid his Gospel '. . . before those of repute. . . '. According to Gal. ii.5, the false brethren also spoke; Acts xv.6, 22.

[22] Most recently, Munck, *Paul and the Salvation of Mankind* (as in §5, n. 30), 119-122.

[23] Cullmann tends in this direction, *Peter, Disciple—Apostle—Martyr* (as in §5, n. 29, Ger. 45), 42.

[24] That has often been supposed since C. Weizsäcker, *The Apostolic Age of the Christian Church* (as in §1, n. 8) (Haenchen, *Apostelgeschichte*, 415). This would then mean that Paul did not mention it at a given situation, in contrast to Acts xvi.4, and that, according to Acts xxi.25, it was made known to him during his final visit in Jerusalem (cf. A. S. Geyser, 'Paul, the Apostolic Decree and the Liberals in Corinth', *Studia Paulina* (as in §5, n. 31), 124-138 and §11, 1 below).

differences the Apostolic Council was a decisive event for Acts and Galatians, an event to which one could refer from then on.

The Apostolic Council also represents a decisive turning point in our picture of the history of primitive Christianity. The ever-widening schism in the Church between Hellenism on one hand and Judaism on the other, which began with the persecution of Stephen, was closed once again through attention being focused on the Church's centre. The men whose word was considered authoritative for each side had now mutually acknowledged the other's respective ministries. Paul and Barnabas continued to stand in the tradition of Jesus' earthly ministry which came from Jerusalem as well as in the confession of the earliest Church. Conversely, Jerusalem acknowledged the Gospel free from the Law as an expression of the one true Gospel. In this manner the two branches of Christianity current at that time were brought together into an ecclesiological fellowship in spite of all the differences in their way of life. This fellowship then expressed itself through an active interchange of emissaries, through which they avoided being absorbed by their religious environment. The Apostolic Council, which is probably to be set in the year 48, also stands chronologically as the decisive turning point of the period extending to 64-70. After the persecution of Stephen a part of the Church had emerged from the shell of Judaism which had protectively surrounded her during the initial stages, but now the turn had been taken which in the following twenty years would force the whole Church from the circle of Judaism, with the result that by the time of the Neronic persecution she would appear to the world as a religion separated from Judaism.

11. THE INNER AND OUTWARD SEPARATION OF THE CHURCH FROM JUDAISM

The time between the Apostolic Council and the Neronic persecution is characterized in Acts by missionary expansion. The question about the Law was considered to be settled, and the actual consequences of this matter are touched upon only briefly in Acts xxi.21. The Pauline Epistles give us insight into the inner problems of the Church. Originating in this period, these Epistles comprise the earliest Christian literature preserved for us, and in contrast to the preceding 'twenty years of darkness' they place this period in the light of the contemporary documents.

1. The Apostolic Council had acknowledged the Gentile Christians as brothers. With this arose the question, as we have learned from the incident in Antioch[1] (Gal. ii.11-21): Were the Jewish Christians in the mixed

[1] T. Zahn, 'Petrus in Antiochien', *NKZ* (1894), 435-448, B. Reicke, 'Der ge-

congregations allowed to give up the Law and to have fellowship with the Gentile Christians in both daily life and table-fellowship? In the Church of Antioch it had apparently been so from the very beginning. Even Peter joined them when he came to Antioch, probably shortly after the Apostolic Council, but when the men sent from James raised an objection to this, Peter, together with all the other Jewish Christians, broke off the table-fellowship. As soon as this came to Paul's attention, he reprimanded them sharply, for in his opinion it followed that if the Gentiles were free from the Law, then all believers were by this very fact free. James, however, did not want this conclusion to be applied to the Jewish Christians, and Peter wavered between the two points of view.

We do not hear further about how the dispute in Antioch ended (pp. 79 ff.), but the Apostolic Decree[2] (Acts xv.28 f; cf. xix f.; xxi.25), which had most probably been directed to the churches of Syria and Cilicia soon after these events in Antioch, required that the Gentile Christians abstain from activities and foods which were also forbidden for the sojourner in Israel according to Lev. xvii.8–14; xviii.6 ff. This abstention was to make it easier for the Jewish Christians to live together with the Gentile Christians. They were still conscious of being bound to the Law, but they set it aside to the extent that a table-fellowship with the Gentile Christians was possible. The Decree, which Paul did not pass on to his churches (see below), was later made operative in the entire Church, but its meaning was modified in the second generation. Rev. ii.14, 20, 24 enjoined its regulations as a confession in opposition to heathen religions and a gnostic, libertine Christianity.[3] In this sense, that which was prohibited in Acts was abhorred as an expression of unholy paganism up to and beyond the second century.[4] At the same time, the Decree received still a third meaning in the second century in that it was applied to the three mortal sins.[5] The original meaning of the Decree was already out of date by the second generation, since the Jewish Christians in the Church

---

schichtliche Hintergrund des Apostelkonzils und der Antiochia-Episode, Gal. 2:1–14', *Studia Paulina* (as in §5, n. 31), 172–187; W. Schmithals, *Paulus und Jakobus*, 1963.

[2] R. Boeckenhoff, *Das apostolische Speisegesetz in den ersten drei Jahrhunderten* (1907); H. Lietzmann, 'Der Sinn des Aposteldekrets und seine Textwandlung', *Amicitiae Corolla* (1933), 203 ff.; H. Waitz, 'Das Problem des sogenannten Aposteldekrets'. *ZKG*, 55 (1936), 227–263; E. Stauffer, *TWNT*, ii, 439, n. 37; Haenchen, *Apostelgeschichte*, 415–419.

[3] This motive is already to be heard in I Cor. x.5 ff., 19 ff.

[4] Abstinence from meat sacrificed to idols (Justin, *Dial.* 34, 7) and eating of blood (Tertullian, *Apol.*, 9, 13; Eusebius, *H.E.*, v, 1, 26; Minucius Felix, 36, 6).

[5] As the Western Text tradition indicates, the 'strangled' was omitted, and the other three prohibitions were understood as the three mortal sins: idolatry, murder, and adultery. By adding the Golden Rule, the Decree was made into a minimal catechism (see Zahn, *Apostelgeschichte* ([4]1927), 546–550).

between Antioch and Rome had to a great extent ceased to live according to the Mosaic ordinances. This departure from the Law was already standard behaviour when Paul went to Jerusalem for the last time c. A.D. 57. He had been accused in the earliest Church of having been responsible for this (Acts xxi.20 f.), and at the request of James Paul was to give evidence that he himself ' . . . lived in observance of the Law' (Acts xxi.24). The record in Acts falsely attributes the viewpoint of James to Paul, even if it does correctly report his conduct. In doing so, Luke intended merely to clear Paul of the accusation of lawlessness rather than to bind the Jewish Christians to an ordinance which they had already left behind by this time. (Luke points out the necessary distinction for the Gentile Christians between the Law of Moses and the 'ordinances' (ἔθη) of Moses.

The problem of the daily fellowship between Jewish and Gentile Christians, which was settled for Syria and Cilicia by the Apostolic Decree, reappeared in the Pauline congregations probably in terms of the tension between the 'weak' and the 'strong' (I Cor. viii–x; Rom. xiv. 1–15, 13).[6] As far as we can tell, the weak were a group of Jewish Christians whose faith was not strong enough to free them entirely from the bonds of Jewish customs. In Corinth they avoided the flesh of animals which had been dedicated to the gods, since for the Jews such meat was the same as that offered to the gods. In Rome they abstained from partaking of meat and wine, just as the pious Jew often did according to Dan. i.8–16 in Gentile surroundings. The weak did not demand that the other Christians abstain in these matters, but they themselves were bound by their own consciences. Paul exhorted the others to take consideration of them in love, but he never, unlike Acts xvi.4, referred to the Apostolic Decree. It is certainly understandable that the Jewish Christians in the churches of the Gentile Christians would not want to be considered permanently as the weak and would, consequently, have discontinued their Jewish customs. Jewish believers in Pauline churches on the whole had probably from the very beginning stopped circumcising their children and living in accordance with the Mosaic ordinances cited in Acts xxi.20 f. Paul had given them the freedom for this without forcing such conduct on them.

2. This conduct by the Jews in Paul's churches (Acts xxi.20) was deeply disturbing to the Palestinian Church and might have set still another judaizing movement in motion after the Apostolic Council (cf. §8, 5). Just as the Judaizers had attempted to halt the break with the Diaspora synagogues prior to the Apostolic Council, so they now attempted to prevent the defection of 'the Jews among the Gentiles' (Acts xxi.21) from the

[6] Literature: *TWNT*, i, 490; Goppelt, *Christentum und Judentum*, 95 f. (= *Jesus, Paul and Judaism*, 127 f.); §10, n. 24.

Mosaic ordinances. At any rate we meet Judaizers again in the Epistle to the Galatians.[7] In the churches of Galatia (Gal. i.2), which are probably to be located in that area of Galatia reached by the second missionary journey (Acts xvi.6; Gal. iii.1), evangelists were demanding circumcision of the Gentile Christians (Gal. v.3, 12; vi.12, 15; cf. ii.3 f.). These evangelists appealed against Paul to the earliest apostles (Gal. i, 11–ii. 21), and, like the Judaizers in Antioch (Acts xv.1; Gal. ii.4), they probably came from Jerusalem.[8] The Christians there were to show by means of circumcision that they acknowledged the Law (Gal. iv.21), even though they did not need to observe the Law in all its details (Gal. v.3). The Gentile Christians, enthralled, accepted this teaching (Gal. iii.1) since it promised them an unqualified affiliation with a privileged ancient religion, its Law, and its promises, but Paul made it poignantly clear that this corrected Gospel was really not a Gospel at all, because ' . . . if justification were through the Law, then Christ died to no purpose' (Gal. ii.21; cf. vi.14 f.).

The Tübingen School of F. C. Baur saw in Galatia the beginnings of an extensive judaizing movement from which came the opponents with whom Paul had to cope in Corinth and Rome. It claimed that the earliest apostles, especially Peter, were forced into the camp of the Judaizers by means of the incident at Antioch (Gal. v.10; I Cor. i.12), and gave the Judaizers the necessary support. Hans Lietzmann[9] and Eduard Meyer[10] have partially revived this viewpoint, but in the meantime it has become clear that Paul's opponents in Corinth (and in Colosse) are not to be interpreted in terms of Galatians (cf. §13, 2). The brief warnings in Rom. xvi. 17–20 and Phil. iii.2 f. (18 f.) remind us more of II Cor. xi.28 ff.[11] It is only in Galatians that Paul counters the demand for circumcision according to the Law. Since the appearance of a legalistic Judaism in Galatia seems so singular in nature, there is now an opposite tendency to interpret it in terms of the problems in Corinth and elsewhere and to view it as a syncretistic and gnostic Judaism.[12] This forced uniformity

---

[7] Literature: introductions and commentaries on Galatians.

[8] According to E. Hirsch, 'Zwei Fragen zu Galater 6', *ZNTW* 29 (1930), 192–197; W. Michaelis, 'Judaistische Heidenchristen', *ZNTW* 30 (1931), 83–89; and Munck, *Paul and the Salvation of Mankind* (as in §5, n. 30), 87 ff., they came from the Gentile Christians in Galatia. A. Oepke, *Der Brief des Paulus an die Galater* (²1957), refutes this.

[9] *SAB* (1930), 153 ff.; *The History of the Early Church*; 107, 155. Further, see Oepke, *op. cit.* (n. 8), on Gal. v.10.

[10] *Ursprung und Anfänge des Christentums* (1923), iii, 434, 441.

[11] Goppelt, *Jesus, Paul and Judaism*, 181 f. (= *Christentum und Judentum*, 136 f.).

[12] According to H. Schlier, *Der Brief an die Galater* (*Meyer Kommentar*, ¹⁰1949), 144 cf. 134, and G. Bornkamm, 'Die Häresie des Kolosserbriefes', *Gesammelte Aufsätze* (1952), i, 148, the 'other Gospel' in Galatians is influenced by apocryphal Judaism whose traces we find in Eth. Ennoch and in the Jewish Christian sects (Elchasites). W. Schmithals, 'Die Häretiker in Galitien', *ZNTW*, 47 (1956), 25–67, replaces the pan-Judaism of the Tübingen school with a fanciful pan-Gnosticism.

contradicts the clear statements of the Epistle, however, for although in Gal. iv.9 Paul placed Judaism theologically on a level with Gentile syncretism, this does not mean that it was syncretistic in terms of the history of religions.

As well as the events in Galatia, a legalistic Judaism may have appeared here and there in the Church; it is seen in the second century in both Asia Minor and Syria, although, in terms of the total picture, the numerical growth of the Gentile Christians made the attempt to turn them back to the Law pointless. Even in I Corinthians and Romans, Paul had to do the very opposite by protecting the Jewish Christians whose conscience was still bound to the Jewish customs (pp. 78 f.). Nevertheless, it was of decisive importance for the further development of the Church that the legalistic Judaism in Galatia was not only overtaken by the Church's expansion but that it was overcome by a Spirit-inspired exposition of the Gospel in Galatians[13] and that this Epistle was preserved as a guide for the Church. It was also just as important that Paul in Galatians (ii.9), as in the later debates, could legitimately assert his essential oneness with the earliest apostles (I Cor. ix.5; xv.ii).

3. The total picture is rounded off when we remember that the Palestinian Church, contrary to its expectations, was driven out of the Jewish community almost immediately after these events, at the beginning of the Jewish insurrection (cf. p. 61). Thus, towards the end of the Pauline period, believers withdrew everywhere, except perhaps in Egypt, from association with the Jewish community. Furthermore, the Jewish Christians living between Antioch and Rome forsook the life according to the Mosaic Law, while those in Palestine, Syria and Egypt still maintained it.

Let us now pursue the growth of the Church in the world of Hellenism and her first struggles with syncretism.

12. THE EARLIEST CHRISTIAN MISSION IN THE WORLD OF HELLENISM

1. The earliest Christian mission in the realm of Hellenism is embedded in the latter's religious movements. The mission entered the Hellenistic world from the background of the Diaspora synagogue, and so grew out of the religious dialogue of Diaspora Judaism with Hellenism. It was only because the Diaspora synagogues were spread like a thick net over the entire area of the Mediterannean[1] that Christianity could expand over

---

[13] They also took part in the collection for Jerusalem (I Cor. xvi.1).

[1] J. Juster, Les Juifs dans L'Empire romain (1914), i, 179–212; G. Kittel, 'Die Entstehung des Judentums und die Entstehung der Judenfragen', in Forschungen zur Judenfrage (1937), i, 43–63; 'Die Ausbreitung des Judentums bis zum Beginn des Mittelalters', in Forschungen zur Judenfrage (1941), v, ibid. (1944), ix; P. Dalbert, Die Theologie der hellenistisch-jüdischen Missionsliteratur unter Ausschluss von Philo und Josephus (1954), 12–21.

the whole *oikumene* within one generation, and only because Diaspora Judaism had always had missionary contact with her environment that Gentiles beyond her limits could be won so quickly for the message of Jesus.

This was the 'missionary age' of the Jewish Religion. Although the literature preserved for us from Hellenistic Judaism is in the main apologetic with only a few writings of a missionary character,[2] the apologetic material did build personal and intellectual bridges with the Hellenistic world. Diaspora Judaism assimilated the Hellenistic ideas and combined them with Biblical concepts, so becoming Hellenistic Judaism. We are not to consider Philo, a contemporary of Jesus, as the only representative of Diaspora Judaism, since writings such as the Wisdom of Solomon were widely circulated.[3] The translators of the Septuagint above all expressed the Old Testament concepts in a magnificent manner and with universal appeal through the use of Greek words. The work itself was created for the Diaspora Jews who were no longer familiar with Hebrew,[4] but it became the most important foundation for the Jewish and Christian mission.

The Diaspora communities did not send out missionaries. The Jews who sought to win converts from among the Gentiles for the faith of Israel, as we see reflected in Rom. ii.17 ff., acted on their own initiative just as had the Pharisees of the mother country (Matt. xxiii. 15) who sought to convert proselytes (not 'God-fearers'). The synagogues supported the mission in that they made it easier for the Gentiles who were interested in the religion of Israel to take part in the services and to join the community. Affiliation was not only granted to the proselytes who completely joined Judaism through immersion, circumcision and subjection to the Law, and in doing so became eligible for a Jewish marriage, but also to the 'God-fearers', who embraced the major commandments of the Old Testament and monotheism in particular.[5] In the synagogue, the Gentiles not only found the Old Testament preaching but also Hellenistic thought and Hellenistic style and form. The synagogue preaching adapted for itself the form of the diatribe[6] and the revelatory discourses.[7] In all this, though, neither the Judaism of the motherland nor

---

[2] See *ibid.*, 7, supplemented by J. Jeremias, *Jesus' Promise to the Nations* (as in §6, n. 1, Ger. 10 f.), 12 f.

[3] Probably written in Alexandria during the first century A.D. (O. Eissfeld, *Introduction to the Old Testament*, 1965, 600 ff. Ger. 742 ff.).

[4] *Ibid.*, 701 ff. (Ger. 855 ff.).

[5] Acts xiii.50; xvi.14; xvii.4, 17; xviii.7; cf. §10, n. 17. For discussion of this difference see Dalbert, *op. cit.*, 22, n. 5.

[6] H. Thyen, *Der Stil der Jüdisch-Hellenistischen Homilie* (1955), esp. 62 f.

[7] H. Becker, *Die Reden des Johannesevangelium und der Stil der gnostischen Offenbarungsrede* (1956), 41–53.

that in the Diaspora gave thought to a mission to the nations of the world, but only thought about winning individual Gentiles[8]—a means used by other oriental cults to gain their respective members.

Characteristic of the situation at that time was the fact that Hellenistic thought adopted Jewish ideas merely from the latter's literature while being completely independent of personal contact with the synagogues. For example, the authors of the *Hermetica*, which was written in the period extending from the end of the first century to the third, used the Septuagint in a manner similar to their usage of the Platonic and Stoic literature.[9] They were not the only ones who had such an interest in that mysterious book belonging to the Jews.[10]

When the Christian mission began, the setting of Hellenistic religion[11] was characterized by the age of Augustus. Caesar Augustus had brought peace and order to the world after a period in which it had badly damaged itself. The leading Roman poets of his time conveyed to the people a consciousness of his being the saviour and the one who brought the golden age.[12] Augustus attempted to instil new life into the ancient Roman religion which had already been subdued to the Greek religions and had collapsed under philosophical scepticism.[13] It then became a cult of the state which was closely bound to the house of Augustus. At the same time, he introduced a religious veneration of his person[14] conferring upon himself titles such as *divi filius* and σεβαστός, although in Rome he avoided the divine veneration which was readily granted to him in the East where rulers had long been viewed as gods. Augustus was genuinely revered in

---

[8] See S. Aalen, *Die Begriffe 'Licht' und 'Finsternis' im Alten Testament, im Spätjudentum und im Rabbinismus* (1951), 202–232 and Munck, *Paul and the Salvation of Mankind* (as in §5, n. 30, Ger. 259–265), 264–271. Both correctly limit the exaggerated portrayal of the Jewish mission by G. Rosen G. Bertram, *Juden und Phönizier* (1929).

[9] C. H. Dodd, *The Bible and the Greeks* (²1954).

[10] *Ibid.*, 243 f.

[11] Literature: *P.W.* and *RAC*, *passim*; P. Wendland, *Die hellenistisch-römische Kultur* (³1912); F. Cumont, *Oriental Religions in Roman Paganism*, 1911, r.p. 1956 (Eng. trans. of *Les Religions Orientales dans le Paganisme Romain*, ²1909); W. W. Tarn, *Hellenistic Civilisation* (³1952); K. Prümm, *Religionsgeschichtliches Handbuch für den Raum der altchristlichen Umwelt* (²1954); H. Preisker, *Neutestamentliche Zeitgeschichte* (1937); F. G. Grant, *Hellenistic Religions, The Age of Syncretism* (1953); R. Bultmann, *Primitive Christianity in its Contemporary Setting* (1956) (Eng. trans. of *Das Urchristentum im Rahmen der antiken Religionen*, ²1954); 'Zum Thema: Christentum und Antike', *ThR*, 23 (1955), 207–229; M. Rostovtzeff, *Die hellenistische Welt. Gesellschaft und Wirtschaft* (3 vols. 1955–56); C. K. Barrett, *The New Testament Background: Selected Documents* (1956).

[12] Wendland, *op. cit.*, 143; Barrett, *op. cit.*, 6–10. The subject of the Virgil's *Ecologue*, iv, is still not certain.

[13] Wendland, *op. cit.*, 137–145; Barrett, *op. cit.*, 5 f.

[14] Wendland, *op. cit.*, 146 ff.; *P.W. Supplement* iv, 806 ff.; Preisker, *op. cit.*, 201 f., more literature given. L. Cerfaux et J. Tondriau, *Le culte des souverains dans la civilisation Gréco-Romain*, 1957.

this way because he had brought what one expected from a deity, peace and security. In the following generations the emperor cult was further expanded to such an extent that the artificially revived cult of the state eventually faded away.

The real religious need, however, could not be satisfied in this manner. 'Caesar has brought freedom from war but not freedom from cares.'[15] As a result, magic and astrology became the secret religion of the masses.[16] Simultaneously a popularized religious philosophy[17] concerned itself with the education of the people. It was carried into private homes by Cynic and Stoic peripatetic philosophers and preached to audiences in the streets in the style of the diatribe. This philosophy developed a practical ethic and built a bridge to the traditional gods by means of its allegorical interpretations of the myths, while the propaganda by the mystery religions was much more restrained;[18] by means of dedicatory rites in a closed cult, they imparted participation in the fate of the deities as they die and come again to life. The representatives of the Hermetic Writings proclaimed a cultless, sublime religion in philosophic garb. They did so as pneumatics to whom the *gnosis* of existence had been revealed.[19]

This propaganda met a universal religious need of the people, who were seeking a personal satisfaction for their intense religious desires. The search which Augustine's *Confessions* describes was so typical of the age that we meet it again in Justin (*Dial.* 2, 3–3, 1), in the *Metamorphoses* of Apuleius whose hero finally discovers fulfilment in the Isis mysteries, and even in the *Vita Josephi* written in keeping with the tastes of that period. This search took as its point of departure the concept that in the different religions the same divine element was always present, Hellenism being essentially syncretistic, but behind this relativism stood a remarkable tendency towards monotheism.

Thus the Christian mission did not break into a static religious structure such as a fixed national religion, but became like one of the oriental redemptive religions in which many had sought freedom from an inward emptiness and a devotion to a materialistic, hedonistic existence. They expected religious satisfaction in the form of a moralistic monotheism and were prepared to accept it wherever it was evidenced by a moral way of life. This desire was met by the Christian message when it was carried into the Hellenistic world primarily by way of the Diaspora synagogues.

---

15 Epictectus, *Discourses*, 3, 13, 11.

16 Preisker, *op. cit.*, 175–189 (further literature); Barrett, *op. cit.*, 31–36.

17 Wendland, *op. cit.*, 75–91.

18 R. Reitzenstein, *Die hellenistischen Mysterienreligionen* (³1927); Barrett, *op. cit.*, 91–100; *TWNT*, iv, 810–814; G. Wagner, *Das religionsgeschichtliche Problem von Röm. 6, 1–11* (1962), 69–270.

19 C. H. Dodd, *The Fourth Gospel* (1953), 10 ff.; Barrett, *op. cit.*, 80–90; §13, lc.

2. How did this message read? We have already seen how the proclamation of the Gospel free from the Law became the fundamental missionary sermon[20] for the Gentiles in the Diaspora synagogues (cf. p. 74), but what was the form of the proclamation which went directly to the Gentiles? The only example in Acts is Paul's sermon on the Areopagus (Acts xvii.22–31; cf. xiv.15 ff.).[21] Even according to Luke, this was not supposed to represent the usual missionary sermon to the Gentiles, but it does correspond to the outline which we can deduce from 1 Thess. i.9 f. and Heb. vi.1 f. We find here an outline agreeing to a great extent with the form of the Hellenistic revelatory discourse which we meet in Hermetic literature and in the literature of Hellenistic Judaism.[22] This outline involved the following elements:

(1) Since the Christian message had a special revelation to proclaim, it called the pagan existence ignorance (ἄγνοια).[23] The Gentiles did not know God because they could not recognize him (I Cor. i f., especially ii.10–16), because they inexcusably failed to acknowledge the reality of God which had been shown to them (Rom. i.18–20), or because they inexcusably misunderstood the rule of God which had been shown to them by the order of nature and history (Acts xvii.23–29), and thus condemned themselves. The first passage (I Cor. i, and ii.10–16) spoke of their 'not knowing' in a manner similar to the Hermetic *gnosis*, the second (Rom. i.18–20) in a manner similar to that of Old Testament Judaism and the third (Acts xvii.23–29) in a manner similar to that of the Stoics and Jewish wisdom literature.[24] Ignorance was combined with ἐπιθυμία, i.e., with their self-centred desires (Rom. i.24–27; Eph. iv.17–19; I Pet. i.14), just as it was in the respective analogies, but unlike the non-Biblical analogies,

[20] Literature: A. Oepke, *Die Missionspredigt des Apostels Paulus* (1929); K. Pieper, *Die Missionspredigt des heiligen Paulus* (1921); Harnack, *The Mission and Expansion of Christianity*, 86–100 (Ger. i, 114–129); G. Schrenk, 'Urchristliche Missionspredigt im ersten Jahrhundert', in *Auf dem Grunde der Apostel und Propheten (Festschrift* for Wurm, 1948); Bultmann, *Theology of the New Testament*, §9; J. Munck, 'I Thess. i.9 and the Missionary Preaching of Paul', *NTS*, 9 (1963), 95–110.

[21] Literature: E. Nordon, *Agnostos Theos* (⁴1956); Dibelius, *Studies in the Acts of the Apostles* (Ger. 29–70); recent literature in W. Eltester, 'Schöpfungsoffenbarung und natürliche Theologie im Frühen Christentum', *NTS*, 3 (1956–57), 100, n. 1. In my opinion B. Gärtner has developed an interpretation which is correct to a great extent, *The Areopagus Speech and Natural Revelation* (1955).

[22] Nordon, *op. cit.*, 3–30, 125–140; Becker, *op. cit.* (n. 7), and Thyen *op. cit.* (n. 6).

[23] Acts xvii.30; I Cor. i.21; Eph. iv.18; I Pet. i.14.

[24] The terms ἀγνοέω (xvii.23) and ἄγνοια (xvii.30) which set the tone of the Areopagus address do not mean a lack of knowledge as in the Stoic teaching (so M. Pohlenz, 'Paulus und die Stoa', *ZNTW*, 42 (1949), 69–104), but in keeping with the usage in Acts (iii.17) and the context (xvii.30 ὑπεριδών), as well as with the primitive Christian missionary sermons in general, it meant an inexcusable and condemning, to be sure forgivable, misunderstanding from which a special act of God alone (xvii.30: 'He announces to all men everywhere to repent') can save one. Up till now this aspect has not received sufficient consideration in the research.

to Paul this ignorance appears as an inexcusable and condemning bondage (as in Acts xvii). Consequently, the reference to the true God came not as enlightening instruction nor as an awakening call to remembrance, but as a proclamation of grace and repentance.

(2) Just as in the case of Israel, the aim of the missionary sermon was repentance (μετάνοια) to the one true God, a repentance which was both demanded and granted through Jesus (Acts xvii.30; Heb vi.1; cf. I Thess. i.9). The Stoics at this point summoned one to knowledge (ἐπιστήμη); the Hermetics, under the influence of Old Testament Judaism, summoned one to μετάνοια.[25]

(3) This summons to repentance was supported, as in the case of Israel, by pointing to Jesus' resurrection and his coming appearance as Judge of the world (I Thess. i.10; Acts xvii.31; Heb. vi.2). His resurrection was not only interpreted from his function as Judge of the world but also in terms of his earthly ministry in a manner similar to the Marcan tradition. This was all placed in the light of the Septuagint which filled it with meaning, giving shape to the proclamation of the one true God.

(4) Just as in the case of Israel, the missionary sermon led the Gentiles into baptism (Heb. vi.2), which was also generally practised by the Gentile Church (Rom. vi. 2 ff.).

Did Paul abandon this general outline of the missionary sermon when he, as he asserted, preached only the crucified Jesus (I Cor. ii.1–5; Gal. iii.1)? As the context of these passages shows, he did not intend to say that he preached only the Crucified One but that he placed everything in relationship to the Crucified One. This is the missionary sermon when it characterizes the way to God in terms of guilt and grace and does not, as did the Jewish sermon, appeal to the understanding and will of man nor teach wisdom in the manner of the Stoics or the Gnostic movements (I Cor. i.18–ii.16).[26] We can no longer determine in detail how Paul preached to the Gentiles, since in Rom. i–iii he spoke to the Church about a paganism and a Judaism which faith had to overcome at the same time as the 'old self' (Rom. vi).[27] In his missionary sermons, however, Paul certainly did not simply speak of the raising of 'a Man', as in Acts xvii.31, but he also included the Crucified One and thus condemned even more strongly the religion of the Gentiles.

This missionary *kerygma* was always presented accompanied by a claim to absolute truth found elsewhere only in the Jewish mission and with a universalism which was quite unique. Whereas the Jewish mission

---

[25] Norden. *op. cit.* (n. 21), 134–140.

[26] U. Wilckens, *Weisheit und Torheit, Eine exegetisch-religionsgeschichtliche Untersuchung zu I. Cor. 1 und 2* (1959), esp. 270.

[27] Thus the 'point of contact', as in Acts xvii.23, is missing here. To be sure even in Acts xvii it only had an informative meaning.

had only thought about winning individuals, the missionary *kerygma* not only asserted that mankind could be saved through this message alone (Acts iv.12), but it expected in faith that the 'full number of the Gentiles', i.e., not every individual but the nations of the world as a whole, would comply and 'all Israel (would) be saved' (Rom. xi.25 f.). Paul certainly did not stand alone in this bold prophecy; whereas he could only look forward to the salvation of all Israel by means of a miracle of grace prior to the consummation, James, the Lord's brother, struggled for the conversion of the entire nation (cf. §8, 5). A generation later, it became clear that 'the full number of the Gentiles' would not take part in the salvation. 'Many are called, but few are chosen', was asserted in Matt. xxii.14 in the parable of the marriage feast representing the universal invitation. According to John's Gospel, Jesus as the good shepherd separated only 'his own' from Israel and the nations of the world (John x.3, 14 ff.), and 'the world' hates them (John xvii.15 f.). The Apocalypse sees the Church as the chosen flock in the midst of a world which has rejected them and their Lord and which will finally fall to the Anti-Christ and crush the Church (Rev. xiii.7 f.), only to be destroyed itself in a presumptuous attack on God and his Christ (Rev. xvii.13). Yet the universal claim remains (Matt. v.13 f.; xxviii.19; John i.9 ff.; viii.12; Rev. xi.10) and the Church stands at the end as an innumerable flock from all the nations before God's throne (Rev. vii.9; xi.12; xiv.5). This claim refers to the universal eschatological people of God. When Christianity became a state religion under Constantine and later first a tribal and then a national religion under the North European Peoples, a part of this original universal claim on all nations was expressed in spite of all the distortions.

3. Thus the strongest motivation for propagating this message lay in its own content. Here was not only one man who was just as conscious of being sent to all the nations of the world as the first apostles were of being sent to the whole of Israel, but also a situation in which every believer was conscious of being appointed to be 'the salt of the earth' and 'the light of the world' (Matt. v.13 f.).[28] Apart from the general situation, this witnessing to which everyone was conscious of being called became especially effective through a series of circumstances to which we now turn.

Because the mission began in the Diaspora synagogues, the message from the very start did not come to the Gentiles in the majority of the larger cities as isolated discourses but through a living congregation. The congregation most probably took part in the missionary gatherings

[28] There was, therefore, a 'self-supporting mission' similar to that represented in modern missions by R. Allen, *The Spontaneous Expansion of the Church* (²1956); cf. *RGG³*, i, 240 f.

which Paul, for example, held daily in Ephesus for two years in the hall of the orator Tyranius (Acts xix.9 f.). At the same time the church services were effective missionary agencies just as was the case in the synagogue (I Cor. xiv. 24 f.). The Christian mission was probably seldom conducted in the streets in the fashion of the peripatetic philosophers, but converts were recruited in a fashion similar to that of the mysteries by person to person and from house to house (cf. Matt. x.12 f. par. Luke, Luke xix.5).

We hear again and again that 'whole households' were baptized. This meant families including small children and servants,[29] so that the Church contained from its very beginnings an element of the 'state church'. It did not merely consist, like the mystery groups, of converted individuals, but like the synagogue it consisted of families involving a younger generation. Baptism on this basis gave the congregation concrete form. Families who opened their houses to other believers for regular gatherings[30] became the initial centres of the congregation,[31] and in all probability the 'local congregations' in the larger cities often consisted of a number of such 'house-congregations' since a regular combined gathering was not possible (cf. §22, note 9).

A very important principle for the mission was at work in the incorporation of the household into the congregation. As was seen in the earliest Church (cf. §5, 4), the believers remained in the world, and they were conscious of their obligation to the social and created orders by which life in that world was preserved. 'Every one should remain in the state in which he was called', even the wife of an unbelieving husband and the slave of an unbelieving master (I Cor. vii.20–24). This instruction, according to Paul, was in keeping with the will of the Lord:[32] since this world was created by God through Christ and for Christ, the Christians were to adapt themselves to the social and created orders for the purpose of preserving the life of mankind for its redemption through Christ.[33] Thus they were to fulfil their worldly tasks in their worldly (social) order, but they were to do so in such a manner that it would become a witness for the Lord whom they served just as they were to bear witness in a different way within the Church (I Cor. vii.16; I Pet. iii.1 f.). Since they had to

[29] I Cor. i.16; Acts xvi.15, 31, 33; xviii.8; cf. xi.14; Luke xix.9; J. Jeremias, *Infant Baptism in the First Four Centuries* (as in §6, n. 29, Ger. 23–28), 19–24.

[30] Acts ii.46; v.42; xx.20.

[31] Rom. xvi.5; I Cor. xvi.19; Col. iv.15; Philem. 2; cf. I Tim. iii.4; v.4; II Tim. i.16; iv.19; Tit. i.11.

[32] Col. iii.18–iv.1, seven references to the Lord!

[33] L. Goppelt, 'Der Staat in der Sicht des Neuen Testaments', in *Macht und Recht* (1956), 14 ff.; 'Die Freiheit zur Kaisersteuer', in *Ecclesia und Res Publica* (*Festschrift für K. D. Schmidt*, 1961); D. Schroeder, 'Die Haustafeln des Neuen Testaments' (unpublished dissertation, Hamburg, 1959).

live together with others in the social orders with their established customs, and yet to live differently from the others who were not Christians, the believers became witnesses through their speech, through their lives and through their suffering (I Pet, ii.12; iv.3 f.). From the very beginning, the path of the Christian mission in the Hellenistic world was of necessity accompanied by conflicts, but the most intense conflict began for the first time at the end of the Pauline period (cf. §15, 1).

The mission also made use of other sociological factors. In particular, it followed the paths of the international traffic, so that it took root at first in the larger centres, and then from the several centres it spread simultaneously into the surrounding areas. For example Epaphras, subsequent to his conversion through Paul, carried the message from Ephesus to his own homeland, into the cities of Lycostales, Colosse, Hierapolis, and Laodicea (Col. i.7; iv.12). At the same time an organic link between the churches in the entire *oikumene* arose naturally without any planned organization because of the structure of the empire. The large centres were linked with one another through the international traffic and stood in close contact with the surrounding areas as well. The lists of greetings in the Pauline Epistles disclose to us the personal connections which took the place of an organizational system.

4. Apart from this all-embracing mission of the Church, the New Testament accounts stress in particular the mission of Paul. Paul himself viewed his work apocalyptically as the eschatological event immediately preceding the end. As he declared in Rom. xv.19 ff. after concluding his work in the East, he had carried the torch of the Gospel through the eastern half of the *oikumene* as one of the messengers (Rom. x.15) promised in Isa. lii.7 for the end times, and he now intended to complete this work in the western hemisphere. This was not merely a vision of grandeur but an eschatological understanding of reality. As an apostle he had laid the foundation among the nations of the world (Rom. i.5, 14 f.; xi.13; xv.15 f.) for the building of the redeemed community of the end times which would soon be completed (Rom. xv.20 f.; I Cor. iii.10; Eph. ii.19–22; iii.8 f.).

Even Luke limited himself to tracing the footsteps of this one torch-bearer and remained silent about the emergence of the churches in Syria and Italy (Acts xxviii.13 f.) which took place during the same period, but he sees things from a more historical standpoint. For him, the area into which Paul carried the Gospel was not the eastern half of the *oikumene* but the Greek world. Athens appears as a high point in his account.[34]

---

[34] The Greeks before whom he often places Paul (xi.20; xiv.1; xviii.4; xix.10, 17; xx.21) are men who speak the Greek language for him (*TWNT*, ii, 507 ff.); for Paul this means the non-Jews (*TWNT*, ii, 505).

The aim was not to traverse the *oikumene* in a short time but to reach Rome as the capital of the world from which point the Gospel was to radiate further (Acts i.8; xxviii.30 f.).[35] The end is delayed and, in a fashion similar to Matt. xxiv.14 (cf. Mark xiii.10 par. Luke), is postponed until the Gospel is proclaimed to all nations. The decisive point for Luke, however, is that he consciously traces the Church's development along the principal line of redemptive history which led from Jerusalem through Antioch to Rome, including the work of Paul. This becomes particularly clear from the way in which he permits the traditions about Apollos and the disciples of John in Ephesus to merge into this line of development.[36]

Both viewpoints, Paul's and Luke's, contained legitimate elements. The work of Paul was actually a laying of theological foundations in a unique way, and at the same time it became historically the decisive factor in the missionary movement. This was so not merely because it made inroads into the Greek world which furnished the cultural background for the empire but also because the Church separated itself clearly from Judaism and syncretism only in those areas where Paul had worked. It was not by coincidence that the links between Ephesus and Rome in the second century became the basis of the *ecclesia catholica* which rescued the Church in Syria, Palestine and Egypt from Judaism and syncretism as far as was still possible. Luke did not intend to describe this *ecclesia catholica* in advance, but he did draw the actual guide line which it followed—naturally, as a result in part of his representation.

From the work of Paul it becomes clearly evident that the 'spontaneous expansion' could not have been carried out without a deliberate mission

---

[35] Differently in Rom. i.7, 15; xv.22–24.

[36] Luke does not intend to recount the incorporation of the splinter groups into the *una sancta catholica* of the Twelve (*contra* E. Käsemann, 'Die Johannesjünger in Ephesus', *ZThK* 49, 1952, 144–154 and in *Gesammelte Aufsätze*, 1960, i, 158–168). Luke never presents the Church of the initial period as an ideal Church. Rather, in all probability, he intended to work out a continuous development along the lines of redemptive history moving from Judaism to the Gentile Church which is world-wide in character (so E. Schweizer, 'Die Bekehrung des Apollos', *Ev. Theol.*, 15 (1955), 247–254). The 'Disciples' in Ephesus (Acts 19 : 1) were not actually disciples, i.e. Christians, but were followers of John the Baptist. John's Gospel also combats (iii.25 f.; cf. i.19–27) a movement which honoured John the Baptist as the Messiah and rejected Jesus (§17, n. 13). The Mandaeans are an outgrowth of this movement (9, 13, n. 12). However, Apollos was not a Christian missionary when he came to Ephesus whom Luke had reduced to a half Christian in order to have him then brought into line (Käsemann), rather more probably a Jewish missionary (Schweizer). He had been taught 'the way of the Lord' (Acts xviii.25), i.e. terminology from the Baptist circles (Mark i.3; I QS viii.13 f.). Apollos was probably a Jewish missionary who had had contact with the Baptist movement and perhaps even with Jesus. He became a Christian missionary through Aquila and Priscilla, and Paul could give him full recognition (I Cor. iii.5–7): 'I laid a foundation, and another man is building upon it' (3 : 10). Earlier literature: W. Michaelis, *NKZ* (1927); H. Preisker, *ZNTW*, 30 (1931).

by men who were specially commissioned, just as the service of all believers for one another cannot be without the pastoral office. The special commissioning of Paul took place in different ways. He was called by the exalted Lord (Gal. i.15 ff.; Acts ix), sent for by Barnabas as a fellow worker (Acts xi.25 f.) and sent out by pneumatics in the Church (Acts xiii.1 ff.). Those sent out were commissioned by a congregational act of prayer and the laying on of hands during the church service (Acts xiii.3), and they reported to the church upon their return (Acts xiv.27 f.). Such a procedure may well have been frequently repeated in different forms. Paul himself strongly emphasized his direct calling by the Lord, and yet he valued the fact that he was 'sent forward' by the churches.[37] This was not a mere gesture of affection but rather an expression of spiritual and economic support. Although the course of the journey was planned, as is obvious from the route of the second missionary journey in Asia Minor, it was not so firmly fixed that it could not be open to the leading of the Spirit (Acts xvi.6–10; cf. Rom. i.13; xv.22).

The course of the greater part of the apostle's missionary work is usually described in keeping with the account in Acts of a second and third missionary journey. This is only an arrangement for convenience, because the journey from the mission field to Antioch, prior to the work in Ephesus (Acts xviii.21 ff.), was merely for a visit and not to begin a new journey. The story of these journeys has often been told.[38] Rather than relating it again we only want to point out what appears to us to be the characteristic traits of Paul's work.[39]

Paul presented his message in every place which he 'passed through', but he concentrated mainly on several crucial centres, above all on Corinth and Ephesus, the capital cities of the Provinces of Achaia and Asia Minor. Here, especially in Ephesus, he worked for quite a time not only to make great inroads into every sphere of pagan religiosity (Acts xix.1–20, 25 f.) but also to help clarify the internal problems of the churches, which were increasing in number. The missionary work was combined no less with pastoral care for the congregations here (Acts xx.20 f., 31) than it was in Jerusalem. Here on the unsteady basis of Hellenism the pastoral task was much more important and difficult than its counterpart in Jerusalem, and because Paul could not carry this out personally or through his fellow workers, he preserved contact with the congregations which he

[37] 'προπέμπειν' is fixed expression of the missionary language (O. Michel, Der Brief an die Römer (Meyer Kommentar, ¹⁰1955), on Rom. xv.24), cf. Rom. xv.24; I Cor. xvi.6, 11; II Cor. i.16; Acts xv.3; Tit. iii.13; III John 6; most striking: Acts xx.38; xxi.5.

. .[38] L. Schneller, Paulus (1933), popularly written; H. Metzger, Les routes de St. Paul dans l'Orient grec (1954); cf. §10, n. 5.

[39] H. Turlington, 'Paul's Missionary Practice', Rev. and Exp. 51 (1954), 168–186.

had founded by means of his Epistles from Corinth and Ephesus, thus playing also the part of overseer to the churches. In these Epistles he gave fundamental instruction about questions which were vital for the life of the Church at that time as well as in principle for all times. He explained the Gospel in its opposition to Judaism and syncretism and directed the inner organization of the Church, writing the two Thessalonian Epistles from Corinth, and from Ephesus I Corinthians and probably Galatians. The Epistles to Corinth give us a more precise insight into how Paul, while in Ephesus, had struggled with this congregation—and probably not only with this one; even before writing our I Corinthians he had addressed a letter to them (I Cor. v.9). In I Corinthians Paul replied to news which had come to him (I Cor. vii.1). When the visit to Corinth announced in this Epistle (I Cor. xvi.1–9; Acts xix.21) was delayed and the difficulties in Corinth came to a head, he intervened by means of a brief visit (II Cor. ii.1–4; xiii.1) and by means of a harsh letter, the 'sorrowful letter' (II Cor. ii.4; vii.8), but it was Titus' lot, as Paul's fellow worker, to bring the congregation back on to the right road. On the basis of Titus' report Paul wrote II Corinthians from Macedonia, where he had travelled to meet Titus (II Cor. ii. 12 f.; vii.5 ff.), in order to prepare for the third visit to Corinth (II Cor. xii.14; xiii.1). It has often been suggested that our two Corinthian Epistles contain parts of other letters which were later inserted into them,[40] but this cannot be established. During the ensuing three-month stay in Corinth (Acts xx.2), Paul prepared the transfer of his work into the western half of the world, to Rome and to Spain (Rom. xv.19–26), by means of his Epistle to the Romans. Before he set out on this mission which was so attractive to him, he personally delivered to Jerusalem the collection from the churches around the Aegean Sea (I Cor. xvi.1; II Cor. viii f.) in spite of the many possible difficulties (Rom. xv.30 f.). Paul wanted to do this in order to establish firmly the heart of the Gentile Church by means of its bond with Jerusalem (Rom. xv.27).

13. THE GROWING INNER CONFLICT WITH SYNCRETISM

1. Neither the philosophers in Athens nor the representatives of Artemis in Ephesus appear in Acts as the most dangerous opponents of the Christian missionaries, but two men, Simon and Elymas, designated as magicians (Acts viii.9–13; xiii.6–12). For the fathers of the Early Catholic Church,[1] Simon was the father of the largest and most dangerous heretical move-

---

[40] Recently, Schmithals, *Die Gnosis in Korinth* (1956), 9–22 (*contra* G. Bornkamm, *ZThK*, 53 (1956), 346 ff.); G. Bornkamm, *Die Vorgeschichte des sogenannten zweiten Korintherbriefes* (*SAH*, 1961).

[1] Irenaeus, *Haer.*, I, 23, 4: '. . . From them [Simonians] "Knowledge, falsely so called", received its beginning, as one may learn even from their own assertions.'

ment in the Christianity of the second century, namely Gnosticism. We can see today that the system of second-century Simonianism does in fact go back in its starting point to Simon himself, and that the basic characteristics do correspond to the system of the Christian Gnosticism in the second century. However, in the first century Simon was only a representative of a larger religious movement which one must designate, in a broader sense of the word, as Gnosticism. Beginning with Paul, the New Testament Epistles fought the appearance of this movement in the Christian churches, since this incipient Gnosticism was the form in which syncretism threatened to take control of the Church. To discuss this problem, we must first attempt to clarify the background and essence of this movement, and we will do this by enlarging on the three theses about Simon stated above.

a. According to the statements of Acts which are reliable in substance, Simon[2] was revered by his followers as 'that power of God which is called Great', i.e., as the embodiment of the Most High (Acts viii.10; cf. I Cor. i.24). This was the sense in which he called himself 'Great' (Acts viii.9). It is not coincidental that when Simon met the Christian mission he tried to gain the ability to mediate the experience of the Spirit rather than, for instance, to be able to work miracles. The movement which in its essence was related to him was also concerned with the *pneuma* (cf. p. 99) 'The Spirit' was for him, like 'the power of God', a supernatural tonic which was at one's service with the help of special devices. In his ideology, the Old Testament Samaritan concept of God was completely reshaped in the form of Hellenistic syncretism. According to all appearances he must have performed miracles (Acts viii.9 ff.) as an expression of a supernatural demonstration of salvation, just as did the Christian missionary who entered the scene as his competitor.

His work was later interpreted increasingly along these lines by his followers. According to Justin, who himself came from Samaria, a large segment of the Samaritans in his day, which would have been the first half of the second century, revered Simon as the highest God and ' . . . a woman, Helena, who went about with him at that time, who had formerly been a prostitute, and whom they say is the first idea (*Ennoia*) generated[3] by him'. The system of Simonianism reproduced by Irenaeus (*Haer.* I. 2.) showed the intellectual background to Justin's statement. This system was

[2] Sources for Simon and the Simonianism: G. Quispel, 'Simon en Helena', *Ned. Theol. Tijdschr.* 5 (1952), 45–70; E. Haenchen, 'Gab es eine vorchristliche Gnosis?' *ZThK* 49 (1952), 316–349; G. Kretschmar, *Ev. Theol.* 13 (1953), 357 ff.; Goppe , *Christentum und Judentum*, 132 f. (= *Jesus, Paul and Judaism*, 176 f.); J. McL. Wilsc , *The Gnostic Problem* (1958), 99 ff. For Essene influences on the Samaritan Gnos. , cf. *ThLZ*, 80 (1955), 147, n. 8 and 81 (1956), 145, n. 59.

[3] Justin, *Apol.* i, 26.

thus in existence in its basic outlines at the latest around the turn of the second century, and it goes back for its starting point to Simon's under-standing of himself.[4]

b. This system of Simonianism, however, corresponds to the basic schema of the myth of the redeemer which was the basis for the forms of Christian Gnosticism of the second century.

(1) It explained the existence of this world by means of a cosmology. The world did not come directly from the hand of the most high God, but Ennoia proceeded from him and brought forth the angels, who then created the world and subjected it to their laws. At the same time they seized Ennoia and enclosed her in a human body. She passed from one body to another and fell lower and lower in status until Simon dis-covered her in the form of a prostitute of Tyre and ransomed her.

(2) The most high God, who was unknown to the angels, descended unrecognized by them and appeared in Simon in order to reunite his Ennoia again with himself. This is a very old interpretation of the Gnostic idea of the redeemer who redeems the divine element which has fallen and become entangled in the world by uniting the divine element again with himself.

(3) The meeting of Simon and Helena represents in an elementary form the redeeming knowledge, the *gnosis*, which makes possible the return of the lost divine element to its origin and frees it from the rule of the temporal powers and their law. We can no longer determine to what extent the mythical story of Simon and Helena, as symbolic (liturgical) proclamation, mediated *gnosis* or established the use of magic in Simonian-ism. Each merges into the other.

c. From the standpoint of the history-of-religions school, even on the basis of this correspondence between the Simonian and Christian Gnosti-cism, it is clear that it is not sufficient to define Gnosticism with Harnack as 'the acute Hellenization of Christianity'.[5] There is no reason for not designating the non-Christian system of Simonianism as Gnosticism. Since the epoch-making works of Richard Reitzenstein, the history-of-religions school had discovered other non-Christian systems to which the same conclusion applies. Without doubt *Poimandres*, the first Hermetic tractate, which was probably written at the beginning of the second century in Egypt,[6] reflects a Gnostic system which arose independently

---

[4] If Simon was only a 'Samaritan *Goet*' who pretended to be an epiphany of God (Schweizer, *Erniedrigung und Erhöhung*, Ger. 161), he was already more than a *Goet*! It is still quite debatable whether Helena is an historical (Foakes-Jackson and Lake, *The Beginnings of Christianity*, v, 155 f.) or merely mythical figure (G. Quispel, *op. cit.*, 339–345; Haenchen, 'Gab es eine vorchristliche Gnosis?', *ZThK* 49, 1952, 341).

[5] *History of Dogma* (Ger. i, 250), i, 228; F. C. Burkitt, *Church and Gnosis* (1932).

[6] Dodd, *The Bible and the Greeks* ([2]1954), 209.

of Christianity.[7] The same holds true for both the *Naassenerpredigt*, also written about this time in Phrygia,[8] as well as for the *Chaldean Oracles* which were recorded around A.D. 180.[9] Whether the 'Hymn of the Pearl' in the Acts of the Apostle Thomas, which contains the classic form of the Gnostic redemption drama, originated towards the end of the first century[10] rather than during the third century[11] in Syria, as most have supposed, must remain open. The writings of the Mandaeans, who still live today in Iraq and derived from the Jewish baptistic sects of Palestine, would be of value for us if we could successfully isolate reliable elements of tradition which go back to the early Christian period.[12] At the same time, it becomes clear that the movements opposed by a number of New Testament writings, above all by the Epistles to the Corinthians and Colossians, the Pastorals, I John and the letters to the churches in Revelation, as well as by Jude and II Peter, represent essential traits of that redemption schema. Consequently, these traits are to be classed as Gnostic, or at least Gnostic in tendency so that Gnosticism appears as a religious movement which came into prominence in the course of the first century both within and without the Christian movement in diverse situations mainly independent of one another. When one attempts to analyse these phenomena from the standpoint of the history of religions, they can be understood as an accidental product of the late classical syncretism, a mixture of oriental mythology and Greek philosophy,[13] Upon closer examination, however, there are two closer attributes which have been ascertained by the studies of the last generation.

(1) It has become evident through the existential analysis developed by Hans Jonas[14] that a new understanding of the world and one's self came to expression in these concepts and ideas of late classical man. From their

---

[7] R. Reitzenstein, *Poimandres* (1904); E. Haenchen, 'Aufbau und Theologie des "Poimandres" '; *ZThK* 53 (1956), 149–191.

[8] Hippolytus, *Phil.* 5, 7, 3–9, 9. Original form in Reitzenstein, *op. cit.*, 83–98.

[9] Fragments in W. Kroll, *De oraculis Chaldaicis* (1894), cf. 'Chaldica logia', *P.W.*, iii, 2, 2045.

[10] A. Adam, *Die Psalmen des Thomas und das Perlenlied als Zeugnisse vorchristlicher Gnosis* (1959), 59: '. . . As author . . . a Syrian . . . who was familiar with both the late Jewish as well as Parthian thought-world.'

[11] *Ibid.*, 61, n. 68.

[12] See S. Schulz, *Komposition und Herkunft der johanneischen Reden* (1960), 170–182; *ThR*, 26 (1960–61), 301–329, for the direction of recent studies; C. Colpe, *RGG*[3], iv, 709 ff. K. Rudolf, *Die Mandäer*: vol. i, *Prolegomena: Das Mandäerproblem* (1960), vol. ii, *Der Kult, Theogonie, Kosmogonie und Anthropogonie in den mandäischen Schriften*, 1965, has attempted to analyze the various strata of tradition.

[13] R. Reitzenstein, *Das iranische Erlösungsmysterium* (1921) and G. Widengren, 'Der iranische Hintergrund der Gnosis', *ZRG* (1952), 97–114, stressed the first factor; H. Leisegang, *Die Gnosis* ([4]1955) stressed the second factor.

[14] H. Jonas, *Gnosis und spätantiker Geist: Teil i, Die mythologische Gnosis* ([3]1964) and Teil ii, *Von der Mythologie zur mystischen Philosophie* ([2]1958).

own existential situation, various representatives of this religion, under common religious influences yet completely independent of one another, discovered their real self which had descended from another world, from the truly divine world. These then sought to remove themselves as far as possible from the bounds of physical and historical existence in this world which had become simply a plaything for spiritual powers of questionable character. They understood this discovery to be a revelation which came to them directly from above.

Nevertheless, we are not to speak of Gnosticism every time we find elements of this understanding of one's existence and its corresponding dualistic mode of expression. Since the discovery of this principle, such a tendency has been cultivated particularly by one section of German scholarship. On the contrary, we are to use the term only where this understanding of one's existence expresses itself in the schema of redemption given above (cf. p. 94). This schema is basic to the systems unequivocally and generally recognized as Gnostic. Such a limited use of the nebulous concept 'Gnosticism' has often been demanded, and rightfully so in recent years.[15] Incipient and divergent forms of this Gnosticism proper can be seen from the middle of the first century and appear in the Hellenistic philosophy and religion (e.g., in the mystery religions), in Hellenistic Judaism (above all in Wisdom of Solomon xviii[16] and Philo)[17] and also in Palestinian Judaism (in Essene dualism[18] and in the apocalyptic writings).[19] The apocalyptic writings used dualism to devalue the present world in terms of a coming world which at the same time was already at hand as the world above. Such incipient and divergent forms are to be designated as pre-Gnosticism, pre-Gnosis,[20] or Gnostic in tendency.

(2) When one overlooks these pre-Gnostic elements and concentrates

---

[15] For Discussion on Gnosis; R. P. Casey, 'The Study of Gnosticism', *JTS*, 36 (1935), 45–60; Dodd, *The Interpretation of the Fourth Gospel* (1953), 97–114; G. Quispel, *Gnosis als Weltreligion* (1951); W. Foerster, 'Das Wesen der Gnosis', in *Die Welt als Geschichte* (1955), 100–114; H.-J. Schoeps, 'Zur Standortbestimmung der Gnosis', *ThLZ* 81 (1956), 413–422; G. Kretschmar, *RGG*³ ii, 1656–61; R. McL. Wilson, *The Gnostic Problem* (1958), 65–71; *Vig. Christ.* (1955) 193 ff., and (1957), 93 ff.

[16] Adam, *op. cit.*, 31 ff.

[17] U. Wilckens, *Weisheit und Torheit, Eine exegetisch-religionsgeschichtliche Untersuchung zu I Kor. 1 und 2* (1959), 139–150 (further literature on p. 139). *Contra* the ideas of N. Friedländers, *Der vorchristliche jüdische Gnostizismus* (1898) see A. Büchler, *Studies in Jewish History* (1956), 245–274.

[18] B. Reicke, 'Traces of Gnosticism in the Dead Sea Scrolls' *NTS*, 1 (1954–55), 137–141; H.-J. Schoeps, 'Das gnostische Judentum in den DSS', *ZRG* (1954, 276 ff.).

[19] Goppelt, *Christentum und Judentum*, 131, n. 2, cf. *Jesus, Paul and Judaism*, 175, n. 12.

[20] Quispel, 'Christliche Gnosis und jüdische Heterodoxie' *Ev. Theol.*, 14 (1954), 476; B. Reicke, *op. cit.*, *NTS*, 1 (1954–55), 137–140; R. McL. Wilson, 'Gnostic Origins', *Vig. Christ.* (1955), 211.

merely on Gnosticism proper as just defined, a second observation must be made which various scholars, independent of one another, have made in the last decade. A non-Christian Gnosticism has only been identified to date in the first and second centuries in the documents cited above. It is hardly coincidental that they all emerge at one particular intersection of various religious traditions. In all of these documents we meet Iranian-Oriental mythology, Greek philosophy of Stoic-Platonic character, and Old Testament-Jewish influences, and it has become clear that the third factor, Old Testament-Jewish influences, was obviously a necessary presupposition for the emergence of Gnosticism.[21] Consequently, Gnosticism emerged only on the periphery of Judaism and/or Christianity. Although the movement arose simultaneously in various places, all the evidence indicates that it appeared for the first time in the course of the first century, so one cannot postulate that a fully developed pre-Christian Gnosticism, already widespread in the environment of primitive Christianity, had come to light in the pre-Gnostic and Gnostic movements identifiable in the first century.[22] The further analysis of the Pauline and Johannine writings from a history-of-religions point of view shows that the 'Gnostic' terms and concepts appearing in these works were not taken over from a pre-Christian Gnosticism but were products of a many-layered process in which Christianity itself had also taken part.[23] This is revealed especially by an examination of I Corinthians which recounts the earliest struggle with a pre-Gnostic element in primitive Christianity.

2. The interpretation of the events in Corinth to which Paul addressed

---

[21] After the precedent set by F. C. Baur, *Die christliche Gnosis* (1835), and Dodd, *The Bible and the Greeks* (²1954), 99 ff., this has resulted in the following studies since 1953 independent of one another: G. Quispel, *Eranos–Jahrbuch* 22 (1953), 195–234, and *Ev. Theol.*, 14 (1954), 474–484; G. Kretschmar, *Ev. Theol.*, 13 (1953), 354–361; Goppelt, *Jesus, Paul and Judaism*, 178 f. (Ger. 134 f.); Cullmann, *JBL*, 1955, 213 ff.; McL. Wilson, *The Gnostic Problem* (1958), who has thoroughly substantiated this. This is also the most substantial element in the very one-sided thesis of E. Percy, *Der Ursprung der johanneischen Theologie* (1939), 287–299: Gnosis arises primarily as an outgrowth of Christianity. The conclusions drawn with reference to the emergence and essence of Gnosticism (pp. 329–334), in the helpful survey of the research by S. Schulz, 'Die Bedeutung neuer Gnosisfunde für die neutestamentliche Wissenschaft', *ThR*, 26 (1960), 20–166, 301–334 on the basis of the wealth of new text materials corresponds to a considerable degree with the viewpoint developed above.

[22] In particular, Bultmann, *Primitive Christianity*, 167–176 (as in §12, n. 11, Ger. 181–192); *Theology of the New Testament*, §15, 1; *contra* such a view of Gnosticism, and correctly so, are the works cited in n. 15 from Dodd, Foerster, Schoeps, Quispel, and Kretschmar.

[23] E. Schweizer, *Erniedrigung und Erhöhung*, 130 ff. and C. Colpe, *Die religionsgeschichtliche Schule, Darstellung und Kritik ihres Bildes vom gnostischen Erlösermythus* (1961) demonstrate this for the christology of Phil. ii.6–11. F. Mussner, *Christus, das All und die Kirche, Studien zur Theologie des Eph.* (1955), demonstrates this to be the case in the Body of Christ concept as does W. Nauck, *Tradition und Charakter des I Joh.* (1957), for the Johannine 'dualism'.

himself in I Corinthians is the key which discloses the inner structure of the oldest Hellenistic church.

New Testament scholarship developed successively two major solutions to the problem. The first, which was most popular from F. C. Baur to Johannes Weiss and still has considerable influence,[24] took I Cor. i.12 as its point of departure. It considered the congregation to have been threatened by means of various parties existing side by side, each appealing in an exclusive manner to Paul, Apollos, Peter or Christ. Peter had not personally been in Corinth as had the other two, but Palestinian evangelists had appealed to him there. Had Peter been there personally, Paul would have had to mention him along with Apollos in I Corinthians. This viewpoint has occasionally eliminated the 'I belong to Christ' group, taking I Cor. iii.21 f. as a gloss,[25] but this is not correct since this group occurs again in iii.23. Baur thought that the group appeared again in II Cor. x.7 as a designation for the opponents of II Cor. x–xii, who were, he suggested, behind the Christ-party. They were extremist Jews whose prime aim was to gain influence and thus to impose their own demands, e.g. circumcision. On the basis of this interpretation of the Corinthian situation Baur and those following his approach looked for just such parties and schools throughout all of primitive Christianity.

In contrast to the first solution, it was made evident, mainly through the works of Lütgert[26] and Schlatter,[27] that I Corinthians was directed throughout against one and the same attitude. The parties addressed in I Cor. i.12 were only one of its manifestations. According to Lütgert, 'libertine pneumatics and Gnostics' who had misunderstood Paul's preaching on the Spirit and freedom were involved, rather than legalistic Jews. The movement did not come into being merely through this misunderstanding of Paul, but, as Schlatter has demonstrated, it was introduced by teachers from Palestine. This is quite evidently the case since the discussion in I Corinthians is carried on entirely on the basis of Jewish presuppositions. Two recent works[28] have gone beyond this to find an unqualified Gnostic system in Corinth, but they have done so only by interpreting the key words of the movement found in I Corinthians by means of the Gnostic writings of the second century. This interpretation is related to Bultmann's history-of-religions hypothesis that a pre-Christian Gnosticism already existent in the environment of the Pauline churches comes to light in these later writings. This hypothesis has been proven more and more untenable (cf. p. 97)—not least of all by the Corinthian Epistles themselves.

[24] F. C. Baur, *Die Christuspartei in Korinth* (1831), further by G. Heinrici (*Meyer Kommentar*, 1896) and most recently in the Introductions of Feine–Behm and Michaelis.

[25] Heinrici, *op. cit.*, 20, 60; J. Weiss (*Meyer Kommentar*, [10]1925) on I Cor., vii f.; Wilckens, *Weisheit und Torheit* (1959), 17.

[26] *Freiheitspredigt und Schwarmgeister in Korinth* (1908).

[27] *Die Korinthische Theologie* (1914); *Paulus der Bote Jesu* (1934).

[28] W. Schmithals, *Die Gnosis in Korinth* (1956); U. Wilckens, *Weisheit und Torheit* (1959), cf. n. 29.

The errors to which I Corinthians refers were not individual relapses into paganism for the congregation but expressions of Christian liberty. The association with the prostitute, like participation in the cultic meal, was based on the slogan: 'All things are lawful for me!' (vi.12; x.23). This represents an odd reversal of the Jewish question: 'What is lawful for me?' Everything is lawful for him who 'possesses knowledge' (viii.1), i.e. 'the spiritual man'. He is the one who 'searches everything' and ' . . . judges all things, but is himself to be judged by no one' (ii.10, 15).

Paul himself emphasized that the Spirit makes one free, and for this reason the slogan was particularly alluring for his churches. Paul, of course, referred to the Spirit of Christ, but in Corinth it was 'a different spirit' (II Cor. xi.4), and it showed its character in its works. First, this *pneuma*, as I Cor. i.18–ii.16 makes clear, bore witness to a preaching, a discourse on wisdom, which was the antithesis of the word of the cross (i.17 f.). On the basis of this 'wisdom', groups emerged which gave allegiance to individual teachers as mystagogues, so that divisions (σχίσματα) and groups (αἱρέσεις) arose. This was perfectly understandable among the Jews and the Greeks, but it was objectionable in the Church for whom there was only one Teacher (xi.18 f.). While this wisdom-*kerygma* did thrust the cross into the background, it had not yet been developed into a docetic Christology.[29] Instead it had only been used initially from an ethical standpoint.

Secondly, in ethics, the conclusion was drawn that the body had become of no consequence for the spiritual man, so that some could surrender the body to the prostitute (vi.12 ff.), while others wanted to withdraw the body from sexual relations in marriage altogether (vii.1 ff.). For the same reason, some could not understand why the woman should remain bound to different social customs than the man during the gathering of the congregation (xi.2–16; xiv.34 ff.), and some even called into question the resurrection of the body (xv.12, 35 ff.; II Cor. v.1 ff.). This devaluation of the body contradicts the Spirit of Christ, because Christ brought redemption *of* the body rather than *from* the body in that he himself was raised bodily from the dead (vi.13 f.). The spirit at work in Corinth thought quite highly of the pneumatic manifestations and very little of fellowship (xi.17 ff.; xiv.17), and it led to an elevation of one's self, whereas the Spirit of the Crucified One is the Spirit of love who destroys all self-exaltation (i.18–25, 30 f.; ii.1–5; xiii).

The Corinthians, like Simon Magus, understood the Spirit to be a

---

[29] Schmithals, *op. cit.*, 45 ff., and Wilckens, *op. cit.*, 121, both have taken up the exegesis which has repeatedly been suggested (*Meyer Kommentar*, 1896 *in loco*) i.e. the 'Anathema Jesus' in I Cor. xii.3 is the call of a docetic orientated pneumatic (cf. further, Wilckens, 70–73). This exegesis has generally been rejected, and rightly so.

supernatural power which makes one a demi-god. At this point the background of this appearance in the history of religions becomes evident. The conception of the Spirit was hellenized[30] and placed especially, as with Simon, in Gnostic contexts. This is evident in the terminology: for example the difference between spiritual men (πνευματικόι) and un-spititual men (ψυχικόι) (ii.14), the unique absolute usage of the term knowledge (γνῶσις) (viii.1) and also the dualistic devaluation of the body —a concept which actually goes beyond the material common to Hellenism. Since, however, a distinct system is not yet evident, we can call this phenomenon a pre-Gnostic pneumaticism. It arose, as one can conclude from its structure, when a Jewish-Christian pre-Gnosticism penetrated into Corinth and provided the impetus for a Hellenization of Paul's preaching.

We hear about similar intrusions in II Corinthians. In II Cor. x–xii, personal opponents become visible. They wanted to be what Paul was: 'Apostles of Christ' and 'servants of righteousness' (II Cor. xi.13, 15; cf. x.7), but Paul had to reject them precisely because of their understanding of the apostolic office.[31] In order to justify their authority they emphasized their roots in Palestinian Judaism (xi.22 ff.), their contacts with the earliest apostles whom Paul then ironically called the 'superlative apostles' (xi.5; xii.11), and thus their contact with the historical Jesus (v.16). In addition, they stressed their pneumatic abilities such as their lofty thoughts (x. 4 f.), their resourceful discourse on wisdom (xi.6) and their miracles (xii.12). They authorized themselves both as Jewish apostles by means of letters of recommendation (iii.1) and as Gnostic emissaries[32] by means of the *pneuma*. They wanted—but failed—to be apostles of Christ in this way, but brought instead 'another Jesus', 'a different Spirit', and 'a different Gospel' (xi.4). It was necessary to say to them just as to the pneumatics in I Corinthians: 'Let him who boasts, boast of the Lord' (I Cor. i.31; II Cor. x.17).

The teachers rejected in II Cor. x–xii, therefore, exhibited the same essential character as the movement opposed in I Corinthians, but they were more Jewish and less Hellenistic. They might well have been the ones who brought the spark to Corinth from which the movements countered in I Corinthians were ignited under the influence of Hellenism. They represented a pre-Gnostic Judaism. This was the form, before the

---

[30] E. Schweizer, *TWNT*, vi, 413 f., 423 ff., 435 f.

[31] Correctly seen by E. Käsemann, 'Die Legitimität des Apostels, Eine Untersuchung zu II Cor. 10–13', *ZNTW*, 41 (1942), 33–71, cf. also Goppelt, *Christentum und Judentum*, 127, n. 1; G. Friedrich, 'Die Gegner des Paulus im 2. Kor.', in: *Abraham unser Vater* (Festschrift für O. Michel, 1963), 181–215; D. Georgi, *Die Gegner des Paulus im 2. Kor.* (1964).

[32] G. Widengren, *The Ascension of the Apostle and the Heavenly Book* (1950).

time of the *Kerygmata Petru*, in which the Jewish Christianity of Palestine attempted to bring the Gentile Church under its sway. It is to be concluded from Galatians and II Corinthians that both movements, the legalistic and Gnostic Judaism, which gained control of the Palestinian Church in the second century (cf. §16. 3), were already present in their initial stages during the Pauline period.

3. Pre-Gnostic Judaism rather than legalistic Judaism, so Baur and his followers thought, was the dangerous trend with which Paul had to contend in his churches. It is probable that the warnings of Rom. xvi.17–20 and Phil. iii.2 f. (18 f.) (cf. §11, 2) were directed against this tendency, and it is clearly the case with the polemic of Colossians and the (post-Pauline) Pastorals. The aberration in Philippi was brought into that church, as in Corinth, by Palestinian Jewish Christians who came as 'workers' (Phil. iii.2 f.; II Cor. xi. 13), i.e. as missionaries and visitors from the Palestinian Church,[33] whereas in Colosse the movement appeared to develop from within the church itself, possibly under the influence of a syncretistic Diaspora Judaism in her surroundings. The deviation which the Pastorals opposed in the churches of Asia and Crete was also introduced by teachers from their own midst. They came from the 'circumcision party' (Tit. i.10), and presented themselves as teachers of the Law (I Tim. i.7), so that we find ourselves before a movement which arose almost of necessity from religious influences and not from some sort of well planned countermission from Palestine.

The character of this movement in Colosse[34] and as depicted in the Pastorals is still the same as that in Corinth. In Colosse, the observance of ordinances concerning ' . . . food and drink, a festival, a new moon or a Sabbath . . .' was demanded of the congregation (Col. ii.16). These were Mosaic ordinances, but in Colosse they had taken on a dualistic and ascetic significance (Col. ii.21). They served the purpose of 'self-abasement and severity to the body' (Col. ii.23) and were to be kept for the sake of the elemental spirits, the *stoicheia*. They were revered (Col. ii.8, 20) quite probably in order that one might gain a share in the abundance of deity (Col. ii.9). This was, as had already been seen by F. C. Baur, a judaizing pre-Gnosticism.

The movement, against which the Pastorals warned[35]—all three

---

[33] J. Gnilka, *Die antipaulinische Mission in Philippi*, BZ 9 (1965), 258–276.

[34] Literature: M. Dibelius, *An die Kolosser, Epheser, an Philemon* (HNT, [3]1953), on ii.8 and ii.23; E. Lohmeyer, *Der Brief an die Philipper, Kolosser und an Philemon* (*Meyer Kommentar*, 1930), on Col. iii.8; E. Percy, *Die Probleme der Kolosser- und Epheserbriefe* (1946), 137–178; G. Bornkamm, 'Die Häresie des Kolosserbriefes', *Gesammelte Aufsätze* (1952), i, 139–156, cf. §14, n. 2.

[35] Literature: *TWNT*, iv, 789 ff.; J. Jeremias, *Die Briefe an Timotheus und Titus* (*NTD*, 1963), *passim*; Goppelt, *Christentum und Judentum*, 140 ff. esp. 142, n. 3; H. Conzelmann, *Die Pastoralbriefe* (HNT, [3]1955), on I Tim. iv.5.

Epistles refer to the same phenomenon—also embodied similar demands. They demanded abstinence from foods and forbade marriage (I Tim. iv.3; Tit. i.14). This was required by 'teachers of the Law' (I Tim. i.7), although these demands did not serve the Law but rather 'bodily training' (I Tim. iv.8), and the abstinence from the marriage relationship clearly betrays a distinct dualistic character. What these teachers of the Law developed from the scriptures, in the fashion of the Jewish Rabbis, was comparable to the Greek myths, the pagan stories of the gods (I Tim. i.4; Tit. i.14). When some go so far as to maintain that ' . . . the resurrection is past already' (II Tim. ii.18), they move along the same line as the Corinthian perfectionism. The movement called its own teaching 'Gnosis' (I Tim. vi.20). This betrays its real nature, although its judaizing character places the movement near the end of the Pauline period, since such traits were missing later in the Gnostic movements of the Gentile Church after A.D. 70 when Judaism had lost its appeal. Indeed Ignatius also accuses his opponents of ἰουδαίζειν (cf. §17. 3), not because they appealed to Jewish tradition but because he wanted to destroy any validity for their teaching (Ign. *Phld.* vi.1; *Magn.* viii.1). Furthermore, the absence of the Docetism, which was combined repeatedly with Gnosticism towards the end of the first century, also locates the Pastorals at the close of the Pauline period.

14. THE CLOSE OF THE PAULINE PERIOD AND THE CHURCH'S CONFLICT WITH THE PUBLIC UNTIL NERO

1. When Paul wanted to demonstrate on the occasion of his bringing the collection to Jerusalem that he was not an apostate, he was accused by his bitterest opponents, the Jews of Asia, of desecrating the Temple, a crime for which the Romans themselves had imposed the death penalty.[1] He would have been killed by the aroused mob had the Romans not arrested him. One should not put it beyond the governor Felix of delaying Paul's trial for two years on purpose, in the hope of receiving a bribe (Acts xxiv.26 f.), as Tacitus wrote that he wielded ' . . . the power of a king with all the instincts of a slave' (*Hist.* v.9). When his successor Porcius Festus wanted to settle the case in Jerusalem, Paul appealed to Caesar in order to escape being murdered (Acts xxv.11). In this way he finally reached his goal of Rome as a prisoner after a very eventful trip at sea.

How did the trial end? Acts closes with the familiar sentence of Acts

---

[1] Acts xxi.27–40 and commentaries *in loco*; H. Schürmann, 'Das Testament des Paulus für die Kirche, Apg. 20, 18–35', *Unio Christanorum* (*Festschrift* für L. Jaeger, 1962), 108–146.

THE CHURCH OF JEWS AND GENTILES

xxviii.30 f. in keeping with its intent to portray the basic missionary development of the Church (Acts i.8). Does Acts, practising the reserve also found in Hebrews and I Clement, hint by means of the announcement in xx.25, 38 that the two year imprisonment in Rome ended with Paul's martyrdom? On the other hand, Acts relates the course of Paul's trial so favourably that one would not expect his being sentenced to death, this being supported by the rest of the tradition on the subject.

During those two years in Rome, Paul most probably wrote the so-called 'Prison Epistles'. According to the testimony of Colossians, Ephesians and Philemon, all three stem from the same period. Tychicus, the bearer of both Colossians (iv.7–9) and Ephesians (vi.21), was accompanied by the runaway slave, Onesimus, on whose behalf Philemon was written (Col. iv.9; Philem. 10). Ephesians, which contained no address in the earliest manuscripts, could well have been a circular Epistle to the churches of the surrounding areas of Ephesus where it was later preserved. According to present criticism, its authenticity is quite probable, and the authenticity of Colossians has been generally acknowledged.[2] The details concerning the situation of the Church which we can draw from both Epistles point to the close of the Pauline period (cf. pp. 101 f., 104). This group of Epistles takes for granted, as did Philippians, that the churches were already aware of Paul's imprisonment, which must therefore have lasted for months, or even years (Col. iv.3, 10, 18; Philem 1; Phil. i.7, 14, 17). Paul was only in such a situation in Caesarea or Rome, certainly not in Ephesus.[3] The way in which Paul refers to events in his surroundings, and especially the fact that he expected an early decision on his trial, speak for Rome. He hoped to be released and to be able to visit his churches in the East (Phil. i.25 f.; ii.24; Philem. 22).

The Pastorals presuppose, as Eusebius (2, 22, 2 ff.) noted, that Paul was actually released from the first Roman imprisonment and that he once

---

[2] E. Percy, *Die Probleme der Kolosser- und Epheserbriefe* (1946), 1–9, gives a report of the discussion. Both Epistles were rejected as being Pauline by the Tübingen School as well as by Bultmann and his students, Käsemann and Schlier, because the Epistles supposedly presuppose an ecclesiastical situation which first enters the scene in the post-Pauline period, e.g. a stronger influence from Gnosticism and a stronger emphasis on the unity of the Church. By contrast, H. J. Holtzmann, *Kritik der Epheser- und Kolosser-Briefe* (1872) and the careful evaluation by M. Dibelius and H. Greeven (*HNT*, [2]1953) considered Colossians to be authentic, but not Ephesians. E. Percy, in the study cited above, which he justified in *ZNTW* 43 (1950–51), 178–194, in reply to Käsemann's review (*Gnomon* (1949), 342–347), maintains the authenticity of both Epistles. According to G. Schille's, 'Der Autor des Epheserbriefs', *ThLZ*, 82 (1957), 325–334, at any rate, the former arguments against the authenticity of these Epistles are not valid, and even H. Schlier, *Der Brief an die Epheser* (1957), 15–28, has ruled accordingly. We can only say in reference to this discussion that all that can be deduced about the ecclesiastical situation from these Epistles speaks in favour of the authorship claimed for them at the close of the Pauline period.

[3] *Contra* W. Michaelis, *Einleitung in das Neue Testament* ([2]1954), 204 ff.

again worked in Asia and Macedonia as well as on Crete. In II Timothy, Paul, a prisoner in Rome, was expecting his death (i.8, 15 ff.; ii.9; iv.8), but he had recently been in Asia Minor (iv.13), and this does not fit into the first Roman imprisonment. Furthermore, I Timothy and Titus were written during journeys which are impossible to incorporate into the period prior to the first Roman imprisonment, even if it is clear from the forms of expression that these Epistles did not stem directly from Paul. They may have been reworked later, but they are without doubt to be dated at the close of the Pauline period in keeping with their details about the situation of the Church (cf. pp. 102, 191). The author having been intimately connected with Paul had no reason to offend his readers, who at that time were well aware of Paul's death, by an unhistorical portrayal of the situation.

Thus it is probable that Paul was released from the first imprisonment in Rome and that he visited once again his areas of missionary activity in the East. According to his Prison Epistles he had already postponed his earlier plan to travel to Spain (Rom. xv.24, 28), and the execution of this plan was permanently hindered by the new imprisonment. When I Clem. v.7 says that ' . . . he had reached the limits of the West', this could also apply to Rome in view of the passage's dramatic style. The *Canon Muratori*, which was the first to maintain a visit to Spain, probably came to this conclusion on the basis of Rom. xv and I Clem. v, since we have no other direct tradition for such a visit.

I Clem. v.4–7 names Peter and Paul as victims of the Neronic persecution, but according to II Tim. iv.16 Paul was involved in a genuine trial, and according to an old tradition (Tertullian, *De Praescr. Haer.* 36) he was put to death by the sword. He probably pursued his individual path to the very end and suffered martyrdom shortly before the Neronic persecution, perhaps in the year A.D. 63.

In the Epistle to the Romans, Paul had summarized his *kerygma* and the course of his missionary work independently of any local questions. In Ephesians he summarized the result, the development of the Church as a new unity from Jews and Gentiles (Eph. ii.11–19), built 'on the foundation of the apostles and prophets' (ii.20–22). Here the historical conflicts, which could still be heard as live issues in Philippians, had moved into the background; a concern for that which was primary, that which was ordained by God, had moved into the foreground, although the unity of the Church comprised of Jews and Gentiles and built on the foundation of the apostles was not yet taken for granted in a manner characteristic of the writings from the period after A.D. 70.[4] It was considered instead

[4] John x.16; Matt. xxviii.19; cf. the discussion in Percy, *ZNTW*, 43 (1950–51), 187 f.

to be an unprecedented miracle of God's redemptive plan which had been brought to realization through Paul (Eph. iii.4 ff.).

2. Paul's death sheds light on the position of the Christians in society.[5] Luke relates his trial in detail since it reflects the situation of the Church at the close of the Pauline period. The Church, having been brought under suspicion by the Jews and suspected by the government officials, now stood before the forum of the empire. Initially the developing Christian churches were considered by the public to be an appendage to the Diaspora synagogues, but the Jews tried to remove themselves as far as possible from the Christians and to cast suspicion on Christianity[6] as a ' . . . new superstition dangerous to the public good'.[7] This charge was not always disproved by the general public nor by the government officials, as it had been in Corinth (Acts viii.12 ff.), so that serious difficulties often arose in the churches (cf. I Thess. ii.14 ff.). Apart from this agitation by the Jews, Christianity itself provoked criticism and persecution by spreading out so intensively among the Gentiles,[8] yet all these elements of opposition were local in character.

Even the Neronic persecution,[9] which brought the period to its close, was not a move against the Christians throughout the empire but was locally orientated and limited to Rome. Only Tacitus (*Annals* xv.44, A.D. 116–117) has precisely described and given the motivation behind Nero's actions which Suetonius (*Nero* 16, c. A.D. 120) and others reported. In all probability, Tacitus places it correctly in the context of the burning of Rome in July 64. The Emperor, he supposes, tried to clear himself of any suspicion of having started the fire himself by blaming ' . . . a class of men, loathed for their vices, whom the crowd styled Christians', and by distracting the people through having the Christians put to death in public games. We have no evidence for the opinion[10] that the Jews had brought the Christians to the attention of the state, which is unwarranted but often expressed.

[5] Literature: M. Dibelius, 'Rom und die Christen im ersten Jahrhundert', in *Botschaft und Geschichte* (1956), ii, 177–228; E. Stauffer, *Christ and the Caesars*, 1955 (Eng. trans. of *Christus und die Cäsaren*, ⁴1954); J. Vogt, 'Christenverfolgung I' (historical, assessment by pagans and Christians), *RAC* (1954), ii, 1159–1173 and H. Last, 'Christenverfolgung' (juridically), *RAC*, ii, 1208–1213 (further literature there); J. Moreau, *Die Christenverfolgungen im römischen Reich* (1961).

[6] Acts xiii.50; xiv.19; xvii.5–9, 13; xviii.12 f.

[7] Suetonius, *Nero*, 16.

[8] Acts. xvi.19 f.; xix.23 ff.

[9] A. Durfess, 'Der Brand Roms und die Christenverfolgung im Jahre 64', *Mnemosyne* iii, 6 (1938), 261–272; on the arguments against Tacitus s. *RAC*, ii, 1166 f. 1210 f., and Dibelius, 'Rom und die Christen im ersten Jahrhundert' (as in n. 5), 205 ff.

[10] Harnack, *The Mission and Expansion of Christianity* (Ger. 569); P. Styger, *Juden und Christen im alten Rom* (1934), 41 ff.; cf. *ThR*, 17 (1948), 39.

The early Christian writings only make mention of this shattering experience with very reserved hints—especially in I Clem. vi.1 f., and probably in both Heb. x.32 f.; cf. xi.32 ff. and Rev. xvii.6. According to the early Church tradition, Peter[11] suffered martyrdom under the Neronic persecution (Eus. 2, 25; cf. I Clem. v.4 f.; John xxi.18 f.). After leaving Jerusalem, Peter had worked for a lengthy period in Syria (cf. Gal. ii.11 ff.) with Antioch as his base, going to Rome shortly before his death (I Pet. v.13; cf. I Clem. v.4; Ignatius, Rom. iv.3). This large metropolis had attracted him just as Antioch once had, and his arrival there was occasioned neither by special circumstances in Rome nor by any political considerations within the Church.[12]

Since the second century Nero has been considered as the first persecutor of the Christians (Melito in Eus. 4, 26, 9). He did not intend to suppress the Christian religion so much as to further his own interests, like the silversmith in Ephesus, by means of a local measure, and yet a new situation was presupposed as well as introduced by his actions. It presupposed that the Christians had a bad reputation among the people in the capital of the world and thus in the provinces as well. It allowed—indeed it stimulated—the government officials to initiate proceedings against the Christians. Neither the act of setting fire to Rome nor any of the scandalous acts (flagitia) with which they were charged could ever be proven before a court. The only possible exception could have been the charge of 'hatred against mankind' (Tacitus). The Jews had previously been accused of 'odium generis humani' since they had withdrawn themselves from the daily and cultic fellowship accompanying the ideological foundation of the Hellenistic empires. The charge was valid in the case of the Christians, in that they ' . . . are separated from ourselves[Romans] by a greater gulf than divides us from Susa or Bactra or the more distant Indies' because they ' . . . made [their] own a life apart and irreconcilable, [they] cannot share with the rest of mankind in the pleasures of the table nor join in their libations or prayers or sacrifices . . .'.[13] The Jewish nation had ensured state protection for their exclusive religious position by means of agreements with Caesar and his successors. Even after the Jewish war every Jew who paid the fiscus Judaicus enjoyed this protection. Could the

---

[11] Extensive discussion of all reports in Cullmann, Peter: Disciple—Apostle—Martyr (as in §1, n. 25). K. Heussi, Die römische Petrustradition in kritischer Sicht (1955) has most recently disputed Peter's death in Rome. By contrast, the classical work of H. Lietzmann, Petrus und Paulus in Rom (1915, ²1927); T. Klauser, Die römische Petrustradition im Lichte der neuen Ausgrabungen unter der Peterskirche (1956); E. Dinkler, 'Die Petrus-Romfrage', ThR, 25 (1959), 189–230. 289–335; 27 (1961), 33–64. An earlier comprehensive portrayal: E. Fascher, 'Petrus', P.W. (1938), xix-2, 1335–1361.

[12] See §5, 3; 17, 1a on his position in the primitive Church.

[13] Philostratus, Vit. Apol. v, 33, further in Dibelius, 'Rom und die Christen im ersten Jahrhundert' (as in n. 5), 209.

Christians not also have become in like fashion a *religio licita*? Celsus,[14] c. 160, expressed the attitude of the Hellenistic world when he declared Judaism to be tolerable since it was a national religion inherited from the forefathers in spite of its despicable peculiarities, but condemned Christianity as an absurd violation of the order of the world because it drew to itself people from every nation and social order in view of its claim to absolute truth. It was not merely accidental, therefore, that the empire under Trajan refused in principle to grant the Church the status given the Jews, this decision bringing the development started by Nero to a temporary conclusion (cf. §15, 1).

[14] Origen, *Contra Celsum*, 5, 25, 33 ff., 41; Cf. Goppelt, *Christentum und Judentum*, 280 f.

CHAPTER IV

THE CLOSE OF THE APOSTOLIC PERIOD: THE CONSOLIDATION OF THE CHURCH AND HER GOSPEL IN OPPOSITION TO SECULARIZATION

BETWEEN the years A.D. 65 and 70 the drastic historical events of the Neronic persecution, the violent deaths of the two most important apostles, the catastrophe of Palestinian Judaism, the splitting asunder of the Palestinian mother Church and the significant transition to the second generation which accompanies every religious movement all contributed to the beginning of a new chapter in the Church's early history. This period, which moves less abruptly into the succeeding one between A.D. 115 and 135, has often been designated in Protestant scholarship as the post-Apostolic Age, whereas Catholic presentations view it as the Johannine Age, the successor to the Petrine and Pauline Age, in which the Apostolic Age reached its peak. In fact, as will become evident in what follows, it was a period of transition from apostolic Christianity to Early Catholicism. Nevertheless, it was a period not of mere imitation, nor of attempts to cling to what had preceded, but of new and fundamental revisions of thought. Questions vital to the Church's life were considered for the first time and were solved in the Church's own way once and for all. A solution, which one might schematically call Early Catholic, was thus set up alongside the essentially apostolic solution. The boundary between the two forms of Christianity is not chronologically determinable, though the transition from the second to the third generation occurring at the middle of this period meant a considerable break. Actually the distinction runs throughout the period under consideration, so the time is best specified as the close of the apostolic period.

We do not have any historical portrayals corresponding to Acts for this period and we have only a few documents which shed such direct light on it as did the Pauline Epistles for their period. Both the primitive Christian writings preserved for us and the sparse tradition which was recorded later present us more with the problems and their fundamental solutions than with people and events. This is seen even in the central question to which we now turn, the relationship of the Church to the public. Until now, the Church had lived within the framework or shadow of Judaism, but since the Neronic persecution she had become a separate and at the same time a most questionable religious fellowship.

15. THE CHURCH AND THE WORLD: THE MISSION OF THE CHURCH AND
HER RELATIONSHIP TO THE EMPIRE[1]

1. Let us consider first the attitudes of the Church and the world towards each other.

a. The church fathers in the second century had the Neronic persecution followed by a second persecution under Domitian (Melito in Eus. 4, 26, 9; Tertullian, *Apol.* 5, 3 f.). This portrayal distorts both the action by the Emperor as well as the total situation.

Domitian had just as little intention systematically to suppress the Christian religion as had Nero. The Christians were affected by the measures which he directed, especially in the final years of his rule, against all who did not take his increasing claim for divine honour seriously; he was the first Emperor to take the title 'Our Master and our God' while he was still alive (Suet. *Dom.* 13). According to the sparse reports, measures had apparently been taken against the Christians particularly in the two areas where Christianity had become widespread and where the Emperor's claim was strongly enforced. Dio Cassius (67, 14, 1 f.) reports that the Emperor had his cousin, the consul Flavius Clement, put to death in Rome on account of 'atheism'[2] and his wife Flavia Domitilla banished. Many others were either sentenced to death or had their goods confiscated because they had ' . . . erred into Jewish ways'. Just as Eusebius (3, 17–20) supposed and as the name 'Coemeterium Domitillae' for one of the oldest Christian catacombs of Rome suggests,[3] those concerned had in fact been Christians, so that it could well be that the affliction of the Roman Church mentioned in I Clem. i.1; vii.1, was a hint at this action by Domitian in the later years of his rule.

The other area affected was western Asia Minor. During excavations in Ephesus, a temple for Domitian was discovered, as well as the remains of a gigantic statue of the Emperor which had been violently destroyed after his death.[4] This manifestation of the emperor cult was probably the cause of the Book of Revelation, although very little can be inferred from this Book about the implications of the cult (cf. pp. 111 f.). Pliny (A.D. 112–113) refers to several former Christians who had given up their

---

[1] Literature; see §14, n. 5.
[2] *Martyrdom of Polycarp*, ix, 'Away with the Atheists!'
[3] P. Styger, *Die römischen Katakomben* (1933), 63–80; L. Hertling–E. Kirschbaum, *Die römischen Katakomben und ihre Märtyrer* (1950); A. M. Schneider, 'Die ältesten Denkmäler der römischen Kirche' (*Festschrift* for Akademie Göttingen, 1951), ii, 183–186. Cf. §14, n. 11.
[4] J. Keil. *Österr. Jahresheft* (1932), xxvii, *Beiblatt*, col. 53 ff.; R. Schütz, *Die Offenbarung des Johannes und Kaiser Domitian* (1933).

faith—some three years earlier, others several years earlier and some even twenty years earlier. This reference was to those who in the days of Domitian, possibly under official pressure, had left the faith. Soon after A.D. 110, the Bishop of Antioch, Ignatius, became a victim of a wave of persecution, although the churches in Asia which he contacted while on the way to his martyrdom in Rome were apparently not harassed at this time (*Phild.* xi; *Smyr.* x f.).

The 'persecution' by Domitian was thus only a particular intensification of a continual menace. The persecution *logia* of the Gospels,[5] as is the tendency of Acts (cf. p. 105), written between A.D. 65 and 90, take for granted a continuous opposition and persecution which was often started by one's closest relatives and which could result in an appearance before the government officials and their courts.

When the last part of I Peter (iv.12–v.11), written from Rome to Asia Minor, speaks of a 'fiery ordeal' which had come upon the readers (iv.12),[6] this must by no means be understood to refer to the acute 'persecution' under Domitian, particularly since ' . . . the same experience of suffering is required of your brotherhood throughout the world' (v.9). At no point does the Epistle refer to the divine veneration of the Emperor which is evident in the Book of Revelation (xiii. 4,15) and in Pliny. The oppression in I Peter did not stem from government officials but from the pagan society. It consisted at first of malicious insinuations: ' . . . They speak against you as wrong doers . . .' (ii.12; iii.16), but later the Christians were led before courts where they could be condemned 'as Christians', i.e. solely on account of their belonging to the Christian religion, even when they could prove the other accusations to be unjust (iv. 15 f.). It was just such a feeling against the Christians which Nero used to his advantage (cf. pp. 105 f.). At the same time his action reinforced this attitude of the public as did corresponding measures taken by the government officials based on the right of *coercitio*.[7] It could well be that I Peter was written soon after this turn of events by Sylvanus in Peter's name (i.1 f.; v.12).

b. I Peter does not deal with details but describes the situation of the Church in the world by taking up traditional teaching and reworking it.

---

[5] Mark xiii.9–13 par.; cf. iv.17 par.; viii.34–38 par.; Matt. v.10–12, 44 par. Luke. Cf. D. W. Riddle, 'Die Verfolgungslogien in formgeschichtlicher und soziologischer Beleuchtung', *ZNTW*, 33 (1934), 271–289.

[6] For all the details cf. the excellent commentary by E. G. Selwyn, *The First Epistle of St. Peter* (1952); more recent discussion by W. Nauck, 'Freude im Leiden', *ZNTW*, 46 (1955), 68–80, and K. H. Schelkle, *Die Petrusbriefe, Der Judasbrief* (*Herder-Kommentar XIII*, 2, 1961).

[7] That is the authority given to the ruler to punish crime and disobedience and to demand obedience in those cases where the laws do not specify otherwise.

As the Epistle correctly saw, the Christians provoked the opposition of their environment simply by the fact that they had removed themselves from the usual pagan way of life (iv.3 f.). Even in this critical situation, however, they were urged to remain bound by the institutions of this world, even if the master of the Christian slave should be 'overbearing' and the husband of a believer be a non-believer. They were 'to do good',[8] i.e. within their faith to do what was proper and reasonable in worldly matters, and in this way to disprove the insinuations levelled against them and to become witnesses of Christ by means of their conduct, especially when they had to suffer unjustly as his disciples (ii.12, 18 ff.; iii.1–5). I Peter thus held firmly to the tables of household duties, but it also inserted the reference to conflict (Acts v.29) and suffering. Suffering in this Epistle was one of the essentials of Christian existence in the world (iv.12–19). The Christians were 'aliens' in the world, but they, like Israel in Egypt, were to live in the world as 'exiles' and not to emigrate (ii.1; ii.11 f.)— they could only let themselves be driven out.

The Apocalypse,[9] like John's Gospel (ix.22 f.; xii.42; xvi.1 f.; xvii.14 f.) focused on this last point. The Seer John was on the Isle of Patmos (i.9) 'on account of the word of God', probably having been banished there (Eus. 3, 20, 9). A vision of the final events was disclosed to him, starting with the exaltation of the Crucified One (Rev. v,) and concluding with the consummation through his second coming (Rev. xix), with their climax in the conflict between the Church and the empire (Rev. xii. 14). The empire becomes the concrete form of the will of mankind which had defied God, rejected his salvation and attempted to create salvation on its own terms (Rev. xiii). The Book of Revelation did not, like the Jewish apocalypses, describe the course of world history with particular reference to contemporary historical events in order to be able to describe the emperor and his officials as merely ephemeral phenomena.[10] Instead, like early Christian prophecy, it traced the essential character of the final events, in particular the picture of the world ruler of the end times in order that the Church, in spite of all the deceiving appearances and threats to its comfort, might not worship the Emperor rather than God, asking him for both daily bread and salvation. With reference to the history of the Church, one can only deduce from Revelation that the conflict between

[8] W. C. van Unnik, 'The Teaching of Good Works in I Peter', NTS, 1 (1954–55), 92–110.
[9] On the interpretation of the Apocalypse, L. Goppelt, 'Heilsoffenbarung und Geschichte nach der Offenbarung des Johannes', ThLZ, 77 (1952), 513–522; M. Rissi, Time and History: A Study on the Revelation (Eng. trans. of Zeit und Geschichte in der Offenbarung Johannes, 1952, ²1965).
[10] Contra Dibelius, 'Rom und die Christen im ersten Jahrhundert' (as in §14, n. 5), 227.

the Church and the world came to a climax for the first time during the days of the Seer in the struggle with a rudimentay realization of the world ruler, the Antichrist of the end times, in Domitian and the Emperor cult. We can, however, no longer see how the conflict affected the churches. Although according to the letters to the churches, whose historical relationship to the prophecy still remains an unsolved problem, the churches were oppressed in many ways, they were not the object of a persecution by the state, and only a single martyrdom is mentioned (ii.13).[11]

The decisive factor is that Revelation does not demand a basically different stance towards the Emperor who was taking on the traits of the Antichrist than did I Peter toward the 'overbearing master' and I Cor. vii.15 toward a non-believing husband. Christians were to endure unjust suffering (xiii.10) until they were excluded from trade and traffic and the mouth of the witnesses be silenced by force (xi.7; xiii.15 ff.). This is the way of the 'overcomer' (xiv.1–3). There is nothing about a zealot-like insurrection nor any hint of a refusal to pay taxes nor of engaging in a messianic war; there is no summons, in spite of the picture of the removal of the woman into the wilderness (xii.14), to withdraw from this world as the Qumran community had done. In Revelation, as in all the Johannine writings, there is no word about the Christians' conduct in the concrete social orders, in marriage or as a member of the state, nor about the mission to the world (cf. p. 116). Contrary to what has often been thought, therefore, Revelation does not propose an apocalyptic rejection of the attitude of apparent recognition of the state which runs from Jesus' saying about paying tax through Rom. xiii to I Pet. ii.13 ff.[12] Instead it substantially supports the attitude of recognition, since the latter really proclaims that the Christians, as aliens, are both free from the world yet under obligation to it (Rom. xii.1; I Pet. ii.16). They must not only bear witness to the Gospel in the world but also preserve the world as God's creation by serving in its institutions until the day of visitation (I Pet. ii.11 ff.; Col. i.16–20). The Apocalypse forbids neither the serving of the world, nor intercession for it, but warns against worshipping it. The

[11] Rev. xvii.6: 'The Harlot Babylon', i.e. the capital of the world, is '. . . drunk with the blood of the saints and the blood of the martyrs of Jesus.' This is a picture of the nature of things reminiscent of the Neronic persecution.

[12] More recent discussion and conceptions of the early Church up to Constantine in F. A. Strobel, 'Schriftverständnis und Obrigkeitsdenken in der ältesten Kirche' (unpublished dissertation, Erlangen, 1956, cf. ThLZ, 82, 1957, 69 ff.). Literature on the attitude of primitive Christianity towards the State: L. Goppelt, 'Freiheit zur Kaisersteuer' in Ecclesia und Res Publica (Festschrift für K. D. Schmidt, 1961), 40–50; R. Schnackenburg, Die Sittliche Botschaft des neuen Testaments (1954), §12 and 25; O. Cullmann, The State in the New Testament (Eng. trans. 1962, of Der Staat im Neuen Testament, ²1962).

very nature of the intercession to which I Tim. ii.1 f., in accordance with Old Testament Jewish tradition, summons his readers excludes any worship of the state. Conversely, I Peter calls Rome apocalyptic Babylon (v.13) in spite of the fact that it reflects the exhortation of Rom. xiii in ii.13–17.

I Clement strikes a strange note in this regard. This Epistle was written in the name of the Roman Church to the Church in Corinth immediately after the oppression under Domitian. It no longer saw man's relationship to this world as that of a free alien but as an obligation to the order of creation which was endorsed and explained through Christ (I Clem. xx) and to which the political cosmos corresponds (lx.4; lxi.1). In this way the rule 'all things in their order' became the final principle (xl.1), although I Clement certainly did not outdo the philosophy of the empire during that time by a demand for unconditional acceptance of and submission to the Emperor in order to compensate for the refusal to make offerings to him.[13] He described quite clearly the evil-doers who disrupt God's order by the persecution of the righteous (xlv); and, following the reference to the rulers (lx.2) and prior to the prayer of intercession for his sovereigns (lxi.1 f.), I Clement placed the request in his common prayer: 'Deliver us from them that hate us wrongfully' (I Clem. lx.3). Clement's reservations were, however, merely the product of a Christian explanation of the world's order. The dominant motif was the harmonious unity of Church and cosmos which had been suggested by both Old Testament-Jewish as well as Hellenistic-Stoic thought. The eschatological aspect of being an alien in this world is missing. Consequently, I Clement spoke of Paul's martyrdom ' . . . in terms which one is accustomed to use of Heracles', and the same holds true for the discussion of the martyrs under the Neronic persecution (v.1–vi.2).[14] By so doing, I Clement wanted to characterize them as sufferers and warriors for the restoration of this world, and so chose a path which the apologists of the second century followed[15] and which the empire under Constantine made all its own.

c. At first the men of the empire and Hellenistic culture saw the insoluble opposition between Christianity and the Hellenistic empire more clearly than did the Christian apologists. After Domitian's death a *dam-*

---

[13] *Contra* C. Eggenberger, *Die Quellen der politischen Ethik des I Clemensbriefes* (1951), 176 f.; cf. A. W. Ziegler, *Neue Studien zum ersten Klemensbrief* (1958), 38 ff.; H.-U. Minke, 'Die Schöpfung nach dem I. Clem. und der Areopagrede' (Diss. Hamburg, 1966).

[14] Dibelius, 'Rom und die Christen im ersten Jahrhundert' (as in §14, n. 5), 217, 193–199.

[15] Cf. Melito, in Eusebius, *H.E.*, 4, 26, 5–11; E. Peterson, *Der Monotheismus als politisches Problem* (1935).

natio memoriae no doubt followed. His temple in Ephesus was dedicated to Vespasian, and his statue together with its dedicatory inscriptions were destroyed. Nevertheless, we learn fifteen years later from an exchange of letters between Pliny, the governor of Bithynia, and Trajan (112–113) that the Christians continued to be suspected by the populace and were prosecuted by the government officials. The Edict of Trajan became generally known when Pliny published these letters and it remained the legal norm until Decius (249–250). Judicially, it was highly contradictory in its demands: first, simply belonging to Christianity as such was punishable; proof of a criminal offence was not necessary. Secondly, the Christians were not to be deliberately hunted; they could only be prosecuted through an officially lodged protest. Thirdly, all those who declared their veneration for the patron gods of the empire and for the Emperor by means of offerings were to go free. Accordingly, the Christians were denied the usual legal privileges. The Edict served a purpose of political expediency by avoiding unrest among the people as well as a mass persecution and by preserving some semblance of legal character. It outlawed the Christian religion and deprived the Christians of legal rights. There was no other choice for the empire as long as it did not want to exchange its ideological foundation for that developed by the Christian apologists.

2. As we see in Pliny's letters, the attitude of the empire towards Christianity from then on depended to a great extent on the latter's further expansion.[16] The exchange of letters had become necessary because the Christian religion had expanded so rapidly in Bithynia that practice of the official cult had been noticeably disturbed and the populace had become alarmed. It was felt that the expansion should be curbed and yet permitted as well, since the possible consequences of any radical action were to be feared. On the other hand, as we see from the Book of Revelation to I Clement, Christianity's desire to persevere in its mission to the world was not lessened by public pressure. The tradition of this period does not report any missionary work, but it does permit us to see quite clearly the desire for missions and to conclude something about its intensity from the expansion of Christianity.

In the course of the second and third generations the expansion became more intensive in the areas previously covered and more extensive in the areas beyond. For example, in Asia the network of churches according to the letters of Revelation i–ii and Ignatius is much more extensive and thicker than at the time of Colossians (iv.13). In neighbouring Bithynia,

---

[16] Harnack, *The Mission and Expansion of Christianity* (Ger. 529–533, 621–628), and B. Kötting, 'Christentum I' (Expansion), *RAC*, 1954, ii, 1138–1159, for further literature.

Christianity, which was first mentioned there in I Pet. i.1, had already gained a strong foothold in the countryside, according to Pliny. Such an intensive expansion was probably possible elsewhere only in Rome at that time, while the expansion was being consolidated in the other mission areas, in Palestine, Syria, Asia Minor, Macedonia, Greece, Cyprus and Crete, Dalmatia and Middle Italy. It had spread beyond these regions into eastern Syria, northern Egypt, and the then Greek colony in southern Gaul (Marseilles),[17] although in Spain and northern Africa very little work had apparently been done in establishing churches.

This expansion was carried out even more than in the first generation through the continual witness of every church member (cf. I Pet. ii.11 f.; iii.1). The missionary discourses and commissions in the Gospels, the emphasis on the office of evangelist (cf. p. 191) as well as the mention of 'apostles' in Did. 11, 3 (cf. p. 179), suggest that missionary work was also under way in this period, and a mission of this type was also carried on in the second century.[18]

The dominant motif behind the course of the mission was further modified. The mission had been an urgent event of the end times just prior to the final consummation for the earliest Church and for Paul (cf. pp. 33 f., 89), but now Matthew's Gospel explained the delay of the second coming by saying that the Gospel had to be proclaimed to all nations before the final end (Matt. xxiv.14). The Eleven, who had been sent out as missionaries to the nations of the world (Matt. xxviii.19), were understood now, without detracting from their original significance (Matt. xvi.18), to be the representatives of all witnesses and to be the recipients of a long unfulfilled commission (v.13 ff.). According to Acts, the universal missionary command (Luke xxiv.27; Acts i.8) was only carried out in its first phase by the Twelve with the further phases accomplished by many others, so that everyone could expect a call to help in the realization of this redemptive plan. The mission had become progressively a historical process which, although the link had been established between Jerusalem and Rome, was to continue for a long time (Acts i.8; xxviii.31). In the Apostolic Fathers the statement of faith that the apostles had founded the universal Church became historicized by means of legends (I Clem. xlii.4; Hermas 9, 17; Mark xvi.20),[19] but it also remained an expression of a still unfulfilled claim of the Gospel on all mankind.

[17] E. Mâle, La fin du paganisme en Gaule et les anciennes basiliques chrétiennes (1950), 10 f.; on Tit. ii.10, cf. Harnack op. cit. (Ger. 625, n. 9).

[18] All reports concerning places where churches were mentioned until the time of Trajan can be found in Harnack, op. cit. (Ger. 622 ff.) and in the first index.

[19] Origen, Contra Celsum, 3, 9; cf. Harnack, op. cit. (n. 16, Ger. 360 f.), 349 f.

The Johannine conception[20] contrasts considerably with the views just mentioned. In John's Gospel the Shepherd does not go to search for the lost one (Luke xv.4 ff.) but sends forth his own witness to himself which 'his own', the chosen ones, receive while the others naturally reject it (John x.3, 16, 27 f.; xi. 52), although the Evangelist wrote this mainly with reference to the Church and not to those who are to be called. He intended to make the Church certain of its salvation in view of the world's rejection (John x.27 f.). The Church is in no way, like the Essenes, simply to wait for the sons of light (cf. § 6, 1) whom she would attract solely by means of her existence; instead a call is to go out for all (iii.16; iv.35–38; xx.21) and a witness is to be given to everyone (i.40–50). Indeed, the Evangelist himself was concerned with casting the Gospel in a form suitable to the Hellenistic world. He does not intend to say, though, that the call kindles the sparks in the lights of the souls as in Gnosticism, but only that it would inspire faith in keeping with God's election (John vi.36–45). Consequently, this call causes simultaneously a post-Christian Judaism to emerge as representatives of post-Christian mankind. In a similar way, the testimony of the two witnesses in Revelation who represent the witness of the Church (xi.3–10) was given to a world which rejected its Lord. This witness never leaves the world in peace even to the very end, yet it does not win her. Instead, the witness itself is finally silenced by the representatives of this post-Christian world (xi.8; xiii.7). Thus the Johannine writings emphasize that the call which has meaning for all people (Rev. xiv.6) depends upon election by God, but while gathering the elect it allows the reality of an anti-Christian world to emerge simultaneously. Matthew also combines persecution *logia* together with the missionary discourse (x.16–25; cf. II Cor. iv.7 ff., whereas Luke in x.3 (Q) does not emphasize this and contradicts Mark xiii.10 in xxi.13.).

Not only is the prophetically-explained experience of the second generation evident in this Johannine view of the course of the mission, but a Christo-centric ideology is also present which viewed the way of the Church exclusively in terms of the way of Christ. It excludes the conception that the Church and the world would merge into one another through an evolutionary process, a conception which set in with the apologists, but it did not exclude the Lucan viewpoint. The Church at the end of the Apostolic Age could see the results of their mission only in the polar tension between the Lucan and Johannine views. Above these two viewpoints, Rom. xi.25 f. remains valid as an ultimate promise

[20] Cf. K. G. Kuhn, 'Das Problem der Mission in der Urchristenheit', *EMZ* (1954), 161–168; 167 f.

to be clung to in a continually changing form, since it was thought out from the starting-point of the cross.

As well as the Church's developing relationship to the Hellenistic world emphasized in this period, the relationship with Judaism was also important in several respects.

16. JUDAISM AND CHRISTIANITY BETWEEN A.D. 70 AND 135

1. The history of Judaism in this period[1] is marked by three large insurrections. At the beginning (66–70) and at the end of this period (132–135) the Jewish nation rose up in arms in Palestine; between these two points (116–117) the Diaspora rose up in arms in Mesopotamia, Egypt, Cyrenaica and on Cyprus. The insurrections of such a small nation against a world empire were politically senseless; behind them stood a more or less conscious expectation of a Messiah which had not been satisfied by Jesus' coming.

These insurrections and their unfortunate end brought about one of the most disruptive upheavals in the long history of the Jewish nation. Judaism forfeited much of its reputation and its privileges in the Hellenistic world and withdrew within itself as the public became more and more distant from it. The first insurrection cost Judaism its centre of religion and its privilege of self-government recognized by Rome. This was continually brought to the memory of every Jew by the transfer of the Temple tax into an offering for the temple of Jupiter Capitolinus in Rome. The uprising by the Diaspora broke the Jew's economical and political position of power in Egypt and hastened the extinction of Hellenistic Judaism. After the last insurrection, Jerusalem was rebuilt as a purely Hellenistic city with the name of Aelia Capitolina, and the Jews were forbidden to enter the city or its surroundings. Entrance to the Wailing Wall, the western wall of the Temple, was granted to the Jewish pilgrims after the beginning of the third century, but only on the anniversary of the city's destruction. Circumcision was also prohibited by the death penalty, and although this prohibition was lifted by Antonius Pius for Jewish children, it continued to remain in effect for proselytes.

These measures were intended mainly as a punishment. Otherwise,

[1] Literature: H. Graetz, *Geschichte der Juden von den ältesten Zeiten bis auf die Gegenwart* (1853), iv; E. Schürer, *The History of the Jewish People at the Time of Jesus Christ*, Div. I, Vol. ii, 207–321 (Ger. i, 600–704); A. Schlatter, *Geschichte Israels* ([2]1906), 322–381; S. Dubnow, *Weltgeschichte des jüdischen Volkes* (1925), iii; F. M. Abel, *Histoire de la Palestine* (1952), i, ii; S. W. Baron, *A Social and Religious History of the Jews* ([2]1952); Goppelt, *Christentum und Judentum*, 151–164, specific references and literature; special: A. Schlatter, *Synagogue und Kirche bis zum Barkochba-Aufstand*, 1966; H. Bietenhard, 'Die Freiheitskriege der Juden unter den Kaisern Trajan und Hadrian und der messianische Tempelbau', *Judaica* 4 (1948).

pagan Rome continued to grant Judaism the protection of a *religio licita*. Christian Rome in its attempt to root out all pagan religions forced Judaism into the ghetto for the first time.

The Jews were not prevented from starting anew the internal rebuilding of their community after the catastrophes. Soon after the destruction of the Temple, Rabbi Johannan ben Zakkai (died 80–85), the sole survivor of the Jerusalem Sanhedrin, established in Jamnia, a town near Jaffa, a Sanhedrin which was comprised only of rabbis from among the Pharisees. The decisions and directions of this body were authorized by the Law alone and no longer by the Romans, and yet they were acknowledged throughout the Diaspora. The second leader of this Sanhedrin, Rabbi Gamaliel II, gained the postition of a patriarch only because he subjected himself continually to the vote of the majority. After the second insurrection, a Sanhedrin in Galilee took over at Gamaliel's request the government of a people which had become a Diaspora in their own land.

Especially in the days of Gamaliel II, the Sanhedrin took decisive measures to ensure the perpetuation of the national and religious character of the Jewish community without the Temple and a recognized self-government. It made the views of Pharisaism, which prior to the destruction of the Temple was only one group among others, binding for all. All were now to submit to 'the tradition of the fathers', the *halachoth*, which Jesus had rejected according to Mark vii.9. The temple services were to be replaced by a new emphasis on the synagogue and religious duties and by the regular recital of the *Shʿma* and the Eighteen Benedictions. The atonement accomplished by offerings was replaced by the giving of alms, prayer, and suffering. In order to impose this religious way of life uniformly, the people were made amenable by means of social and economic pressure, and the other groups which had stood alongside Pharisaism were now eliminated. For this purpose the *Birkath ha Minim* was taken over c. A.D. 90 into the Eighteen Benedictions. The term *min* (=αἵρεσις) which had previously been a designation for a separate group now took on the meaning of a heretical party. All the separate Jewish groups which opposed the Pharisees were now considered to be heretical, the Essenes as well as the Hellenistic Judaism of Philo. The members of these groups, if ever they did not submit to the Pharisee position, were forced from the synagogues by means of the curse formula in the *Birkath ha Minim*, and their writings were rejected. These writings have only been preserved for us by the church fathers and the caves in the wilderness of Judea. Some of the Essenes in those days may have tried to join the Jewish Christians in Trans-Jordan, but the Nazarenes were particularly named as *minim* in the original form of the curse formula. They were no longer called to account by the synagogues, as Matt. x.17 states, but were expelled from them. John ix.22; xii.42 has adapted Jesus' saying to the new conditions.

The Old Testament Canon came to be sharply distinguished from the Apocrypha, and at the same time the writings contradictory to the orthodoxy of the Pharisees were rejected. The Septuagint, which had accepted these in part, was set aside; in the meantime, it had become the holy scriptures of the Greek-speaking Church, but it contradicted the new direction of Judaism by its universalist tendency. At the instigation of the learned ones in Jamnia the proselyte Aquila translated the Old Testament in an extremely literal fashion into Greek. In all this, the Old Testament became understood more and more as a Book complete in itself rather than a Book pointing beyond itself. The tradition based on the Law and the interpretation of scripture which corresponded with such a viewpoint was finally put into writing in the Mishnah c. A.D. 200, having been orally transmitted prior to this time. From the reworking of the Mishnah (c. A.D. 450) arose the canonical textbook of Judaism, the Babylonian Talmud.

In the course of these changes, both the attraction of Judaism for Hellenistic man and the desire of the synagogue to gain proselytes became paralyzed. Even though Judaism still accepted a few isolated proselytes until the prohibition of a Christian emperor made this impossible, it became more and more ingrown and took refuge under the cloak of the Law and tradition, being sustained through the centuries only by the burning messianic hope which stands at its heart. Thus between A.D. 70 and 135 a transformation took place which has stamped Judaism up to the present, a transformation which was ultimately determined by its inward denial of Christianity.

2. The relationship between the Church and Judaism[2] in this period takes various forms according to the different regions, but the following traits are generally valid.

Judaism's inward denial of Jesus expressed itself in a polemical attitude towards the Church. The rabbis derided Christianity internally and Josephus remained silent about it in his writings c. A.D. 100,[3] not only to create a better understanding between the Jews and Romans but also because it was no recommendation for the Jews to have brought this questionable superstition into the world. Beginning with Justin, the church fathers increasingly raised the charge that the widespread defamation of their faith had originated mostly from the Jews,[4] and, in any case, the Jews gave the pagan polemic its weightiest arguments. For

[2] Literature: Goppelt, Christentum und Judentum, 15, n. 2.
[3] Literature in Goppelt, Christentum und Judentum, 156, nn. 4 f.
[4] Goppelt, Christentum und Judentum, 145, n. 2.

example, they spread the explanation that the disciples had stolen Jesus' body (Matt. xxviii.15; cf. further Rev. ii.9; iii.9). They refuted the proofs from prophecy about Jesus' Messiahship, and they voiced the accusation that the Church had usurped their holy scriptures without really living according to them.[5]

The Church countered this criticism, as Justin (Dial. 133) explained, with intercession for the Jews,[6] but after A.D. 80 she no longer concerned herself outside the realm of Syria and Palestine with a mission to the Jews. The extensive Christian literature which interacted with Judaism sought basically to justify the Church for her own members and for the Gentiles rather than to convert the Jews.[7] This was already the case to an extent for Matthew's Gospel and even more so for Justin's Dialogue and the whole body of literature which was published under similar titles.

An entirely different side of this relationship to Judaism becomes visible when Matthew's Gospel (vi.1 ff.) and the Didache (8, 1 f.) deplore the intrusion of Jewish customs into the Church, yet at the same time Christian customs in the Didache had already been formulated legalistically in keeping with those of the Jews. The churches were now externally separated from the synagogues almost everywhere, but the influence of Jewish tradition[8] became stronger than ever in the third generation. Since Christianity now had to establish itself permanently in the world, it grasped conceptions and religious ways of life which had been developed by the Old Testament Jewish community in the same situation. Consequently it was receptive to a stream of Jewish tradition which worked its way into the formation of the liturgy and of the Church's structure, customs and even theology. For example, in I Clement the influence of the western Diaspora synagogue is quite obvious just as the Essene tradition can be seen in Hermas[9] and the Palestinian apocalyptic tradition in Papias. In particular, Christianity absorbed much from both the apocalyptic writings and later from the Hellenistic literature of Judaism.

3. While the relationship to Judaism influenced the development of the Church at large only in a few, if very important, aspects, it was determinative for the Church in Palestine,[10] whose history we should trace in this context during this period (cf. §8, 5).

---

[5] Goppelt, Christentum und Judentum, 282 f.
[6] Cf. Syr. Didascalia, 108, 2 ff. (Goppelt, Christentum und Judentum, 207).
[7] Goppelt, Christentum und Judentum, 302 f.
[8] Goppelt, Christentum und Judentum, 149 f. et al.
[9] J. P. Audet, Rev. Bibl., lx (1953), 41–82.
[10] Literature: A. Schlatter, Synagoge und Kirche bis zum Barkochba-Aufstand, 1966; K. Pieper, Die Kirche Jerusalems bis zum Jahre 135 (1938); H.–J. Schoeps, Theologie und Geschichte des Judenchristentums (1949), literatire there; Goppelt, Christentum und Judentum, 164–176; J. Daniélou, Théologie du Judéo-Christianisme (1958); J. Munck, 'Jewish Christianity in the Post-Apostolic Times', NTS 6 (1960), 103–116.

The Christians of Palestine refused to participate in the two messianic insurrections. As a result they were themselves persecuted as traitors and both times they fled into the Trans-Jordan and spread their faith as missionaries into the entire Syrian-Arabic border region between Beroea (east of Antioch), Damascus, and the eastern edge of the Dead Sea.[11] Only a few returned after the first insurrection to rebuild churches in the devasted land, in Jerusalem and in the towns of Judea and Galilee. After the last insurrection the area of Jerusalem remained closed to the Jewish Christians as well as for all who were circumcised, so that the churches which developed in the Hellenistic city of Jerusalem were all established by Gentile Christians. The Jewish Christians of Palestine were limited to the villages of Galilee and Caesarea.

According to rabbinic legends, the group which returned after A.D. 70 made such an impression on the rabbinic students themselves by means of their active missionary witness that the Nazarenes were mentioned specifically in the curse formula against the *minim* (cf. p. 118) and the rabbinic polemic had to become particularly intense around the turn of the second century. The small book by the Jewish Christian Aristo of Pella, *Disputes between Jason and Papiscus over Christ*, written shortly after A.D. 135 and now lost to us, was an account of this missionary struggle.[12]

The Palestinian Church between A.D. 70 and 130 was no longer the mother church for Gentile Christianity, as she had been in the Pauline period, but she did maintain contact with it. In all probability the Epistles of James and Jude were connected to her, since in Palestine the Lord's relatives occupied a special place in accordance with the Jewish principle of inheriting a spiritual honour.[13] After James, the Lord's brother, Simon bar Clopas, a cousin of Jesus, directed the Jewish Christian Church until he apparently suffered martyrdom late in life under the Emperor Hadrian. Like James, Simon occupied more the postion of a patriarch than that of a bishop. Under Domitian, two grandsons of Judas, the Lord's brother, who were indicted as Davidites, were said to have been tried and freed after proving themselves to be lowly farmers of Galilee. They then returned to their homes and continued to lead their churches even into the period of Trajan.

Only after the last insurrection did Jewish Christianity which had been forced *en masse* into the Trans-Jordan gradually lose contact with the Gentile Church and sink into a judaizing sectarianism. According to Justin (*Dial.* 47), some of the Jewish Christians still recognized the freedom from the Law for the Gentile Christians, although they themselves lived

[11] Schoeps, *op. cit.*, 270–277, 296–304.   [12] Goppelt, *op. cit.*, 165 f.
[13] Schoeps, *op. cit.*, 282–289.

according to the Law, and for this reason Justin, unlike others, regarded them as brethren. According to Irenaeus (*Haer.* I. 26, 2), on the other hand, all Jewish Christians who lived according to the Law were heretics since they repudiated both Paul and the developing canon, and were said to hold a crude adoptionist christology. Actually the Jewish Christians formulated their own Gospels in the course of the second century, which reflect the two major directions of this group: the Nazarene Gospel (so-called by the modern editors of the fragments) corresponds to the basic legalistic tendency, and the Gospel of the Ebionites corresponds to the particular Gnostic-syncretistic stream.[14]

From these latter elements the sect of the Prophet Elchasai (or Elxai) emerged around the turn of the second century.[15] He wrote a book in the year 116 which contained the revelation which he had received c. 101 east of the Dead Sea. This revelation offered, as a rough parallel to that of Hermas, forgiveness for even the worst sins by means of a second baptism. The religion which surrounded this message was in its essence more magical and Gnostic than Jewish Christian.

This Gnostic Jewish Christianity came into prominence in a sublime philosophical format directed at the West in the *Kerygmata Petru* which were probably written around 160 and were later reworked in (Catholic) pseudo-Clement.[16] They did not represent, as H.-J. Schoeps has contended,[17] the theology of Jewish Christianity as such, but the pre-Gnostic tendency which, as we now see, was greatly influenced by the Essenes.[18] From a history-of-religions standpoint this was certainly the active part of Jewish Christianity. The *Kerygmata Petru* wanted to gain a hearing in the larger Church, and the sect of the Elchasites undertook a futile advance towards the West at the beginning of the third century. In the history of religions, this direction finally merged into Manichaeism and Mohammedanism,[19] while the legalistic Jewish Christianity died of its own accord in the fourth century.[20]

---

[14] Ph. Vielhauer, in Hennecke [3]i, 75–108. The Jewish Christians of Egypt probably used 'The Gospel according to the Hebrews', which gave itself the title.

[15] J. Irmscher, in Hennecke [3]ii (1964), 745 ff. (Ger. 529–532); H.-J. Schoeps, *Theologie und Geschichte des Judenchristentums* (1949), 325–334: arose first in the second century; by contrast, J. Daniélou, *Théologie du Judéo-Christianisme* (1958), 76–80. Goppelt, *Christentum und Judentum*, 168–171.

[16] G. Strecker, in Hennecke [3]ii, 103–220 (Ger. 63–80); Goppelt, *Christentum und Judentum*, 171–176; the history of research up to 1954 on p. 171, n. 8, G. Strecker, *Das Judenchristentum der Pseudoklementinen* (*T.U.* 70, 1958).

[17] Discusssion in H.-J. Schoeps, *Urgemeinde, Judenchristentum, Gnosis* (1956), 1.

[18] O. Cullmann, 'Die neuentdeckten Quamrantexte und das Judenchristentum der Pseudoklementinen' (in *Festschrift* for Bultmann, 1954), 35–51; J. A. Fitzmyer, *JTS* 16 (1955), 335–372 (literature); H.-J. Schoeps, *op. cit.* (n. 17), 68–86.

[19] Schoeps, *Theologie und Geschichte des Judenchristentums* (1949), 332–342.

[20] *Ibid.*, 304 f.

These developments help shed light on the situation within the Church herself.

17. THE REGIONAL DEVELOPMENT OF THE CHURCH

1. At the beginning of this period the organization of the Church changed considerably.[1]

a. In the Pauline period an organizationally closed mother church in Palestine contrasted with a developing mission Church, Gentile in character, whose poles were Antioch and Rome and whose focal point was the area of the Pauline mission around the Aegaean Sea (Rom. xv). Even towards the end of the Pauline period the Palestinian Church had noticeably lost some of its importance since many of her most important witnesses, notably Peter, had placed themselves in the service of the Hellenistic Church. Furthermore the Hellenistic Church had developed a new centre of gravity primarily as a result of Paul's work. When the Jewish War forced the Christians in Palestine to flee, many of them chose the road to the Church of Asia and Syria. After A.D. 70 the Hellenistic Church could no longer look to the salvaged remnant of the earliest Palestinian Church as the mother church, but looked instead to those earliest witnesses, Peter in particular, who were working in the Gentile world, and by the end of the second generation to the places, mainly Rome and Ephesus, where these witnesses had left their legacy.

When the Hellenistic Church of the second and third generation came to designate Peter and/or the Twelve as their founders (cf. p. 115), this claim, although legendary in form, contained both a personal and a traditional basis in history. The mission had moved on to Hellenistic soil from the Palestinian tradition, even through Paul himself (I Cor. xi.15). This tradition had been brought to the Hellenistic Church during the Pauline period by means of the messengers and missionaries of Jerusalem and had spread intensively at the beginning of this period in Syria, Asia and in Rome. In it, apart from the Palestinian and Syrian Jewish Christianity (*Kerygmata Petru*), there was never a tendency to supplant Paul.[2] Memories of him were kept alive and his Epistles were preserved (cf. p. 162) in the Church between Rome and Ephesus. In Syria, Matthew's Gospel and James's Epistle did not polemicize against Paul but against a liberalism

---

[1] K. Holl, 'Der Kirchenbegriff des Paulus und sein Verhältnis zu dem der Urgemeinde', *Gesammelte Aufsätze* (1928), ii, 44–67; W. Bauer, *Rechtgläubigkeit und Ketzerei im ältesten Christentum* (1934); Goppelt, *Christentum und Judentum*, 164–267.

[2] F. C. Baur found a polemic against Paul in the Apocalypse (*Das Christentum und die christliche Kirche*, 81); A. Hilgenfeld and H. J. Holtzmann found such in Matt. v.19 (*Lehrbuch der neutestamentlichen Theologie*, [2]1911, 505).

which had made use of Pauline formulae (Matt. v.19; James ii.14–26). His Epistles had also gained recognition here in the third generation (II Peter and Ignatius), and indeed, the Church between Rome and Antioch allied Paul more and more with Peter and the Twelve as founders of the Church just as did Acts and the Palestinian and Syrian tradition which Acts had reworked. In this way the second generation of the Gentile Church sought to acknowledge Paul together with Peter, just as they had preserved his Epistles as well as the Palestinian tradition.

Because of this influx of Palestinian teachers and traditions into the Greek Church, it is no longer possible to classify the Palestinian and Syrian form of Jewish Christianity after A.D. 70 (cf. the detailed study by H.-J. Schoeps) as a branch of primitive Christianity of equal rank to that of Hellenistic Christianity. After A.D. 70 the Palestinian Church, in spite of all her distinctions, was nothing more than one of the regional churches into which the Hellenistic Church itself had now split.

b. The Hellenistic Church, although consisting of many levels, had remained uniform throughout as a result of the mission situation and the overlapping work of Paul. Now the various regions began increasingly to take on different forms. This was caused by a variety of local forces, historical events, ecclesiastical traditions, and influences of the respective environments. Paul had already recognized the imprint of a particular region on the Church and had partially approved it and partially corrected it. He addressed the Church as an entity when he spoke of the churches of Galatia, Macedonia, Achaia, etc. (Rom. xv.26; I Cor. xvi.1; II Cor. viii.1). He also sanctioned the growth of each church in its own way (I Cor. iii), but he preached just as emphatically the traditions (I Cor. vii.17; xi.16; xiv.36) and obligations of the Church as a whole (I Cor. xvi.1 ff.). Just as she had done in Palestine, the Church now began to take on her own distinctive form in Syria, western Asia Minor, Rome and Egypt without disrupting the development of the entire Church as a unity. This regional development took place until c. A.D. 120 when trends in the Church as a whole began to lead again to a stronger unification during the course of the second century.

Consequently, some of the older works portrayed the various regions separately when considering this phase of church history. An example of this is the work of J. Weiss (R. Knopf) on Judea, Syria, Asia Minor, Macedonia-Achaia, and Rome, since when the sources for such a consideration have increased considerably. The Hellenistic and Jewish environment which constitutes the background for such studies has been further investigated, particularly in terms of archaeology.[3] The Christian documents of this period are still just as difficult to arrange chronologically

[3] Cf. in particular, *RAC.*

as they were before, but investigations carried on in terms of a history of religion and a history of tradition have resulted in several clarifications. *c.* The early Church divided the Christian writings of this period into four groups. First of all she accepted into the canon a number of writings as 'apostolic'. Secondly, she temporarily placed another group of writings on practically the same level as the first, but in the end she merely preserved them without canonizing them. These writings have been grouped together since the seventeenth century under the designation of the 'Apostolic Fathers'.[4] The writings themselves differ considerably from one another both in background and content, yet they are unified in that they represent the Christianity which emerged towards the end of the second century in the Early Catholic Church. Unlike the first and second groups of writings, the third group, consisting of the literature of the Christian Gnostics, and the fourth group, writings from the separatist Jewish Christianity, were destroyed as far as possible by the early Church, so that except for the primary sources preserved by the desert sands of Egypt, we are left with only reports and quotations.

When we arrange, as far as possible, this total corpus of literature in a diagram according to place and time (cf. pp. 224 f.), we notice that the four groups are distinguishable from one another in neither time nor place. Apostolic and post-apostolic, Gnostic and Ebionite writings arise side by side in the same Church, indeed even at times in the same regional churches. Several stand on the border between the four divisions. Did, therefore, these different points of view live together unseparated in the same church during this period, as W. Bauer thought, and only later come to be separated as orthodoxy and heresy towards the end of the second century? Naturally legalistic Jewish Christianity separated itself into separate churches on the basis of circumcision and observance of the Law, but within the Gentile Church there was no organizational separation for various reasons (cf. p. 169). Contrary to Bauer, the emergence of the Gnostic movements was not debated as though they were schools of thought, but they were directly repudiated as pseudo-Christian. Let us now attempt to characterize briefly the several regions.

2. We hear the Church of Rome[5] speaking in I Clement, which was

---

[4] Editions: F. X. Funk–K. Bihlmeyer, *Die Apostolischen Väter I* (²1956) (without Hermas); K. Lake, *The Apostolic Fathers* (Loeb 24, 25, 1912–13) (text and Eng. trans.); *The Apostolic Fathers* ed. J. B. Lightfoot (rev. text with intro. and Eng. trans.); H. Kraft, *Clavis Patrum Apostolicorum*, 1963 (Concordance).

[5] Literature: H. Vogelstein und P. Rieger, *Geschichte der Juden in Rom* (1896); P. Styger, *Juden und Christen im alten Rom* (1934); A. Harnack, *Analecta zur ältesten Geschichte des Christentums in Rom* (*T.U.* 13, 2, 1905); H. Katzenmayer, 'Entstehung und erste Schicksale der Kirche Gottes in Rom', *IntKZ*, 31 (1941), 36–45; 43 (1953), 65–72 (on Ignatius, *Rom.* iv.3); L. Hertling–E. Kirschbaum, *Die römischen Katakomben*

written c. A.D. 96 in her name to Corinth. The revelations of Hermas written in sections between A.D. 110 and 140 address themselves to the central internal problem in the Church of Rome. Hebrews and Luke are related to both of these books by a common tradition. Hebrews could well have been written around A.D. 80 to a house-congregation (cf. xiii.24) by a teacher of the Roman Church who had come from the Hellenistic synagogue. Luke's works could also have been written around the same time, in the Church of the West to which he directed his readers. Before this, the earliest of the Gospel writings, Mark's Gospel, had originated in Rome around A.D. 65–70, and, in all probability, the oldest written sermon, II Clement, also belongs to this area (c. A.D. 130).

The Church of Rome had already gained a certain superiority early in the history of the Church. It became prominent as the church of the capital of the world (Rom. i.8; xvi.16), as the meeting point of the entire Church (cf. the greetings in Rom. xvi; Col. iv; I Peter v.13), as the abode of Peter and Paul (Ignatius, *Rom.* iv.3; I Clem. v.4 f.) and as the first great church to suffer as a martyr (Rev. xvii.6). Because of all this, as Luke points out, she became to a certain extent the successor of Christian Jerusalem, and as I Clement demonstrates, she thus assumed the responsibility for the other churches. Like the Roman synagogues previously, she now had connections with the high, and even the highest, positions of the empire, so much so that Ignatius had cause to fear lest she might prevent his martyrdom (Ignatius, *Rom.* ii.1; iv.1 f.). She had these connections through personal contacts in influential homes and also towards the end of the century through certain highly positioned Christians among her members (cf. §15, 1). The reverse was also true; she was the first to incur expressions of the Emperor's displeasure. In this city of about a million inhabitants, the Church could only gather in groups in private homes (cf. pp. 204 f.), but there was such a bond of unity among these groups that one hears again and again about the church in Rome, even in a sociological sense.

Surprisingly enough, the Christianity of this church has the same characteristics in all of the writings preserved for us from her area. The language of Gnosticism and the struggle with this error are totally missing in the writings, extending from Paul's Epistle to the Romans to the writings of Hermas, although one does always find the thought of legalistic Judaism reflected in these writings. From Rom. i f. through Acts xvii to I Clement, however, this thought presents itself in a synthesis with the popular Stoic philosophy which had already been constructed by Hellenistic Judaism. From the Christian tradition, the Palestinian and

---

Synoptic terminology of atonement, repentance and forgiveness had in particular combined with this thought. Paul's concept of justification was only rarely used in this context, and the so-called Pauline or Johannine 'Christ-mysticism' is totally missing. There were two themes in particular which were handled in these thought-forms. On the one hand, from Rom. xiii to I Pet. ii and from Acts to I Clement, a positive relationship was sought, even if in quite a varied manner (cf. §15, 2), to history and the empire. On the other hand, within the Church itself repentance stood as the theme for Hebrews and Hermas as well as for Mark (i.4, 15) and the missionary sermons of Acts. On the whole we are confronted by a Christianity which is averse to all enthusiasm, all mysticism and Gnosticism, which has deliberately turned its attention to historical reality and its laws, and which has focused attention on the repentance, the forgiveness and the actual obedience effected by Christ. On the basis of this attitude Rome became, along with the Church in Asia, the centre of the Early Catholic Church in the course of the second century.

3. In no area of the Empire had Christianity spread so intensively during this period as in western Asia Minor,[6] and as a result she also experienced far more persecutions from the Jewish and Hellenistic population. Hellenistic syncretism, popular philosophy and the Jewish mission had penetrated this area to an unusual extent and made it receptive to the Gospel. At the same time, however, through these influences, it had also become a source for a contagious syncretism as well as for Judaizers. Colossians and the Pastorals were already warding off a judaizing Gnosticism. The Book of Revelation (ii. f.), I and II John and the Epistles of Ignatius counter various appearances of a strong Gnostic movement around the turn of the second century (cf. pp. 142 f.). The movement had now cast off the Jewish cloak; the Judaism which Ignatius (Magn. viii–xi; Phild. v–ix) fought as well as Gnosticism was in general probably no longer combined with the latter.[7] It is a different kind of Judaism from that of the Pauline period; it accepted Jewish customs (Magn. viii.1; ix.1; x.3) and Jewish exegesis of the Old Testament (Magn. viii.1; Phild. vi; viii.2), but it did not make the Law obligatory for the believers. The

[6] J. Weiss, 'Kleinasien', R.E. 10, 535–563; V. Schultze, Altchristliche Städte und Landschaften: vol. ii, Kleinasien (1922–26); J. Keil, Ephesos, Ein Führer durch die Ruinenstätte und ihre Geschichte (⁴1957); G. Kittel, 'Das Kleinasiatische Judentum in der hellenistisch-römischen Zeit', ThLZ, 69 (1944), 9–20; B. Kötting, Peregrinatio religiosa (1950), 32–57, 171–183; S. E. Johnsen, 'Early Christianity in Asia Minor', JBL., 77 (1958), 1–17; see in addition nn. 7, 23, 25.

[7] So, C. Schmidt, 'Gespräche Jesu mit seinen Jüngern nach der Auferstehung', T.U. 43 (1919), 388–396 (ibid., 403–452 on the supposed Judaism of the Gnostic, Kerinth, who appeared in Ephesus c. A.D. 100), and H. W. Bartsch, Gnostisches Gut und Gemeindetradition bei Ignatius von Antiochien (1940), 11–17, 34–39; differently W. Baur, HNT on Ignatius, Trall. 10.

Didache counters such a form of Judaism in Syria, and the church fathers and synods in both Asia Minor and Syria fought it even into the fifth century.[8] It was nothing more than the exaggeration of the tendency in the Early Catholic Church which had been branded as ἰουδαΐζειν (Ignatius, *Magn.* viii.1; cf. ix.1, for the first time).

These anti-Gnostic voices were diverse in character and background. The author of the Book of Revelation, according to the testimony of his own writing, was a Jewish Christian by the name of John who was held in high repute throughout all Asia (Rev. i.1, 4, 9; xxii.8). According to Papias, he was one of the Lord's disciples (Eus. 3, 39, 3 f. 7, 14). Justin (*Dial.* 81, 4) identified him with John, the son of Zebedee, one of the 'pillar apostles', and a tradition which appeared in Irenaeus (3, 1, 1) identified him with the author of the Fourth Gospel and the Johannine Epistles. Since the nineteenth century these reports have been called into question, not because the tradition as such was incomplete but because the Fourth Gospel appears in form and content to contradict authorship by an eye-witness from Palestine.[9]

Today one can say with a degree of certainty about the background of the Fourth Gospel that the author left it behind in its unfinished form, and it was published by a circle of men who were intimately connected with him (John xxi.24 f.). The author did not simply edit written sources, as the literary criticism once thought,[10] but reworked an essentially homogeneous tradition which existed largely in oral form.[11] This tradition had first been formulated by men who were closely related to the Jewish baptist sects of Palestine. Both the modes of expression,[12] as has become quite clear through the Qumran texts, and the conflicts with a baptist movement which had attached itself to John the Baptist, point to this origin.[13] During the passing on of the tradition, the mode of expression became modified in the disputes with Gnosticism and corresponded to it

[8] M. Simon, *Verus Israel* (1948), 382 f.

[9] Most recently, E. Haenchen, *ThR*, 23 (1955), 30 f.

[10] From J. Wellhausen until E. Hirsch and R. Bultmann; survey of the research: E. Haenchen, *ThR* 23 (1955), 295–335; S. Schulz, *Untersuchung zur Menschensohn-Christologie im Johannesevangelium* (1957), 39–95.

[11] E. Ruckstuhl, *Die literarische Einheit des Johannesevangeliums* (1951); B. Noack, *Zur johanneischen Tradition* (1954); C. K. Barrett, *The Gospel according to St. John* (1955), 20; cf. also W. Wilkens, *Die Entstehungsgeschichte des vierten Evangeliums* (1958); R. Schnackenburg, *Das Johannesevangelium* (*Herder-Kommentar*) I (1965), 59 f. 131–134.

[12] H. Odeberg, *The Fourth Gospel* (1929); A. Schlatter, *Der Evangelist Johannes* (1930); E. Stauffer, *Die Theologie des Neuen Testaments* (³1947) appendix ii; *ThLZ*, 81 (1956), 135–150; F. M. Braun, *Rev. Bibl.* 62 (1955), 5–44; M. Burrows, *More Light on the Dead Sea Scrolls* (1958), 124–131; S. Schulz, *Komposition und Herkunft der johanneischen Reden* (1960).

[13] R. Schnackenburg, *Histor. Jhrb.* 77 (1958), 'Das Vierte Evangelium und die Johannesjünger', 21–38.

in such a way that the tradition came to be addressed to men from a Hellenistic background without losing the basic Old Testament terminology.[14] This tradition was formed and conveyed neither by a congregation[15] nor a *chabura*[16] but by a school comparable to that which we find around Paul and Peter and like the one which stands behind Matthew's Gospel. It is distinct from the other tradition about Jesus, yet it demonstrates an amazing historical reliability (cf. §19, note 20). Consequently, one can class the Gospel as a thorough *kerygmatic* interpretation of Jesus' appearance in history.

It is therefore possible, as the one who published the Gospel claimed (xxi.24 f.), not only that a witness stood behind this tradition who had understood Jesus better than had Peter,[17] considered to be the authority behind Mark's tradition, but also that he was an eye-witness who had originally been a disciple of John the Baptist (John i.35 ff.). The circle which was formed around this eye-witness and which conveyed this tradition took part in the missionary struggles with the Samaritans, according to John iv. In this way they came into contact with Gnosticism at an early date as well as with the Jewish baptist groups which ended in Samaritan Gnosticism (cf. §13, note 2). Is it mere coincidence that together with the Hellenists,[18] who, however, had an entirely different conception of the Temple to John iv (Acts vii), only John, the son of Zebedee, should be named in the primitive Christian tradition, at times with his brother (Luke ix.54) and at times with Peter (Acts viii.14; pseudo-Clem. *Rec.* i, 57), as the leading combatant in these struggles?[19] Other indications also suggest that the 'pillar apostle', John, stands as the authority behind the Johannine tradition. Why should not a school develop around him just as it did around Paul, Peter, and James? (cf. §19, 4a).

The relationship of the Fourth Gospel to Revelation supports this conclusion. There is no other early Christian writing which stands so close to the Gospel in its unique theological conceptions and terms as does Revelation.[20] As in the Johannine corpus, we find apocalyptic and dualistic modes of expression side by side in the Qumran texts, but the difference in language between the fourth Gospel and Revelation excludes the

[14] C. H. Dodd, *The Interpretation of the Fourth Gospel* (1954).

[15] E.g. E. Haenchen, *ThR* 23 (1955), 30 f.

[16] O. Michel, 'Die Fleischwerdung des Wortes', *Zeitwende* 27 (1956), 85; S. Schulz, *Komposition und Herkunft der johanneischen Reden* (1960), 183 ff.

[17] Most recently on the problem of the 'Beloved Disciple', A. Kragerud, *Der Lieblingsjünger im Johannesevangelium* (1958).

[18] According to O. Cullmann (*NTS*, 5, 1959, 157–173) the bearers of the Johannine tradition could well have belonged to this group.

[19] C. K. Barrett, *op. cit.* (n. 11), p. 133 as well.

[20] Goppelt, *Christentum und Judentum*, 250, 260 ff.

possibility of both stemming directly from the same author, so that the complex relationship between the two writings could best be explained in terms of a common tradition preserved by a school. This leaves the question open whether John of Ephesus, the author of Revelation, was identical with John, the 'pillar apostle'.

The connection between the Johannine writings and Ignatius, as well as the Odes of Solomon, can then be explained by the spreading of this tradition into Syria from Palestine. It is still a puzzle, however, why Ignatius remained silent in his Epistles to churches in Asia both about the Johannine writings, with which he no doubt was familiar,[21] and about John of Ephesus;[22] he had had close contact with Polycarp of Smyrna,[23] the pupil of John of Ephesus. Yet there is no reason in the history of religions nor in the history of tradition to suggest that John's Gospel and the Johannine Epistles were written in Syria.[24] Everything speaks in favour of the Church's ancient tradition according to which these, as well as Revelation, were written in Asia.

John of Ephesus and the circle around him were the most important representatives of a considerable number of Palestinian Jewish Christians who had emigrated to Asia.[25] Of these Jewish Christians, Eusebius names the Evangelist Philip (Acts viii)[26] and Aristion,[27] one of the Lord's disciples, as well as John. The emigration was probably occasioned by the Jewish War and not by an intention to occupy Asia, as it were, on the part of the earliest Church after Paul's death.[28] It led in no way to the establishment of Jewish Christian churches,[29] but instead the emigrants placed themselves at the service of the Gentile Church, as their writings attest. The Pauline heritage was not supplanted but simply overlaid by many layers. In the accompanying letter which Polycarp of Smyrna sent with Ignatius' Epistles to Philippi immediately after the latter's visit on his way to Rome, he quotes sayings of Jesus from the Synoptics and pas-

---

[21] C. Maurer, *Ignatius von Antiochien und das Johannesevangelium* (1949).

[22] K. Aland, 'Der Montanismus und die kleinasiatische Theologie', *ZNTW*, 46 (1955), 109–116: In light of Montanus it is probable that John's Gospel was written in Asia, and at the same time it would thus be understandable that Ignatius and the Roman sources should not have mentioned it.

[23] Irenaeus in Eusebius, *H.E.*, 5 : 20, 6; 5, 24, 16.

[24] *Contra* A. Jülicher, *Einleitung in das Neue Testament* ([7]1931), 259 ff., 419; W. Bauer, *Das Johannesevangelium (HNT)*, [2]1925, 237, and W. Nauck, *Die Tradition und der Charakter des ersten Johannesbriefs* (1957), 165.

[25] T. Zahn, 'Apostel und Apostelschüler in der Provinz Asien', in *Forschungen zur Geschichte des neutestamentlichen Kanons*, etc. (1900), vi, 1–224.

[26] Eusebius, *H.E.* 3 : 37 (confused with the Apostle Philip since Polycrates, *ibid.*, 3, 13, 3; 5, 24, 2).

[27] Eusebius, *H.E.* 3, 39, 3 f.

[28] *Contra* K. Holl, 'Der Kirchenbegriff des Paulus und sein Verhältnis zu dem der Urgemeinde', in *Gesammelte Aufsätze* (1928), ii, 66.

[29] *Contra* E. Schwartz, *ZNTW*, 31 (1932), 191.

sages (without citation) from the Pauline Epistles, I Peter, I Clement and I John. He himself developed a Paulinism in the mould of that found in the Pastorals. This diverse group of writings represented for him, unlike Gnosticism and the judaizing tendency, 'the Catholic Church', i.e. the universal Church (Ignatius, *Smyr.* viii.2). By identifying himself with this large group of witnesses, while others of his surroundings chose a more limited selection, [30] Polycarp led the way to the canon of scriptures which the early catholic fathers developed.

Irenaeus[31] referred to Polycarp as well as Papias[32] as one of the presbyters who had imparted to him the correct understanding of the apostolic message. Papias called the apostles and the Lord's disciples 'presbyters', and the author of II and III John used the same title for himself. The title in accordance with the Palestinian usage meant the authorized bearers of tradition.[33] The Church's tradition represented by the presbyters of Asia became in its diversity the most important theological foundation of the Early Catholic Church. It is important that not only the Paulinism of Polycarp but also the Pauline Epistles, not only the apocalyptic Palestinian traditions of a Papias but also the prophetic word of Revelation, not only the Epistles of Ignatius but also those of I John and above all John's Gospel together with the Synoptic tradition should have continued to live together in this tradition. With the witness of the Johannine literature, the brilliance of the apostolic (in its most literal sense) proclamation, which had already faded in the other regions of the Church, reached its climax.

This movement, which culminated in the Early Catholic Church, clearly emerged in Asia as it did in Rome at the end of the period, although it prevailed only after difficult struggles with other currents, especially Gnosticism. The period ended quite differently in Syria and Egypt.

4. The situation in Syria[34] is reflected in the fictional legends of the pseudo-Clem. *Acts of Peter.*[35] In these legends Simon Magus and Simon Peter, who follows him, move competing with each other from Caesarea in Palestine through the region of Phoenicia to Antioch. At the beginning of the period, men from the Palestinian Church were still intervening in the churches of Syria which, since the turn of the century, had expanded from

---

[30] Goppelt, *Christentum und Judentum*, 265 f.

[31] Eusebius, *H.E.* 5, 20, 5; Irenaeus, *Haer.* 3, 3, 4.

[32] Eusebius, *H.E.* 3, 39, 3 f.

[33] A. Schlatter, *Der Evangelist Matthäus* ([6]1963) on Matt. xv.2 and Zahn, *op. cit.* (n. 25), 78–88.

[34] Literature: V. Schultze, *Altchristliche Städte und Landschaften: vol. iii, Antiocheia* (1930); C. H. Kraeling, 'The Jewish Community at Antioch', *JBL* 51 (1932), 130–160; O. Eissfeldt, *Tempel und Kulte syrischer Städte in hellenistisch-römischer Zeit* (1941); reports on the excavations: *Antioch on-the-Orontes* (1934–52), i–iv.

[35] J. Irmscher in Hennecke [3]ii, 532–535 (Ger. 384–398).

Antioch into Phoenicia and farther eastward. They had intervened in order to help in the struggles both with Judaism which was nowhere, apart from Palestine, so intense as in Syria and with Gnosticism which had also developed considerably here. One of these men, in view of the struggle against Judaism, gave written form around A.D. 80 to a Gospel tradition which had been transmitted for some time in Palestine, by combining it with Mark's Gospel to form Matthew's Gospel (cf. §19, 4).[36] The Epistles which were probably written from Palestine to Syria in the name of James, the Lord's brother (A.D. 62–80) and Jude (c. 80) frequently concur in terminology and theological standpoint with this Gospel.[37] The former counters a liberal, the latter an antilegalistic and Gnostic, disintegration of Christianity. The Didache, the oldest book of Church regulations, was written towards the end of the first century, perhaps in eastern Syria,[38] and it also embodies Palestinian material. Unlike James and Jude it reflects merely a position of opposition to Judaism similar to that of Matthew.

According to the traditions of the ancient opponents of heresy in the Early Church, the flood of Gnosticism increased around the turn of the second century. Ignatius' sharp polemic against itinerant Gnostic teachers in Asia indicates that he was well acquainted with Gnosticism. In the last decades of the first century the Samaritan Menander,[39] a 'pupil' of Simon, came to Antioch. He no longer claimed to be the manifestation of the supereme power, as had Simon, but the one sent by the supreme power. He promised, by means of his magic, mastery over the angels who had created the world, and, by means of his baptism, a resurrection to immortality. At the beginning of the second century Saturninus[40] converted the Samaritan Gnosticism into a Christian Gnosticism; the redeemer was no longer called Simon or Menander, but Christ. At the same time the cosmology was conceived with more attention to the Old Testament accounts and related to a particular approach to the Old Testament and to the God of the Old Testament. It is possible, as the

[36] A. Schlatter, Die Kirche des Matthäus (1929); G. D. Kilpatrick, The Origins of the Gospel according to St. Matthew (1946); K. Stendahl, The School of St. Matthew (1954); N. A. Dahl, 'Die Passionsgeschichte bei Matthäus', NTS (1955–56), 17–32; G. Strecker, Der Weg der Gerechtigkeit (²1966); W. Trilling, Das Wahre Israel (³1964); G. Bornkamm, G. Barth and H. J. Held, Tradition and Interpretation in Matthew (as in §1, n. 16).
[37] Goppelt, Christentum und Judentum, 189–191; E. Lohse, ZNTW, 48 (1957), 1–22. F. Mussner, Der Jakobusbrief (Herder–Kommentar) xiii, 1, 1964), 1–23.
[38] A. Adam, 'Erwägungen zur Herkunft der Didache', ZKG, 68 (1957), 1–47; B. Altaner, Patrologie (⁶1960), 43 f.; J. P. Audet, La Didache, Etudes Bibliques (1958), 187–210.
[39] Justin, Apol., 26; Irenaeus, Haer. i, 23, 5.
[40] Irenaeus, Haer. i, 24, 1 f. = Hippolytus, Phil. 7, 28; Epiphanius, 23; further, see A. Hilgenfeld, Die Ketzergeschichte des Urchristentums (1884), 14 ff.

opponents of the heresies report,[41] that Basilides also took Antioch as his base of departure. The groups of profane Gnosticism which have been gathered together under the general term of 'Ophites' appear also to have had their roots in Syria.[42]

We know of only one voice which was raised at the beginning of the second century against this stream of Gnosticism in Syria, that of Ignatius.[43] He himself had fallen prey to a pre-Gnostic, Hellenistic thought which no longer allowed him to understand Jesus' appearance in terms of the Old Testament God-man relationship. For example, he understood the two fundamental terms, 'flesh' and 'spirit', in a Hellenistic fashion. Nevertheless, in contrast to all Hellenistic Gnostic thought, he developed the conception that Christ had brought the unity of flesh and spirit, which was forced on him by his belief in the reality of the incarnation and the sufferings of Christ. By so doing, Ignatius delineates for the first time a form of Hellenistic Christianity which would eventually lead to the Greek Catholic Church rather than to Gnosticism.[44] As well as Ignatius, the Odes of Solomon[45] also confessed their belief in the creation, Christ's physical body and the clothing of the redeemed soul with a body, contrary to the teachings of Gnosticism. These hymns were written at the beginning of the second century in Syria, and they combined in a unique manner pre-Gnostic modes of expression and conceptions with those of the Old Testament. It could possibly have been the hymnbook of Ignatius' congregation.

Thus the struggle among the diverse forces in Syria took a different course from that in Asia. Ignatius requested in his Epistles that the churches of Asia should declare their affection for the Church in Syria by means of letters and personal representatives.[46] They were, as was most probably the actual purpose of this request, to bring support for him in Syria. Nevertheless, Syrian Christianity developed around the middle of the

[41] Irenaeus, *Haer.* i, 42, 1.

[42] C. Schmidt, *RGG*[2], iv, 730; G. Kretschmar, *RGG*[3], iv, 1959.

[43] H. W. Bartsch, *Gnostisches Gut und Gemeindetradition bei Ignatius von Antiochien* (1940); C. Maurer, *Ignatius von Antiochien und das Johannesevangelium* (1949); Goppelt, *Christentum und Judentum*, 197–201; R. Bultmann 'Ignatius und Paulus', in *Studia Paulina* (as in §5, n. 31), 37–51; V. Corwin, *St. Ignatius and Christianity in Antioch*, 1960; cf. also §18, n. 15.

[44] Of all the literature from the ancient Church, the Byzantine Church had confidence only in the writings of Ignatius and the Areopagites which they copied without taking any dogmatic offence (Harnack, *Geschichte der altchristlichen Literatur* (1897), ii–1, xli).

[45] Edition: R. Harris and A. Mingana, *The Odes and Psalms of Solomon* (1916–20), i, ii. M. Testuz, *Papyrus Bodmer* (1960) x–xii (*Od. Sol.*, 11, Gr.). Literature: B. Altaner, *Patrologie* ([6]1963), 53; R. M. Grant, 'The Odes of Solomon and the Church of Antioch', *JBL* 63 (1944), 363–377.

[46] *Phild.* x; *Smyr.* xi.2 f.

second century in such a manner that the early catholic fathers could no longer find any witness there for their tradition. This explains why we have no news about Christianity from this region any more than from Egypt for the following decades. Both areas had been flooded by Gnosticism.[47]

5. Furthermore, we lack any knowledge of the Church's first three generations in Egypt.[48] Christianity comes into the light of history there for the first time around 180. In this area, it had found conditions quite similar to those in Syria; most probably Christianity had already taken hold in Egypt during the Pauline period, although the earliest indications date back only to the beginning of the second century. We know from Clement of Alexandria that two apocryphal Gospels were used in the first half of the second century: the Gospel according to the Egyptians and the Gospel according to the Hebrews.[49] The former was probably used by Greek and Egyptian congregations and the latter by Jewish Christian congregations which had been established in the exclusively Jewish settlements. The fragments of both Gospels demonstrate pre-Gnostic admixtures, which led W. Bauer to suggest that from its very beginning Christianity in Egypt had been 'heretical', to use the language of the Early Catholic Church, and that 'orthodoxy' had first taken root with Bishop Demetrius of Alexandria (189–239).[50] Since then, however, papyrus discoveries have shown that the Synoptic Gospels and John's Gospel were also known in the first decades of the second century,[51] so that the Church here was diverse in character at the beginning of the second century. Both the apostolic witness as well as the tendency leading toward the Early Catholic Church were present. The latter tendency is represented by the Epistle of Barnabas,[52] which was quite probably written in Egypt c. A.D. 135. This letter lacked incisive influence, however, perhaps because it had not known the personal word of the apostolic witnesses. Towards the close of this period Christianity in Egypt took on more and more Gnostic colouring, and Egypt eventually became the stronghold of the

---

[47] So W. Bauer, Rechtgläubigkeit und Ketzerei im ältesten Christentum (1934), 67 f. 49.

[48] Literature: A. Heckel, 'Die Kirche von Ägypten . . . bis zur Zeit des Nicänums' (unpublished diss., Strassbourg, 1918); H. J. Bell, Jews and Christians in Egypt (1924); Juden und Griechen im römischen Alexandreia (1926); L. Fuchs, Die Juden Ägyptens in ptolemäischer und römischer Zeit (1924); W. Schneemelcher, 'Von Markus bis Mohammed', Ev. Theol. 8 (1948–49), 385–405; F. Zucker, Ägypten im römischen Reich, by the Akademie der Wissenschaft, Leipzig, 1958); M. Hornschuh, 'Die Anfänge des Christentums in Ägypten' (unpublished diss., Bonn, 1958).

[49] Ph. Vielhauer, in Hennecke [3]i, 158–178 (Ger. I, 104–117).

[50] Rechtgläubigkeit und Ketzerei im ältesten Christentum (1934), 57–60.

[51] Pap. Rylands Greek, 457 (W. G. Kümmel, Introduction, 363; Ger. 380) and Pap. Egerton 2 (ZNTW, 34, 1935, 285–291); cf. E. Haenchen, Die Botschaft des Thomas-Evangeliums (1961), 9.

[52] B. Altaner, op. cit. (n. 45), 66 f.

Gnostic schools. Just as its representatives carried her teaching to the rest of the Church, especially to Rome, so the reverse was true as the Gospel papyri show. They continually received representatives from the rest of the Church so that Egyptian Christianity was not simply left to the syncretistic forces of her environment.

This survey of the inner development of the Church has demonstrated an unusually strong differentiation among the individual regions in which various dominating forces emerged towards the close of this period. The Palestinian Church, having been forced into the regions of the Trans-Jordan, sank into a Judaistic sectarianism. In Syria and Egypt, Gnostic formulations of Christianity became dominant. In Rome and Asia, the tendency which prevailed was the one which recognized the later canonized writings as its guiding line and which formed the Early Catholic Church towards the close of the second century. Even in this tendency we do not find theological consistency nor even complete conformity with the writings for whose canonization this tendency was responsible. This becomes evident when we examine the common problems and their solutions within the Church during this period.

18. THE COMMON PROBLEMS WITHIN THE CHURCH

1. There were also common problems within the Church which transcended all local differences and which left behind the questions of the Pauline period. Paul had fought against legalistic Judaism and a Judaistic pre-Gnosticism. After A.D. 70 both of these tendencies disappear from the Hellenistic Church as a whole. They survived only in the Jewish Christian Church of the Palestinian and Syrian realm. The problem of fellowship between Jewish and Gentile Christians remained acute for her alone, since the Hellenistic Church was now concerned with other questions. She was endangered in general by a relaxation of the Christian conduct, a relaxation which led to a relapse into the secular way of life. In the eastern regions of the Church in particular, she was threatened by a Gnostic disintegration of her teaching which, although proclaiming the radical desecularization of the higher 'ego', actually resulted in conformity to syncretism and its way of life.

2. This relapse into the secular way of life is dealt with in a particularly impressive manner by two writings directed to the Roman Church. Hebrews compares in typological terms the conduct of the Christian congregation with Israel's murmuring in the wilderness (iii.7–iv.13). They had moved out of the house of slavery, out of this world, and had followed the call to eschatological existence (vi.1–5; xiii.12 ff.), but rather than finding the promised land they had found only adversity (xii.1–13),

had become tired, and, longing for the temporal way of life (not some sort of Judaism), they were now becoming discontented. Many were closer to the precipice of ' . . . falling away from the living God' than they thought (iii.12 f.). They were like Esau, tired and at the point of selling their birthright without concern for a single meal (xii.16 f.). The single meal was no more than the every-day life of this world. One generation later Hermas sees in one of his visions the Church as an old woman who explained to him that she had become weak and senile because she had offered herself to the activities of this life (*Vis.* 3, 11, 1–3, 13, 4).

At the time of Hebrews, Matthew's Gospel was summoning the Christians in Syria by means of a series of parables on the second coming (24 f.) to an obedient watchfulness. He most certainly meant it allegorically when he says of 'the evil servant' (from Q): ' . . .[He] says to himself, 'My master is delayed', and begins to beat his fellow servants, and eats and drinks with the drunken'.

This relaxation is attributed to the delay of the parousia: the servants became tired because the time was long—not because their expectation of an imminent end was disappointed.[1]

> The 'consistent eschatological' viewpoint which supported the latter position[2] has been conclusively disproven. It falsely ascribed to Jesus the Jewish apocalyptic concept of the Kingdom of God and thus considered him, as well as earliest Christianity, to be conditioned primarily by his consistent response to an imminent future beyond the worldly life. The disappointment of this expectation is supposed to have been the decisive problem which created the crises of the second generation. However,'a look at the literature between A.D. 65 and 130 shows the following: first, the Church's questions about the imminent end were seldom treated and then always superficially (James v.8 f.; Heb. x.36–39; I Clem. xxiii; II Clem. xi; II Pet. iii). This observation alone excludes the possibility that an extensive part of the Synoptic tradition had developed partially as an apology and partially as a reinterpretation of the expectation of the imminent end.[3] When one sees that Jesus' earthly ministry took the announcement of the nearness of the Kingdom as its point of departure and yet directed the disciples to his resurrection and a redemptive period of time between the resurrection and the parousia,[4] one

---

[1] Literature: M. Werner, *Die Entstehung des christlichen Dogmas* (³1953); W. G. Kümmel, *Promise and Fulfillment* (Eng. trans. 1957, of *Verheissung und Erfüllung*, 1956); E. Grässer, *Das Problem der Parusieverzögerung in den synoptischen Evangelien und in der Apostelgeschichte* (1957); A. Strobel, *Untersuchungen zum eschatologischen Verzögerungsproblem* (1960); G. Ladd, *Jesus and the Kingdom* (1964); O. Cullmann, 'Parusieverzögerung und Urchristentum', *ThLZ* 83 (1958), 2–12; O. Cullmann, *Heil als Geschichte* (1965), 10–29 (= Eng. trans. 1967, 28–40).

[2] Werner, *op. cit.*, 115 ff.

[3] *Contra* Grässer, *op. cit.* (n. 1).

[4] Kümmel, *op. cit.* (n. 1), 64 ff. (Ger. 58 ff.).

discovers how relatively limited the further development of this theme actually was in the Synoptic tradition. An example of this would be the composition of the Synoptic apocalypse in Mark xiii par.

Secondly, the authors of this literature could not have been dominated by this disappointment because, surprisingly, they emphatically reiterate the announcement of the imminent end (I Cor. vii.29 ff.; Rom. xiii.11; I Pet. iv.7; James v.8 f.; Heb. x.36–39; Rev. xxii.20; Did. 10, 6; I Clem. xxiii.5; II Clem. xii.1, 6; Barn. iv.3; Hermes, *Vis.* 3, 8, 9; *Sim.* 9, 12, 3; 10, 4, 4). The expectation of the imminent end, then, did not depend on the temporal limit which Jesus had set to comfort the disciples, 'even in this generation' (Mark ix.1; xiii.30). On the basis of this saying it was expected initially that the majority of the Church would experience the parousia and only a few would die. Paul in I Thess. iv.15 and I Cor. xv.51 f. put himself in the former group; in II Cor. v.1–10 and Phil. 1.21 ff., however, he placed himself with the latter group (without modifying his theology in the process). Mark ix.1 limited Jesus' pronouncement in similar fashion to 'some', and John xxi.23 corrected the popular expectation that at least one of the disciples would 'remain'. The expectation of the imminent end held its own without being dependent on these references to a limited period. Only two writings fail to take it into account, and this was probably intentional: Luke, who concentrated on the development of the Church with the help of his sayings concerning the redemption (Acts i.6 ff.), and John's Gospel, which focused on the presence of the eschaton in Jesus' appearance and on its proclamation (John vi.27; xi. 24 ff.). Both set forth in a one-sided manner the goal of Jesus' earthly ministry and the decisive factor in the apostolic preaching from the very start. This was the presence of the eschaton and its correlative which was the development within history of the redeemed community of the end times, although this was evident only for believers who without trying to calculate the time waited for the end, and for whom the Lord was 'always at hand' (Phil. iv.5).

Thirdly, and in keeping with the first two points, the cause for the relaxation and relapse in Hebrews, as with Hermas, was the slackening of that tension produced by the presence of the eschaton rather than the disappointment of the expectation of an imminent end. Because the time had grown long, the believers were no longer able to maintain the tension between the eschatological existence of being aliens in this world and everyday life as people within secular history. They had been called to maintain this tension at all times by every command in the Sermon on the Mount, but on the other hand, they were not only imprisoned in this life within history but were also obliged to remain therein. Thus the problem of the second generation, a problem which appears in every religious movement,[5] arose in primitive Christianity with a particular intensity.

[5] Cf. W. Freytag, 'Das Problem der zweiten Generation in der jungen Kirche', *EMZ*, i (1940), 198–210.

The question of how the tension between the eschatological and historical existence could be maintained over a lengthy period of time thus became the central theme of the Church's literature in the second and third generations. The strengthening of the believers' hope, in particular the hope of the expectation of the imminent end, is only one aspect of the development of this theme.

3. Two entirely different solutions for this question were developed in keeping with its two parts.

a. Hebrews and Hermas both classify the relaxation on the part of the Christians as the sin which puts into jeopardy their actual participation in the redeeming grace granted at their conversion, but each of these two writings counters this sin in an entirely different way.[6] Hebrews opposed this temptation of the Church with nothing else except preaching, a mere sermon which did not simply repeat the Gospel but considered the new situation through a new, grandoise interpretation. Christ is the eschatological High Priest (viii.1-10, 18), as an extensive typological comparison with the Old Testament priesthood shows. In spite of all appearances to the contrary, he who confesses Christ stands already on the ground of that new abiding world (xii.27 f.), and he who denies him will perish at the end (vi.4 ff.; x.26-31; xii.16 f.). Since Christ's work before God is the final redemptive work, conversion is now an eschatological event, bestowed once for all time, but also an action that involves one's total lifetime. Hebrews does not casuistically describe the point beyond which there is no longer any hope of salvation, but warns *kerygmatically* that the man of faith who backs away nears the precipice behind him and does not know whether or not the next step will bring his fall. The entire congregation is therefore to ' . . . see to it that no one fails to obtain the grace of God' (xii.15, e.g. Matt. xviii.15 ff.). In this way the entire congregation becomes involved, but everything hinges on the preaching.

By contrast Hermas opposes the relaxation by means of a comprehensive legal system of repentance which rations out grace. There is only one repentance, so he taught in keeping with Hebrews (*Mand.* 4, 3, 1 f.), and this is the baptism of repentance. Founded on Christ's sacrifice, this cancels all the sins committed up to that point, but those baptized will only be saved in the judgment if they have lived blamelessly in accordance to the Law of Christ after their baptism (his statements about the work of Christ, *Sim.* 5, 6, 2 f., and baptism, *Mand.* 4, 3, 1 f. *et al.*, are probably to be related in this manner). Those baptized have failed to do this, however, and the continuous exhortation to repentance (as in II Clement) has not

---

[6] Literature: J. Behm, *TWNT*, iv, 972 ff.; B. Poschmann, *Paenitentia secunda* (1940); K. Rahner, 'Die Busslehre des Hirten des Hermas', *ZKTheol.*, 77 (1955), 385-431.

brought about any changes (*Vis.* 1, 2 f.). Hermas therefore proclaimed a unique second repentance on the basis of a prophetic revelation. Everyone who accepted the message in active penitence received once more the remission of all guilt and would be saved if he continued to live blamelessly (*Vis.* 2, 2, 1–5; *Mand.* 4, 3). When the imminent end expected by Hermas failed to come, the early catholic institution of penance developed from this message of a unique second repentance. This led to the later, but consistent, regulation of the Middle Ages which stated that every baptized person should seek forgiveness through penance at least once a year for sins committed. In this way the problem of the existence of sin and grace within time was resolved in a way similar to that once found in Israel's Day of Atonement.

The Reformation under Luther stepped in at just this point. He broke through this system of repentance whose roots went back to Hermas, and the conception that baptism is merely a closed, historical act and that the repentance of the Christians was thus something else. According to Rom. vi, as Luther's Small Catechism again pointed out,[7] repentance is on the contrary the experience of baptism which involves all life. Hermas removed the eschatological element from baptism as well as from the work of Christ, so that the work of Christ was divided into an atoning offering and the giving of a law, both of which were only relatively better than that of the Old Testament. According to Hebrews, on the other hand, Christ stood in person as the perfect, heavenly High Priest with his self-offering before God, and he so cleansed from sin that he drew others into the obedience of discipleship. Here indicative and imperative and, in a different way, the sinfulness and the righteousness of man run so to speak parallel to each other and are joined by the *kerygma*, whereas they were separated into a chronological succession for Hermas so that he had to combine them in a pedagogical, legal way. The viewpoint of Hermas corresponds in its starting point with the teaching of the Early Catholic Church. He is in this sense 'early catholic', while Hebrews belongs with the apostolic preaching (cf. pp. 172 ff.).

b. Like the offer of grace, the ethical demand was also adapted pedagogically to history.[8] The ethical instructions of Hermas compared with those

---

[7] 'What does such baptizing with water signify? It signifies that the old Adam in us should, by daily contrition and repentance, be drowned and die with all sins and evil lusts, and, again, a new man daily come forth and arise, who shall live before God in righteousness and purity for ever.' Here is described in the language of the sixteenth century what we call the eschatological character of baptism.

[8] M. Dibelius, *Der Brief des Jakobus* (*Meyer Kommentar*, [8]1956), 30 f. and 44; M. Dibelius, *Der Hirt des Hermas* (*HNT*) on *Sim.* 2 : 5; G. Kittel, 'Der Jacobusbrief und die Apostolischen Väter', *ZNTW*, 43 (1950–51), 54–112; Goppelt, *Christentum und Judentum*, 187; P. Meinhold, Die Ethik des Ignatius von Antiochien, *Histor. Jhrb.* 77 (1958), 50–62; Mussner, *op. cit.* (§17, n. 37), 33–53.

of James are just as 'de-radicalized' and modified in keeping with what was practical for this world as was the Didache compared with Matthew's Gospel. Whereas James, like the sayings of Jesus, had radically summoned the rich from their wealthy existence (i.9 ff.), Hermas developed a theory of counterbalance which we find frequently in different forms in the Early Catholic Church: the rich in the congregations were to support the poor, and the poor were to pray for the rich (*Sim.* 2, 5–10). In much the same way, Did. 1, 3 and 2, 7 changed the commands of the Sermon on the Mount into proverbial rules. Thus Jesus' radical command, which as an eschatological summons to repentance led to an alien existence in this world, was again brought into line with the law of this world (Matt. xix.8). In the process, the tension between eschatological existence and life within temporal history was modified so that it could be borne more easily over a lengthy period of time.

c. Another aspect of this problem is the somewhat overlapping question of the Church and history. At this point the Johannine writings draw an abrupt distinction. Although '. . . the world was made through him', belongs to him, and will be saved through him (i.3, 9 ff.; iii.17), 'his own' stand in a dualistic contast to 'this world' and to 'the Jews' who represent it (John viii.44 ff.; xv.19; xvii.7, 14 ff.). Consequently, the instructions for conduct concentrated on the command to love one's brethren (John xiii.34; I John ii.7 ff., *et al.*) and did not, for example, touch on the area of the tables of household duties.

Luke, on the other hand, propounds a positive relationship between the Church and history.[9] He intended to give to the Church a historical self-awareness, and this was the *kerygmatic* tendency of his work as a whole. The development of the Church is itself history which has been inserted into world history, yet it is history in its own particular way. First, for Luke the Church grows out of Judaism through a continuing process of development and gains its place in the Greek world. In the view of the Church alone, the Church was only to be found where its continuity with devout Israel and with the path of the Gospel from Jerusalem through Paul to Rome had been recognized. In the view of those outside, Christianity was a *religio antiqua*. Secondly, this history of the Church has been inserted into world history which God's 'strong arm' had formulated (Acts xvii.26 f.). God brought it to pass by means of the decree from Caesar Augustus that the Promised One would be born in Bethlehem (Luke ii.1), and he caused Paul to be brought by the governor and soldiers of the Emperor to Rome in order that Paul might preach there unhindered

---

[9] H. v. Baer, *Der Heilige Geist in den Lukasschriften* (1926); H. Conzelmann, *The Theology of Saint Luke* (Eng. trans. 1960, of *Die Mitte der Zeit, Studien zur Theologie des Lukas,* [2]1957).

(Acts xxviii.30 f.). Thirdly, the history of the Church itself is history of a particular kind; her history is an event determined by the Spirit of God which, as the third period in redemptive history, follows both the period of Jesus as well as its predecessor, the period of the prophets.

Is this Lucan viewpoint, rather than John's Gospel, the second or early catholic solution to the problem? In the last decade it has often been maintained that Luke had removed the eschatological element from Jesus' mission and from the Church.[10] For Paul, Christ is the end of history; for Luke he is 'the centre of history'. This thesis misunderstands the Pauline concept of the eschaton. Paul does say in Rom. x.4: 'Christ is the end of the Law' (and thus the end of history), but he is the end of history 'for those who believe', who are still living 'in the flesh' (Gal. ii.20) within history. The eschaton is therefore paradoxically present in the centre of history. It cannot be defined philosophically, only theologically, The end of history is present where the realtionship with God promised in the Old Testament for the time of salvation is realized, and this is taking place now through God's grace within history contrary to all expectations. Thus Christ is, if one must use these unsatisfactory terms, both the end and the centre of history. In any case the Church is essentially both eschatological and historical. Luke, unlike Paul or John's Gospel, does permit the eschatological aspect of the Church to recede into the background in favour of historical continuity, and with it Jesus' antithesis to the Law and the antithesis of the Church to Israel, creation, and history; nevertheless he does not surrender the eschatological aspect. He does not subordinate the eschatological and pneumatic aspect of the Church to the historical and institutional. This occurs for the first time in I Clement. As soon as one compares Luke with I Clement—a task which has been omitted up to now—it becomes evident that Luke stands in strong contrast to Paul and John's Gospel, and so he has done an important service for the Church's way by revealing the historical aspect of her existence.

It was I Clement[11] rather than Luke[12] who adapted the Church and her message to the cosmos which he conversely interpreted in terms of the Church. Justification and the resurrection correspond to the cosmic order which has always been present in history and which was merely confirmed and ratified universally by Jesus. We were made righteous ' . . . through faith, by which Almighty God has justified all men from the beginning of

---

[10] Bultmann, *Theology of the New Testament*, 116 f., 126 f. (Ger. 462 f., 471 f.); E. Dinkler, *RGG*[3], ii, 1476–81; cf. Conzelmann, *op. cit.* and in *RGG*[3] ii, 665–672 (literature).

[11] Literature on I Clem. see §15, n. 13 and §18, n. 25; K. Beyschlag, *Clemens Romanus und der Frühkatholizismus*, 1966.

[12] *Contra* Ph. Vielhauer, 'Zum "Paulinismus" der Apostelgeschichte', *Ev. Theol.* 10 (1950–51), 1–15, esp. 15.

the world' (I Clem. xxxii.4). 'Let us consider, beloved, how the Master continually proves to us that there will be a future resurrection, of which he has made the raising of the Lord Jesus Christ from the dead the first-fruits . . .', by means of the change from day and night, sowing and harvesting, even indeed by the myth of the bird called Phoenix (I Clem. xxiv. f.). Since the blueprint of the cosmos is found in the structure of the Church, the structure of the Church's offices, for example, should correspond to the cosmic order (I Clem. xl). In this way the eschatological element in the Church and her message was actually removed, and both were given a place in a cosmic context; in this way I Clement set out along the path which the apologetes pursued and which the early catholic fathers pursued further, with some corrections to conform to the apostolic writings which had since been canonized. I Clement can therefore be called 'early catholic'.

During this period, then, the literature, which the ancient Church regarded as belonging to the Church and consequently preserved, evolved again and again the same two contrasting solutions, in their various forms, for the decisive problem. The Gnostic movement offered a third solution in the eastern regions of the Church. It announced the radical 'de-secularization' of the higher '*ego*', but in fact, according to the view of the apostolic witnesses, it brought simply a pseudo-pneumatic justification of secularization (I John iv.5 f.).

4. The Gnostic movement, which arose at this time in Asia Minor, Syria and Egypt did not therefore appear to the apostolic witnesses as a solution to the problem of secularization, but as a cause of its intensification.

a. Actually the movement was instigated and brought to a climax by the influence of the Jewish syncretistic environment as well as by means of the existential tendency, apparent from I Corinthians on, to fill in the gap between the Church and the Hellenistic Jewish world. We only know about particular events from the polemic of the Church's literature preserved for us, so the movement's reconstruction is uncertain in parts, but quite straightforward on the whole.

Without doubt the opponents attacked in the letters to the churches in Revelation, by I John, Ignatius, Jude and II Peter belonged to Gnosticism.[18] It also appears in this period as a movement within the churches rather than in the form of a separate entity. According to Revelation and I John

---

[18] Literature: W. Hadorn, *Die Offenbarung des Johannes* (*ThHK*, 1928), 65 f.; R. Schnackenburg, *Die Johannesbriefe* (1953), 13–20; H. Windisch, *Die katholischen Briefe* (*HNT*, ²1930), on II Pet. ii.22; W. Bauer, 'Die Briefe des Ignatius von Antiochia und der Polykarpbrief' (*HNT*) on *Trall*. 10; P. Meinhold: ' "Schweigende Bischöfe". Die Gegensätze in den kleinasiatischen Gemeinden nach den Ignatianen', *Glaube und Geschichte* (*Festgabe* for J. Lortz, II 1958), 467–490.

the heresy was passed on by prophets, according to Ignatius by teachers. It was thus continually represented by members of the primitive Church's pneumatic circles, but speculations about deities and creation were not yet cited as belonging to the content of the teaching as they were in the second century. However, a docetic christology not mentioned during the Pauline period was now a feature of the teaching (I John, Ignatius, Polycarp, *Phil.*), as was a definite deficiency in the area of ethics. The criticism of the ethical teaching was not simply an *ad hominem* attack on the part of theological opponents, but the Gnostic movement fluctuated from its very beginning between a liberal ethos conforming to the world (I Corinthians) and a legalistic ethos damning this world (Colossians, Pastorals). In this period the opponents were accused by Jude (par. II Pet. ii) of a libertine dissipation (Jude 4, 8, 16); in the letters to the seven churches, they were accused of worldly conduct, including participation in the religious ceremonies and erotic practices of the pagans (Rev. ii.14, 20; cf. I Cor. vi.8–10). In I John they were accused merely of worldly conduct, 'walking in darkness', i.e. in the fashion of this world, and lack of brotherly love (I John i.6; ii.4, 9 *et al.*). In II John 4–7 this deficiency in the ethical realm was expressly related to docetism; because they disregarded the body they could not find the proper relationship to physical responsibilities. The opponents of the Church act throughout as pneumatics who have elevated themselves as religious individuals far above the Christian life of the congregation (Jude 16), but in fact they have fallen prey to the spirit of this world (I John iv.5; Jude 12, 19; cf. Rev. ii.20). Their conception of the body and the spirit is actually Hellenistic rather than Old Testament or early Christian (cf. I Cor. x.1 ff.). They contrast an earth-bound psychic and material nature with that of a free pneumatic supra-nature, and in so doing they release the tension of pneumatic and eschatological existence 'in the flesh', i.e. in history. They preach pneumatic 'de-secularization' and yield themselves completely to the conduct of this world. Since the Gnostic movement met in this manner the underlying negative tenor of its time, each carried the other mutually to its peak. In the literature which countered the gnostic movement the same two contrasting solutions to the problem of this period come again to the surface.

b. I John opposed Gnosticism—in a manner comparable to the Book of Hebrews—with a witness to the redemptive event, a witness which is focused on the particular situation by using a dualistic language closely related to that of Gnosticism. It placed before the Church unequivocal antitheses and summoned her continually to a rejection of pseudo-faith and worldly conduct. This summons to rejection was not designed as a sermon to secure individual conversion, but like Rom. vi. it reiterates the baptism event[14] and aims at its realization in the life of the congregation and not merely in the life of the individual (I John v.16). It appears to be a sermon which brought about a crisis of faith.

By contrast Ignatius, if we may use a caricature, led to a separation from the Gnostics by stressing a hierarchical and cultic representation of the Church.[15] He countered the conventicles of the Gnostic teachers with the exhortation to enter into the unity of the Church assembled around the bishop and celebrating the eucharist.[16] This call was perfectly under-standable in this situation of the Church, and it contained without doubt correct elements, but it obscured the mysteries of the worship service and of the office. From the proclamation which brought salvation developed the instructions on the use of the sacramental institution of salvation, and from the office ' . . . of the ministry of reconciliation' (II Cor. v.18) developed that of the mystagogue.

c. The tendency which appeared in Ignatius bearing his own personal stamp had already existed in the Church prior to and contemporary with him, since it was conditioned by the particular situation of that age; for example, Ignatius found the monarchical episcopate already at hand in Asia Minor. Consequently, it is not surprising that John's Gospel by implication not only stood with I John against Gnosticism, but also countered the 'early catholic' tendency by stressing the proclamation, par-ticularly in the way in which it spoke of the sacraments and Church office.[17] John did not report any institution of the sacraments because they were not to be independent institutions, but he so formed Jesus' words in the relevant places that it becomes clear that the word which imparts salvation is only fully received when one accepts it in its concrete form of the sacra-ment (John iii.5; vi.51c–58).[18] In the same way he refuted the view that the office was an institution in itself. No designation of the office appears in either the Fourth Gospel or I John. Jesus alone is the Shepherd, although all the members of his Church are directly 'taught by God' (John vi.45 according to Jer. xxxi.33 f.; I John ii.20, 27) and are called to be his witnesses. By this token there may and indeed should be a special pastoral service in the Church,

---

[14] Cf. Nauck, *Die Tradition und der Charakter des ersten Johannesbriefs* (1957), 65 f.

[15] Cf. C. Maurer, *Ignatius von Antiochien und das Johannesevangelium* (1949); H. Köster, 'Geschichte und Kultus im Johannesevangelium und bei Ignatius von Antiochien', *ZThK*, 54 (1957), 56 ff.

[16] Ignatius, *Eph.* xx.2; *Rom.* vii.3, *et al.*

[17] Correctly observed already in A. Schlatter, *Die Theologie der Apostel* (²1922), 209–217.

[18] See E. Schweizer, 'Das johanneische Verständnis vom Herrenmahl', *Ev. Theol.* 12 (1952–53), 341–366 and L. Goppelt, *TWNT*, vi, 143 f. *contra* the literary-critical elimination of the Johannine references to the sacraments by E. Hirsch, R. Bultmann and G. Bornkamm (*ZNTW*, 47, 1956, 161–169); Th. Fritschel, 'The relationship between the Word and the Sacraments in John and in Ignatius' (Diss. Hamburg, 1962).

which is expressed accordingly in the appended chapter: 'Simon, son of John, do you love me more than these?' '. . . Feed my lambs' (John xxi.15 ff.).

5. Therefore, apart from Gnosticism's response, the same two contrasting solutions to the central problem within the Church appear continually at the close of the apostolic period. The teaching of the Church sought to make her existence in history possible in two different ways. One solution placed everything in terms of the proclamation, proclamation which was founded on historical tradition, given concrete form in the sacraments, and conveyed by the entire congregation through exhortation, intercession and church discipline. The other solution developed a pedagogical system of repentance, an adaptation to the natural ethos, an ordering of the Church and her message in a cosmos which was interpreted from a Christian viewpoint; and it came close to a mystery-type understanding of the Church as an institution of salvation. The former solution is represented on the whole by the writings of this period which were later canonized; the second is represented by the so-called Apostolic Fathers. The first appears as 'apostolic', the second as 'early catholic'. The first is not only supplemented by the second through the development of a more fixed form, but in many respects it was restricted and repressed. The first way preserved the dialectic tension between the eschatological and historical side of the Church characteristic of Paul, i.e. the tension between Spirit and institution. The second way chose to relax this tension by subordinating the first element to the second, while Gnosticism did the reverse. The Gnostics subordinated the institution to the spirit, but in doing so, they fell prey to 'another spirit'.

The recognition of this distinction between the two solutions is an extensive exegetical and theological decision in a discussion which goes all the way back to those early days of the Church. The discussion itself centres around three questions which blend into one another: First, where does the boundary lie between the apostolic and early catholic word? Secondly, what is the essence of each? Thirdly, how did Early Catholicism come about? The discussion has run its course in three stages.

a. How did the problem appear to those who were themselves involved? Although the early catholic viewpoint had set in quite early, we find no polemic against it in the apostolic writings; John's Gospel merely presents an indirect counter to it.[19] On the other side, however, the Apostolic

---

[19] The supposition that a conflict between Diothrephes, a monarchial bishop, and the Presbyter as a representative of Johannine Christianity stands behind III John (E. Käsemann, *ZThK*, 41, 1951, 292–311) has been refuted by R. Schnackenburg, 'Der Streit zwischen dem Verfasser des 3. Joh. und Diotrephes und seine verfassungsgeschichtliche Bedeutung', *Münch. Theol. Z.*, 4 (1953), 18–26 (cf. *TWNT*, vi, 671). On the *alogoi*, see Goppelt, *op. cit.* (n. 8), 266 f.

Fathers were fully aware of being the representatives of the first post-apostolic generation which looked back to its authoritative apostolic teachers. These fathers did not claim for themselves the authority of those earlier teachers, but they did consider themselves to be at one with them.

This claim by the Apostolic Fathers was questioned by Gnosticism, especially by Marcion, and by Jewish Christianity, both of whom had laid exclusive claim to specific apostles for themselves, but it was acknowledged to such an extent in the developing Early Catholic Church that I and II Clement, Hermas and Barnabas were considered at times to be on the same level as the apostolic writings (cf. pp. 123 f.). Should a difference in teaching be noticed, the Apostolic Fathers were usually given the preference unconsciously. As Tertullian, the Montanist, bitterly remarked, the 'pastor of adulterers' (Hermas) was favoured over Hebrews because the thought of the time was like that of Hermas and thus the passage on the once-for-all character of repentance in Hebrews was understood to be the rejection of this practice of repentance.[20] Even though James was at hand as an early apostolic document, it was apparently not read during the services, since his rigorous ethos had no place in a Church which thought along the lines of Hermas;[21] it was canonized quite late. The ancient Church ultimately drew the line of canonicity according to apostolic authorship. Basically, this insufficiently founded boundary line coincides strikingly with the distinction drawn above between what was apostolic and what was early catholic. Our distinction comes to us based on the criteria of the material, so that the delimitation of the canon appears to be the work of divine providence.

b. The Reformation under Luther was the first to lead to a material criterion for the canon and so to a material difference between the apostolic and post-apostolic writings of the Church. While Humanism sporadically applied historical criticism to the boundary of the canon, Luther dialectically combined his fundamental recognition of the traditional canon with the principle that the canon was to be evaluated in terms of its middle point, Christ.[22] According to this criterion he questioned the apostolic character of James, Jude, Hebrews and Revelation on the ground of an exegetical misunderstanding. Later, the earliest church history of the Reformation, Centuriae Magdeburgenses, maintained by this Reformation principle that the developing Catholic Church had begun already by the

[20] De Pud, 20.
[21] This Epistle was presented at the very latest c. A.D. 90 (cf. p. 138) and yet it still belonged to the antilegomena for Eusebius, H.E. 2, 23, 24 f.
[22] Forewords to the Septemberbibel (WA Deutsche Bibel 7), esp. 387, cf. J. Leipoldt, Der Neutestamentliche Kanon (1908), ii, 60–88; W. G. Kümmel, Das Neue Testament, Geschichte der Erforschung seiner Probleme (1958), 16 ff.

beginning of the second century to fall away from the apostolic truth in her constitution and in specific doctrinal elements.[23]

c. The modern historical study of primitive Christianity[24] has rejected the category of apostacy and has attempted to explain the various movements in terms of a historical development. Like Marcion, F. C. Baur believed that the main divisions were present even at the beginning, in the antithesis between the Judaism of the earliest apostles and Paulinism. This antithesis was then gradually resolved after an approach from both sides in the synthesis of Early Catholicism around 150 which could be seen in John's Gospel and in the Church of Rome. By contrast, A. Ritschl and A. Harnack found Catholicism already existent in the Apostolic Fathers,[25] especially in I Clement, and they explained it as the emergence of Hellenistic Christianity which was influenced but not dominated by the apostles. Harnack carried on an exhaustive debate about the nature of Catholicism with R. Sohm and Catholic theologians. For the history-of-religions school, the great hiatus in the history of primitive Christianity was the transition from Palestinian to Hellenistic Christianity. The adjective 'catholic' appeared only on the margin of their investigations, but at a most surprising place: they called the teaching on the sacraments which Paul had taken over from Hellenistic Christianity 'catholic'.[26] At this point, they understood Paul to be completely catholic, because they interpreted him solely in terms of Hellenistic analogies. By means of its exegesis, this school of thought thus brought about later exactly what had taken place of its own accord in the Church of the second century under the influence of her environment.

After the first world war, Bultmann attempted to use the historical analysis of the history-of-religions school to arrive by means of a theological, existential interpretation at the actual Gospel which was the kerygma

---

[23] *Centuriae Magdeburgenses; vol. ii, Norimbergiae* (1759), *praef.*

[24] Sources for the following, see pp. 1 f., 62 f. and Goppelt, *Christentum und Judentum*, 4–11.

[25] A. Ritschl. *Die Enstehung der altkatholischen Kirche* ([2]1857), 271 ff.; A. v. Harnack, *Entstehung und Entwicklung der Kirchenverfassung und des Kirchenrechts in den ersten zwei Jahrhunderten* (1910), esp. 173–186: The designation 'Catholic' should first be used for the period of Tertullian. ' "Catholicism" cannot be defined as the equating of the Church as an official body with the true Church of Christ' (R. Sohm), rather: 'Both the remoulding of Christian faith into a revealed philosophical-Hellenic teaching which is predicated apostolic and passed on through holy orders, through authority and thought as well as the equating of the empirical Church directed by the "apostolic" episcopate as an official body with the Church of Christ characterize the essence of Catholicism' (184 f.). This is prefigured in I Clement (Harnack, *Einführung in die alte Kirchengeschichte*, 1929). R. Sohm, *Wesen und Ursprung des Katholizismus* ([2]1912); P. Batiffol (cath.), *Urkirche und Katholizismus* (Ger. trans. 1910; E. Peterson, *Theologische Traktate* (1951), 193–321; exchange of letters with Harnack and whose ideal of Christian fellowship was that of the Quakers!

[26] W. Heitmüller, *Taufe und Abendmahl bei Paulus* (1903), 14 f.: 'Baptism was a

behind the text.[27] After 1945 the term 'early catholic' was used by his followers to differentiate elements, levels, and writings of the New Testament from its *kerygmatic* centre. Bultmann himself, without using the actual designation, had found a 'redaction by the Church' of this character in the Fourth Gospel.[28] It has now been ascertained by use of the older principle of examining the underlying tendency that the redaction of Luke[29] and Matthew's Gospel is supposedly early catholic. Not only is II Peter, whose canonicity certainly raises some questions, named as 'the clearest witness of Early Catholicism',[30] but 'strong traces of Early Catholicism' have also been found (which is logically to be expected) in Paul.[31] In general the criterion has been the removal of the eschatological thrust of the message and the subordination of the *pneuma* to the institution. These characteristics correspond to our observations. In these studies, however, the relationship of the eschaton and the *pneuma* to history has been understood in the onesided manner described above (cf. pp. 140 f.) and the questionable passages have been interpreted just as onesidedly in the opposite direction. Furthermore, these scholars have failed to undertake a comparative study of the unequivocal documents of Early Catholicism.[32] Such a comparison would have shown first that Luke and John's Gospel stand together with Paul on the opposite side to I Clement and Ignatius and secondly that the message of Luke, John and Paul which encompasses the two polar elements has rightly earned the designation 'apostolic'. Such a comparison might perhaps have brought about a revision of the hermeneutic principle which led to these distortions.

---

sacramental action for Paul which . . . worked *ex opere operato* (in the true Catholic sense)'; thus 'away with the principle of scripture and with the literal meaning and to the true Gospel with Luther' (p. 56)! P. Wernle, *Die Anfänge unserer Religion* (²1904), 196 f.: Paul is not the 'creator' but the one who '. . . develops the Catholic teaching of the sacraments'.

[27] So explained H. Schlier, *Bekenntnis zur katholischen Kirche* (⁴1956) and *Die Zeit der Kirche* (1956), postscript: The exegesis which he as a student of Bultman had both learned and taught forced him to go 'the way to the church', namely, the way to the Catholic Church, since he did not want to replace the canon of Scripture with the 'canon of the revelatory event' as did the *kerygmatic* theology. Cf. L. Goppelt, 'H. Schliers, "Weg zur Kirche"', *Ev.-Luth. K.Z.* (1956), 443–446.

[28] R. Bultmann, *Das Evangelium des Johannes* (Meyer Kommentar, ¹¹1950), *s.v.* 'Redaktion'.

[29] Ph. Vielhauer, *op. cit.* (n. 11), 15; E. Käsemann, 'Paulus und der Frühkatholizismus', in *Exegetische Versuche und Besinnungen* (1964), ii, 239–252.

[30] E. Käsemann, 'Eine Apologie der urchristlichen Eschatologie', *ZThK* 49 (1952), 296.

[31] E. Fuchs, 'Jesu Selbstzeugnis nach Matthäus 5', *ZThK* 51 (1954), 30, in reference to I Cor. v. 1–5.

[32] Thus F. Mussner (*Trierer Theol. Z.* (1959), 239, in a review of W. Marxsen's *Der 'Frühkatholizismus' im Neuen Testament* (Bib. Stud., 21, 1958) can call the picture of Catholicism, which is occasionally used, a 'primitive simplification which removes every theological difference'.

6. The concept, 'early catholic', becomes clear for us when we attempt to ascertain, as far as is summarily possible, just how its appearance came about. We have already seen in the survey of scholarship above what the history of the development has had to say as clarification of the term 'early catholic'. Naturally Early Catholicism was not a relapse setting in around the turn of the second century from the heights of a Church strongly influenced by the apostles, but the emergence and convergence of currents long present in the Church. The history-of-religions and history-of-tradition analysis which has been carried out since Harnack allows us now to view the writings of primitive Christianity as an intersection of a confusing plethora of Christian and pre-Christian traditions. It shows that the early catholic orientation arose among the Apostolic Fathers because the Old Testament-primitive Christian tradition had taken on an alien character through Hellenistic and Jewish influences. In other words, it had been Hellenized and Judaized. Just as the traditions of the Essenic-Palestinian Judaism had become dominant in Hermas,[33] so the conceptions of Stoicism imparted through the Hellenistic synagogue had become dominant in I Clement, and the influences of Hellenistic Gnosticism as well as the mysteries are found in Ignatius.[34] In Barnabas it was the hermeneutic principle of Alexandrinian Judaism. The Hellenistic influence had forced its way in through the environment from which these fathers themselves had arisen (unlike the majority of the New Testament authors) and partly through the Diaspora synagogue. The Jewish influence came through the traditions which had continually been passed on by means of personal contact, community tradition and the later Jewish literature, a large part of which was taken over at this time. These traditions had been particularly attractive since they had preserved the Old Testament community in the same Diaspora situation from disintegrating into syncretism.[35] (The development of the Early Catholic Church has indeed a certain analogy in the development of Judaism.)

The history of tradition, nevertheless, does not explain why these currents in the Church should have become prominent at just this point nor why these religious influences should become so strong. We also need to examine the conscious *kerygmatic* intent of these writings and their place in the Church. This shows that: first of all, the Apostolic Fathers wanted to preserve for their churches the apostolic witness as well as the reality of salvation to which this witness testified. The documents acknowledged by them as being authoritative were truly apostolic in character, and it

---

[33] J. P. Audet in *Rev. Bibl.* lx (1953), 41–82; R. Joly, *La Nouvelle Clio*, 5 (1953), 483–519.

[34] H. Schlier, *Religionsgeschichtliche Untersuchungen zu den Ignatiusbriefen* (1929).

[35] Cf. the introduction to *Kerygma Petru* in Hennecke, ³ii, 94 f. (Ger., II, 69 f.).

was proper that they should have accepted the documents in their entirety rather than have selected from them as did Gnosticism and Judaism. Secondly, they naturally had to apply the apostolic witness to their own situation, as Paul had to do for the Gentile Church and Hebrews or I John for the second generation; however, the application was free from any of the temporally, locally, or personally conditioned onesidedness which is usually characteristic of preaching relevant to a specific situation. Whereas the apostolic witness in Paul, Hebrews and I John was actually preserved in its new specific application, it was always truncated in the same fashion by the fathers. These writings no longer stand in proper relationship to the Old Testament nor to an eschatological grace, and this is their most distinguishing factor,[36] so that one cannot explain them as being mere supplements to the apostolic preaching with view to their particular situation. For example, what Hebrews had to say about repentance was more supplanted than supplemented by the system of repentance under Hermas.

Thirdly, this truncation of the message did not result primarily because the oral tradition of the Church, from which they had drawn, for example, the traditional sayings of Jesus, had become progressively vague in the post-apostolic period, nor because the Hellenistic Jewish influences had become increasingly stronger. The modification arose because it was believed not only that a setting of the Church in historical forms was necessary—this was the actual task of that generation—but also that the Church had to be made secure through these forms in order that she might be able to exist in history. The authoritative word which summoned one to obedience in faith was thus subordinated to the authority of a constitutionally established office, to the sacraments which functioned in a manner similar to the mystery religions, and to a system of repentance. They believed themselves to be directed to the institution by the Spirit (pp. 193 ff.), yet they fitted the Spirit into the institution.[37] The development of Early Catholicism was therefore also a 'falling away'.[38]

Fourthly, this modification of the message could only become the prevailing preaching of the Church during this period because the Church lacked Spirit-inspired teachers. Indeed, the spiritually active teachers, supposedly pneumatic in character, had to a great extent lent their voices to Gnosticism and betrayed the message to the spirit of the times. Finally, these men leading to Early Catholicism had nevertheless preserved the

---

[36] L. Goppelt, *Typos* (r.p. 1966), 24 ff.; J. Klevinghaus, *Die theologische Stellung der Apostolischen Väter zur alttestamentlichen Offenbarung* (1948); T. F. Torrance, *The Doctrine of Grace in the Apostolic Fathers* (1948).

[37] Cf. *TWNT*, vi, 449 f.

[38] So also O. Cullmann according to M. Werner, *op. cit.* (n. 1), vii.

apostolic witness in its broad scope and had basically subordinated their word to it,[39] so their congregations had remained the 'Church'. Had they not done so, the Gnostic movement might have caused Hellenistic Christianity to end in syncretism, just as Jewish Gnosticism brought Jewish Christianity to its end. On the basis of the apostolic witness preserved as a norm for the Church, some of the bias of the Apostolic Fathers was able to be corrected by the theologians of the Early Catholic Church.

This summary interpretation of the entire development during this period will be further clarified when we examine the development of the historical forces which gave form to the Church, the authorized (recognized) tradition which conveyed the proclamation, the preservation and delimitation of this tradition, the organs of the Church which represented and guarded this tradition, and its representation in the service of worship.

[39] Harnack (*Die Entstehung des Neuen Testaments* (1925), 25) takes this too lightly, and unjustifiably so: 'The Age of "enthusiasm" (literal sense) is closed and for the present the Spirit has been in the words of Tertullian (*adv. Prax.* 1)—"chased away". He has been chased into a book.'

CHAPTER V

THE DEVELOPMENT OF THE FORCES WHICH GAVE
FORM TO THE CHURCH

19. THE CHURCH, THE WORD, THE TRADITION
AND THE CANON

1. THE power within history which created, shaped and carried the
Church was a message which from its content was called 'the Gospel' and
from its origin 'the Word (of God)'.[1] It was issued in keeping with its
theological character as 'witness' to God's redemptive act through Jesus,
the redemptive act which 'fulfilled the scriptures', and hence was eschatological in nature. The message had the form of *kerygma*, which confronted
one personally as a 'proclamation', of 'teaching', and of 'prophecy'. Each
was passed on in keeping with its *Sitz im Leben* as a missionary summons
for the non-Christian to conversion and baptism, as a sermon and instruction for those baptized or as a pastoral word from brother to brother.
The transmission of the message in the Church became personally and
collectively effective in the celebration of the Lord's Supper (John vi.51c
ff.; cf. 1 Cor. xi.26) and focused on the individual in the granting of forgiveness as well as in the withholding of forgiveness and fellowship
(§20, 3).

Because the message became personal and individual in this manner,
it formed an *ecclesia* rather than a movement with a particular world-view
as did, for example, the popular philosophy of that day. For Paul this
ecclesia, as we are able to see particularly in I Corinthians, was an organism
with various manifestations. It was the flock of those called and baptized
by whom and among whom the word was preached, a flock who gathered
for the Lord's Supper, who separated itself as a sign from the unrepentant
(I Cor. v.11), and who on the basis of faith responded to the Gospel through
confession of faith, prayer, and service (I Cor. i.2; xii). Preserved by God's
faithfulness (I Cor. i.8 f.; x.13), the *ecclesia* follows the way of the cross to
the resurrection (I Cor. iv.7–13; II Cor. iv.7–18; Col. i.24). Each of these
facets of the life of the *ecclesia* is an extension of the message. Thus a

[1] J. Schniewind, *Euangelion* (vol. i, 1927, vol. ii, 1931); R. Asting, *Die Verkündigung
des Wortes Gottes im Urchristentum* (1939); E. Gaugler, 'Das Wort und die Kirche
im Neuen Testament', *IntKZ* (1939), 1–27; C. H. Dodd, *The Apostolic Preaching and
its Developments* (⁹1960); H. Schlier, 'Verkündigung im Gottesdienst der Kirche', in
Die Zeit der Kirche (1956) 244–264; *TWNT*, s.v.

fellowship is only an *ecclesia* to the extent that it lives from the Gospel, and can only then be recognized as such through a faith which itself knows the Gospel (II Cor. ii.3 f.); it was all important that the message of the Church remain the Gospel and that the Gospel maintain the central position in the Church. As we have seen, false teaching and Early Catholicism had called this into question in various ways.

Since the message was the witness to God's redemptive act in history, it could only be preserved as tradition. Only from the 'scriptures' could Jesus' appearance become known as God's eschatological redemptive act and be truly appreciated as the final fulfillment of faith in the God of the Old Testament; this oral tradition had to be transmitted as well as the scriptures which had already been set apart in principle (cf. p. 119). These scriptures were what II Cor. iii.14 designated for the first time as 'the Old Testament' in keeping with their central content (cf. pp. 38 f., 66, 162).

2. The problem of having a historical tradition[2] within an eschatological Church becomes apparent as early as the two Corinthian Epistles. In I Corinthians, Paul appealed to his apostleship and the tradition (I Cor. xv.1–11) against a distortion of the message which had been founded in terms of the *pneuma*. In II Corinthians, however, he appealed to the *pneuma* (II Cor. iii.1 ff.; xii.9 f.) against the office holders who had attempted to make their position and their tradition historically legitimate. In New Testament studies, too much emphasis has been placed on either the one or the other; according to one approach[3] the proclamation of primitive Christianity was always the application of a fixed tradition about the Christ event, but this fails to recognize that Paul only passed on the formula in I Cor. xv to the extent that he proclaimed it as the Gospel and interpreted it in terms of the current situation. This is the only type of interpretation which does justice to the Gospel's content and the Church's essential character. This formula can only be repeated as a confession of faith and thus transmitted as proclamation which itself summons to faith. In the Church of the New Covenant there cannot be a rabbinic office, as Jesus himself said (Matt. xxiii.8–10), nor can there be simply a historical tradition or authorized bearers of this tradition, because the Church was to be taught directly from God (Jer. xxxi.34; cf. John vi.45), through the Holy Spirit.

---

[2] Literature: A. Deneffe, S.J., *Der Traditionsbegriff* (1931); J. Ranft, *Der Ursprung des katholischen Traditionsprinzips* (1931); O. Cullmann, *Die Tradition als exegetisches, historisches und theologisches Problem* (1954); G. Gloege, 'Offenbarung und Uberlieferung', *ThLZ*, 79 (1954), 214–236; G. Ebeling, *Die Geschichtlichkeit der Kirche und ihre Verkündigung als theologisches Problem* (1954); L. Goppelt, 'Tradition nach Paulus', *Kerygma und Dogma* (1958), 123–233.

[3] E.g. J. N. F. Kelly, *Early Christian Creeds* ([2]1952), 11 f. and H. Schlier, *Die Zeit der Kirche* (1956), 216 f.

As a result, the opposite view[4] has held that there could only be a transmission of the Christ-event in the self-propagating proclamation interpreted in terms of the current situation. This view derives from the concept that the proclamation originated from the Easter faith which interpreted the cross. In fact, however, the proclamation was the witness or testimony of those witnesses who had been personally called, and it was based on the self-disclosure of the Risen One (§2, 4a). It is therefore appropriate that Paul should transmit a fixed formula in I Cor. xv and designate it expressly with the rabbinic terminology as historical tradition; yet at the same time he called it the Gospel which summons to faith.[5] Thus Christian tradition, according to its very nature, is simultaneously historical and *kerygmatic-pneumatic*. This twofold aspect of the tradition corresponds to the character of the Christ-event as well as the Church. Consequently, it is a characteristic of all types of genuine Christian tradition.

3. Paul took for granted that his churches were familiar with four different contents of the tradition. These four were then divided into two groups which belonged together: (1) the earliest *kerygma* in I Cor. xv.3–5 and (2) the account of the institution of the eucharist in I Cor. xi.23 ff., i.e. a part of the Gospel tradition. The latter was tradition 'from the Lord', just as the *logia* were cited as 'words of the Lord' (I Cor. vii.10; ix.14; I Thess. iv.15; cf. Acts xx.35). The words transmitted from the Christ who appeared in history were an absolute authority (I Cor. vii.10)—naturally within the framework of the *kerygma*—and, in the sense of I Cor. xii.3, they were also the norm for the work of the Spirit. However, instructions proclaimed as the word of the Exalted Lord through the Spirit were subject to the judgment of the Spirit working in the Church (I Cor. vii.25, 40; xiv.37 f.), and the same was true a generation later. No one had equated the word of the Exalted One in the Book of Revelation (i.10 ff.) with the interpreted word of the One who had appeared in history in John's Gospel (§6, 4c).

The Pauline Epistles also indicate where the Gospel tradition had its *Sitz im Leben*.[6] It is found in the Epistles almost solely in the *paraenesis* which occasionally cited words of the Lord or which were based on them —not because Paul thought so little of the tradition from the Jesus who had appeared in history but because this simply was not the place for its

---

[4] E.g. Bultmann, *Theology of the New Testament*, §§33, 5; 54, 2 f., and Ebeling, *op. cit.*, 67.

[5] I Cor. xv.1–3; cf. Goppelt, *op. cit.* (n. 1), 215 f.

[6] Literature: The Introduction of Feine-Behm-Kümmel, Michaelis, Wikenhauser; in addition K. Stendahl, *The School of St. Matthew* (1954); C. H. Dodd, 'The Primitive Catechism and the Sayings of Jesus', *New Testament Essays* (Studies in Mem. of T. W. Manson, 1959), 106–118; B. Gerhardsson, *Memory and Manuscript, Oral Tradition and Written Transmission in Rabbinic Judaism and Early Christianity* (1961), literature there; E. Larsson, *Christus als Vorbild* (1962), 26 f.; cf. §1, n. 19, and §7, n. 14.

transmission. The later primitive Christian Epistles, which obviously pre-supposed the Gospel tradition, used it just as sparingly. The Epistles correspond to the congregational sermon, which developed what the Exalted One had to say to the Church, but the main concern of the Gospel tradition was to show who the Exalted One is. The Gospel tradition, in a theologically reworked form, therefore, stood behind the Pauline Epistles; but, as the mnemonic formulation of the Synoptic tradition indicates, it was communicated in catechetical instruction and later, as Matthew's style indicates, in the liturgical readings. The communication of the Gospel tradition was thus far more remote from the Church's *kerygma* and far less influenced by it than the classical 'form criticism' supposed.

As well as the earliest *kerygma* and the Gospel tradition, which had to be tradition in view of its origin and content, Paul also classified other elements as tradition. These were elements which had arisen from the interpretation and application of this tradition to the particular situation of the Church. In the current terminology of today Paul recognized an 'ecclesiastical tradition' as well as the 'apostolic tradition'.

(3) In I Cor. xv. 3 ff., the earliest *kerygma* was passed on in the form of the Church's confession. A form-critical analysis of the Pauline Epistles reveals a number of doctrinal or confessional formulae which Paul had inserted into his expositions without expressly quoting them. These formulae were to a considerable extent tradition; for example, some even go back to the Palestinian Church.

(4) Finally, Paul frequently classified ethical instructions as tradition (I Cor. xi.2; II Thess. ii.15; iii.6; cf. I Thess. iv.1; Phil. iv.9?). He did not quote formulae in this case, but set forth basic principles. An analysis of the history of the tradition demonstrates that he was not simply taking over a primitive Christian moral catechism,[8] but was drawing on a stream of ethical traditions[9] which were continually being developed. These traditions, such as the tables of household duties,[10] frequently had their origin in pre-Christian Jewish and Hellenistic traditions. From this stream of tradition specific guide lines were singled out as valid for 'all churches' and thus became tradition in its true sense (I Cor. iv.17; vii.17; xiv.33). In this way the individual was not left alone with his conscience and the instructions of the Spirit, but he was referred to the practice of the

[7] Rom. x.9; I Cor. xii.3; vii.6;—Rom. i.3 f.; iii.25 f.; iv.25; viii.34; I Cor. x.16; I Thess. i.9 f.;—Phil. ii.6–11; Col. i.15–20.

[8] *Contra* A. Seeberg, *Der Katechismus der Urchristenheit* (1903).

[9] P. Carrington, *The Primitive Christian Catechism* (1940); E. G. Selwyn, *The First Epistle of St. Peter* (1952), Essay ii, 365–466.

[10] D. Schroeder, 'Die Haustafeln des Neuen Testaments' (unpublished diss., Hamburg, 1959).

Church of God (I Cor. xi.16); there was no evident casuistry. The guide lines were both applied and developed *kerygmatically;* they were not ordinances.

4. How did this fourfold tradition develop during the close of the apostolic period? The earliest *kerygma* merged into two other forms of 'apostolic' tradition: (a) it combined with the Gospel tradition, which had now emerged in an important role, to form a complete picture of Jesus' earthly ministry; and (b) it was unfolded in the apostolic *kerygma* or Gospel. Romans is the classic example of the latter, which was directly related to the Church's development of doctrine and confessions. From this latter form a third emerged (c) the tradition of the confessional formulae. This became in the course of the second century the expression of the *oral* apostolic tradition, whereas the original apostolic tradition (a and b) went into the canon. The stream of ethical tradition continued to flow and was developed further in the process, although ethical instructions were no longer introduced as tradition as they had been by Paul, but were passed on without any substantiation as a fixed commandment and ultimately as 'the new Law of our Lord Jesus Christ' (Barn. ii.6), despite the fact that they had only recently been taken over to a considerable extent from the Jewish and Hellenistic tradition. The commandments of the Shepherd of Hermas as well as the teaching of the Two Ways in Barn. xviii–xx par. Did. 1–6 are two examples of this. Let us now examine more closely these three elements which were classified as tradition in the post-Pauline period.

a. The Gospel tradition,[11] of which Luke i.1–4 speaks, had existed since the end of the Pauline period, fluctuating between oral tradition and Gospel writings. It continued in this manner until the latter emerged predominant at the end of this period around A.D. 120.

The ancient missionary outline of Jesus' earthly ministry (§6, 4c) was most probably portrayed in a complete written form for the first time in Mark's Gospel.[12] This written portrayal has been called a 'Gospel' ever since Justin first used the term.[13] Within a few years this Gospel, probably written between A.D. 64 and 70, had become so widespread and so respected in the Hellenistic Church that it was logically used as a text not only by Luke's Gospel, originating around A.D. 80 in the western Church, but also by Matthew's Gospel which had been written in Syria just a short time before Luke's Gospel.[14] Yet both Matthew and Luke,

[11] Literature on the following, see n. 6.
[12] V. Taylor, *The Gospel according to St. Mark* ([2]1966), 26–32 and 67–77.
[13] *Apol.* i, 66; Iren. 4, 20, 6.
[14] For the time and place of the writing of Matt., Mark, Luke, see Goppelt, *Christentum und Judentum*, 178 ff., 225 f. (lit.) and G. Bornkamm, 'Evangelien', *RGG*[3], 753–766.

as the Lucan foreword expressly states and an analysis of the history of the tradition substantiates, drew much from the stream of oral tradition as well. They reworked the Marcan material in terms of their redactional goals and also combined it occasionally with oral, parallel tradition so that we can no longer reconstruct the form of the Gospel which they had in front of them, although they remained amazingly close to the Marcan text. That which had been written was of more importance than the oral tradition, in spite of the fact that the latter had been referred to with such emphasis.

We can no longer determine with any degree of certainty to what extent Matthew and Luke reworked other written sources, Gospels or collections of pericopes and sayings, such as a written *logia* source (Q). Although Luke i.1 speaks of many other Gospel writers, no other Gospel appears at the beginning of the second century with anything comparable to the widespread acceptance and respect attained by these three Gospels.[15] Some of the apocryphal Gospels[16] of which we hear in the course of the second century have definite local importance, like the Gospel of Peter and the Gospel according to the Egyptians; others, like the Jewish Christian or Gnostic Gospels, are directly related to a separate theological movement or, like the Infancy Gospels and the Apocryphal Acts, are individual concoctions. To the extent that the sparse fragments allow a judgment, they have mostly taken the Synoptic Gospels as their point of departure and have also made use of numerous *agrapha*,[17] which often have the character of the Synoptic Gospels in style and terminology. Significantly, there is no trace of any Johannine *agrapha*.[18]

This fact shows that John's Gospel occupied an enigmatic place of its own within this development. It was familiar with the Synoptic tradition which had already been spread from Jerusalem to Rome in Paul's day, but it did not make use of it.[19] Instead it relied upon its own information

[15] T. Zahn, *Einleitung in das Neue Testament* (²1900), 16 f.

[16] W. Michaelis, *Die apokryphen Schriften zum Neuen Testament* (1956); E. Hennecke, *New Testament Apocrypha* (ed. R. McL. Wilson 1963) (Eng. trans. of *Neutestamentliche Apokryphen*, ed. W. Schneemelcher, ³1959), i; W. C. van Unnik, *Newly Discovered Gnostic Writings* (Eng. trans., 1960, of *Evangelien aus dem Nilsand*, 1960).

[17] A. Resch, *Agrapha* (²1960); J. Jeremias, *Unknown Sayings of Jesus* (Eng. trans., 1964, of *Unbekannte Jesusworte*, ²1951).

[18] A. Resch, 'Ausserkanonische Paralleltexte zu Johannes', *T.U.* x (1896–97), 61 f.: 'Source remnants like those behind the origin of the Synoptics are missing here!' Neither are there any points of contact between John's Gospel and the traditions peculiar to the Gospel according to Thomas which arose c. A.D. 160 (van Unnik, *op. cit.* (n. 16), 55).

[19] H. Windisch, *Johannes und die Synoptiker* (1926); T. Sigge, *Das Johannesevangelium und die Synoptiker* (1935); discussion in P. Menoud, *L'Evangile de Jean d'après les recherches récentes* (²1954), 27 ff.; E. Haenchen, 'Aus der Literatur zum Johannesevangelium, 1929–1950', *ThR* (1955), 295–335 and *ZThK* (1959), 19–54.

about Jesus' earthly ministry which gave a different picture of the whole and yet has proven itself to be historically reliable at numerous points.[20] This information did not underlie the Gospel in the form of personal memoirs but as tradition which was essentially oral rather than written in form (§17, 3), and it presented a terminology, particularly in the discourses, which Jesus did not use. Thus the tradition of Jesus was, so to speak, translated into a new terminology. At the same time the tradition was so conditioned by this terminology that the new interpretation went considerably beyond the scope of the tradition. For the most part it is no longer possible to differentiate between the two. The Gospel as a whole, apart from the fact that it is an unpretentious, redactional compilation, is undoubtedly the homogeneous work of a very unusual man. However, the terminology and the corresponding formulae were not created by him, but were developed in a stream of tradition which allows us to see both the distribution of the Johannine portrayal of Christ as well as the path this distribution took.

The terminology, style and thought-structure of John's Gospel and I John approach those of Ignatius, 'the Bishop of Syria', and the Odes of Solomon which also arose in Syria, but these elements are even closer to those of the Book of Revelation which was written in Asia Minor and they simultaneously refer back to Palestine (§17, 3) as well. It is therefore quite possible that certain men of the Palestinian Church had presented the tradition of Jesus through this mode of expression in their own homeland, then in Asia Minor and probably also in Syria. According to several indications John, the 'pillar apostle', and John of Ephesus, the author of Revelation whose identity must remain open, were the very heart of this movement whose choicest fruit was the Fourth Gospel. As early as c. A.D. 115 we meet a copy of this Gospel in Egypt (§17, note 51), which was certainly not its place of origin. Copies of it must therefore have been distributed just like those of the first three Gospels. Even the *Alogoi* themselves, who had rejected this Gospel, could not dispute the fact that it alone was recognized around the middle of the second century by the entire Church as belonging together with the three Synoptic Gospels.

In spite of this distribution of the Gospel writings, the Apostolic Fathers usually continued to quote the oral tradition,[21] unlike Justin who simply quoted from his memory of written material.[22] Thus the oral tradition was

[20] E. C. Hoskyns, *The Fourth Gospel* ([2]1948), 21–35; Dodd, *The Interpretation of the Fourth Gospel* (1954), 445; Dodd, *Historical Tradition in the Fourth Gospel* (1963); to the following cf. F.–M. Braun, *Jean le Theologien et son Evangile dans l'Eglise Ancienne* (1959).

[21] *The New Testament and the Apostolic Fathers* (1905); H. Köster, *Die synoptische Überlieferung bei den apostolischen Vätern* (T.U. 65, 1957), 258 ff.

[22] W. Bousset, *Die Evangelienzitate Justins d. Märtyrers* (1891).

still alive during the third generation in the *paraenesis*, and it is this category to which the literature of these fathers belong. The Gospel writings, on the other hand, were used in the liturgy and catechesis and thus achieved an authoritative role. This became increasingly necessary with the passing of time. Unlike the Gospels written in the second generation, oral tradition coming to light in the Apostolic Fathers had become considerably modified in an apocryphal manner by means of the environmental influences and the needs of the Church. These modifications corresponded to the tendency observable throughout the third generation as a whole, so they permit one to draw only qualified conclusions concerning the previous development of this tradition. They do make clear what an examination of the extra-canonical tradition, in particular the *agrapha*,[23] reveals: seen in terms of the whole, the only genuine tradition of Jesus which extends beyond the third generation was that which entered our four Gospels. The stream of oral tradition had disintegrated.[24]

That which was preserved in this written manner was in no way an arbitrary choice from the tradition of Jesus; instead, the *kerygmatic* character of this tradition permitted the elements themselves to emerge which told the Church who Jesus was. They were even preserved at times as duplicate traditions. As well as the accounts of the first Easter, the earliest apostolic *kerygma* also went into the Gospels as their starting point (I Cor. xv)

b. The earliest *kerygma* was also evolved with reference to the Church, particularly as seen in the Pauline Gospel for the Jews and Gentiles (Romans). How was this to have been preserved for the Church? The Pastorals were the first to handle this question which became even more acute after the loss of the apostles.[25] Here 'Paul' does not speak as in his authentic Epistles of various traditions which he himself had received, but calls all the message which stems from him, in other words his Gospel, as παραθήκη, i.e. the deposit (trust) which Timothy was to maintain and to represent (I Tim. vi.20; II Tim. i.12–14). The Pastorals did not use the *paradosis*-terminology which we met in Paul, but speak of a

[23] J. Jeremias, *op. cit.* (n. 17), 32 f., found only 21 of the large number of agrapha which '. . . could lay the same claim to authenticity as the traditional sayings in the four Gospels'. On the Gospel according to Thomas, cf. above all: van Unnik, *op. cit.*, (n. 16); O. Cullmann 'Das Thomasevangelium und die Frage nach dem Alter der in ihm enthaltenen Tradition', *ThLZ*, 85 (1960), 321–334; E. Haenchen, *ThR* 27 (1961), 147 ff., 306 ff.; W. Schrage, *Das Verhältnis des Thomas-Evangeliums zur synoptischen Tradition und zu den koptischen Evangelienübersetzungen* (1964).

[24] E.g. the Didache (1, 3–6) softened the commands of the Sermon on the Mount and applied them to the practice of the Church. E. L. Wright, *Alterations of the Words of Jesus as quoted in the Literature of the Second Century* (1952, 15–71 and Köster, *op. cit.* (n. 21), 261 ff., cite motives for the transition into the apocrypha element.

[25] Literature: H. v. Campenhausen, *Kirchliches Amt*, 169 ff., 176; M. Dibelius–H. Conzelmann, *Die Pastoralbriefe* (*HNT*, ⁴1955).

παραθήκη. Perhaps this change in terminology resulted from the fact that the Gnostic opponents here had appealed in a fashion similar to that in Colosse (Col. ii.8) to *paradosis*. At any rate, the intention behind this difference was to describe the Gospel of Paul as an unchangeable, fixed quantity which one can only preserve. Does this correspond to the intention of the Apostle Paul?

It has frequently been maintained ever since Jülicher[26] that only the scriptures and the Lord were authorities for Paul. Moreover, Paul himself expected from the churches founded by him merely 'a respectful reception of and an obedience to' his writings. In fact, however, Paul was conscious of being called to a witness by means of a unique revelation of Christ which only the earliest apostles had experienced. This was a witness which was the foundation for all future witnesses (Gal. i.16 f.; I Cor. xv.1–11). As the apostle to the nations of the world he presented this witness to the church of the world's capital. Thus the Pastorals had only neglected the fact that Paul also spoke of the preaching of the earliest apostles (I Cor. xv.11) and had let it be known that the apostolic Gospel was to be continually interpreted anew, as for example in Hebrews, which contains an interpretation based on an early oral witness. The Pastorals did then bring to bear in the post-Pauline situation a definite intention of Paul which they narrowed but did not distort. For example, they did not combine the principle of tradition with that of succession, but stressed that the tradition could only be preserved through the Spirit (II Tim. i.14).

The Apostolic Fathers[27] also wanted to maintain the apostolic Gospel. They named 'the apostles' as well as 'the prophets,' i.e. the Old Testament, and 'the Lord' (this meant above all the *logia*) as the authority which determined faith and practice (Ignatius, *Phild.* v.1 f.; Polycarp, *Phil.* 6, 3; II Clem. xiv.2; II Pet. iii.2). However, that which in the opinion of the author had become the proper teaching and order for the Church was simply claimed, without reflection, to be the instruction of the apostles (Did., *inscr.*, I Clem. xlii.1–4). Thus the apostles' instruction became law, whereas it only had authority for Paul and the New Testament writings of the second generation to the extent that it unfolded the earliest witness through the Spirit.[28] It is significant that the apostles' instruction was also

---

[26] *Einleitung in das Neue Testament* ([7]1931), 455, 458; on the discussion, most recently: H. v. Campenhausen, *Die Begründung kirchlicher Entscheidungen beim Apostel Paulus* (SAH, 1957); Bultmann, *Theology of the New Testament*, §34, 1; G. Blum, *Tradition und Sukzession: Studien zum Normbegriff des Apostolischen von Paulus bis Irenäus*, 1963).

[27] Jülicher, *op. cit.*, (n. 26), 458–466.

[28] Gal. i.16 f.; I Cor. xv.1–11; Luke i.2: 'Just as they were delivered to us by those who from the beginning were eyewitnesses and ministers of the word'; John xxi.24; I John i.1 ff.; Eph. ii.20; Matt. xvi.18; Rev. xxi.14

sought in the Epistles of Paul by I Clement, Ignatius and even by II Peter,[29] while Acts and the Pastorals did not refer to them. Thus for the third generation, oral tradition and written documents also stood side by side in the transmission of the apostolic Gospel. This relationship was clarified for the first time when the Valentinians and other Gnostic schools appealed to a secret 'apostolic tradition',[30] which led to the discussion in which the early catholic fathers (in the West) finally fell back upon the apostolic writings and the *regula fidei*.[31] The apostolic Gospel has been preserved in its essence only in the former, in the actual application to the particular situation, but the confessional and liturgical formulae of the second century corresponding to the actual preaching in a given situation were further developments of the formulae by which the primitive Church had summarized her response to the Gospel. These earlier formulae have been preserved for us only in the canon.

c. Even Paul took a confessional tradition[32] of the Church for granted, although he only used the terms ὁμολογία and ὁμολογεῖν for the actual practice of confession of faith (Rom. x.9 f.). In the Pastorals, Hebrews and I John, the term ὁμολογία acquired the meaning 'confessional formula'.[33] In Jude 3 and II Pet. ii.21, confessional formulae were expressly designated as tradition. The communication of such formulae was in keeping with the essence of confession as long as it continued to be interpreted *kerygmatically*, as Hebrews reflects in an exemplary manner,[34] so that it really was repeated as the response of faith, and as long as it remained open for a new confession which could be demanded by a new situation of the Church. For example, the early confession of the Hellenistic Church, Jesus is Lord (I Cor. xii.3; Rom. x.9; Phil. ii.11), did not suffice against docetism. To counter this, one needed to confess according to I John iv.2, 'Jesus Christ has come in the flesh'. This sentence was repeated literally in Polycarp, *Phil.* 7, 1 and in substance by Ignatius (*Smyr.* v.2; cf. vii.1). It had become, as I John intended, a confessional formula

---

[29] I Clem. xlvii.1 ff.; Ignatius, *Eph.* viii.1; xii.2; *Rom.* iv.3; Polycarp, *Phil.* 1 : 2; 3 : 2; 11 : 3; II Pet. iii.15 f.; T. Zahn, *Grundriss der Geschichte des neutestamentlichen Kanons* (²1904), 35 ff.; E. Käsemann, 'Paulus und der Frühkatholizismus' *Exegetische Versuche und Besinnungen* (1964), ii, 239–252.

[30] We find this phrase for the first time in a letter from Ptolemaeus to Flora (Epiphanius, *pan.* 33, 7).

[31] H. v. Campenhausen, *Kirchliches Amt*, 172–194; H. E. W. Turner, *The Pattern of Christian Truth* (1954), 309–386.

[32] Literature: H. Lietzmann, 'Symbolstudien', ZNTW, 21 (1922), 1–34; (1923), 257–279; (1925), 193–202; (1927), 75–95; F. J. Badcock, *The History of Creeds* (1938); O. Cullmann, *Die ersten christlichen Glaubensbekenntnisse* (1943); J. N. D. Kelly, *Early Christians Creeds* (²1952).

[33] O. Michel, *TWNT*, v, 210 f. 216 f.

[34] Heb. viii interprets 'sitting at the right hand' as a part of the confession (iv.14; x.23).

in the liturgy. As long as the earlier formula had a definite meaning, the new confessional formula did not invalidate the old formula. There was a multiplicity of formulae in the primitive Church, having the form of one, two, or three lines, and speaking from the very beginning about God's work. They were used mainly at baptisms but also in services, especially at ordinations (I Tim. vi.12 f.), against false teaching (I John iv.2) and as a witness against opponents.[35]

5. How were the writings that were later canonized related to the oral tradition in the period up to A.D. 120?[36] We see today that these writings, the Gospels included, were not collections of tradition, but were a particular *kerygma*, which might contain varying amounts of tradition, for a definite situation in the Church. The Epistles at any rate had unthinkingly been considered in precisely this manner by the close of the apostolic period, and so were distinguished from the tradition.

I Clement in Rome, Ignatius and Polycarp (*Phil.*) in Asia Minor and Syria had presupposed even around A.D. 100 a collection of the Pauline Epistles[37] which in all probability contained the majority of our Pauline Epistles apart from the Pastorals, but these Epistles were not quoted in the same way as the Old Testament. It alone stood as the 'scriptures'.[38] The Epistles of the Apostle Paul were, however, respected as that for which they were intended, as the word in the form of a sermon for one particular time and yet a word that was to remain and to give direction.

The Epistles would not have had this import around A.D. 100 had they not been exchanged from the very beginning, between the churches as they occasionally demanded,[39] and read in the services in place of the sermon but not in place of the scripture reading. It was only because the

---

[35] Cullmann, *op. cit.* (n. 32), 13–29.

[36] Literature: a history of the canon is to be found in most of the New Testament introductions; the older literature in Jülicher, *op. cit.* (n. 26); a classic is T. Zahn, *Die Geschichte des Neutestamentlichen Kanons* (2 vols., 1888–92); *Grundriss der Geschichte des neutestamentlichen Kanons* (²1904); J. Leipoldt, *Geschichte des neutestamentlichen Kanons* (2 vols., 1907–08); A. v. Harnack, *Das Neue Testament um das Jahr 200* (1889), *contra* Zahn; *Die Entstehung des Neuen Testaments* usw. (1914); on the basic principles, A. M. Hunter, *The Unity of the New Testament* (1952); R. Bultmann, *Theology of the New Testament*, §55; W. G. Kümmel, 'Notwendigkeit und Grenze des neutestamentlichen Kanons', *ZThK*, 47 (1950), 277–313; W. Schneemelcher, in Hennecke ³i, 28–60 (Ger. 1–31).

[37] I Clem. xlvii.2; Ignatius, *Eph.* xii.2; Polycarp, *Phil.* 3 : 2. Cf. W. Hartke, *Die Sammlung und die ältesten Ausgaben der Paulusbriefe* (1917); A. v. Harnack, *Die Briefsammlung des Apostels Paulus und die anderen vorkanonischen Briefsammlungen* (1926); cf. G. Bornkamm, *op. cit.* (§12, n. 40), 35, n. 132 (further literature).

[38] G. Schrenk, *TWNT*, i, 750–761.

[39] I Thess. v.27; Col. iv.16; Polycarp sent Ignatius' epistles to Philippi at the request of the church (Polycarp, *Phil.* 13 : 2 = I *Phil.* 1 : 2). The sermon which II Clement has recorded was read publicly (II Clem. xix.1). I Clement was also read regularly in Corinth (Eusebius, *H.E.* 4, 23, 11).

Pauline Epistles had come to be appreciated in this way that it became the practice in the post-Pauline period to impart exhortations and encouragement to the churches in letter form, even when there were no personal messages involved, as in James or I John. II Peter, which could hardly have originated later than A.D. 120, placed itself and I Peter alongside the Pauline Epistles (iii.1 f., 15 f.). Thus the early collection of the Pauline Epistles gave rise to the writing as well as to the collection of corresponding Epistles. They actually became one of the nuclei for the later crystallization of the canon.

The other nucleus with Revelation, which was itself intended to be preserved as a Book (xxii.7, 9, 18 f.) and which attracted other apocalypses, was the Gospels. Around A.D. 80, Mark's Gospel had gained validity for itself in the entire Church alongside the oral tradition, as did Matthew's Gospel around A.D. 100 (cf. pp. 156 f.). Luke's Gospel and John's Gospel were the only others to follow in this manner. The first impetus to combine these Gospels, which had generally been accepted as one collection, probably resulted from the fact that John's Gospel placed itself emphatically alongside the Synoptic tradition and its Gospels, while simultaneously taking their presence for granted. It is not merely coincidental that the origin of such a Gospel collection[40] appeared for the first time in the homeland of John's Gospel in Asia Minor. When Papias' presbyter explained around A.D. 100 that Mark had not represented Jesus' work in its proper order and that Matthew had collected the Lord's sayings in Hebrew, he was probably attempting to justify the position of John's Gospel alongside them (Eus. 3, 39). Papias accepted this collection, and Irenaeus from Asia Minor had been familiar with the 'Fourfold Gospel' since his youth, c. A.D. 140 (Haer. 3, 11, 8). It is quite possible that the canon of the Four Gospels had developed around A.D. 140 in Asia, and in view of similar preparation elsewhere had spread through the Church to such an extent that it was attested for in Rome c. A.D. 180 by the Muratorian Canon. It is not surprising that this collection was found second to the Epistles on the list.

The combination of the Gospel collection with that of the Epistles was foreshadowed in the Apostolic Father's formula, 'the Lord, the apostles, the prophets' (cf. p. 160) and exemplified by Luke's writings. It actually appeared for the first time towards the end of this period in II Peter. According to II Pet. iii.1 f., 'the Epistles' of the apostles were to remind them of ' . . . the predictions of the holy prophets and the commandment of the Lord and Saviour (witnessed) through your apostles'. The third

---

[40] Harnack, Die Entstehung des Neuen Testaments (1914), 46 ff.; O. Cullmann, 'Die Pluralität der Evangelien als theologisches Problem im Altertum', ThZ, 1 (1945), 23–42.

phrase in juxtaposition to the first two could only mean writings as well and would thus refer most probably to the Gospels.

The setting of these three side by side indicates that II Peter was the first document prior to Justin which placed the apostolic Epistles (as well as the Gospels) deliberately and emphatically on the same level as the writings of the Old Testament. In iii.14 f., Paul's Epistles were classified just like the Old Testament (cf. i.20) as γραφαί, 'scriptures'. The author was conscious of what he was saying when he used the term 'scripture', since he excluded the apocryphal quotations when quoting from Jude in II Pet. ii, and so differentiated sharply between canonical and apocryphal writings. The classifying of the apostolic writings as scripture was neither coincidental nor traditional; it resulted from the theological principle which the author used in his attempt to procure a standing for the Gospel. II Peter developed the principle of scripture, and in so doing he encountered its hermeneutical problem (i.20 f.; iii.16). The latest writing of the New Testament thus set the seal of canonicity to the apostolic writings. This Epistle itself stands on the margin of the canon, but its theological principle comes much closer to that of the New Testament starting point than to the theological principle of I Clement or Ignatius.

Another occasion for the evaluation of the primitive Christian documents as 'scripture' had already arisen earlier, when the Gospels came to be read as well as the 'prophets' in the liturgy of the service. This was expressly mentioned first by Justin (c. A.D. 150, §22, 5a), but the material of Matthew's Gospel could have received its style as a result of being used as a liturgical reading.[41] The Synoptic tradition and the Gospels, including John, were initially devised with a view to the catechesis and might well have also taken the place of the sermon. (Justin was the first to combine unequivocally the term 'Gospel' with the formulae which one used when quoting the Old Testament.[42] In so doing he assimilated these theologically with the evaluation of the scriptures being developed at that time.)

Thus the beginning of the New Testament Canon did not result from a search for Christian 'scriptures' which corresponded to the Old Testament. It resulted on the one hand from the basic principle that the Church lived by the apostolic witness, which was bound up with the witness of the Spirit and the scriptures (John v.39; xiv.26; Rom. i.2; I Cor. xiv.37 f.), and on the other hand from a number of writings which claimed to apply *kerygmatically* a genuine witness directly from the apostles (Gal. i) or

[41] G. D. Kilpatrick, *The Origins of the Gospel according to St. Matthew* (²1950).

[42] Justin, *Dial.* 100, 1, 'It is written in the Gospel'. Prior to this, quotations were introduced by 'For the Lord says in the Gospel' (II Clem. viii.5, cf. Did. 8, 2) or 'remembering the words of the Lord Jesus which he spoke' (I Clem. xiii.1 f.; xlvi.7 f.; Acts xx.35). When Barn iv.14 and II Clem. ii.4 introduce sayings of Jesus with 'it is written' and/or 'the scripture says', it is uncertain whether or not the author meant to quote the Old Testament.

from the tradition (Luke i.1 ff.). This claim was so confirmed by the Spirit that the writings came to be used regularly in the churches. The Church did not of itself and for itself create a canon then, but the apostolic writings brought about their own acceptance through the dialogue between their own claim and the witness of the Spirit at work in the Church. The Church first took this into account when she coined the concept and the name of the New Testament Canon in her struggles between A.D. 130–180 with Gnosticism. She placed its three elements in this relationship: the collection of the Gospels, the collection of the Epistles and Revelation—all connected together by Acts. The Church later marked off the whole after a lengthy process.

The development of tradition, like the development of the canon, took place in the continual struggle against a false Gospel.

20. THE PURITY AND UNITY OF THE CHURCH: HERESY AND THE SINS OF THE CHRISTIANS

1. We have already seen how the Church distinguished herself at the centre of her message from the religion of the Jews and pagans, the un-believers, through her unique claim to absolute truth. She withdrew in a similar manner from the false faith within her own walls.[1] Besides mis-sionary and apologetic struggles with her surroundings, the struggles with these appearances later called 'heresies' were most influential in leading to a theological development of the message; indeed it occasioned a con-siderable part of the early Christian literature from Paul to Ignatius. Ever since the Apostolic Council it had led to consolidation within the Church as well as to splits, both of which took on organisational form after this period. Seen from a historical perspective, heresy was neither apostacy nor a falling away from a previous teaching; it was a development of a still unexplored possibility which furthered the total development through the byplay of effect and counter-effect. The men of the earliest Church, however, viewed this interaction theologically, and in doing so grasped the heart of the matter.

Paul permitted an amazing variety in the forms of life and teaching within the Church. He joined together not only with Peter but also with

---

[1] Literature: On the content of the various false teachings see the introductions and excurses in the commentaries; on the basic principles: W. Bauer, *Rechtgläubigkeit und Ketzerei im ältesten Christentum* (1934); G. L. Prestige, *Fath and Heretics* (1940); O. Schmitz, 'Die Grenze der Gemeinde nach dem Neuen Testament', *Ev. Theol.* 14 (1954), 6–22; H. E. W. Turner, *The Pattern of Christian Truth* (1954); L. Goppelt, 'Kirche und Häresie nach Paulus', in *Beiträge zur historischen und systematischen Theologie* (*Gedenkschrift* for W. Elert, 1955), 9–23; Bultmann, *Theology of the New Testament*, §55, 4 f.

James and the churches under the latter's influence (I Cor. xv.11; cf. Gal.
ii.1-10), suddenly drawing an absolute limit when a form of teaching
entered Galatia and Corinth which was no longer the Gospel and whose
representatives were no longer brethren, i.e. members of the Church
(Gal. i.6 ff.; II Cor. xi.4 ff.). The men of Jerusalem might have judged
this teaching differently, but they also had made known their fellowship
with Paul (Gal. ii.9) and had fought against false prophets and teachers.
The latter is demonstrated by the warnings of Matt. vii.15-20; xxiv.11
and Rev. ii.20; xiii.11 ff. which stem from the Palestinian tradition.
Even in the writings of the post-Pauline period, an extraordinary variety
in the Church's life and teaching was recognized again and again, yet
at the same time certain forms of teaching and its corresponding life were
radically repudiated.

This distinction had taken place so much in terms of the particular
situation that an appropriate terminology had not yet been developed
even by the close of this period.[2] The error was mostly referred to in the
Old Testament fashion by compounds with ψευδ- and ἑτερο-. The
Pastorals alone developed a term for correct teaching when they spoke
of the 'sound words' or the 'good doctrine', but the more philosophical
formulae with ὀρθός, 'correct', which conveyed the meaning of a correct
system rather than the true, redeeming message, were also missing here.
The phrase αἱρετικὸς ἄνθρωπος (Tit. iii.10) appears occasionally in
the Pastorals. The αἵρεσις[3] was originally a school or group within the
Church, as among the Jews and Greeks, and it had nothing to do with
false teaching. Paul condemned this appearance of αἱρέσεις, accepted
as perfectly natural by the Jews and Greeks, and also the σχίσματα which
were conditioned more by personalities than by the subject matter itself,
since both had emerged from an exaggerated emphasis on the particular
individual rather than on the multiplicity of service (I Cor. xi.18 f.; Gal.
v.20). Tit. iii.10 was intended for the followers of a group, which at the
same time suggested an erroneous teaching, although 'group' and 'erroneous teaching' were still not yet identical, not even in Ignatius (Eph. vi.2;
Trall. vi.1). The term αἵρεσις first acquired the second meaning of
'heresy' in Justin, Dial, 80, 4, in Irenaeus and in the Muratorian Canon (65).
In these the Church appeared as a continuous, world-wide unity whose
teaching was an unvarying quantity; by contrast, the 'heresies' appeared
as locally and temporally limited groups which had fallen away from the
established truth (Irenaeus, Haer. 20). The self-designation καθολική (catholica) thus characterized the Church not only as universal (Ignatius,
Smyr. viii.2) but also as apostolic and orthodox (Mur. Can. 61 f., 66, 69;

[2] Bultmann, ibid., §55, 4; TWNT, ii, 701.
[3] TWNT, i, 180 ff.

Clem. Alex. *Strom.* 7, 106 f.). The Pastorals, in keeping with their concept of tradition appear to approach this early catholic viewpoint,[4] but the teaching remained a message for them rather than a given system. The majority of the teaching was certainly not handed down to Paul but was developed from the Gospel against a particular error (I Cor. xv. 1 ff). Because of this, primitive Christianity had a different conception of heresy to that of Early Catholicism.

What was the essence of these appearances which were condemned over and over again and which we shall call 'heresy' for the sake of brevity? For Paul heresy had a twofold characteristic. First of all, it brought 'a different Gospel, a different Christ, and a different Spirit' (Gal. i.6–9; II Cor. xi.4). Yet it wanted to represent the genuine as well as the entire message, and attempted to substantiate this by appealing to the earliest apostles (Gal. i.17; II Cor. xi.5) or to tradition (Col. ii.8) as well as by demonstrating it to be pneumatic in character (I Cor. xii.3; cf. I John iv.2; Rev. ii.20). The 'other Gospel' was deceptively similar to the true one, and yet was just its counterpart stamped by the spirit of this world, an expression of anti-Christianity, according to I John iv.3. The second characteristic was therefore its perversion of the Christian existence, a false faith (Gal. v.11; vi.12). The warnings in Matt. vii.15–20, 23, and in the letters to the churches (Rev. ii.6, 20) judged the corrupting elements by their 'fruits' alone, i.e. by their total conduct,[5] This second criterior, even if it was crudely understood in the Pastorals,[6] Jude and II Peter, should not be misunderstood as a moral defamation by a different theological thought. False teaching is not simply a different theological opinion but a pseudo-Gospel which of necessity must have a corresponding pseudo-faith.

2. While the majority of the New Testament writings simply addressed the particular heretical message apodictically and pointed directly to the resultant fruits, Paul, and in part Ignatius, characterized it by means of theological reasoning. They did not examine it historically or systematically nor did they judge it solely from a prophetic standpoint, but put it in the context of the Christian tradition from both its historical and pneumatic side. Paul emphasized that he had received his Gospel in the same manner as the earliest apostles, through a revelation of Jesus (Gal. i), and linked his witness in I Cor. xv.3–8 with that of the apostles. Only the message which stems from this original authorized witness is Gospel. However, since this message could not be reduced to a sum of its statements, its origin was not substantiated historically, e.g. by means of letters

[4] Goppelt, 'Kirche und Häresie nach Paulus' (as in n. 1), 11, 18 f.
[5] Cf. *TWNT*, vi, 858, 18 ff.
[6] I Tim. i.19; vi.3 ff.; II Tim. ii.18; iii.8.

of recommendation demonstrating a kind of succession (II Cor. iii.1 ff.; v.16); instead, this message bears witness to a reality which has been established *heilsgeschichtlich*, i.e. in the final and exclusive mediation of salvation in Christ, and yet is only realized in a pneumatic, existential fulfillment. The criterion by which Paul judged the content of the message was this reality of salvation, a redemptive existence through Christ alone, not with legalistic achievements or by accompanying cosmic means (Gal. ii.21; Col. ii.8), and so from God alone and not from ourselves (I Cor. i.31; II Cor. x.17). The historical witness and this, its substance of reality, are only and always given together, and it can only be understood in faith through the Spirit. Therefore, according to I Cor. xii.10, the function of determining the spirits was a charisma. That which was the truth, in opposition to the 'other Gospel', could only be proclaimed *in actu* through a believing theological understanding, and it could only be confessed on the basis of faith.

At the same time, this was the fundamental attack against false teaching. In countering such teaching Paul did not simply quote formulae which had come to him, but unfolded through his teaching the apostolic witness with reference to the new question. Since the false teaching involved a false faith, it could only be positively overcome by means of the word which leads to faith. Paul demonstrated the authority of his witness for the truth in that he spoke the anathema over the representatives of the false teaching. This took place in a conditional form in order that the possibility of repentance might remain open: 'If anyone should preach to you another Gospel . . . let him be accursed', i.e. singled out for God's judgment. The excommunication of the unrepentant from the congregation (cf. I Cor. v.9; I Tim. i.20) corresponds to this delivery of one to God's judgment. With the same authority, I John contrasted, once again in antithetical form, truth with false teaching. At the same time he placed the Church under an obligation to withhold the prayer of intercession from him who persisted in false teaching as one who commits ' . . . the sin which is mortal'. (I John v.16). In the case of the member who tends in the direction of false teaching, the Pastorals recommended that the office holder use a procedure which was prescribed in Matt. xviii.15 ff. against brethren who had sinned in the Church.[7] Ignatius bound the Church members to a fellowship under the bishop similar in kind to the mystery religions in order to withdraw them from the Gnostic conventicles, but he did not develop any procedure against the Gnostics themselves.[8] In this way the struggle with heresy became more institutional.

---

[7] Tit. iii.10; cf. I Tim. i.3, 20; II Tim. ii.24 ff.; iv.2 f.; Tit. i.9–14, cf. H. v. Campenhausen, *Kirchliches Amt*, 156 f.

[8] v. Campenhausen, *ibid.*, 155 f.

Unlike the later second century, as far as we can tell, no organizational groups resulted from the struggle with heresy during this period. This was not because the differences were viewed merely as varieties of theological movements, whereas in the second century one movement had become more or less absolute and had marked the others out as heresies (cf. Justin, *Dial.* 80, 4), a phenomenon seen in Judaism after A.D. 70.[9] If such had been true, the leading Church would have been 'the most successful heresy',[10] and Paul would have rejected the opponents in Galatia more because of their intolerant dogmatism than the content of their teaching.[11] In fact, even the men of primitive Christianity had seen here irreconcilable opposites, but these opposites could only then be marked off organizationally after organization and teaching had become more consolidated. This consolidation was partly inherent in the development itself, but also partly due both to the rapid growth of the organization along constitutional lines and lines comparable to the mystery religions and to the approximation of the primitive Christian type of teaching to a type more like that of a philosophical system. Thus, in the second century, a historical, static element developed out of the eschatological and dynamic without the latter disappearing.

3. While the confrontation with heresy contributed greatly to the creation of both the theology and the Church on a larger scale, the problem with the sins of the Christians,[12] which corresponded in many ways with that very confrontation, conditioned the everyday experiences of the local congregations and the individual believers. This is seen especially in the prototypes of the forms which we now call priestly guidance, confession, repentance and discipline. This same problem had also been felt very strongly by the Jewish community, and it led to the practice of repentance and banishment, to the differentiation between sinners and righteous and to the movements of the Pharisees and Essenes. Jesus thoroughly opposed this differentiation, just as he did the Jewish conceptions of repentance, so the earliest Christian churches which came from

[9] W. Bauer, *op. cit.* (n. 1), *passim.*
[10] M. Werner, *Die Entstehung des christlichen Dogmas* ([2]1953), 138.
[11] W. Bauer, *op. cit.* (n. 1), 237 f.
[12] Literature: on the essential principles: H. Windisch, *Taufe und Sünde im ältesten Christentum bis auf Origines* (1908); P. Althaus, *Paulus und Luther über den Menschen* ([3]1958); J. Behm, *TWNT*, iv, 972–1004; B. Poschmann, *Paenitentia secunda* (1940); A. Kirchgässner, *Erlösung und Sünde im Neuen Testament* ([2]1951); Bultmann, *Theology of the New Testament*; on Church discipline: v. Dobschütz, *Die Briefe an die Thessalonicher* (*Meyer Kommentar* [7]1909, on II Thess. iii.15; R. Bohren, *Das Problem der Kirchenzucht im Neuen Testament* (1952); W. Doskocil, *Der Bann in der Urkirche* (1958); v. Campenhausen, *Kirchliches Amt*, 135–162, 244, n. 4; on the Old Testament-Jewish background: E. Sjöberg, *Gott und die Sünder im palästinischen Judentum* (1938); *S.-B.*, i, 739 f.; iv, 93 ff.; I QS vi.24–vii.25; viii.16–ix.2.

this background of the Jewish problem approached the question with a totally different pre-supposition.

Not one early Christian writing up to Hermas proposed the theory that the baptized ones were to live a sinless life. This 'theory of sinlessness' stemmed in Hermas, as in the modern protestant studies,[13] from a 'de-eschatologized', psychologized misunderstanding of the primitive Christian statements. In Hermas the prophetic expectation of an imminent end was an additional factor.

The indicative under which Paul had placed the Church did not describe a condition already present, but proclaimed what God had done for man and how he therefore looked upon him: you have died by means of the cross and baptism to that power of sin which had previously controlled you, in order that you may live for God with the living Christ.[14] The Pauline imperative did not mean to be a continuation of the evangelistic sermon[15] but a summons based on the word of God which continually leads through the Spirit to faith. This is the faith which allows the indicative to become valid and effective in one's life (Rom. vi.11). The preaching must be continually given in the indicative and imperative for the baptized community because the man of faith, who himself lives by this preaching, never chronologically leaves the old man behind him but lives in faith, so to speak, with the old man subdued in him until death (Rom. vi.1–14; Gal. v.13–24). Thus the Pauline Epistles focused in their imperative content more or less on a concrete correction for the baptized ones under temptation. Doubtless all who spread the proclamation in the Pauline churches attempted to correct in similar fashion those who had failed (Gal. vi.1).

The Church was to support this correction by means of her conduct towards the one who had been corrected. As II Cor. ii.5–11 and vii.8–12 reports in one case, the offender was to be reproved by all so that a wholesome repentance and conversion might result. Should he disregard the exhortation, then the congregation was to remove itself from him and refuse him their fellowship, in particular their table-fellowship. This was to be done not because he had sinned but because he did it as a 'brother', i.e. he had disregarded the grace which was summoning him to repentance (II Thess. iii.6, 14 f.; I Cor. v.9–11). This procedure, according to II Thess. iii.14 f., was to support the correction and effect repentance. By contrast, the purpose recommended in I Cor. v.13 was simply to 'drive out the wicked person from among you' (Deut. xvii.7). The first principle was later developed into the pedagogical rule of Did. 14, 2; 15, 3

---

[13] Established by Windisch, *op. cit.* (n. 12).
[14] II Cor. v.14 f.; Rom. vi. 1–10; Col. ii.11 f.
[15] *Contra* Windisch, *op. cit.* (n. 12).

and Polycarp, *Phil.* 11, 1, 4. The latter approaches the procedures which Paul in the same chapter of I Corinthians wanted applied to the one who in the name of freedom had committed incest. The assembled community was to 'deliver [him] to Satan for the destruction of the flesh, that his spirit might be saved . . .' (I Cor. v.5). According to all the indications, both church discipline in order to support the instruction leading to repentance and final expulsion from the redeemed community in the hope that the one expelled might be saved through God's grace on the day of judgment were current in the Pauline Churches.[16]

The Synoptic tradition has preserved ancient rules from the Palestinian Church which placed the brethren under an obligation to correct those who had sinned (Matt xviii.15–17 par., Luke xvii.3) and which gave them the authority through the saying about the 'keys to the Kingdom' to forgive him who was repentant (Matt. xviii.18; cf. xvi.19). In so doing, the congregation itself was involved in the action (Matt. xviii.17); it was placed under the obligation of 'binding' finally, i.e. of judging a particular conduct, not as a transgression of the Law but as a disregard and misuse of grace. Accordingly, the congregation was to exclude those who so persisted.[17] By this Palestinian tradition also, it was the sin against the Spirit alone (Matt. xii.31 par.; cf. Acts v.3, 9), i.e. the misuse of grace, which was unpardonable before God and his Church (Acts v.1–6). In Acts v, as in I Cor. v.1 ff., the presence of such sin was disclosed by the spirit of prophecy, and in Acts v it was judged immediately through this disclosure (cf. Rev. ii.22). According to Matt. xviii.15–17, the unrepentant one was to be expelled if he also failed to observe the correction of the congregation. Neither Matt. xviii nor I Cor. v.5 speak of readmitting the expelled one later.[18] The final exclusion from the Church was a rare and extreme action. The possibility reveals the eschatological seriousness of the correction in the eschatological Church. Whereas the ban, i.e. a

---

[16] II Thess. iii.14 f. is thus no argument for the inauthenticity of this Epistle.

[17] 'Binding and loosening' as Jewish terms meant to declare casuistically with reference to the Law something as forbidden or allowed, or also the banning and lifting of the ban as practised by the synagogues (S.–B., iv, 293 ff.) and expanded by the Essenes (I QS vi.24–ix.2) in order to subject the recalcitrant to the Law and order of the community. Both terms have been transformed in terms of the Gospel. They now mean to condemn or to approve a conduct with reference to Christ and in so doing to refuse or to grant the fellowship of the redeemed community, perhaps primarily in the mission to Israel (Matt. xvi.18). In the Church the order was reversed as the composition in Matt. xviii suggests and the further development of the saying in John xx.23 in conjunction with I John v.16 shows. (In the further development the difference between the Synoptic call to repentance and the Johannine redemptive discourse are also reflected.) The saying has been applied more legalistically to the practice of confession since Tertullian, *De Pud.* 21 and Origen, *Com. in Mt.* xii, 14.

[18] With v. Campenhausen, *op. cit.* (n. 7), 139, 3.

separation from the fellowship generally limited in time, was frequently used as a part of the Law in the Jewish communities, as a penal measure with a pedagogical intent, the expulsion from the redeemed community through the word after an unsuccessful attempt at correction corresponded to the direction of the Gospel in such a crisis. Even though church discipline in Palestine and Syria may have leaned more towards the Jewish practice than in the Pauline areas, the basic principle was the same.

In the second generation, the combination of both elements which we have seen again and again appears on the scene. In the preserved writings which come to grips with this problem in a great variety of situations, everything is significantly focused on the *kerygmatic* warning against a final fall from which there is no salvation. Matthew's Gospel, having taken over for the contemporary Church the rules in Matt. xviii already noted from the Palestinian tradition, threatened the one invited to the marriage feast and who had arrived without a wedding garment with the final expulsion (Matt. xxii.11–14 (M)). This threat did not mean the tares to be weeded out (Matt. xiii.24–30, 36–43, 47–50 (M)) in order to produce a relatively pure Church of the same type as the community of the Pharisees and Essenes; it was intended instead as a summons to the direct circuit between God's forgiveness and our forgiveness. To break this circuit meant death (Matt. v.23 f.; vi.12; xviii.23 ff. (M)).

Hebrews warned all who were falling away in faith against the fall from which there was no salvation (vi.4 ff.; x.26–31; xii.16), and so summoned each person to watch over the others (xii.15), but it did not say what was to take place when the fall occurred.

In contrast, I John demanded the Church to refuse intercession and with it fellowship for 'the sin which is mortal' (v.16). The unpardonable sin, as in Hebrews, was the unrepentant surrender of grace, which took place in concrete behaviour rather than in a basic declaration (Heb. xii.16). I John, however, placed all the other sins of the Christians under the condemnation and forgiveness of the cross. This forgiveness which the Epistle proclaims in general was given concrete expression in the Johannine form of the saying about the 'keys to the Kingdom' (John xx.22 f.). This took place both when a brother corrected another (xviii.15 ff.) and when a brother confessed his sins to another (in New Testament only in James v.16) or before the congregation in a service of worship. The latter occurred in the case of new converts (I Cor. xiv.24 f.; Acts xix.18) and of public sins on the part of Christians (I Clem. li f.; Did. 14, 1; 4, 14a par. Barn. xix.12). Like the Lord's Prayer, the earliest common prayer contained a general confession of sin (I Clem. lx.1 f.).

In the Pastorals, the obligation of the individual Church member or rather the Church as a whole in all the voices heard up to this point, was now laid upon the office holders of the Church[19] and applied in particular against them (I Tim. v.19 f.; cf. Polycarp, *Phil*. 11, 1), although they were not to replace the others but merely to lead them in a particular way. This, as we see in Acts v.1 ff.; I Cor. v.1 ff.; Matt. xvi.18 (cf. xviii.18) and elsewhere, was the fundamental meaning of the special offices. I Tim. v.22 did not speak, according to its context, about the 're-admission of penitent sinners or "penitents" ' by the leader of the congregation in an act during the service of worship,[20] but about the installation of the office holder.

In all these different statements, the emphasis in the New Testament writings lies on the preaching of the forgiveness from the cross which punishes and overcomes the sin, as well as on the warning against the fall from which there is no salvation. This proclamation took on such a form in the life of the Church that priestly guidance, confession, repentance and discipline were not institutions but a responsibility borne by the entire Church. By contrast, a legalistic and pedagogical character which reminds one of the Jewish practice comes to the fore in the writings of the third generation. The rules of the Didache were aimed at producing pedagogically an improvement by means of a temporary expulsion (Did. 14, 12; 15, 3), which in certain cases was also expressed in a public confession of sin during the Church service (Did. 14, 1; cf. 4, 14a par. Barn. xix.12). Hermas (cf. pp. 138 f.), however, taught the once-for-all-time character of the baptism of repentance to a congregation in which a continual repentance had been demanded and practiced (I Clem. vii f.; II Clem.) without any real consequent renewal of life. Nevertheless, Hermas misunderstood this view of baptism in terms of the Old Testament, Jewish meaning. On the basis of Christ's offering, it granted pardon for the past guilt in a fashion similar to the Day of Atonement, but it was to be followed by a sinless life in keeping with the Law of Christ;[21] however, those baptized had sinned, so Hermas proclaimed in a prophetic manner a unique second repentance which was to be the last one before the imminent end and which was to bring about a sinless life which did not come to pass after baptism—and naturally could not come to pass. A rationing of grace and the Law were to bring about pedagogically what only an uncurtailed grace could effect according to the New Testament writings. Hermas himself (as a prophet) did not develop an ecclesiastical institution from his teaching on repentance, but the theological starting-point of the Catholic institution of penance comes to light in it, a starting-

[19] I Tim. v.1 f.; II Tim. iv.2; Tit. i.9; ii.15.
[20] *Contra* v. Campenhausen, *op. cit.* (n. 7), 161.
[21] *Mand.* 4, 3, 1 f.; *Sim.* 5, 5, 3; 5, 6, 3.
[22] *Vis.* 2, 2, 1–5; *Mand.* 4, 3.

point which was first broken down when Luther understood that baptism according to Rom. vi was the beginning rather than the end of an existence *sola gratia*.[23] Unlike the repentance practiced by Pharisaic Judaism, Hermas offered, in a fashion similar to John the Baptist or the Essenes, the final total repentance in view of the imminent end, but he did not speak from the standpoint of the present eschaton.

With the removal of the eschatological element from baptism and repentance, the conception of the purity of the Church was also distorted. According to Hermas, of the masses baptized only the few who actually lived according to the Law of Christ belonged to the true Church;[24] others could still gain entrance through penance, and not a few would fall away. Thus we have for the first time the theological distinction between the visible Church of those baptized and the invisible, true Church of the righteous. The New Testament writings did not know this difference (for Matt. xiii.24 ff. see above, pp. 171 f.), since for them the Church at that time consisted of those baptized who lived in conversion and in discipleship, or under the indicative and the imperative. A relatively pure Church is not then to be produced through the expulsion of the unrepentant, but this was carried out to prevent the leavening of the 'new dough' and to declare figuratively that grace is not the cloak of sin but its death.

4. The unity of the Church[25] is to be considered in the same way as its purity. Paul could only express both matters in the indicative and imperative. The Church, as represented by every gathering for a service of worship, as well as by the life of the local church, and the Church as a whole, is a unity because one God, one Lord and one Spirit (I Cor. xii.4–6) are at work in her through one Gospel (I Cor. i.10–13; Gal. i.6–9), one baptism and one bread (I Cor. xii.13; x.17; Gal. iii.27). Paul bore witness to this indicative which Eph. iv.4–6 (cf. ii.13–16) broadly summarizes in order to summon the Church in the imperative to its realization (cf. Eph. iv.3, 13). Even here the indicative stands behind the realization of the imperative, although without suspending the imperative. Paul himself actually brought the *koinonia* of the whole Church established by Christ to realization both by means of his common confession of faith in the one Gospel at the Apostolic Council (Gal. ii.9) and by means of the collection

[23] *WA* 6, 529; see Goppelt, *Christentum und Judentum*, 242 ff.

[24] *Vis.* 3, 5, 1–7, 3; *Sim.* 9, 183 f.

[25] Literature: K. Holl, 'Der Kirchenbegriff des Paulus in seinem Verhältnis zu dem der Urgemeinde', *Gesammelte Aufsätze* (1928), ii, 44–67; E. Stauffer, *TWNT*, ii, 438 ff.; S. Hanson, *The Unity of the Church in the New Testament* (1946); P. I. Bratsiotis, 'Paulus und die Einheit der Kirche', *Studia Paulina* (as in §5, n. 31), 28–36; H. Schlier, 'Die Einheit der Kirche im Denken des Apostels Paulus', in *Die Zeit der Kirche* (1956), 287–299; J.-L. Leuba, *Institution und Ereignis* (Ger. trans. 1957), esp. 90–118.

which was given out of love for Jerusalem. According to this he emphasized that his Gospel was at one with that of the Jerusalem apostles (I Cor. xv.11) and that his basic instructions were valid for 'all churches' (I Cor. iv.17; vii.17; xi.16; xiv.33–36). The unity of the Church is thus neither a purely indicative element arising solely through her origin, Christ,[26] nor is a purely imperative element through the acknowledgment ' . . . by all the members of the Church . . . of the binding unity in the *regula fidei*'.[27] It is in fact the New Testament combination of both.

On the other hand, the men of Jerusalem, whose concept of the Church we can conclude only indirectly from traditions in the Gospels, Acts and Revelation as well as from their conduct, might well have considered the unity of the eschatological people of God more from an institutional and less from a *kerygmatic* standpoint than did Paul. For them the new people of God had a geographical focal point, Jerusalem (Acts i.4; viii.1; Rev. xx.9; xxi.10), and a hierarchy of personnel, the Twelve with Peter as the primate, and later the 'Three Pillars'. Both had a soterial and eschatological meaning rather than a cultic and juridicial function[28] as did Jewish Jerusalem and its Sanhedrin. The Twelve, as did the Three later, represented the unique eschatological body of witnesses (§7, 5). These authoritative bodies were not therefore given permanency by successors but disappeared when the individuals themselves had died. James and the elders who had guided and represented the Church of Jerusalem from around A.D. 50 did not consider themselves any longer to be the representatives of the Church as a whole[29] but, at most, as the representatives of Palestinian Christianity or Jewish Christianity.[30] However, did not the visitors from Jerusalem, who not only appeared at the founding of the churches in Samaria and Antioch but even in the Pauline mission fields, as well as the collection brought by Paul to James around A.D. 57, suggest a claim to primacy on Jerusalem's part? The visitors did not bring legal instructions as did the 'apostles' of Jewish Jerusalem.[31] Instead they simply represented, even if in the form of a Judaistic distortion (II Cor. xi.5, 13),

[26] G. Ebeling, *Die Geschichtlichkeit der Kirche und ihre Verkündigung als theologisches Problem* (1954), 76.

[27] H. Schlier, *op. cit.* (n. 25), 297.

[28] *Contra* K. Holl, *op. cit.* (n. 25). Considerably stronger than Holl, P. Gaechter, S.J., 'Jerusalem und Antiochien. Ein Beitrag zur urkirchlichen Rechtsentwicklung', *ZKTheol.* (1948), 1–48: Christian Jerusalem had a legal priority, since it was the seat of the central government of the Church, of the Twelve and above all of Simon Peter. This centre was shifted with his departure.

[29] James is the leader of the entire Church for the first time in the Epist. Petri in Pseud. Clement. Cf. Hennecke, [3]ii, 106 (Ger. 69 f.).

[30] I cannot see that Peter, as leader of the Jewish mission, was administratively dependent on Jerusalem (Gal. ii.12) (cf. Cullmann, *Peter: Disciple–Apostle–Martyr* (as in §1, n. 25), 42.

[31] *TWNT*, i, 417.

the continuity of all believers with the apostolic tradition which had originated in Jerusalem, a continuity which Paul had also recognized.[32] The collection was not a legal obligation[33] corresponding to the Temple tax, but a spiritual obligation by which the Gentile Church expressed thanks for the spiritual gifts and declared their *koinonia* (Gal. ii.10; Rom. xv.26). Jerusalem thus viewed the unity of the Church more from its historical, Paul more from its pneumatic side, yet neither excludes the other (§21, 3).

In the second generation, Luke in no way intended to give the impression that 'the apostles and elders' in Jerusalem had maintained a kind of leadership for the Church as a whole, but he did mean to see the Church as gathered around a line of redemptive history which led from devout Israel through the 'apostles' in Jerusalem and Paul to Rome. In contrast to this historical view, in which Palestinian conceptions and traditions were strongly at work, John stressed the *kerygmatic* view. A unity had been established through Christ's redemptive act and intercession which summoned all beli3vers to a oneness with one another (John x.16; xi.52; xvii.11, 20–23). Both viewpoints were so developed that they could remain open to each other.

In the third generation, I Clement and Ignatius made it clear that the members were conscious of the oneness in the Church as a whole and that each member accepted the responsibility for the others apart from any organizational unity through emissaries, letters and visits. It was only in the following generations that one began to leave this exchange more and more to the bishops, but in I Clement, Rome as a church addressed her sister in Corinth, although strange overtones in the basic principles are also present here. In order to restore unity in Corinth, I Clement stated the principle, 'all things done in order', which according to Paul (I Cor. xiv.40) was to be added to the pneumatic principle as an ultimate rule,[34] and developed accordingly an order of office in keeping with the principle of succession (I Clem. xlii.1 ff.). Hermes' viewpoint agrees with that of I Clement: 'The apostles, bishops, teachers' and other representatives of the true Church represent her purity as well as her unity because ' . . . they always agreed among themselves, and had peace among themselves and listened to one another' (*Vis.* 3, 5, 1; *Sim.* 9, 15, 4–9; 17, 4 took up Eph. iv at the same time). As well as this legal and

---

[32] W. G. Kümmel, *Kirchenbegriff*, 53, n. 85; Munck, *Paul and the Salvation of Mankind*, 104 f. (Ger. 96 f.).

[33] *Contra.* K. Holl, *op. cit.* (n. 25), 60 f. For the discussion, N. A. Dahl, *Das Volk Gottes* (1941), 315, n. 60; v. Campenhausen, *Kirchliches Amt*, 36; *TWNT*, iv, 285 f.

[34] The central exposition of office in chap. xl–xliv of I Clement stand under the key word τάξις in xl.1, cf. xli.1. In a similar fashion words from this root occur frequently in chap. xx in reference to the world.

moralistic distortion, there appeared a type of Gnostic mystery in Ignatius. The individual church as it gathered around the bishop, the presbytery and the deacons to celebrate the eucharist, depicts the unity of the Church as a whole represented through God, Christ and the apostles (*Eph.* xi.2; *Trall.* ii.2; iii.1; *Smyr.* viii.1; *Phild*, v.1; *Magn.* vi.1). Both starting-points lead to a hierarchical misunderstanding of the Church's unity. Whereas the apostles were considered as the foundation stones of the Church from Ephesians to Revelation, they were not named among the factors comprising her unity (Eph. iv.4 ff.). Thus the question about the Church's unity and purity leads us to the question about the organism which conducted her activity.

21. THE CHURCH OFFICE[1]

1. The Greek language offered many designations from personal or cultic associations for the Church's office, but instead of accepting these the Church developed a new designation which was common to neither the Jewish nor the Hellenistic environment, διαχονία 'service', or διαχονεῖν 'to serve'.[2] Since this term occurs in the Synoptic as well as the Pauline terminology, it was already present in all the Early Apostolic Church. It was the usual term for functions within the framework of the Church and not, significantly enough, for the services to one's neighbour or within the social orders.[3] Διαχονία is the service performed for the unifying and preservation of the Church, the service which establishes and maintains the faith; thus it is the office of the Church.

According to the Synoptic tradition, the Church had been given this new designation by Jesus; she had not developed it of her own accord. Indeed, the term had been used in conscious and express antithesis to the official terminology of the surroundings. In the Synoptics, the logion according to Mark x.44: " . . . Whoever would be great among you must be your servant (δοῦλος)' is repeated six times with only minor

---

[1] Literature: older works, see n. 22 below and the survey of research on this in O. Linton, *Das Problem der Urkirche* (1932), 3–131 and F. M. Braun, *Neues Licht auf die Kirche* (1946); survey of the more recent discussion which has been heavily influenced by ecumenics: P. H. Menoud, *L'église et les ministères selon le Nouveau Testament* (1963); comprehensive portrayal: E. Schweizer, *Church Order in the New Testament* (Eng. trans. 1963, of *Gemeinde und Gemeindeordnung im Neuen Testament* (1959); K. E. Kirk, *The Apostolic Ministry* (1946), traditional Anglicanism; T. W. Manson, *The Church's Ministry* ([2]1956); H. v. Campenhausen, *Kirchliches Amt und geistliche Vollmacht in den ersten drei Jahrhunderten* (1953); J. K. S. Reid, *The Biblical Doctrine of the Ministry* (three lectures, 1955), presbyterian; E. Käsemann, 'Amt und Gemeinde im Neuen Testament', *Exegetische Versuche und Besinnungen* (1960), i, 109–134.
[2] Schweizer, *op. cit.* (n. 1) 171–180 (Ger. 154–164).
[3] Rom. xiii.4 is the only exception!

variations. According to the context, the logion intended to differentiate the relationships within the circle of disciples from those of other personal relationships. Among the disciples no office was to be allowed which would correspond to that of the political rulers (Mark x.44 par. Matt.; cf. Mark ix.35 (par. Luke)) or to that of the Scribes (Matt. xxiii.11, cf. vs. 8–10). The one is constituted by right and power, the other by right and knowledge. Certainly these factors could not be totally excluded from the Church's action, but they were not to constitute it. Later the office of the Church was marked off just as unequivocally against magic (Acts viii.18) and against a priesthood (Hebrews). The determining factor behind this designation was Jesus' own work, just as the positive basis of the principle logion indicates (Mark x.45 par. Matt.; Luke xxii.27): 'Which is the greater, one who sits at table, or one who serves? . . . But I am among you as one who serves' (διακονῶν in its basic meaning). This is then unfolded in grand fashion by John xiii.4 f., 12 ff. Jesus, as the one who serves, brings God's reign. The Kingdom of God did not come in the manner expected by all the Jewish groups, in a legal event in keeping with the Law and by means of a display of power; instead it came by means of an *Anaw* for the *anawim* (Matt. v.3; xi.28 ff.), it came concealed for those of faith by means of 'serving'. Any work of Jesus' disciples and any office within the circle of his disciples was then only meaningful to the extent that it was 'service'. 'To serve' means to demonstrate love to mankind out of a faith which forgoes the use of right and power and seeks God's help in Jesus. This love is to be demonstrated for the same purpose as it was by Jesus, to inspire a faith in God and compassion for others.

This service has been given to all disciples according to the Synoptic tradition as well as according to Paul. Both, however, give prominence to a special service which is found within the service of all, that is the service of the apostolate. The Synoptic tradition also traces this special office back to Jesus.

2. The much debated question concerning the origin, meaning, and history of the apostolate[4] is best clarified by taking the historically tangible statements of Paul as our point of departure. At times the word ἀπόστολος

4 Literature: K. H. Rengstorf, *TWNT*, i, 406–446 (older lit.); *Apostolat und Predigtamt* ([2]1954); G. Sass, *Apostelamt und Kirche* (1939); 'Die Apostel der Didache', in *Gedenkschrift* for Lohmeyer (1951), 233–239; A. Fridrichsen, *The Apostle and his Message* (1947) H. v. Campenhausen, 'Der urchristliche Apostelbegriff', *Stud. Theol.* i (1947), 96 ff.; H. Mosbech, '*Apostolos* in the New Testament', *Stud. Theol.* ii (1949), 166–200 (176 ff. survey of the discussion); E. Lohse, 'Ursprung und Prägung des christlichen Apostolates', *ThZ*, 9 (1953), 259–275; K. H. Schelkle, *Jüngerschaft und Apostelamt* (1957); J. Dupont, *Le Nom d'Apotres atil été donné aux Douze par Jésus* (1957); G. Klein, *Die zwölf Apostel, Ursprung und Gehalt einer Idee* (1961); J. Roloff, *Apostolat– Verkündigung–Kirche* (1965); cf. §13, n. 32.

meant for him those 'sent out' by the churches, in keeping with its Greek meaning (II Cor. viii.23; Phil. ii.25). Nevertheless, when it is used absolutely it is a *terminus technicus* whose meaning is expressed in the genitive construction, 'Ιησοῦ Χριστοῦ: the 'sent one' is the 'sent one of Jesus Christ'. In these passages it is a designation of office and is to be translated as 'apostle'.

Paul defined most clearly the way in which he applied this designation to himself. He was an apostle because the Crucified One showed himself as the Living One to him in a revelation which was basically the same as the Easter appearances. In so doing the Living One had also commissioned Paul with the missionary preaching of the redemptive event announced in this revelation (I Cor. ix.1 f.; xv.8 ff.; Gal. i.1, 12, 15 f.). Paul was an apostle because the Son had been revealed to him 'in order that [he] might preach him' (Gal. i.16).

Paul assumed the same calling for all those whom he called apostles. This is seen in the fact that he stressed in I Cor. xv.7 that the Easter revelation had been granted to 'all the apostles'. This could well have been the case for all to whom he had ascribed this designation, for Cephas and James, the Lord's brother (Gal. i.18), for Barnabas and the Lord's brothers who were quite possibly included in I Cor. ix.5, and even for the two men of Rom. xvi.7, otherwise unknown, since they were his 'kinsmen' and 'in Christ before [him]'.

There is only one passage where the designation appears in a different sense, in II Cor. xi.13. Here we find men who were rejected as 'pseudo-apostles'. They were not witnesses of Easter but itinerant missionaries called by the Spirit. These missionaries coming out of Palestine had called themselves apostles, but appealed at the same time to the apostles in Jerusalem (Gal. i.15) as though to a higher authority. Paul therefore named the latter ironically 'superlative apostles' (II Cor. xi.5; xii.11). This double meaning of the word 'apostle' confronts us again later in the traditions from the Syrian and Palestinian realm. Frequently, 'the apostles' refers in the same writing to both the pneumatic itinerant missionaries (Acts xiv.4, 14; Rev. ii.2; Did. 11, 4–6; pseudo-Clem. *Hom.* 11, 35) and the witnesses of Easter (Acts, *passim*; Rev. xxi.14; Did. *inscr.*). It has been suggested that the broader meaning was the more original[5] and that Paul was the first to introduce the narrower usage.[6] In fact, Paul took for granted that the narrower meaning of the word was already current in the Church, and he vigorously claimed that he himself was an apostle in this sense (Gal. i.1, 15 ff.; I Cor. ix.1 ff.; xv.9). He did not expressly reject the usage of the word in its broader meaning which had developed

---

[5] R. Bultmann, *Theology of the New Testament*, §52, 3, *et al.*
[6] Mosbach and Lohse, *op. cit.* (n. 4).

as a secondary extension of the term in Palestine—he did not call the opponents in Corinth 'false apostles' on account of what they called themselves (cf. p. 100)—but he did not use this meaning himself. In this way, 'the least of the apostles' definitely influenced the development of the term 'apostle'. By establishing his claim, Paul formulated the term theologically; he prevented it from simply melting away, and he made the Church aware of what it meant when it called men such as Peter an apostle. Nevertheless, Paul was only expressing again here with theological precision what Jesus had given to the Church.

If the term 'apostles' already had this meaning for the Church in Jerusalem by the time of Paul's conversion one to three years after the end of Jesus' earthly ministry (Gal. i.17), then there can be no doubt about the Synoptic tradition that Jesus himself instituted the apostolate. The framework of the pericopes about the mission is redactional (Mark iii.13–19; vi.7–13, 30 par. Luke; Luke x.1–16 Q, cf. Matt. x), but the *logia* of the mission found in Mark as well as Q attest the fact of the entrusting of the mission. Moreover, these *logia* do not correspond to the situation of the primitive Church (cf. pp. 34 f.).[7] Jesus sent his disciples out as his personal representatives, and in so doing he created an office which was unique to his environment. All of the special Jewish groups maintained the Old Testament Jewish offices of prophets, priests and scribes, which represented the Torah, whereas the office of Jesus' disciples could only represent him personally. The form of this new office was already given in the legal institution of the *schali*^{a}*ch*, 'the one who is sent'; such a one was the authorized representative of his employer.[8]

The sending of the disciples in the earthly ministry, which had understandably become faded in the tradition, was a commission limited temporally and geographically. Those sent out were only called 'apostles' until their return, according to Matthew and Mark. The Synoptic tradition reports in agreement with Paul that a renewed commissioning for life was the result of the appearances at Easter (Matt. xxviii.19; Luke xxiv.46–49; Acts i.4–8). Contrary to Paul, however, the commissioning was limited in the Synoptic tradition to the Eleven and re-defined as a universal, itinerant mission. The experiences and viewpoints of the second generation are thus to be seen in the context of the commissioning, but the commissioning as such is historically indisputable.

The creation of the commission leads us from the earliest beginnings beyond Paul to the second generation's concept of apostle. Luke developed

---

[7] V. Taylor, *Mark*, on iii.14 and vi.30.

[8] Set forth in detail by K. H. Rengstorf, *TWNT*, i, 414 ff. This derivation has hardly been denied and in no way convincingly challenged, e.g. by Mosbach (*op. cit.*, 187 f.) and A. Ehrhardt (*The Apostolic Succession in the First Two Centuries of the Church*, 1950, 18 ff.).

his sharply defined and influential conception of the apostles from this latter viewpoint. 'The apostles' for him were identical with the Twelve whose circle was completed again by the election of Matthias to replace Judas after the latter's death. Luke received this conception from a Palestinian and Syrian tradition which we meet in Rev. xxi.14; Did. *inscr.* and also in Matt. xxviii.16-20 and John xx.21, 24. (In I Cor. xv 'the apostles' (vs. 7) are a further circle, whose number was not fixed but was nevertheless limited in principle to a certain group, as well as 'the Twelve' (vs. 5). It probably included the Twelve. Originally, the Twelve as such had indeed had a function which was to be differentiated from that of the apostolate (§5, 3).) Luke strictly followed this concept which remained unstressed in the tradition, and he called Paul and Barnabas, 'ἀπόστολος', (Acts xiv.4, 14) only in a secondary sense as missionaries having been sent out by the Holy Spirit (Acts xiii.4). He underlined the limitation of this designation by means of a corresponding definition. The apostles were the chosen eyewitnesses of both the resurrection and the earthly ministry, beginning with the baptism at the River Jordan (Acts i.21 f., 26; cf. Luke i.1). Luke was brought to this definition of the apostolate less by his Palestinian and Syrian tradition than by his intention to protect from vanishing (Did. 11) and misuse (Rev. ii.2) an office which had determined the direction of the Church's development (Acts, *passim*) and established her preaching (Luke 1.1-4).

Luke's conception was instrumental in the third generations's consideration of Paul alone as being an apostle with the Twelve, since Paul's Epistles had been accepted. Wherever the local tradition suggested it and the Pauline Epistles were recognized, as in Rome, Peter and Paul were named whenever the names of apostles were mentioned.[9] Otherwise, one spoke of 'the Twelve Apostles' (Did. *inscr.*; Barn. v.9; viii.3) without deliberately intending to exclude Paul. It was only when Marcion and later Jewish Christianity began to play Paul against the earliest apostles that thought was given to the circle of the apostles, and the Early Catholic Church maintained that 'the Twelve and Paul' qualified as apostles.[10]

The conception of the apostles' commission and work was changed even more in the third generation. According to Luke as well as according to Matthew, they had received the commission and promise of the universal witness and were its representatives who really laid the foundation for the witness, although the actual execution of the commission developed far beyond the temporal or geographical realm of their work

[9] I Clem. v.4 f.; II Clem. v.3 f.; Ignatius, *Rom.* iv.3; Polycarp, *Phil.* 3 : 2; 9 : 1; only the (later) Papias fragments name more names.

[10] J. Wagemann, *Die Stellung des Apostels Paulus neben den Zwölf in dern ersten zwei Jahrhunderten* (1926); J. Munck, 'Paul, The Apostles and the Twelve', *Stud. Theol.* 3 (1950), 96–110; J. Dupont, *op. cit.* (n. 4); G. Klein, *op. cit.* (n. 4).

(Acts i.8; Luke i.1-4; Matt. xxviii.19). In I Clement there appeared for the first time the idea that the apostles themselves were personally to have carried out the basic missionary work among the nations of the world.[11] This conception of the missionary commission became increasingly the general view of the Church. For the New Testament writings of the second generation then, they were like the first witnesses (Matt. xvi.18; Acts i.21; Eph. ii.20; Rev. xxi.14), the foundation stones for the Church; for I Clement, on the other hand, they were such in the final analysis because they ' . . . appointed their first converts . . . to be bishops and deacons of the future believers . . .', and they arranged that they should be succeeded (xl.4; xliv.2), so appearing as the founders of a succession of office holders. According to Matthew and Luke, they represented, as well as the missionary office or function, the pastoral office or function of the Church (Matt. xvi.18; cf. xviii.18; Acts xx.17-38; John xx.22; xxi.15 ff.); according to I Clement, they founded this office as an institution, and they authorized the constitution and order of the Church as being a part of the tradition established by them (I Clement xliv.1 f.; cf. Did., inscr.).

Here we are confronted by the question which has been raised on this subject since the very beginning, a question which still divides the opinions concerning the Church office today in ecumenical circles: how was the special office of the earliest witnesses instituted by Jesus to continue working as his representative in those parts of the Church which these witnesses themselves had neither temporally nor geographically reached?[12] The function of the office of apostle was not completed in the forming of the original witness. (So it cannot come to its end in the canon). The apostles were not writers of memoirs; they formed, represented and guarded the earliest witness as missionaries and as pastors of the churches. The special service of the witness was performed as a service for the edification of the Church. Its special nature consisted in the basic responsibility both for the witness and for the Church as a whole (Matt. xvi.18; Gal. i.2; II Cor. xi.28).

This special ministry, established with the apostolate but independent of its unique commission, can be supplemented by the service of all, but it can not be replaced, and so from the very beginning, other offices were created to take over parts of this special service. When the itinerant missionaries were called apostles in Palestine, this was an unconscious attempt to relate this service too directly to those who followed. This

---

[11] I Clem. xlii.1-4 as in Herm. *Sim.* 9, 16 f.; 9, 25, 2; Barn. viii.3; Polycarp, *Phil.* 6, 3, Justin, *Apol.* i, 39, 3.
[12] For discussion: F. M. Braun, *Neues Licht auf die Kirche* (1946), 158-165; E. Schweizer, *op. cit.*, 213 (Ger. 194) (Schweizer views the office too much from the service of the congregation and too little from the content of the service and hence from the apostolate); further in n. 46 below.

attempt remained of necessity merely an isolated episode. The other offices within the Church which arose to spread the message of life according to the Gospel distinguished themselves from that of the apostolate through the difference in name, although at first there was no clear indication to what extent these offices were viewed as the recipients of the ministry represented by the apostolate or as a further development of the service shared by all. The same was true of the formation of the offices as a whole.

Let us now trace the development of the offices alongside the apostolate and then examine the meaning of this development as a whole and in particular the relationship of these offices to the apostolate.

3. The documents which give us our first reliable picture of the Church as a whole and her offices are the Pauline Epistles, especially I Corinthians. This was a church which had arisen under Paul's mission in the Hellenistic area and in which there was already a service shared by all as well as special services. Paul placed this church under the *kerygmatic* conception of the Body of Christ in order to counter by means of their inter-relationship the spreading distortion of these ministries. Just as a person exists historically with a body (Rom. vi.12 f.), so Christ acts historically by means of the members of his Church; they are his mouth and his hands (I Cor. xii.12-27; Rom. xii.4 ff.; Eph. iv.11-16). Accordingly, the offices in the Church are not uniform but manifold. The Spirit gives different charismata (I Cor. xii.4 ff.) based on the historical needs of the Church. Such a charisma is not a supernatural power but the call of the Spirit to a service, a call which also enables one for a specific task. People are therefore graced with a charisma only when they allow themselves to be taken into service through God's working in them. The ministries are united since they are ultimately from the same origin, God's redemptive work through Jesus in the Holy Spirit, and since they have the same ultimate goal, the edification of the eschatological community, but they are also diverse since the origin and goal occur within history. Therefore the apostolate stands at the top of the list.

When Paul ennumerates the ministries or rather the charismata, he refers partly to designations of office and partly to functions: 'God has appointed in the church first apostles, second prophets, third teachers, then workers of miracles, then healers, helpers, administrators and speakers in various kinds of tongues' (I Cor. xii.28; cf. Rom. xii. 4-8; Eph. iv.11-16). This does not say that one group of ministries was bound permanently to an office holder and others were practised solely as a specific function for the actual situation. The gift of prophecy, for example, fell now and then on members of the congregation other than the prophets, the ones from whom one would normally expect it (I Cor. xiv.31). On the other hand, the two most important functions named, 'helping and administrating',

were practised in Corinth over an extended period of time, since I Cor.
xvi.16 exhorts the members to be 'subject to the first converts of Achaia',[13]
who were named by name. I Thess. v.12 and Rom. xii.8 have the same
service in mind when they speak of the '*προϊστάμενοι*'.[14] This word
connotes in extra-Biblical Greek the *function* of managing and supporting,
as found for example in the role of the father in his household (I Tim.
iii.4). A few years later an *office* was constituted for this function. Phil.
i.1 mentions for the first time 'bishops and deacons' (*ἐπίσκοποι καὶ
διάκονοι*).

Harnack divided these office holders into two groups: apostles, prophets and teachers were charismatic; bishops and deacons were officers of
the congregation.[15] The former were for the entire Church, the latter
were limited to the local church. The first distinction, at best, is congruent
partly with the view of the third generation but certainly not with that
of Paul or Luke (Acts xx.28). The latter distinction is basically correct,
even though prophets and teachers often remained for a lengthy period
in one place and the 'administrators' were not limited permanently to one
locale. Both groups were expressly and consciously differentiated by the
Church for the first time towards the end of the second generation
(Did. 15, 1).

The uniqueness of the Pauline concept of the offices becomes clear for
us when we see it alongside the contemporary Palestinian concept. The
latter must be reconstructed from bits of information which we have.
Here we find on the whole the same offices for the entire Church: the
offices of an apostle, which were expanded quite early by the use of
'apostle' in the broader sense, prophecy and teaching, which since 'Pentecost' had been a function. Prophets soon appeared on the scene as office
holders (Acts xi.27; xv.32; xxi.9.f.), but teachers, perhaps in keeping
with their own tradition (Matt. xxiii.8 ff.), were not given the title, although they were certainly active in the Palestinian Church (Matt. xiii.52;
xxiii.34).

These offices, however, operated in Palestine under a considerably
different, though unwritten, constitution (§7, 5). Authoritative bodies
were characteristic of this constitution, a characteristic which we do not

---

[13] H. Greeven, *ZNTW*, 43 (1952–53), 37, concludes from the absence of both
functions from the repetition in I. Cor. xii.29 f. that they were performed by the
prophets and teachers. That might have been the case at times, but the public proclamation and teaching by nature did not belong together with administration
(*προϊστάμενοι*).
[14] In a similar fashion *ἡγούμενοι* was used for some time: Heb. xiii.7; xvii.24;
Acts xv.22; I Clem. i.3; xxi.6; Hermas, *Vis.* 2, 2, 6; 3, 9, 7 (F. Büchsel, *TWNT*, ii,
909 f.).
[15] 'Die Lehre der zwölf Apostel', *T.U.* 5 (1886), 93 ff.; for discussion see Schweizer,
op. cit. (n. 1), 181, 188 (Ger. 164, 171).

find in the Pauline area. First of all, the Twelve directed and represented the Church with Peter as the primate, then came the 'Three Pillars', and finally James, the Lord's brother, with a body of presbyters (§5, 3). Paul disassociated himself from this conception in Gal. ii.1 f., 6, on the grounds of his own self-awareness, but he did not enter into a controversy over it. At the Apostolic Council he did not confer, so it seems in the further developed Palestinian tradition of Acts xv, with an authoritative body representative of the entire congregation, but as the apostle to the Gentiles with the apostles to Israel (Gal. ii.7). He also claimed as the apostle to the Gentiles an authority over the entire Gentile Church, even over the church in Rome which had not been founded by him (Rom. i.5, 9 ff., 14 f.), and he spoke in Jerusalem as the Gentile Church's representative. This authority was, however, realized in a purely *kerygmatic* fashion. The authoritative bodies in Jerusalem to which representatives of the Palestinian Church in the Pauline churches appealed (Gal. ii.12; II Cor. iii.1) were institutional. Nevertheless the Palestinian Church identified themselves ultimately with the one common basis (I Cor. iii.11) in that it subjected those bodies again and again in favour of the leadership of the Lord in history (§7, 5; §20, 4).

We find a corresponding difference in the offices limited to the local church. Authoritative bodies were also present on the local level in Palestine as seen especially in the body of elders and perhaps also in the Seven among the Hellenists of Jerusalem (§7, 6)[16] (the body of elders were designated as πρεσβύτεροι, 'the presbyters', 'the elders' in I Tim. iv.14 and also as τὸ πρεσβυτέριον, 'the presbytery'). This institution which is unequivocally confirmed c. A.D. 57 (Acts xxi.18) had in all probability already been developed between A.D. 40 and 50.[17] It had obviously been taken over from the constitution of the synagogue community which was governed by a group of seven elders,[18] but only because it corresponded to the need of the churches. Like the Jewish elders, the Christian elders represented their churches to the outside (Acts xi.30; xxi.18; cf. Luke vii.3), cared for order and the economical concerns and, above all, concerned themselves with those who were struggling in the faith. Nevertheless, they did all this on the basis of the Gospel and not like their Jewish counterparts on the basis of the Law. This we can deduce from the later statements which go back to Palestinian traditions. According to I Pet. v.1–4 they were to tend the Church as shepherds, following the example of Christ, and according to James v.14, they were to care for

[16] Literature: W. Michaelis, *Das Ältestenamt der christlichen Gemeinde im Lichte der Heiligen Schrift* (1953); G. Bornkamm, *TWNT*, vi, 662–680 (further lit. on 652).

[17] The formula, 'apostles and elders', Acts xv.2, 4, 6, 22 f.; xvi.4 is a secondary construction by Luke. Cf. Acts xi.30.

[18] *TWNT*, vi, 660 f.

the sick. Yet in this very Palestinian tradition every church member was responsible for the troubled brother (Matt. xviii.10–18), but to carry out this responsibility in terms of the whole congregation and to direct her numerous concerns demanded a special office as the Church continued to grow, and so the office of the elder was taken over from the constitution of the synagogue. The final decisions, as in the case of an expulsion of a member, remained the perogative of the congregation as a whole (Matt. xviii.17).

The elders attended to the task which was essentially that of the 'helpers and administrators'. This was the task for which the offices of bishop and deacon were later developed in the Pauline Church. In view of this point of contact it is even more remarkable that (apart from the Pastorals) the elders were not mentioned in the Pauline Epistles,[19] although Acts reports that Paul and Barnabas had appointed elders on the first missionary journey into the southern parts of Asia Minor (xiv.23) and that Paul had taken his leave of the elders in Ephesus (xx.17). We cannot determine geographically the limits of the Palestinian influence, but Luke did include the names of the offices common during his time in the account of Acts xx (cf. p. 189) and therefore quite possibly did so in Acts xiv. In the churches on Hellenistic soil then, at least in the Pauline churches of Greece and Macedonia, there were no elders in the first generation, but was this because this name for an office was foreign to Hellenistic man, even to the Hellenistic synagogues,[20] or was it because there was no place 'in principle' for an office of this type in the Pauline Church?[21] In what way did it differ from the office of the 'προϊστάμενοι'? Those in charge, and even the bishops in Acts xx.28, were not addressed as an authoritative body nor on the basis of their position but in view of their individual calling by the Spirit: 'Age is not a spiritual gift'. This latter statement, however, oversimplifies the difference. The office of elder was certainly related at times with one's age (I Pet. v.1, 5; I Tim. v.1, 17), but the presbyters were those who had been proven in the faith (cf. I Tim. iii.6). The first converts from Paul's missionary work had become those in charge (I Cor. xvi.15; cf. Rom. xvi.5). Furthermore, the office of the presbyter certainly involved a considerable legal and institutional element, and in the long run administrative rights and pastoral duties were transferred to it. In the Corinthian Epistles, however, Paul had wanted to give freedom to faith in accordance with its character and in opposition to Palestinian and Hellenistic influences. In so doing he opposed the historical and legal as well as the spiritual authorities, although the dislike

19 Goes as well for Didache.
20 TWNT, vi, 661 ff.
21 H. v. Campenhausen, Kirchliches Amt, 71.

which he displayed of the institution of elders should not be seen as an artificial opposition.

The constitution which Paul represented was not, as has often been maintained from Sohm[22] to von Campenhausen,[23] purely pneumatic and charismatic. Even in I Corinthians it contained a legal and institutional element. As well as the mutual service out of love which was to characterize the life in the Church, a 'self-subordination' was also necessary (I Cor. xvi.16; cf. I Thess. v.12), since everything was to take place in the Church, 'in order' (I Cor. xiv.40). This order corresponds in its character to the order which is preserved fundamentally by the temporal rulers according to Rom. xiii.1 ff.,[24] and it is an order which can only be realized with the help of legal authority. This 'self-subordination' corresponds to the familiar *terminus technicus* of Rom. xiii.1 and the tables of household duties for the obedience to men who have been authorized to give instructions as a means to the realization of order. In this sense subordination was also commanded, according to I Corinthians, in the Church, and to the elders in I Pet. v.5. I Corinthians in no way represents an authoritative ideal of the Pauline constitution, but corresponds to the strong pneumatic movement found during the initial period in Corinth and more generally to a transitory stage in the Pauline constitution. The constitutional difference between the Palestinian office of the elders and the Pauline office of those in charge, the bishops, is thus simply relative, so much so that I Peter can place the 'charisma constitution', the only non-Pauline writing which he mentions (iv.10 f.), together with the constitutional office of the elders (v.1–5).

This becomes even clearer when it is seen that the office of the bishop[25]

[22] According to R. Sohm, *Kirchenrecht* (1892), and *Wesen und Ursprung des Katholizismus* ([2]1912), in keeping with the essence of the Church only the Spirit and not the legal authority which first became prominent in I Clement should hold sway in the Church. In contrast to this, Harnack, *Entstehung und Entwicklung der Kirchenverfassung und des Kirchenrechts in den ersten drei Jahrhunderten* (1910), demonstrated that there not only was but had to be legal orders in the Church from the very beginning. We can no longer use the purely historical methodology of Harnack nor can we view the Church, as Sohm, in its primitive Christian aspect as the invisible fellowship of pneumatic-enthusiastic individuals. Furthermore we cannot confine ourselves to Bultmann's statement (*Theology*, §51) that the eschatological-pneumatic revelation constructed traditions of historical necessity. We must rather add that this revelation is given as a personal witness and the Church in her essence is not only eschatological-pneumatic but also historical-physical, since it has pleased God to save those who believe through the weakness of the human message.

[23] v. Campenhausen, *Kirchliches Amt*, 69. Paul is practically placed in the category of the pneumatic perfectionism which he had repudiated in I Corinthians!

[24] Cf. the frequency of the terms with the root τάξις in Rom. xiii.1 ff.

[25] Literature: H. W. Beyer, *TWNT*, ii, 607–617; R. Schnackenburg, 'Episkopos und Hirtenamt', in *Episkopus* (*Festschrift* for Faulhaber, 1949), 66–88; A. Adam, 'Die Entstehung des Bischofsamtes', *Bethel-Jahrb.* (1957), 104–113 (cf. n. 27).

was not originally developed simply because of the needs of the Christian Church at that time, but it too had Old Testament and Jewish roots, just like the office of the presbyter.

The office of bishop does stem partly from its Greek surroundings. The Greek word 'ἐπίσκοπος' was a name for governing offices in both cities and associations and would have been familiar as such to anyone who spoke Greek. It was the Christian Church's own particular needs which caused her to take over the term, as is seen most clearly in the fact that the bishops were always mentioned in conjunction with the deacons from Phil. i.1 on (I Tim. iii; I Clem. xlii). The office of the deacon,[26] however, had most probably developed from the function at the communal meal, to judge by the root meaning of the word διακονία (cf. pp. 177 f.). Contrary to an opinion which goes back as early as Irenaeus,[27] Acts vi.1 ff. does not refer to its institution (the term does not even appear in this passage), but probably refers to the situation which caused the demand for it. At the communal meal the deacons performed the service of waiting at table (cf. Ignatius, Magn. vi.1; Trall. ii.1), but the bishops functioned as overseers in order to see that all went according to order and to carry out the church discipline which reached a climax at the meal. The picture of the communal meal in I Cor. xi does not specifically mention such a service, but the situation does call for it. Both offices had corresponding services to perform in the Church as well as in the gathered congregation. Thus, according to the Pastorals which speak from Pauline tradition, the bishops and deacons were to be 'in charge' of the Church just as a father is over his household (I Tim. iii.4 f., 12; Tit. i.6 f.).

The pastoral superintendence as well as the ordering of the various affairs, both of which actually constitute the essence of the office, point to a second derivation. The Greek root ἐπισκεπτ- corresponds in the Septuagint to the Hebrew root pāqåd. In 1QS vi.14 pāqid, 'the overseer' appears parallel to mᵉbāqqēr (vi.12, 20) as a name for an office. The powers of the overseer or overseers were quite limited in the Manual of Discipline, and the details are not clear. In the Damascus Scroll, on the other hand, the overseer, who was designated exclusively as mᵉbāqqēr, has a position comparable to that of a monarchical bishop. Was this background of the term influential in the development of the office of bishop? This seems to have been the case in view of the fact that the root ἐπισκεπτ- appears together with the root ποιμαιν- in the statement in Acts xx.28 and I Pet.

[26] Literature: W. Brandt, Dienst und Dienen im Neuen Testament (1931); H. W. Beyer, 'Der Diakon als Amtsträger in der Gemeinde' (TWNT, ii, 89, 93); C. F. D. Moule 'Deacons in the New Testament', Theology, 58 (1955); R. P. Symonds, 'Deacons in the Early Church', Theology, 58 (1955).

[27] Haer, I, 26, 3.

ii.25; v.2 (*v.l.*) about the bishop, a statement which comes from the Palestinian tradition.[28] According to CD. xiii.9 the *m*bāqqēr* was to retrieve those who had wandered astray, 'as a shepherd his sheep'. Several of the many Old Testament passages which contain this root take on added significance through the appearance together of these two roots. In these passages ἐπισκεπτ- implies the action of the shepherd seeking and retrieving his sheep which have gone astray and become scattered (Jer. xxiii.2; Ezek. xxxiv.6; Zach. x.3; xi.16).

The concept of the shepherd was already current in the Church through Jesus' own figure of speech,[29] but the correspondence between the two terms suggests that the office of overseer found in the separate Essene community had influenced the further development of the name and the office of the bishop. It is possible that the Pharisaic communities also had a similar office, but we can only surmise that this was the case. At any rate we have here a valuable analogy: in both the Essenes and the Church, the exaggerated demands of the separate community required an office which could continually serve to rescue those being assailed. In the former, this service was performed through the Law, in the latter through the Gospel. The overseer of the separate community attended, with a greater or lesser degree of participation on the part of the community itself, to approximately the same major responsibilities as did the elders in the synagogue community; perhaps for this reason the elders only appear on the fringe of the Essene writings. Even in terms of background and origin, the difference between the offices of the elder and the bishop was only relative.

4. In view of this strong correspondence between the two offices, it is not surprising that soon after the close of the Pauline period bishop and presbyter came to be used in most areas of the Church to refer to the same office. I Peter and Acts speak of the office of the elder, but they address the elders (Acts xx.17; I Pet. v.1) as bishops (Acts xx.28; I Pet. v.2 cf. ἐπισκοποῦντες; v.4 Christ as the chief Shepherd and in ii.25 the Bishop) when it concerned their actual work. By contrast, the Pastorals think more

---

[28] W. Nauck, 'Probleme des frühchristlichen Amtsverständnisses (I Pet. v.2 f.)', *ZNTW* 48 (1957), 200–220; previous discussion in: B. Reicke, *The Jewish 'Damascus Documents' and the New Testament* (1946), 16, n. 40 and Beyer, *TWNT*, ii, 614 f.

[29] The picture of the shepherd (pastor) which receives its meaning from Jesus, the chief Shepherd (I Pet. v.4) as well as its typological application to the apostles (I Pet. v.1 f.; John xxi.16) gives central expression to the task of the episcopates or presbyters (Ignatius, *Phild.* ii.1; *Rom.* ix.1; I Clem. xliv.3; Hermas, *Sim.* 9, 31, 4–6). It is missing (by chance?) in the earlier Pauline Epistles. In the list of offices in Eph. iv.11 it replaces the 'helpers' and 'administrators' of I Cor. xii.28. Who it is that should fill this role is not given, but the position in the list emphasizes its importance. The designation of the office as 'shepherd' (lat. pastor) is no more present here as anywhere else in the primitive Church. Cf. J. Jeremias, *TWNT*, vi, 497; Schnackenburg, *op. cit.* (n. 25).

of the office of the bishop. They definitely recognized the existence of elders (I Tim. v.17; Tit. i.5), but when the evangelists appointed elders, these were to meet the requirements of 'the bishop' (as a generic type) (Tit. i.7; cf. I Tim. iii.1 ff.).

The next step in the development becomes evident when I Tim. v.17 says in the same context that those of the elders who then 'ruled well' (in contrast to those who had no ruling function) were to be especially honoured, in particular those 'who labour in preaching and teaching'. The role of ruling and teaching, however, according to I Tim. iii.2, 4 f. and Tit. i.9, is the task of the bishop. Apparently, therefore, only some of the elders were active as bishops, and the bishops now emerge into prominence from the circle of the elders.

This distinction made by the Pastorals between the elders and the bishops appeared in Asia Minor and probably led around the turn of the century to the monarchical episcopacy.[30] The bishop became mainly the leader and representative of the church with a presbytery and a body of deacons subordinate to him. Ignatius (c. A.D. 110) took such an order for granted in the churches of Asia Minor;[31] he thought quite highly of the order, but did not urge it upon the Church of Rome where, as in Philippi (Polycarp, *Phil.*), it was not yet known.

In the time of I Clement, 'the elders' still carried out the ἐπισκοπή in Rome (xliv.1, 5). They were called bishops and deacons (xlii.4) and, unlike the elder members of the congregation to whom due honour was paid (i.3; xxi.6), they were described as the 'appointed presbyters' (liv.2; lvii.1). Hermas also took the same situation for granted.[32] Only towards the middle of the second century did the monarchical episcopacy prevail for the first time in Rome. In a large city like Rome this would only have been possible if the individual house-congregations had been bound together for some time by a body of presbyters (cf. p. 205). Whereas the monarchical episcopacy became prominent in all the Church between Rome and Antioch during the first decades of the second century, the development in Palestine, in parts of eastern Syria and in Egypt followed a different course up to the end of the second century when the Early Catholic Church began to get a foothold in these areas as well.

This hierarchy within the offices of the local church was demanded in

[30] That it came to a dispute between the bishops and elders is perhaps to be drawn from Asc. Jes. 3, 24, 29 (c. A.D. 100): 'A great division will arise between shepherd (= bishops?) and elders.' By contrast, the Presbyter of III John is not an elder of the congregation, so his dispute with Diothrephes does not in any way belong within this context (see §18, n. 19).

[31] Ignatius, *Magn.* vi.1; xiii.1; *Trall.* ii; iii.1; vii.2; *Phild.* iv; vii.1; x.2; *Smyr.* viii.1; xii.2; *Pol.* 6 : 1

[32] M. Dibelius, *Der Hirt des Hermas* (HNT 1923), on *Sim.* 9, 27, 3; E. Schweizer, *Church Order in the New Testament* (as in n. 1), 156–159 (Ger. 141–145); cf. §21, 5c.

particular by the fact that they had to take over to an ever-increasing extent the functions of the offices for the whole Church. This was particularly so in the case of the teaching in the service and in the catechesis. Did. 15, 1 refers specifically to this practice which had already appeared in the Pastorals (I Tim. v.17): 'Appoint therefore for yourselves bishops and deacons . . . for they also minister to you the ministry of the prophets and teachers'.

5. In the meanwhile, however, how had the offices for the whole Church developed?

a. Apart from the debatable statements about the author's role as an eyewitness in John's Gospel and in I John, 'apostles' in the true meaning of the word were already a part of the past for the writings of the second generation.

b. It is not coincidental that at the turn of the second generation, an office for the whole Church previously unmentioned in I Cor. xii.28 should appear in Eph. iv.11 alongside the office of apostle, that is the office of the evangelist.[33] Of the early Christian writings up to A.D. 120, Acts and the Pastorals were the only ones to mention the evangelists. Acts xxi.8 called Philip, one of the Seven, an evangelist. He was the one who carried the Gospel to Samaria and later worked with his four prophetically gifted daughters in Caesarea, Asia Minor and finally in Hierapolis. The Pastorals give this title to the recipients of the Epistles, Timothy and Titus (II Tim. iv.5), both of whom had formerly been Paul's fellow workers. The name referred to a circle of men who, partly independent of the apostles and partly as their companions and fellow workers, had carried out the mission and the pastoral care of the churches (II Cor. ii.13; vii.5 ff. concerning Titus; I Pet. v.12 f. concerning a similar circle around Peter). The Pastorals took for granted that such men would continue the missionary and pastoral work after the apostles had left the scene,[34] but they tell us just as little as the other sources about the historical work of these men. We can hardly overestimate their meaning for the Church of the second generation. By means of their work in the Church as a whole, the evangelists in particular, like the apostles, bound the churches together to one another as well as to the origin of the Church, so that they lived on in the tradition of Asia, like other teachers important to the whole Church, with the title of 'presbyter' or 'father'.[35] They were not only missionaries and pastors but also prophets and teachers in an outstanding way. One of their

[33] Literature: G. Friedrich, *TWNT*, ii, 734 f. (older literature); *TWNT*, vi, 666, n. 92; cf. n. 34 below.

[34] E. Kühl, *Die Gemeindeordnung in den Pastoralbriefen* (1885); H. Schlier, 'Die Ordnung der Kirche nach den Pastoralbriefen', in *Die Zeit der Kirche* (1956), 129–147.

[35] *TWNT*, vi, 670 ff.

number, John of Ephesus, if not actually the apostle, wrote the prophetic book of the New Testament; Mark and Luke, who were originally evangelists in this sense, wrote their books as teachers.[36]

c. Thus prophecy was in no way limited in the second generation to the prophets.[37] Its essence is most evident in the prophetic statements of Paul and John. Prophecy by means of a Spirit-inspired speech illuminated the course of the Church and the individual for both the present and the future. Since in so doing they spoke from the standpoint of the Christ-event (Rev. v; xix.10), unlike the Old Testament prophecy but like Jesus' prophetic words, their actual statements did not reveal isolated, pregnant acts and coming historical events,[38] but the essence of the heart (I Cor. xiv.23-25) and the essential characteristics of the soteriology of the end times (Rom. xi.25; I Cor. xv.51 ff.; Eph. iii; Rev. vi-xxi). Corresponding to this, there follows as instruction a call to concrete obedience in faith, rather than directions concerning particular deeds. The Church accepts this call in freedom through the Spirit (I Cor. vii.40), and yet the call itself binds her to an active obedience, For example, Rev. xiii sketched the picture of the essential anti-Christ and the world ruler in order that the Church might deny him veneration wherever she might confront the rudimentary realization of this picture. Thus, on the basis of a direct revelation, prophecy extended into the present and future, as it were, the apostolic witness to the redemptive event. The prophets were therefore always listed as second to the apostles, and prophecy came much closer to teaching here than in the Old Testament, Jewish realm. Teaching also speaks to the present and future in terms of the apostolic witness, and it also speaks in the Spirit; it does not speak intuitively but develops its statements theologically from the scriptures and the Christian tradition. Thus the teaching of I Corinthians does not uncover the grievances in the congregation there in a way much different to that of the prophecies in the letters to the churches of the Book of Revelation, even when I Corinthians says, 'It has been reported to me', (i.11) and Revelation says, 'I know thy works' (ii.2). Furthermore, a development of instructions along the lines of teaching often alternates with a giving of an intuitive instruction in I Corinthians.

Since prophecy lived in the Apostolic Age from a direct original witness

---

[36] The writers of the Gospels were first called 'Evangelists' in Tertullian, adv. Prax. 21, 23 and Hippolytus, Antichrist. 56.

[37] G. Friedrich, TWNT, vi, 842–863, extensive lit. on 781 f.

[38] Acts v.1 ff.; xi.28; xxi.10 f. are peripheral. Luke has also taken the heilsgeschicht-lich–eschatological declaration by Jesus that God's covenant with Israel would be broken and the destruction of the Temple would be the sign of this break and made both into a judgment which took place within history, i.e. the destruction of Jerusalem.

and since it brought the initial and fundamental illumination of the Church's present and future way, it establishes a standard for her and her prophecy; it therefore entered with important declarations, and rightly so, the New Testament Canon. In this sense the Church is '... built upon the foundation of the apostles and prophets' (Eph. ii.20).

As we have already seen, apostles and evangelists in particular were named in the primitive Christian writings as the representatives of this prophecy. The Christian prophets, who were believers with the rare gift of prophecy, were only seldom mentioned.[39] They in no way performed the same role in the pentecostal Church which the prophets had performed in Israel. The primitive Christian prophets were not itinerant preachers who were constantly moving, but generally settled down for a lengthy period of time in a church without being bound to it (Did. 13; cf. Acts xi.27 f.; xxi.10).

In the third generation, Hermas[40] still received important prophetic revelations in the Church of the West, but because of their apocalyptic form he only shared these revelations with the Church by recording them and reading them to the presbyters (Vis. 2, 4, 2 f.). He listed apostles, bishops, teachers and deacons as being the only ecclesiastical office holders (Vis. 3, 5, 1), and of these the apostles and probably the teachers were already a part of the past (Sim. 9, 16, 5). He mentions the appearance of men of prophecy in the circles of the Church solely in order to define the false prophets (Mand. 11), and he does not claim either the title or the position of a prophet for himself. In spite of his prophetic gift, he adopted for himself the order which I Clement had followed. I Clement mentioned in his detailed discussion of the office only apostles, bishops and deacons or presbyters, and overlooked in stony silence prophets and teachers. This he probably did because of the disorder which had emerged in Corinth from such charismatic men. At any rate, he deliberately intended to exclude them. At the same time Ignatius summoned the gathering of the Church in Asia Minor with a prophetic (!) voice: 'Give heed to the bishop, and to the presbytery and deacons' (Phild. vii.1)—in order to supplant the freer teachers who represented the false Gnostic teaching.

Thus the prophets and also the teachers were frequently repressed and replaced in the third generation by the representatives of the offices of the local church because, as we saw in Hermas, the power of genuine prophecy had begun to fail (cf. Did. 15, 1 for Syria) and false teaching (Rev. ii; I John ii.4), fraud and deception (Did. 11, 8; Hermas, Mand. 11; Origen,

---

[39] Acts xi.28; xxi.9 ff. An antimontanist writing from the second century (Eusebius, H.E., 5, 17, 3) can only name Agabus, Judas, Silas, Philip's daughters, Amnia in Philadelphia and Quadratus (the Apologete).

[40] Cf. n. 32 above.

Contra Celsum 7, 9, 11) had taken control of the freer offices. Consequently, the prophets disappeared towards the end of the second century and the freer teachers in the middle of the third century.[41] Eusebius (5, 17, 4) quotes the following principle from an anti-Montanist writing: 'The prophetic charisma, according to the apostolic word, must be present in the Church as a whole until the final parousia'. In fact, prophecy, as well as a pneumatic form of teaching, continued to live in the Church, but under the ascendancy of the institution. It was not until the Reformation that teaching rooted both in the earliest apostolic witness and in the Spirit was again acknowledged for itself.

d. The New Testament writings are full of teaching, but they only mention teachers[42] personally once (Acts xiii.1). The other references are either to the office (I Cor. xii.28; Eph. iv.11; James iii.1 cf. Matt. xiii.52) or to the function (Rom. xii.7; Gal. vi.6). Teaching, which originated with the apostles in the earliest Church (§7, 1), interpreted, in terms of the scriptures and through the Spirit, applied and transmitted the tradition of the Christ-event (II Thess. ii.15). The outstanding teachers in the first generation were the apostles, in the second generation the evangelists and in the third the representatives of the pastoral office in the individual churches like the writers I Clement, Ignatius, or Polycarp, the latter being called an 'apostolic and prophetic teacher' (*Martyrdom of Polycarp* 16). A diversified teaching was necessary in every congregation, however; as in the separate Jewish communities, the congregations had to be taught. Not only was this done in the services of worship, but the new members, the younger generations, and those who were to teach had to be instructed (§7, 1).[43] We can only determine now from a few limited references how this task of teaching was carried out. Perhaps as early as Acts xviii.25 and certainly by II Clem. xvii.1 the rare Greek word κατηχέω, taken over by Paul to mean Christian instruction (Gal. vi.6), had come to imply elementary instruction, while διδάσκω meant the teaching of the Church who could be addressed on the strength of her 'knowing' (Rom. vi.3; I Cor. x.15 *et al.*). In the post-Pauline period, the elementary instruction, which Heb. vi.1 also distinguished from the teaching for the 'mature', took place as 'catecumen instruction' prior to baptism (Justin, *Apol.* i.61), whereas according to the accounts of Acts, in the early period of the Church the converts were baptized. The distinction between the

---

[41] Harnack, *The Mission and Expansion of Christianity*, i, 350 ff.; 354 ff (Ger. i, 361 ff. 365 ff.); H. v. Campenhausen, *Kirchliches Amt*, 195–233; *TWNT*, vi, 161 f.

[42] K. H. Rengstorf, *TWNT*, ii, 138–168; F. V. Filson, 'The Christian Preacher in the First Century', *JBL*, 60 (1941), 317–328.

[43] L. J. Sherill, *The Rise of Christian Education* (1944); W. Jentsch, *Urchristliches Erziehungsdenken* (1951).

teaching in the sermon and that of the instruction, found in the homes (Tit. i.11) where the tradition was passed on, was quite fluid.[44]

Many, ranging from the fathers of households to the apostles, took part in this diversified teaching. The actual name of 'teacher' was given to the men who were especially familiar with the scriptures and the Christian tradition and who were able to reinterpret the Christ-event with reference to both sources in a fashion comparable to that of I Corinthians and Hebrews, and to apply this to the revelant questions of the Church, the name of teacher was thus a recognition of a charisma just as was the name of prophet. When the Church in Did. 15, 1 was told to ' . . . appoint for themselves bishops and deacons . . .' who were to minister . . . the ministry of the prophets and teachers', it remained free to recognize charismata. On the other hand, when according to I Clement the particular office in the Church was to be filled only by bishops and deacons who ' . . . were appointed by them [apostles] or later on by other eminent men with the consent of the whole Church . . .' (I Clem. xliv.3), then the rule of the Spirit invested in the Church had been subordinated to that of an institution.

6. The final result of this history of the primitive Christian offices raises the question about their meaning and structure. The instruction to the Early Catholic Church, as represented by I Clement and Ignatius, emphasized the local church office which soon took on the threefold form of the monarchical episcopate. This instruction established the office as the single legitimate heir to the office of the apostle and excluded more and more the freer office of the prophet and teacher, whereas the Gnostic movement relied upon these latter offices.

From a historical point of view, the development of the offices in I Clement and Ignatius appears logical, since the tendency was towards an organizational solidification; from a theological point of view, it had the relative justification of the path which led to Early Catholicism in its favour (§18, 6). The ancient Church developed her offices in view of this outcome, but basically it was a new starting point. It is at precisely this point that the departure from the New Testament starting point becomes so evident that the Reformation deliberately refused to develop the office of the Church from such a starting point. Instead, the Reformation chose

[44] V. Taylor, *Mark*, 133: indications of a catechetical background for the material found in Mark's Gospel have been preserved in the Gospel: menmonic principles, succession of allied themes, explanations and applications. G. Schille, 'Bemerkungen zur Formgeschichte des Evangeliums' *NTS* 4 (1958), 1–24, 101–114: Mark is the expression of the earlier post-baptismal catechesis; Matthew the forerunner of the ante-baptismal catechesis which is found in the Didache (the.is as a whole quite questionable). Cf. G. Schille on the catechetical elements in Eph. (*ThLZ*, 82, 1957, 325–334) and in Heb. (*ZNTW*, 48, (1957), 270–280).

to go back to the New Testament itself, although this closed at a stage at which the offices of the Church had gained neither a unified nor a clear-cut form. Consequently, in the process of going to the New Testament pattern for the offices, it was easy to legitimize certain stages which had been of temporary and regional character, such as the presbyter constitution of Palestine or the charismatic outline in I Cor. xii. Moreover, it was most easy arbitrarily to set aside the two integrating offices of the apostle and the prophet. One can only do justice to the New Testament statements about the offices when they are viewed in terms of their material starting point in the primitive Christian development of the offices, namely Christ's commission. One must, however, go beyond the Lutheran Reformation, which intiated this approach, and analyse the New Testament formation of the offices as a model with view to their underlying principles. Let us now attempt to trace the structure of the history of the primitive Christian offices in just this manner.

a. Jesus' commission, which set the establishment of Christian offices in motion, becomes visible at the very beginning of the historical development in that Jesus himself had placed all of his followers under the obligation to serve. This was the service which had been created by his own serving and in which his serving was continued. At the same time he called some to a special service, to the apostolate. The apostles were made responsible in a special way for the Gospel, for the Church as a whole, for her mission and for her care. In II Cor. v.18-20, Paul described this commission theologically as being given by God, who had not only brought about the universal redemptive act in Christ's death and resurrection but had also established the word which preached this event, as well as the service to spread this word. This ministry is given within the Church, and its goal is her 'edification'. It has been given to all as the indefinite 'we' in vv. 18-20 indicates, but especially to the apostle. From I Cor. xii it becomes evident just what unifies this ministry and what makes its diversity necessary (cf. p. 183). Both the redemptive event and the Church have an eschatological-pneumatic and a historical aspect simultaneously. The former aspect united all members in the 'priesthood of the believers', while the latter causes a diversity of service, especially the particular offices whose model was the apostolate. Because of the historical aspect, the message comes through historical tradition and necessitates as a responsibility for the Church as a whole the forming of the mission as well as the correcting pastoral care for the struggling believers. This required offices along the lines of the apostolate (§12, 4). The Church was thus neither 'before the office', nor was the office 'before the Church'. The one had always existed together with the other. The Church exists for serving as well as from serving since she lives for Christ and from him

(Eph. iv.15). In this sense, the Church in accordance with Christ's commission is responsible for the realization of this service.

b. How does the formation of the special ministries result from this commission? According to I Cor. xii.27 f., God formed the offices and determined who would fill them by granting spiritual gifts, but the Pastorals appear to be diametrically opposed to this. In other words the problem has been reduced to the following:[45] according to I Corinthians the Church only had to recognize and order the charismata offered to her; according to the Pastorals she had positions to fill (I Tim. iii.1). According to I Corinthians the gift determined the office holder; according to the Pastorals he was appointed on the basis of a probation period and the charisma for the office was imparted through the ordination (I Tim. iv.14). This antithesis, however, is an abstract construction,[46] since it places two possibilities over against each other which in the New Testament, even in I Corinthians and the Pastorals, were always jointly at work in the formation of the offices, even when they received varied emphasis and assessment.

In I Corinthians, Paul sharply rejected the perfectionistic, fanatical conception that the *pneuma* makes the physical, i.e. the temporal and historical element, of no consequence and sets it aside. The Spirit does not set the physical and historical elements aside, but enlists them into service while at the same time judging the old man. Therefore, for example, the physical difference between man and wife was not to be eliminated in the functions of the service of worship (I Cor. xi.2–16; xiv.34 ff., 40, in spite of Gal. iii.28).[47] On the basis of this principle, Paul would not have excluded what took place in Acts vi.1–7, even though he always challenged his readers to permit the Spirit to become effective through faith and to accept his working rather than to establish offices and fill them. He even sent Titus to Corinth (II Cor. viii.16; xii.18) without waiting until one of his fellow workers had volunteered for that difficult conciliatory visit. Thus the Pauline Church had to respect the charismata offered to her, and yet not simply to wait for these. She was to realize the necessary tasks and to concern herself with carrying these out—even when in the final analysis only the Lord of the harvest could request workers for his harvest (Matt. ix.37 f.; II Cor. viii.16).

[45] v. Campenhausen, *Kirchliches Amt*, 122–129; Literature: *Charismen und Ämter in der Urkirche* (1951); G. Friedrich, 'Geist und Amt' *Bethel-Jahrb.* (1952), 61–85; E. Kohlmeyer, 'Charisma oder Recht?' *Z. für Rechtsgeschichte* 69 ʹ ʹ52), 2 ff.

[46] Since v. Campenhausen, *Kirchliches Amt* (122 ff.) has inte reted Paul and the Pastorals each in terms of the two abstract possibilities, they represent for him the polar antitheses of the primitive Christian concept of office. See n. 57.

[47] The position of the woman in the organism of the primitive Christian congregations corresponds to this: A. Oepke, *TWNT*, i, 786–790.

The Pastorals, in spite of a different stress which is not to be overlooked, remain within the framework of this starting point, whereas I Clement does not. According to this letter, the offices of the bishop and deacon were established according to divine instruction in the scriptures by the apostles and were filled by those they had appointed (I Clem. xlii.1-4; xliv.1 ff.). What had occasionally taken place according to Acts xiv.23 was here construed as a general occurrence. With the aid of this historical fiction, offices which had emerged of their own accord were now made into a *jure divino* ordinance. In I Clement we actually have existing offices which are to be filled. Here the rule of the Spirit, who offers the charismata and points out new tasks and thus gives structure to the offices, is eliminated. The disapproving silence about prophets and teachers documents this fact. The tension-filled relationship between the spiritual and the historical, the living event and the institution given to the Church from the character of the redemptive event itself, is relinquished and the former is subordinated to the latter. By contrast, the Pastorals view the offices as being more flexible in terms of the actual commission (cf. I Tim. v.17; II Tim. ii.2) and in no way as a fixed ordinance. I Clement and not the Pastorals developed a starting point which departed from the guide line instituted by Jesus' commission for the formation of the offices.

The New Testament writings did not deduce the special offices from their establishment by the apostles, as did I Clement. The commission for the office of the apostle served as the basic outline and model for their structure. The office of the apostle stood at the top of the list throughout the first generation and was determinative for the other offices. What its disappearance meant for the structure of the office is first expressed in the writings of the second generation. According to Acts and the Pastorals, Paul demanded that his special service be continued, which was the representation of the apostolic tradition, and was performed in the mission as well as in the pastoral service to the local church and in the function of overseer and protector for whole areas of the Church. In Acts xx bishops were called to the former; in the Pastorals evangelists were called to the latter. If we take John xxi.15 ff. as being in the typical Johannine mode of speaking, this passage also indicated that the special commission of the apostolate was to be continued further in the Church to the extent that it was separable from the original body of witnesses. The instructions left room for a diversified structure of this special commission. They also made it possible to separate the care for the physical needs as 'diakonia' in the narrow sense of the term from the 'ministry of the word' (Acts vi.1-7; I Pet. iv.11).

Thus the office of the apostle became the model of the obligatory commission for the Church. The apostles were also the foundation stones of the Church in this respect, but not a basis for a series of office holders which they made legitimate through the principle of succession. The latter was quietly intimated in I Clement (cf. p. 182). Succession is a sequence of office holders who legitimize their successors either legally or sacramentally. The principle was current in the Hellenistic as well as in the Jewish surroundings, yet, and this is significant, it was not taken up at all in all the New Testament. It turns the office into a unique institution which destroys the vital, mutual relationship between Church and office.[48] In order to obviate such tendencies, the Johannine writings emphasized the immediacy of all to their Lord (John vi.45; I John ii.20, 27) and only described the special office as a commission without giving it a name (John xxi.15 ff.).

c. The procedure of filling the special office corresponded to its structure. Only Acts and the Pastorals deal with this in the New Testament. According to these, a nomination and an installation always took place both when the charismata offered were simply to be accepted as well as when particular tasks were to be performed.

The nomination[49] took place, like all of the other activity in the Church, in accordance with a pneumatic rather than a democratic or oligarchic principle. In Acts vi.3 the Church selected them; in xiii.1 f. the prophets named the names (just as in I Tim. i.18; iv.14); in xiv.23 the missionaries installed the first office holders. The Pastorals made it the evangelists' obligation to install office holders, without giving any indications about the congregation's participation (Tit. i.5; cf. II Tim. ii.2). In a letter written from one church to another on the subject of church offices, I Clement maintained the participation of the congregation in the formula which remained valid for a long time in the ancient Church: the office holders were appointed by eminent men '. . . with the consent of the whole Church' (xliv.3). How the nomination was shared by the church and the office holders thereafter is a matter of opinion.

[48] v. Campenhausen, *Kirchliches Amt*, 172 ff., traces the appearance of the principle of succession c. the middle of the second century to the idea of successors in the philosophical schools. E. Stauffer, 'Zum Kalifat des Jakobus', *ZRG*, 4 (1952), 207 ff., traces it back to the succession of the High Priests and rabbis. To be sure, both influences were at work, but *contra* Stauffer und Ehrhardt the principle of succession had not yet entered the scene in Jerusalem by the time of James; rather it quite possibly came towards the end of the first century (quite strong in *Kerygmata Petru*, Hennecke, ³ii, 106 f. (Ger. II, 69 f.). In Asia Minor it was present at least by the time of Papias. For discussion: K. H. Rengstorf, 'Das Wort Gottes und die apostolische Sukzession', in *Die Kirche Jesu Christi und das Wort Gottes*, ed. Zöllner–Staehlin (1937), 187–203; A. T. Ehrhardt, *The Apostolic Succession in the First two Centuries of the Church* (1950); K. M. Carey, *The Historic Episcopate in the Fulness of the Church* (1954); O. Karrer, 'Apostolische Nachfolge und Primat', *ZKTheol.*, 77 (1955), 129–168; G. Blum, *Tradition und Sukzession*, 1963.

[49] Primitive Christian: χειροτονέω (Acts xiv.23; II Cor. viii.19; Did. 15, 1; Ignatius, *Phild.* x.1); on the later usage, see n. 52 below.

From a very early period the nomination had been followed by an installation through the laying on of hands in keeping with an Old Testament Jewish custom. However, in the New Testament one can only designate as ordination[50] the installation through the laying on of hands mentioned with reference to Timothy in the Pastorals and not the events in Acts vi.6 and xiii.3. This is the case because the former alone corresponded formally to the installation called ordination by the Rabbis[51] and later by the Church. For such an installation the phrase 'laying on of hands' took on the special meaning 'to ordain', just as it did among the Rabbis.[52] Both Epistles to Timothy addressed the evangelist on the subject of his ordination and bound him to bring about the ordination of similar office holders who, like himself, would take over the transferable commission of the apostolate (II Tim. ii.2). It thus became a general practice. Ordination was an act performed as part of the service and included the following elements in keeping with the character of the office being conferred: First, the apostolic tradition, probably in formulaic form, was delivered to the one being ordained (II Tim. ii.2). Secondly, he gave confession to this tradition by means of a confessional formula. Thirdly, the presbytery then performed the laying on of hands (I Tim. iv.14).[53] Only II Timothy mentioned (i.6) that Paul also took part in the laying on of hands. The participation of the apostle was mentioned so incidentally that any thought of an apostolic succession must be considered alien to it.[54] This laying on of hands imparted the charisma for carrying out the functions of the office.

The Pastorals reminded the evangelist of his ordination in a fashion similar to the other New Testament writings' reference to baptism,[55] not because it too was a sacramental act[56]—baptism and the eucharist were described even in I Cor. x.1 ff. as unique rites—but because it approximates baptism in several respects. Christian ordination is not, as was the Rabbinic ordination, a legal credential meaning that the one ordained stands now in a line of succession, knows the tradition and is capable of

[50] Literature: E. Lohse, *Die Ordination im Spätjudentum und im Neuen Testament* (1951); J. Heubach, *Die Ordination zum Amt der Kirche* (1956).

[51] Lohse, *op. cit.* (n. 50), 19–66.

[52] Old Testament-Jewish, s'mikkah = ἐπίθεσις τῶν χειρῶν, later in the church fathers, *ordinatio* = χειροτονία (cf. Lohse, *op. cit.* (n. 50), 76, and J. Jeremias, ZNTW 47 (1957), 130 f.).

[53] Differently, J. Jeremias, ZNTW, 47 (1957), 127–132.

[54] *Contra* Schlier, *op. cit.* (n. 34), 144 f.

[55] I Tim. iv.14; II Tim. i.6. As E. Käsemann (*Bultmann–Festschrift*, 1954, 261–268), has made probable, I Tim. vi.11–16 is an ordination paraenesis whose first two verses were taken over from a baptismal paraenesis.

[56] *Contra* v. Harnack, *Entstehung und Entwicklung der Kirchenverfassung und des Kirchenrechts in den ersten drei Jahrhunderten* (1910), 20 and v. Campenhausen, *Kirchliches Amt*, 126.

making doctrinal and disciplinary decisions in keeping with the tradition. Timothy could not boast of this as the opponents in Corinth boasted of their letters of recommendation (II Cor. iii.1), but he was to be certain of the charisma which was imparted to him through the ordination (I Tim. iv.14; II Tim. i.6), i.e. the work of the Spirit which calls and equips one for the service. Accordingly ordination, like its closest analogy in the rabbinic ordination, was an obligation for life. This is indicated by its correspondence to baptism as its relationship to an office which takes over most directly the inheritance of the office of the apostle, an office which was certainly for life.

This form of installing officers corresponded to the intention of the apostolic Gospel, even if it was only mentioned in the Pastorals and suggested by Acts. Jesus himself had called the apostles through a historical act, and this calling meant a simultaneous endowment of authority. He now operated in the same manner but through his Body, the Church. From the earliest period, the gesture of laying on of hands was an expression not only of intercession but of an authoritative impartation of grace (cf. p. 208). In this sense ordination was not only a substantiation or attestation of the calling by God but also its concluding act.

d. The commission and the postition which the ordination assigned to office holders according to the Pastorals were in keeping with the New Testament starting point. I Clement, on the other hand, viewed the office holders' relationship to the Church too much from the principle of legitimacy when his discussions about the office led to the final conclusion that the office holders who had been properly installed and who had performed the duties of the office blamelessly were not to be discharged (xliv.3–6). Even for Paul the freedom of the Spirit was not greater than God's faithfulness (I Cor. i.9; I Thess. v.24), but I Clement did not develop his conclusion from this faithfulness, so much as from the world order which conditions and legitimizes everything.

Just as I Clement introduced a legal misunderstanding so Ignatius introduced a misunderstanding of the position of the office holders similar to that found in the mysteries. He did not make the monarchical episcopate into an obligatory ordinance, but he did assent to it, wherever it had developed a position in the holy order. The monarchical episcopate brought in the rudiments of the hierarchical concepts by means of its relationship to the other church offices and to the Church. This tended to make the Church into a sacramental institution of salvation and the word into directions for her use as such an institution. The presence of the bishop identified a gathering for a divine service to be the redeemed community, and so the preaching of Ignatius' Epistles always enjoined its recipients to join the Church gathered around the bishop to celebrate the eucharist (§18, 4b). The fact that Old Testament analogies were sought was in keeping with the change of attitude towards the office. As a result, the Old Testament difference between priests and laity began to show itself in various forms among the Apostolic Fathers (I Clem. xl.5; Did. 13, 3–7), and at the same time pre-Christian terms for office began to emerge (e.g. λειτουργία (-εω) I Clem. xli.1; xliv.2 f., 6; Did. 15, 1). In contrast to this incipient misunderstanding of the office in Ignatius which departed from the New Testament starting point, the Johannine preaching reminded the Church of her eschatological and pneumatic character without intending to give her a utopian and pneumatic Church order (§18, 4c).[57] What Church and office actually mean is depicted ultimately, as becomes evident in Ignatius, in the service of worship.

22. THE SERVICE OF WORSHIP[1]

1. The primitive Christian concept of the essence of the service of worship is evident in the terminology itself. The termini technici developed by the Septuagint for the (cultic) worship of God (λατρεία) and for the service of the priest (λειτουργία) were taken up in the New Testament writings, but they were related to the general conduct of the believers rather than to the actual service of worship. We have only two verbs which refer to the latter, and they express a coming together or a gathering of the members.[2] Thus the whole life of the believers was a service of worship (Rom. xii.1 f.), and the actual celebration of the service of worship was designated by the gathering of the congregation. In this gathering of the community, the koinonia of the believers with the Lord

---

[57] Thus it is to be maintained with Harnack op. cit. (n. 56), contra v. Campenhausen, Kirchliches Amt, that the decisive new starting points which led to the Early Catholic understanding of office emerge in I Clement and Ignatius, whereas Luke and the Pastorals, in spite of their proximity to the history of development of I Clement, took the situation of the second generation into account basically in a way corresponding to the New Testament starting-point, and John in his onesidedness asserted the central concern of the eschatological message of redemption.

[1] H. Lietzmann, Mass and the Lord's Supper (1964); W. Bauer, Der Wortgottesdienst der ältesten Christen (1930); A. B. MacDonald, Christian Worship in the Primitive Church (1934); A. M. Ramsay, The Gospel and the Catholic Church (²1956); E. Lohmeyer, Kultus und Evangelium (1942); L. S. Thornton, The Common Life in the Body of Christ (1944); O. Cullmann, Early Christian Worship (Eng. trans. 1963, of Urchristentum und Gottesdienst (1944); W. Hahn, Gottesdienst und Opfer Christi (1951); G. Dix, The Shape of the Liturgy (⁷1959); G. Delling, Der Gottesdienst im Neuen Testament (1952); R. Stählin, 'Die Geschichte des christlichen Gottesdienstes', Leiturgia (1954), 1–81; F. D. Moule, Worship in the New Testament (²1962).

[2] συνέρχεσθαι (ἐν τῇ ἐκκλησίᾳ): I Cor. xi.17 f., 20, 33 f.; xiv. 23, 26; Ignatius, Eph. xiii.1; συνάγεσθαι: Matt. xviii.20; Acts iv.31; xx.7 f.; I Cor. v.4; Did. 16 : 2; I Clem. xxxiv.7; later συναξις (Justin, Apol. 65); Jk. 2 : 2 συναγωγή; Heb. x.25 ἐπισυναγωγή.

and with one another was realized (Acts ii.42; I Cor. x.16 f.). This historical realization of the *koinonia* occurs ' . . . where two or three are gathered in my name . . .' (Matt. xviii.20), especially through the Lord's Supper. Witness in word and deed as well as confession and prayer pervaded the whole life of the believers, but the sacrament was peculiar to the celebration of the service of worship. In the primitive Christian writings, the performance of the sacraments was never reserved especially for the office holders. However, since the sacraments enrolled one into the Church, they had been delivered to the Church as a whole and to her representatives, as Ignatius (*Magn.* vii; *Smyr.* viii) correctly pointed out against the individualistic character of the Gnostic conventicles.

In Pauline terminology, the Exalted Lord becomes historically effective in a most immediate fashion through the Spirit during the service of worship in order to construct the redeemed community of the end times, the Temple of God (I Cor. iii.9–15; I Pet. ii.4–6). The Spirit opens one's mouth for preaching, for prayer and for confession of faith (I Cor. ii.12 f.; xii.3, 13; xiv; Rom. viii.15, 26), and He reveals the preaching to the heart of the hearers (John xv.26 f.; Acts v.32; II Cor. iv.6). The Spirit makes use of men (I Cor. xii.4 ff.) and limits itself, even when it speaks prophetically, to the witness of Jesus and to the sacraments (John xiv.26; Rev. xix.10; I Cor. xii.13). This self-limitation on the part of the Spirit never means, as becomes clear in the case of Simon the Magician (Acts viii) and with the opponents of Paul in II Corinthians, that a person could have the Spirit at his disposal by merely reciting correct doctrine and performing the sacraments correctly. It does mean, however, that one can be certain in faith of the Spirit's working on the basis of the promise given with this service (I Cor. ii. 12 f.; I Thess. ii.13). In this way, 'the worship in Spirit and truth' takes place now as a prelude to the eschaton and supersedes the Old Testament and Jewish as well as the Gentile services of worship (John iv.23 f.; II Cor. iii; Rev. ii.22). It is no longer the work of man's efforts but of God's grace (I Cor. xii.3 f.).

2. The Church had begun the practice of gathering mainly on the 'first day of the week' (I Cor. xvi.2; Acts xx.7; Did. 14, 1) quite early.[3] This was called the 'Lord's Day' (Justin, *Apol.* I, 67, 3; 'Sunday'=the day of the pagan week of the planets dedicated to the sun god) for the first time in Rev. i.10 and Did. 14, 1 (cf. Ignatius, *Magn.* ix). The emergence of this particular day resulted from the origin of all Christian services of worship, that on this day the Lord arose (Barn. xv.9) in order to gather his

---

[3] E. Schürer, 'Die siebentägige Woche im Gebrauche der christlichen Kirche der ersten Jahrhunderte', *ZNTW*, 6 (1905), 1–66; H. Lietzmann, *Der christliche Kalender* (1935); E. Lohse, *TWNT*, vii, 29–34 n. 228 for further literature; W. Rordorf, *Der Sonntag, Geschichte des Ruhe- und Gottesdiensttages im ältesten Christentum*, 1962.

own around him (cf. Luke xxiv.1, 36; John xx.19, 26). This stress on the Lord's Day was not based on the Third Commandment until the fourth century. The Hellenistic Church rejected the observation of the Sabbath along with the Jewish feasts as being part of Judaism (Gal. iv.10; Col. ii.16; Ignatius, *Magn.* ix.1), whereas Jewish Christianity living in accordance with the Law kept the Sabbath rest in keeping with their surroundings (Matt. xxiv.20). The only feasts of the pre-Nicean Church were the Passover, which from the very beginning was celebrated as a memorial to the accomplished redemption of the end times with a view to its fulfillment in the parousia,[4] and Pentecost, which developed out of the Pentecost events and, like the Christian observance of the Passover, from the Jewish feast. Pentecost represented (Acts ii.1 ff.) the exaltation ('ascension') of Jesus and the development of the eschatological people of God through the Spirit.[5] Even before the end of the first century, a fast on Wednesday and Friday was instituted in the East, in opposition to the custom of the Pharisees (Did. 8, 1; cf. Luke xviii.12). By contrast, in the West Tertullian only knew about a general fast just prior to the Passover (*Jeiun.* 2). Perhaps this was the point of the reference behind Mark ii.20 and Luke v.35 when they inserted 'in that day/in those days' into the logion concerning the question about fasting.

The place, like the time of the service of worship, was determined entirely by its content. The baptismal service took place as far as was possible in flowing or standing water which made immersion possible. The celebration of the meals together was by nature dependent upon a table (I Cor. x.21) so that private homes, which in the Mediterranean lands were built around a court and thus offered considerable room, were the gathering places until the close of the second century. It is not merely coincidental that the basilica of the ancient Church was developed architecturally from the Roman patrician home. Dix[6] has attempted to depict in detail the role of the individual parts of the Roman house in the gathering for a service of worship, but this remains purely hypothetical

---

[4] Not as memorial to the passion or the resurrection! While the Jews celebrated the Passover until 3 a.m., the Church fasted (for them) and celebrated the Lord's Supper. Perhaps this order is reflected in Luke xxii.15–18 (abstinance from the Passover meal), 19 f. An Early Christian Passover-*haggada* lies at the roots of I Cor. v.7 f. Cf. J. Jeremias, *TWNT*, v, 900 ff.; *Eucharistic Words of Jesus* (1966), 237–255 (Ger. ³1960, 229–246); B. Lohse, *Das Passafest der Quartadecimaner* (1953); H. Schürmann, 'Die Anfänge christlicher Osterfeier', *Theol. Quartalschrift*, 31 (1951), 414–425; O. Casel, 'Art und Sinn der ältesten christlichen Osterfeier', *Jahrb. für Liturgiewissensch.* 14 (1938), 1–78.

[5] In I Cor. xvi.8 and Acts xx.16 the Jewish calendar is used for giving the dates, but Acts ii.1 ff. and others refer to a Christian feast: *TWNT*, vi, 49 f. 52 f.; G. Kretschmar, 'Himmelfahrt und Pfingsten', *ZKG*, 65 (1954), 229.

[6] Dix, *op. cit.* (n. 1), 16–27.

for the primitive Christian period. The single cultic symbol in the Christian homes was the cross, and it appeared as early as the first century.[7] The material concerning the altar in Heb. xiii.10 is purely figurative.[8] Thus the believers in the larger cities could only come together in separate groups,[9] the contact between these groups apparently being established through assemblies of the presbyters (Hermas, *Vis.* 2, 4, 3). In addition, gatherings also took place during the early period in the halls of the Temple (Acts ii.46; v.12) or in the lecture halls of a philosopher (Acts xix.9). Such gatherings had mainly a missionary orientation, and they had probably already died out by the second generation when the Christians had come under the public's suspicion.[10]

Justin gives us the first total picture of a Christian service (*Apol.* I, 61; 65; 67), but certain types of services and their essential elements, even a certain liturgical order, had begun to emerge much earlier. The sparse material can be supplemented by cautiously drawing conclusions from the latter development as well as from the factors then present in the varied religious environment. However, in the use of this method we must not forget the fact that the structure of the service in the period under question was very flexible and differed from place to place. The major sources of the first and second centuries simply represented their respective branches of this development: the Didache represented Syria c. A.D. 100, Justin represented Rome and Asia Minor c. A.D. 150, and Hippolytus' *Apostolic Tradition*[11] represented Rome c. A.D. 200 with eastern influences. Thus we can only point out the basic outlines which appeared here and there in different forms.

3. From the very beginning a separate service developed around the act of baptism[12] (§6, 5). From the standpoint of the history of religions, four

[7] H. Dinkler, 'Zur Geschichte des Kreuzessymbols', *ZThK*, 48 (1951), 148 ff.

[8] *TWNT*, iii, 182 f.; J. Braun, *Der christliche Altar in seiner geschichtlichen Entwicklung* (1924).

[9] *Mart. Justini* 3: Justin (c. 165) states during his trial that the Christians of Rome never come together at the same place and that he only knows of one of the places of gathering.

[10] The Roman Church probably had at their behest subterranean burial places (cemeteries or catacombs) towards the end of the first century, but they did not serve as gathering places for worship services.

[11] We are quoting from the reconstruction in G. Dix, *The Treatise on the Apostolic Tradition of St. Hippolytus of Rom* (1937); cf. A. Elfers, *Die Kirchenordnung Hippolyts von Rom* (1938); further in W. Nauck, *Die Tradition und der Charakter des I Johannesbriefs* (1957), 42 ff.

[12] G. Dix, *The Theology of Confirmation* ([2]1948); J. Jeremias, *Infant Baptism in the First Four Centuries* (as in §6, n. 29); O. Cullmann, *Baptism in the New Testament* (as in §6, n. 29); G. Schille, 'Liturgisches Gut im Epheserbrief', (unpub. diss., Göttingen, 1952), 148 ff.; W. Nauck, *op. cit.* (n. 11), 42–46, 153–182; K. Aland, *Die Säuglingstaufe im Neuen Testament und in der alten Kirche* (1961); cf. §6, n. 29; G. Kretschmar, 'Die Geschichte des Taufgottesdienstes in der alten Kirche', *Leiturgia V: Der Taufgottesdienst*, (1964–66).

similar rites affected the formation of this service in the course of the first two centuries, the proselyte baptism,[13] the initation act of the Essenes,[14] the baptism of John (which was itself influenced by the former two) and the initiation rites of the mysteries.[15]

Under what conditions would one be admitted for baptism? With the Essenes one had to go through a three-year novitiate before one could be ceremonially accepted (1QS iii.6–12; v.7–11, 20 ff.) after numerous examinations by the overseers and the gathered community (1QS vi.13–23; Josephus, B.J. 2, 8, 7). Children of the Essene community were given a rank when they reached their twentieth year following their special upbringing (1QSa vi–xviii). Among the Christians, one raised the question about admittance to baptism with the formula, 'What is to prevent . . .',[16] the fulfilling of the request of faith for baptism which originated with the call of God. This question was not raised liturgically at the baptismal act but prior to it. The decision was made for the 'first converts' (Rom. xvi.5; I Cor. xvi.15) by the missionary, even when the latter did not directly assist in the baptism himself (Matt. xxviii.19; Acts viii.38; x.48; I Cor. i.14 ff). The missionary was then responsible for his decision to the Church standing behind him (Acts xi.1–18). Everywhere that baptism meant enrolment into an existing community, one proceeded with baptism just as one would with the disciplinary situations (cf. pp. 170 f.) since the granting and refusing of baptism was the first application of the 'keys to the Kingdom' (Matt. xvi.18 f.; John xx.21f. in connection with the mission). Baptism, like the promise of forgiveness, could not be refused one who had been 'converted' and who desired it in faith. This rule was in keeping with the essence of the matter; even Jesus had made his redemptive work dependent on faith alone and had granted it on the basis of a believing request for those who could not themselves request it. In the missionary baptism of entire 'houses', the children were probably also baptized.[17] According to Mark x.13–16 par., believing parents were not to 'be hindered' from having their children blessed by Jesus. I Cor. vii.14 does not allow the conclusion that it was any different in Corinth during the time of Paul.[18]

But how was the faith of the one desiring baptism to be determined?

---

[13] Jeremias, *Infant Baptism in the First Four Centuries* 24–40, (as in §6, n. 29, Ger. 29–47); S.–B., i, 108 ff.

[14] Nauck, *op. cit.* (n. 11), 44, 167–173.

[15] C. K. Barrett, *The New Testament Background*, 96–100; C. Schneider, *Geistesgeschichte des antiken Christentums* (1954), ii, 201–204.

[16] Matt. iii.17; Mark x.14 par.; Acts viii.36; x.47; xi.17.

[17] Jeremias, *Infant Baptism in the First Four Centuries* (as in §6, n. 29, Ger. 23–28, 19–24); 'Nochmals: Die Anfänge der Kindertaufe', *Theol. Existenz heute*, 101 (1962), 21–27.

[18] Differently, Jeremias, *ibid.*, 44–48 (Ger. 52–56).

The renunciation of the pagan life and dealings, as well as the turning to the everyday fellowship of the Church, were necessary signs, but in the final analysis, faith could only become clear, as in the miracle healings by Jesus, through a *kerygmatic* dialogue and be recognized by faith. The most direct expression of this faith was the confession of faith (Rom. x.9), so a confession of faith was introduced quite early into the liturgy of the baptismal ceremony. Acts viii.37 is a subsequent insertion into the text of Acts, but we find early formulae in the New Testament writings which were probably confessions of faith given at baptism.[19] Towards the middle of the second century, the basis of the Apostolic Creed developed from the Roman confession of faith at baptism.[20] In the course of the development leading to Early Catholicism, the question about one's faith became more and more an examination of one's knowledge and conduct, so that the conditions for admittance to baptism in the *Apostolic Tradition* of Hippolytus (XVI, 1-8) remind one immediately of 1QS.[21]

In the second generation, a catechetical instruction demanded by the situation developed, which preceded the baptism. In this instruction, the missionary sermon (cf. Heb. vi.2) and the baptismal *paraenesis* (cf. Did. 7, 1 f.) were unfolded doctrinally. This is perhaps implied already in Heb. vi.1 f., probably apparent in Did. 7, 1 f., and certainly present in II Clem. xvii.1 and Justin, *Apol.* I, 61 (§21, 5d). In Justin (*Apol.* I, 61), admittance to the catechetical instruction (also Hippolytus, *Apostolic Tradition*, XVI, 1-8) or to baptism required that the baptismal candidates promise to live according to the Gospel, so that the obligation to desist from evil which Pliny reported (cf. p. 211) could have been connected with baptism, although such an obligation corresponded more to the synergistic initiation act of the Essenes (1QS v.7-11) than to the Christian baptism; it is not coincidental that the New Testament makes no reference to it. On the other hand, it is conceivable that the confession of faith in primitive Christianity might be developed into an express confession of one's sins and a turning to the living God, although such an account in the New Testament referred solely to John's baptism (Mark i.5 par. Matt.). In any case, fasting, which preceded baptism from a very early period in the Church (Acts ix.9, 17 ff.; Did. 7, 4; Justin, *Apol.* I, 61), was an expression of a contrite renouncement of the past (Justin, *Apol.* I, 61) and one's readiness for God's gracious act. Later (Hippolytus, *Apostolic Tradition*, XXI, 6-11 for the first time) the confession of faith was introduced by a renunciation of Satan which was then followed by an exorcism with an annointing by oil.

---

[19] O. Cullmann, *Die ersten christlichen Glaubensbekenntnisse* ([2]1949).
[20] A. Adam, 'Apostolikum I', *RGG*[3], i, 510–513; cf. §19, n. 32.
[21] Nauck, *op. cit.* (n. 11), 162.

After the confession of faith, the baptismal candidate was immersed in the water at the invocation of Jesus' name (I Cor. i.13; Gal. iii.22; Acts viii.16; xix.5). The name of Jesus was not invoked over the water[22] nor over the person as such but over the baptismal act itself in order to make it an act of God. As early as Did. 7, 3, baptism by means of pouring water on the head was permitted,[23] and as early as A.D. 80, a trinitarian baptismal formula appeared in Matthew's Gospel (xxviii.19) and in the Didache (7, 1, 3). This formula corresponded to a triple immersion or pouring and presupposed a commensurate confession of faith. Thus baptism was the ' . . . washing of water with the word' whereby the word was the baptismal formula (Eph. v.26).

The only other gesture connected with this washing with water in the New Testament period was the laying on of hands[24] which followed immediately (Acts xix.6; cf. viii.17; ix.12–17; Heb. vi.2). Just as at the healing of the sick or at the installation into office, this gesture at baptism bestowed upon the individual as an intercessory exhortation what the act imparted. Even in Acts, which (apart from Heb. vi.2) was the only New Testament writing to mention the laying on of hands at baptism, the Spirit was clearly promised with baptism (Acts ii.38) and in spite of Acts viii.17 was not directly related to the laying on of hands. In the second century this gesture was expanded to include the sign of the cross and the anointing with oil.[25] The anointing with oil, which had only been mentioned in the New Testament with reference to healings of the sick (Mark vi.13; James v.14), was a detraction from the actual baptismal event. It was not long before the concept that the anointing imparted the Spirit in a magical way came to accompany the act. It is a mistaken ritualistic interpretation of I John v.7 which considers the series 'Spirit, water, blood' to reflect baptism and the eucharist preceded by an anointing with oil imparting the Spirit, as in the later Syrian liturgy (rather than after the baptismal act as in the rest of the Church).[26]

According to Acts the promised Spirit normally, although certainly not of necessity, became effective through the baptismal act and gave expression of it through an ecstatic praise (Acts x.46; xix.6). It is, therefore, possible that the baptismal ceremony concluded with hymns as in

---

[22] The later *epiklese* which summoned the Spirit to be united with the water (*Apostolic Tradition*, xxi, 1, 2; *Const. Ap.* 7 : 34–45; Tertullian, *De Bapt.* 4) contradicts the nature of the Spirit; cf. L. Goppelt, *TWNT*, viii, 333.

[23] This and other instructions in the Didache with reference to the water are related to the rules of proselyte baptism; cf. L. Goppelt, *TWNT*, viii, 332.

[24] J. Behm, *Die Handauflegung im Urchristentum* (1911); J. Coppens, *L'imposition des mains et les rites connexes dans le N.T.* (1925); N. Adler, *Taufe und Handauflegung* (1951).

[25] *Apostolic Tradition*, xii, 1–4; Tertullian, *De Bapt.*, 7 f., cf. Nauck, *op. cit.* (n. 11), 153 ff.

[26] Nauck, *ibid.*, 152.

Eph. i.3–12a; ii.4–7, 10; Tit. iii.3–7; I Pet. i.3–12.[27] These hymns do not, however, describe personal baptismal experiences but bear witness *kerygmatically* to the fulfillment of the promise of baptism. The hypothesis that a baptismal address stood behind I Pet. i.3–4, 11[28] or that even the entire Epistle of I Peter reflected the liturgy of a baptismal service is based,[29] apart from a few minor points, on a misunderstanding of the Epistle's content.[30]

More important than the effects of such baptismal liturgy on the New Testament writings, the detailed confirmation of which always remains uncertain, is the way in which the baptism was inseparably combined with the preaching. The sermon had the function not of preparing the actual mediation of salvation through the sacrament and then bearing witness to it as *paraenesis*,[31] but of making the mediation of salvation in the sacrament possible *kerygmatically* through the promise pertaining to the sacrament (Acts ii.38) and through the *paraenesis* whose basis is the sacrament (Rom. vi.1 ff.), since the sermon conveys the faith which receives the mediation of salvation through the sacrament. Consequently, baptism was preceded by the missionary sermon and the catechetical instruction as well as a corresponding word in the baptismal ceremony itself. In this sense the sacrament needs the word, not simply the word which as a baptismal formula makes the washing of water a sacrament (Eph. v.26) but the word directed at the sacrament and in terms of the sacrament. Is the converse true? Does the word also need the sacrament?

The missionary sermon did not merely point to the promise of baptism but it imparted through declaration what baptism appropriated personally, that is the Spirit (Acts x.46; Gal. iii.2). However, the sermon needs the sacrament in order to gain physical and historical form in the Church and in ethical actions. Paul always appealed to the sacraments when problems arose concerning the Church and ethics. The experience of missions today also teaches that individual believers do arise through the sermon, but the Church as a corporal, every day fellowship only comes into being through baptism. John's Gospel let the sacraments grow out of the preaching. He so formulated the word that it became evident that the word was only accepted in its entirety when it was received as a

[27] Schille, *op. cit.* (n. 12), 147 ff.; N. A. Dahl, 'Anamnesis', *Stud. Theol.* 1 (1948), 69–95, esp. 81 f.; J. Coutts, 'Ephesians i.3–14 and I Peter i.3–12', *NTS*, 3 (1957), 115–127.

[28] R. Perdelwitz, *Die Mysterienreligion und das Problem des I Petrus* (1911) taken over by H. Windisch, Die Katholischen Briefe, (*HNT*, ²1930).

[29] H. Preisker, Die katholischen Briefe (*HNT* ³1951), 157 and F. L. Cross, *I Peter, A Paschal Liturgy* (1954).

[30] Also E. G. Selwyn, *The First Epistle of St. Peter* (⁴1952), 32, 41.

[31] Contra H. Schlier, 'Zur kirchlichen Lehre von der Taufe', *ThLZ*, 72 (1947), 321–336.

sacrament (John iii.3 ff.; vi.51c ff.), and so the sacrament has the redemptive necessity of being an unrestricted incarnation of the word rather than an ecclesiastical institution (John iii.5; vi.53). This understanding of the relationship between word and sacrament was already fundamentally distorted in Ignatius (§21, 6d).

Immediately after the baptismal ceremony the ones newly baptized, according to Justin, *Apol.* I, 65, were allowed into the congregational assembly in order to celebrate the eucharist. This has been a fixed ordinance since Justin,[32] but it might well reach back into the apostolic period. It was certainly not documented anywhere in this early period, not even in Acts ix.18 f. and xvi.33 f. and even less in I John v.7.[33] The fact that the initiation rite gave one entrance to the communal meals in Qumran[34] is simply a material analogy.

4. The structure of the service of baptism and the eucharist in Justin led further to the central problem of the Church service, to the problem just discussed in terms of the baptism, i.e. word and sacrament. According to Justin and similarly in the consecration of the bishop in Hippolytus, *Apostolic Tradition*, XIV, the first part of the service of worship included the reading of scripture and the sermon at the conclusion of which the catechumen and penitents were dismissed.[35] This had been dropped in the service of baptism and the eucharist. Apparently, as was already evident in the theology of Ignatius, this part of the service did not have the same weight as the part concerning the sacraments. How did these two elements of the Church service originally relate to one another?

The older Protestant scholarship assumed that the two elements, word and sacrament, had originally stood side by side independent of each other in a fashion similar to the synagogue and Temple services (I Cor. xi and xiv), whereas the form found in Justin represented a combination which had only gradually worked its way into the Church.[36] In fact, as Cullmann in particular has shown, the actual service of worship was originally a celebration of a meal which combined teaching and sacrament in an inseparable manner within the framework of a regular meal. This is seen from the evidence of the Jewish sacred meal in Acts ii.42, 46; v.42 for the earliest Church in Palestine and in Acts xx.7–12; I Cor. xi.17–31 for the Pauline, Hellenistic Church. The celebration of this meal was

---

[32] *Apostolic Tradition*, xxii 5, 6; Tertullian, *De Carn. Ressur.*, 8, cf. Nauck, *Die Tradition und der Charakter des I Johannesbriefs* (1957), 153 ff.

[33] Possibly by the structure of Did. 7–9.

[34] I QS ii.25–iii.11; vi.13–23; cf. Josephus, *B.J.*, 2, 8, 7.

[35] Justin, *Apol.* 66, 1; according to the Clementine liturgy, (1) the catechumen, (2) the possessed, (3) those waiting to be baptized, and (4) the penitents were dismissed.

[36] Weizsäcker, *The Apostolic Age of the Christian Church* (as in §1, n. 8), ii, 249 ff. (Ger. 548 ff.); W. Bauer, *Der Wortgottesdienst der ältesten Christen* (1930), *passim*; *et al.*

designated initially 'the breaking of bread' (Acts ii.42, 46; xx.7) and later 'the Lord's Supper' (for the first time in I Cor. xi.20), 'eucharist' (Ignatius, *Smyr.* viii.1, *et al.*) and '*agape*' (Jude 12; II Pet. ii.13; Igantius, *Smyr.* viii.1). The question today is whether, as Cullmann holds,[37] there were apart from baptismal ceremonies only missionary services as well as this celebration of the meal, or whether preaching and prayer services also took place independent of the meal. The discussion revolves around the interpretation of several minor accounts.

If the earliest Church in Jerusalem gathered daily not only in the homes for the breaking of bread but also in the halls of the Temple for the teaching of the apostles (Acts ii.46; v.12, 42), then this was, especially since it stood in conjunction with the Temple worship (Acts iii.1), not merely a missionary effort but a specific service of worship consisting of teaching and prayer.

In all probability, the developing Church in Ephesus did not leave Paul alone with his daily missionary sermons in the lecture hall of the orator Tyrannus (Acts xix.8), but continued the situation in which Paul had previously preached in the synagogue. There is certainly no trace of a service similar to that of the synagogue to be found in the Pauline Epistles. I Corinthians addressed itself to the abuses both of the celebration of the meal (I Cor. xi.20 ff.) and of the service based on the word (I Cor. 14).

We can no longer determine with any degree of certainty whether prophesying, teaching, singing and praying (I Cor. xiv. 15 f.) took place only within the framework of the celebration of the meal, in keeping with I Cor. xi, or whether it also took place in an independent preaching and prayer service, as the presence of unbelievers might suggest (I Cor. xiv.23 f.). As these two chapters indicate, the form of the gathering was still quite flexible. The decisive factor is that we have clearly described here the elements which constituted a Church service for Paul.

According to the Didache, prophecy and teaching also appear to have lived their own particular flexible life away from the gathering for the celebration of the meal, which was fixed by liturgical rules and formulae. Moreover, Did. 4, 1 f. in particular takes for granted that gatherings for services took place daily in small groups. The word stood at the centre of these gatherings to which the catechumen was also admitted. These daily services of worship may have been related to the tradition of the daily morning and evening prayers in the synagogue.

The last of the sparse accounts is the report that Pliny made without any understanding of the matter after the Christians had been tried by the courts (*Letter to Trajan*, X, 96). According to him, the Christians gathered on a fixed day before sunrise in order to '. . . [sing] in alternate verses a hymn to Christ, as to a God, and to [bind] themselves by a solemn oath. . . .' Afterwards they separated and '. . . then [reassembled] to partake of food. . . .' These morning services were probably a baptismal ceremony rather than a preaching service.[38]

[37] *Early Christian Worship* (as in n. 1 Ger. 30 f.), 28 f.
[38] Discussion in Nauck, *op. cit.* (n. 32), 160–164.

Taken together, these sparse references suggest that as well as the celebration of the meal there were also gatherings which at times served more as missionary teaching and as edification through the word and prayer. All the same, these gatherings were considered as church services and were so in the sense of Matt. xviii.20. (This would also correspond to the previously developed apostolic understanding of the basic relationship between word and sacrament.) The service consisting of the word came to be the preparatory element to the celebration of the sacrament in Justin, as the more flexible missionary service had been taken over into the actual Church service and the original combination of teaching with the sacrament had become much looser. The first reason explains both the missionary character of the preaching service which made the break before the celebration of the meal necessary as well as its increasing resemblance to the form of the synagogue service.

5. We can reconstruct the original structure of the primitive Christian celebration of the meal (§7, 2) from its background. It takes as its points of departure both the institution in the night of Jesus' betrayal, behind which stood the table-fellowship of the earthly ministry, and the tradition of the sacred meal in Judaism represented by the Feast of the Passover[39] and the daily communal meals of the Essenes.[40] The mystery feasts and the Old Testament Temple services became influential for the first time later, particularly in the post-apostolic period.

Like the Feast of the Passover, the primitive Christian celebrations took place 'in homes' or rather 'at home' (Acts ii.46). Within the framework of the regular mealtimes they represented God's redemptive act by means of teaching (cf. the Passover *haggada*) and by means of the partaking of special food along with praise, prayer and psalms. Whereas the Passover was only celebrated annually, the Christian celebration of the meal at the beginning of the earliest Church was daily, like that of the Essenes (Acts ii.46). In the Hellenistic Church it was mainly celebrated on 'the first day of the week' (§22, 2).

In the course of this period under consideration, the relationship of the sacrament to the regular meal shifted in three stages until its weight actually broke through the framework of the meal. The first stage (on the earliest Church, see pp. 44 f.) is reflected in the liturgical formula of I Cor. xi.23 ff. which was still valid in Corinth c. A.D. 55. The cup was passed 'after supper', and so was separated from the passing of the bread at the beginning of the meal by the rest of the dinner. This phrase is missing in the words of institution in Mark c. A.D. 65, and a second stage

---

[39] J. Jeremias, *Eucharistic Words of Jesus*, 15–88 (Ger. 9–82).

[40] Josephus, *B.J.*, 2, 129–133; I QS vi.4 ff.; cf. I QSa ii.17–21; K. G. Kuhn, 'The Lord's Supper and the Communal Meal at Qumran', (as in §6, n. 19).

becomes evident. Here the sacramental bread is passed 'as they were eating' (Mark xiv.22). Apparently the sacramental eating and drinking had now been drawn together and placed at the end of the regular meal-time. We meet this order, which had already begun to set in in I Cor. xi.[41] again in the Didache. The prayers in Did. 9 and 10 referred to the regular meal. They are, in the terminology at the close of the second century, *agape*-prayers, and the liturgical formulae at the end of chap. 10 convey the transition to the celebration of the sacrament.[42] By contrast, the same formulae at the end of I Corinthians (xvi.22 f.) did not lead from the regular meal into the sacrament but from the teaching, in this case the reading of the Epistle, to the meal which was bracketed by the sacrament (cf. Acts xx.11). The third stage is found in Justin where the sacrament was completely separate from the regular meal. It is doubtful whether Did. 14 already had this third stage in view. In any case the older form continued to live in isolated cases, particularly in the celebration of the Passover, even after Justin until the end of the second century.[43]

The regular meal was not simply a traditional vehicle for the sacrament because of its origin, but an important material expression of the fact that the Church when she came together was bound into a corporal fellowship of love through her Lord. As a result, the absence of this love was a denial of the sacrament for Paul (I Cor. xi.27 ff.). The regular meal, after being separated from the sacrament, was continued under the designation *agape* (love feast) which in the ancient Church expressed the original meaning of the entire emal. This *agape*-meal was celebrated irregularly during the week, and with the eucharist on Sunday, as a communal meal. Instead of being sacramental, it had the character of service of worship.[44] In the earliest formula of an *agape* celebration (*Apostolic Traditions*, XXVI), the physical elements of the celebration were interpreted as symbolic references to the eternal, as in the prayers of the meal in Did. 9 f.[45]

When the sacrament became separate from the regular meal, as was necessary after a while (I Cor. xi), its integral relationship with teaching, which had been given to it by the Jewish tradition, was also disturbed. This becomes particularly evident in Justin. Consequently, Hellenistic and magical conceptions were able to gain more and more room.

[41] In xi.34, hardly in xi.21 (*contra TWNT*, iv, 15).

[42] This has been convincingly established most recently by A. Adam, 'Erwägungen zur Herkunft der Didache', *ZKG*, 68 (1957), 1–47, esp. 9 ff.; earlier discussion in Stählin, 'Die Geschichte des christlichen Gottesdienstes', *Leiturgia* (1954), 16, n. 43.

[43] E.g., in the *Epistula Apostolorum*.

[44] *Apostolic Tradition*, xxv ff.; Tertullian, *Apol.* 39, 16; *Constitutiones Apostolicae*, ii, 28. Lietzmann, *Messe und Herrenmahl* (³1953); 183–186, 197 f., 202, n. 1, older literature.

[45] Dependent in form to the blessing at the table in the Hellenistic synagogue (M. Dibelius, 'Die Mahlgebete der Didache', *ZNTW*, 37 (1938), 32–41.

6. Let us now consider the individual elements of the primitive Christian service of worship, following their order in Justin.

a. An element appears before the sermon in Justin (*Apol*. I, 67, 3 f.) which was missing at the original celebration of the meal. 'The memoirs of the apostles' (which were the Gospels) or 'the memoirs of the prophets' (which were the Old Testament for Justin) were read. The reading of scripture[46] did not originate in the tradition of the sacred meal since such readings were absent in the Passover and most probably in Qumran, but they did play a central role in the synagogue service.[47] The earliest reference to a reading of the 'holy scriptures' (i.e. of the Old Testament, cf. II Tim. iii.15) in the Christian service is I Tim. iv.13 (later II Clem. xix.1).[48] At the same time, as suggested by the liturgical style of Matthew's Gospel (§19, note 41), a reading of the Gospels appears to have developed in the second generation. The readings in the synagogue were continually before the Christians as a model so that they could easily supply the form for any such need that might have arisen.[49] A familiarity with the Old Testament (I Cor. x.11) necessary for the understanding of Jesus' appearance as well as knowledge about the history of Jesus were undoubtedly imparted to the Church and even to the Gentile Christians to an amazing degree (Rom. vii.1; I Clement) through catechesis, but the liturgical readings first gave central expression to the authoritative meaning of these two fundamental aspects of Christian teaching. The procurement of biblical scrolls (or rather collections of *Testamonia*) was not as difficult for the churches as it once seemed to earlier scholars. The Church soon had her own scribes at her disposal, as the exchange of Christian writings shows, and during the second century she had already developed such a technique that it is quite possible that the codex was invented in her midst. This form was much better suited for extensive use than was that of the scrolls.[50]

The reading of letters to the churches (§19, 5) or of prophetical revelations (Mark xiii.14; Rev. i.3; Hermas *Vis*. 2, 4, 3) is to be distinguished from the liturgical readings. The former took the place of the didactic or prophetic sermon. Apparently sermons were often written for reading,

---

[46] P. Glaue, *Die Vorlesung heiliger Schriften im Gottesdienste* (1907); O. Michel, *Paulus und seine Bibel* (1929).

[47] S.–B. iv, Excursus 9.

[48] See M. Dibelius, H. Conzelmann, *Die Pastoralbriefe* (HNT ³1955) *in loco* and R. Knopf, 'Die Anagnose im II Clement', *ZNTW*, 3 (1902), 266–279; not Luke iv.17!

[49] Acts xv.31; II Cor. iii.14; accordingly they took over the terminology which had seen developed there for cultic rea·ings: ἀναγιγνώσκω and ἀνάγνωσις (*TWNT*, i, 347).

[50] F. G. Kenyon, *The Text of the Greek Bible* (²1950), 18; *Books and Readers in Ancient Greece and Rome* (²1951); B. M. Metzger, *Chapters in the History of New Testament Textual Criticism* (1963).

as for example II Clement (xix.1). We have already discussed in the chapters on the mission and the offices (§12, 2; §21, 4 c,d) the content of the teaching and prophecy in the mission as well as the congregational sermon. Its form was related in many ways to the synagogue sermon.[51]

b. The redemptive work of God was made present and effective through the preaching in the reading of scripture, in teaching and in the sacrament. It brought about the congregation's confession of faith and prayer through said and sung responses. In primitive Christianity as in Judaism, confession of faith and prayer were indispensable elements of every service of worship, both personally as well as collectively. Besides the reading of scripture and the sermon, the confession of the Sch'ma and the prayer of the Eighteen Benedictions were the major components of the synagogue service, and they were also repeated daily by every devout member.[52] At the Feast of the Passover, confession and prayer rang together in the Hallel (Ps. cxiii–cxviii) which was 'sung' here as in the synagogue service, i.e. performed as a chant.[53] These elements of the service of worship had lived since ancient times in the Temple service.

In the primitive Christian service, the older confession and prayer[54] took on a new import (§19, 4c; §7, 3). The Old Testament, Jewish service also praised, for example in the Hallel, the present reign of God, but the radiance of an exultant worship of the end times enveloped the primitive Christian service in an entirely different way. It was a worship which united the redeemed community with the heavenly world that was even now honouring its Creator (Acts ii.46; Phil. ii.10 f.; Rev. v. 9–14). The Church can worship in such a fashion since the eschaton had dawned for her with Easter morning, and its 'guarantee', the Spirit, forms and conveys the confession of faith and prayer, even if she must await the bodily consummation in the midst of trials (I Pet. i.6–9).

The new confession and prayer was distinguished in content by the name of Jesus. In the Hellenistic world the Christians called themselves the ones ' . . . who everywhere call[ed] on the name of our Lord Jesus Christ . . .' (I Cor. i.2). The invocation of the Exalted One was instituted in the earliest Church of Palestine (I Cor. xvi. 22). In the Hellenistic Church the practice became even more direct and frequent, but the Exal-

[51] E.g., similar to that of Hebrews and I Clement.
[52] S.–B., iv, Excursuses 8–10.
[53] Literature: F. J. Dölger, Sol salutis: Gebet und Gesang im christlichen Altertum (²1925); S.–B., iv, 394 ff.; A. Z. Idelsohn, Jewish Music (1928); M. Jenny, 'Musik und Gottesdienst nach dem Neuen Testament', in Musik und Gottesdienst (1948), 97 ff.
[54] Literature: H. Greeven, TWNT, ii, 774–808 (older literature); G. Harder, Paulus und das Gebet (1936); J. M. Nielen, Gebet und Gottesdienst im Neuen Testament (1937); K. G. Kuhn, Achtzehngebet und Vaterunser und der Reim (1950); A. Dietzel, 'Die Gründe der Erhörungsgewissheit nach den Schriften des Neuen Testaments' (unpub. diss., Mainz, 1955).

ted One in no way came to be a sort of cult god for her. In the model prayers from the Lord's Prayer to the common prayer of I Clement lix.3–lxi.3), God was addressed in Jesus' name and in such a manner that the form of address, 'Lord', considered him as being closely related to the Exalted One. The Exalted One, however, was invoked and addressed with brief formulae: in the formula in which one's immediate love speaks to the One who has come and who is coming (Eph. vi.24; I Pet. i.8); in the prayer, 'Come, Lord Jesus' (Rev. xxii.20); in the early confession of the Hellenistic Church, 'Jesus is Lord' (I Cor. xii.3); in the salutations which conclude the letters, 'The grace of the Lord Jesus be with you' (I Cor. xvi.23); and in the doxologies (II Tim. iv.18; Rev. v.9 f., 12; I Clem. xx.12; l.7). The wealth of diversity in the primitive Christian prayers is reflected, as was the case with the preaching of the word, in the abundance of terms used to describe it.[55]

By taking up the Old Testament, Jewish liturgical tradition and developing it further, the new confession of faith and prayer produced a wealth of material fixed in form ranging from the short formulae just named to hymns with several strophes. This has been pointed out to a great degree by the form-critical analysis of the primitive Christian literature. In particular the heavenly service of worship in Revelation echoes 'psalms and hymns and spiritual songs' of the earthly worship[56] (Col. iii.16; Eph. v.19 cf. I Cor. xiv.26; Mark xiv.26 par. Matt.), even if not directly imitating the latter. Perhaps the hymns were also accompanied by the harp on earth (Rev. v.8). The poems in the primitive Christian writings of this period were written entirely in the ancient Oriental rather than Greek (metric) style.[57] Primitive Christianity remained in the stream of Old Testament, Jewish tradition for this most immediate expression of religious life. It began to take over extra-biblical tradition offered to it—also Oriental in style—for the first time in Gnosticism.

The fixed liturgical form was not considered to be any more in opposition to the freer confessions and prayers than the reading of the teaching from an epistle was to the freer teaching and prophecy, since the same Spirit spoke from both, and so one proceeded according to I Thess. v.19 ff.; 'Do not quench the Spirit . . . test everything; hold fast

---

[55] Along with προσεύχομαι and εὐχή: αἰτέω (want to have something), δέομαι, δέησις (request), δοξάζω (praise); ἐρωτάω (only in John), εὐλογέω (in keeping with the Jewish usage: blessing at the table), εὐχαριστέω (thanks), κράζω (the 'calling out' of the Spirit), παρακαλέω.

[56] E.g. Rev. iv.8, 11; v.9, 12 f.; xii.10 ff.; xix.1 f., 6; H. Shephard, *The Paschal Liturgy and the Apokalypse*, 1960.

[57] W. Bauer, *Der Wortgottesdienst der ältesten Christen* (1930), 22–29; and Kuhn, *op. cit.* (n. 54).

what is good'. As we have already seen in another context, the freer word of the Sprit began to recede behind what had been passed on as tradition in the second and third generations (Did. 10, 6). In the service, one person generally led the prayers, and the congregation appropriated them for themselves, as in the Jewish service, by a responding 'Amen' (I Cor. xiv.16).

Primitive Christianity took over the Jewish gestures[58] in prayer and applied these more from the content of the prayers than from the local tradition. The one praying stood[59] or, for purposes of supplication and worship, knelt[60] and raised his hands to heaven (I Tim. ii.8). (A folding of the hands is mentioned for the first time in Judaism by isolated, late Rabbinic passages[61] and in Christianity in the fifth century. Clasping them together was first mentioned in the ninth century.)[62] Prostration, which combines a bow with kneeling, was a silent expression of honour and not a gesture of prayer (Matt. iv.9; Rev. iv.10; xix.10; xxii.8). It is quite improbable that the Christian in prayer turned towards the East for the dawning of the day of the parousia (Luke i.78; II Pet. i.19) in this period, as the Jew in prayer turned towards the holy place in Jerusalem.[63] The Jewish hours of prayer and fasts were taken over quite early for personal prayers.

The benediction[64] went beyond the realm of intercessory prayer. In it intercession and declaration were combined and directed at specific people. Along with the benediction the curse was also taken over from the Old Testament tradition, but the benediction occurred now as a declaration of the grace which appeared in Jesus, and thus in a binitarian or trinitarian form,[65] while the curse was directed at the one who ' . . . has no love for the Lord' (I Cor. xvi.22) rather than at the transgressor of the Law.

c. In I Cor. xvi.20 ff. as well as in the Did. 10, 6, such an anathema was combined in the introduction to the celebration of the sacraments with the request for the present and future coming of the Lord. This introduction contained a fixed liturgy[66] and had already been developed very

---

[58] S.-B., ii, 259 ff.   [59] E.g., Mark xi.25; Luke xxii.46.

[60] Acts vii.60; ix.40; Eph. iii.14; Phil. ii.10.   [61] S.-B., ii, 261 f.

[62] T. Ohm, Die Gebetsgebärden der Völker und des Christentums (1948), 269 f., 273.

[63] E. Peterson, 'Die geschichtliche Bedeutung der jüdischen Gebetsrichtung', ThZ, 3 (1947), 1–15; Dölger, op. cit. (n. 54), 210–219.

[64] Literature: L. Brun, Segen und Fluch im Urchristentum (1932); F. Horst, 'Segen und Segenshandlungen in der Bibel', Ev. Theol., 7 (1947–48), 23 ff.

[65] I Cor. xvi.23; Rom. i.7; II Cor. xiii.13; the Aaronite blessing of Num. vi which was quite common in the synagogue is not apparent in the primitive Christian writings.

[66] Literature: H. Lietzmann, Die Entstehung der christlichen Liturgie nach den ältesten Quellen, Vorträge der Bibliothek Warburg, 1925–26); T. Klauser, Abendländische Liturgiegeschichte (1949); G. Bornkamm, 'Das Anathema in der urchristlichen Abendmahls-

early in the Church. In it we hear all of the essential elements of the worship service.

I Cor.:	Did.:
If any one has no love for the Lord,	If any man be holy, let him come
Let him be accursed	If any man be not, let him repent
Maran-atha!	*Maran-atha!*

This liturgical warning was, so to speak, the last barrier intended to restrain the 'unworthy' from eating and drinking to their judgment. Initially, those not baptized were excluded from the meal. This ordinance, established since Did. 9, 5, corresponded in substance to what Paul had said about the relationship of the Lord's Supper to the baptism and to the Church (I Cor. x.1–5, 17), so it is quite probable that this had been the practice from the very beginning. Further, even in I Cor. v.11 the congregation was not 'to eat together' with unrepentant, public sinners and false teachers (§20, 2 f.), and so the penitents later came to be dismissed with those not baptized at the close of the catechumen service (§22, note 35). However, all who were not included in the church discipline were summoned finally by this liturgical warning to examine themselves (I Cor. xi.28). Everyone was questioned in the end about his faith which accepts God's gift (II Cor. xiii.5) and which shows itself to one's brother as forgiving love (I Cor. xi.20 ff., 27 ff.). The Didache (14, 2) rightly exhorted the hostile church members to reconcile themselves prior to the eucharist. An expression of this mutual forgiving of one another and of the fellowship of love was the 'holy kiss of love', which was already mentioned in 1 Cor. xvi.20 (cf. Rom. xvi.16; II Cor. xiii.12; I Thess. v.26; I Pet. v.14) in the liturgy of the eucharist and preserved in the liturgies of the ancient Church.[67] It is possible that here and there in the primitive Christian period, the general confession of sin mentioned in Did. 14, 4 and 14, 1 followed the exhortation to self-examination and came just prior to the brotherly kiss.

The threefold 'preface' which in Hippolytus' *Apos. Trad.* IV, 3 makes the transition from this preparation to the sacramental meal itself might well contain early material:

The Lord be with you	And with thy spirit
Lift up your hearts	We have them with the Lord
Let us give thanks unto the Lord	(It is) meet and right

---

liturgie', in *Gesammelte Aufsätze* (1952), i, 123 ff.; J. Beckmann, *Quellen zur Geschichte des christlichen Gottesdienstes* (1956).

[67] K. M. Hofmann, *Philema hagion* (1938).

The first part of this corresponds to the benediction, which in I Cor. xvi.23 followed the teaching (reading of this Epistle), the brotherly kiss and the warning. The third part corresponds to the summons which introduced the Jewish prayer of thanksgiving for the cup of blessing,[68] and the second, which is probably echoed in Hermas, *Vis.* 3, 10, 9, possibly replaced the *Maran-atha* which has been absent since Hippolytus.[69]

The decisive element, however, was the 'blessing of the elements'. The earliest interpretation of Jesus' institution in I Cor. x.16 referred to this specifically. According to the terminology which developed from the Jewish usage, the 'blessing' of the cup and the 'breaking of the bread' took place in that praise and thanks were given for the cup and bread as the gift which the Lord offers in keeping with his institution. The elements were 'made holy' through this giving of thanks, just as was the daily food by means of saying grace at the table (I Tim. iv.4 cf I Cor. x.30), i.e. it was taken from the area of the profane and *in usu* made into the conveyer of that which the institution promised. The cup which was blessed is 'the fellowship [participation] in the blood of Christ', when it is drunk. This thanksgiving containing both confessional and *kerygmatic* character is the apostolic form of the 'consecration'; later in the East it was the *epiklesis*, in the West the quoting of the *verba testamenti* which became the 'consecration'.

The earliest formula offers an actual prayer of thanksgiving at this point for the redemption through Christ. This prayer then led directly into the words of institution (*Apostolic Tradition*, IV, 4 ff.). Since the New Testament already had similar summaries of the redemptive event (*e.g.* Phil. ii.5–11; I Tim. iii.16; I Pet. iii.18–22) it is probable that even in the apostolic period thanks was given for the bread and cup along with such a summary followed by the quotation of the words of institution which are indeed present in the New Testament as liturgical tradition.[70]

In Hippolytus' *Apos. Trad.* IV, ii, three elements were added for the first time to this giving of thanks and they appear quite frequently from then on. These were: (1) the *anamnesis*, (2) the offertory prayer, and (3) the *epiklesis*

(1) 'Doing therefore the *anamnesis* of his death and resurrection
(2) We offer to Thee the bread and the cup making eucharist to Thee because Thou hast bidden us to stand before Thee and minister as priests to Thee.
(3) And we pray Thee that Thou wouldst send Thy Holy Spirit upon the offering of Thy holy Church. . . .'

---

[68] Lietzmann, *Messe und Herrenmahl* ([3]1955), 230; Jeremias, *Eucharistic Words of Jesus*, 228 f., (Ger. 109 f.).
[69] F. J. Dölger, *Sol salutis: Gebet und Gesang im christlichen Altertum* ([2]1925), 198–210.
[70] Lietzmann, *op. cit.* (n. 68), 179 f.; *ZNTW*, 22 (1923), 265 ff.; N. A. Dahl, 'Anamnesis', *Stud. Theol.* 1 (1948), 81 f.

Contrary to Lietzmann',[71] these three elements were not indicated in I Cor. x. Instead, the eucharistic *epiklesis* as at the baptism corresponds to a Hellenistic personification of the Spirit, but in its earlier forms, the concept of the offering'[72] being a speculative extension, detracts from the actual import of the celebration and its final form runs into contradiction with the apostolic Gospel. Initially the prayers accompanying the eucharist (Did. 14, 1–3: here for the first time as fulfillment of Mal. i.11; I Clem. xliv.4; and in part Justin, *Dial.* 41, 3; 117, 1) were considered as the offering. Later it was the gifts of nature, the bread and wine, which were offered on the altar (Irenaeus, *Haer.* 4, 17, 5; 18, 4) and finally the sacrament itself as counterpart to the sacrifice of Christ (Cyprian, *Epistles,* 63; Origen, *Dom.* 4, 31). Since Early Catholicism no longer understood the appearance of Jesus as the actual eschatological fulfillment of the Old Testament, the concepts of the offering forced their way in mainly from the Old Testament under the influence of the surroundings. According to the apostolic Gospel, the sacrifice of Christ as a totally unique, eschatological event, and thus effective for the entire eschaton (Heb. x.11–14), can only be a current event through its work and not through repetition. It does not take place through a person looking back in reminiscence, a secondary viewpoint which the *anamnesis* sets forth, but in keeping with the original meaning of the command to repeat the ceremony (I Cor. xi.24 par. Luke), it takes place through the performing of what Jesus had instituted. This is the way Paul interpreted this command in I Cor. xi.26. 'The Lord's death' is proclaimed, i.e. becomes effective in a current sense, 'until he comes' by means of the whole sacrament and not merely by means of the words spoken during it.[73]

The distribution which followed the prayer of thanksgiving was probably accompanied by a formula. The oldest formulae that we have from tradition are already conditioned by the early catholic misunderstanding, as though a heavenly food were served here for the nourishment of individual souls.[74] The original formulae could well have corresponded to the words which accompanied the distribution of the bread and cup in the words of institution. These words in Matthew (xxvi.26 f.) were developed more strongly as a command than in Mark and I Cor. xi:

[71] Lietzmann, *op. cit.* (n. 68), 180 f. 226 f.

[72] *Ibid.,* 82 ff.; W. Hahn, *Gottesdienst und Opfer Christi* (1951).

[73] So *TWNT,* i, 70, cf. G. Bornkamm, *ZThK,* 53 (1956), 333. On the whole: Dahl, *op. cit.* (n. 70).

[74] *Apostolic Tradition,* xxiii, 5, 11: 'Heavenly bread in Christ Jesus!' and the recipient responds, 'Amen'. The three cups of water, milk and wine were offered with the formula: 'In God, the almighty Father—the recipient: 'Amen'—and 'the Lord Jesus Christ and the Holy Spirit and the Holy Church!' and he responds: 'Amen'. *Constitutiones Apostolicae,* viii, 13: 'Body of Christ!' 'Amen!' 'Blood of Christ, cup of life!' 'Amen!'

'Take, eat . . .', 'Drink of it, all of you', and followed directly after the 'giving of thanks' in the celebration at the table.[75] Their plural form corresponds to the meaning of the meal as constituting the Church (I Cor. x.17). Perhaps the remark, 'as often as you drink [the cup[. . .' in I Cor. xi.25 means that the sacramental meal was celebrated at times without the cup.[76] This absence of the cup, probably for technical reasons, had nothing to do with the participation *sub una* which withdrew the cup from the Church.

In the period extending from the institution of the meal in the circle of the Twelve, who were the forerunners of the new People of God, through the daily gatherings of the primitive Church for the breaking of bread and the coming together of the Pauline Church for the Lord's Supper (I Cor. x.17), up to and including the days of the Didache at the close of the apostolic age, the gathering around the 'table of the Lord' (I Cor. x.21) was always the most immediate representation and actualization of the *ecclesia* in history. The meaning of the meal went through some modifications in this period (cf. §7, 2), but there were never two separate guide lines nor did any break appear which changed its essential character. By contrast, during the third generation, a definite change in the understanding of this meal becomes apparent. In Ignatius, so it would seem, the Lord's Supper no longer made real the redeemed community, but instead, the Church gathered around the bishop to celebrate the Lord's Supper was an institution of salvation in which, in a fashion similar to the mysteries, the individual received participation in salvation through the meal. So finally the guide lines appear again which characterized the history of the Apostolic Age and which ushered in a new period in the third generation.

[75] Cf. The Gospel according to the Hebrews (Hennecke ³i, 165; Ger. ³I, 108): ". . . the Lord said: 'Bring a table and bread'. And . . . he took the bread, blessed it and broke it and gave it to James the Just and said to him, "My brother, eat thy bread. . . ." '

[76] *TWNT*, vi, 115, lines 15–20.

CHRONOLOGICAL AND GEOGRAPHICAL SYNOPSIS

1. CHRONOLOGY

THE history of primitive Christianity is related to the following datable events of general history. We can, therefore, determine from these a more or less accurate chronological sequence of events.

1. The death of Herod Agrippa I (Acts xii.): spring of A.D. 44.
2. The famine in Palestine (Acts xi. 28): A.D. 46–48.
3. The expulsion of the Jews from Rome by Claudius (Acts xviii. 1 f.): A.D. 49.
4. Gallio, Proconsul of Achaia (Acts xviii. 12): spring of 52–53 or, more probable, A.D. 51–52.

From this date we can determine the following chronology with reference to Paul.

Prior to it:

> Arrival in Corinth: A.D. 49/50.
> Apostolic Council: A.D. 48.
> First visit to Jerusalem (Gal. ii. 1): A.D. 353/7.
> Conversion (Gal. i. 18): A.D. 33/35.
> (Jesus' death: A.D. 30/33).

Subsequent to it:

> 2½ years in Ephesus (Acts xviii. 21 f.): A.D. 52/53–54/55.
> Journey to Jerusalem with the collection: spring of A.D. 55/56.
> Two-year imprisonment in Caesarea (Acts xxiv, xxvii?): A.D. 55/56–57/58.
> Two-year imprisonment in Rome (Acts xxviii. 30): A.D. 57/58–59/60.

5. Change in governors, Felix Festus (Acts xxiv. 27): A.D. 55/60.
6. Neronic persecution: summer of A.D. 64.
7. The Jewish War against Rome: A.D. 66–73.
   Destruction of Jerusalem (Matt. xxii. 7; Luke xix. 43 f.): A.D. 70.
8. Wave of persecution towards the end of Domitian's rule (I Clem. i; Rev.): A.D. 93–96.
9. The exchange of letters by Pliny and the Edict of Trajan: A.D. 111/113.
10. The insurrection of the Jewish Diaspora: A.D. 116/117.
11. The Bar-Kokba Insurrection: 132–135.

2. CHRONOLOGICAL-GEOGRAPHICAL TABLE

The following synopsis is an attempt to place the most decisive occurrences of primitive Christianity in chronological-geographical order: expansion and important events, the literature of the New Testament (capital letters), the literature of the Apostolic Fathers (in italics), the literature and representatives of Gnosticism (broken line) and legalistic Judaism (with stars). The arrows indicate the origin and goal of the literature and also the exchange between the various areas of the Church.

EMPEROR	ROME (ITALY)	GREECE	ASIA MINOR	PRIMITIVE CHRISTIANITY IN: SYRIA	PALESTINE	EGYPT
Augustus 29BC—AD14						?
Tiberius 14–37						
Caligula 37–41				Damascus Paul's conversion 33/35 Antioch (Syria)	Jesus' death 30/(33). Jerus. (Judea) and Galilee Stephen's persecution Samaria (*Simon*)	
Claudius 41–54	Rome		Cilicia Southern Galatia ("1st Miss. journey")	Apostolic Council 48	James' (Zeb.) death 44 — Apostolic Council 48	
	So. Italy — ROMANS ←	Corinth (Achaia) — Macedonia — PAULINE EPISTLES	Ephesus (Asia) ("2nd Miss. journey")			
Nero 54–68	Paul's death Neronic persecution Peter's death.		Pontus Bithynia Cappadocia → I PETER	JAMES? →		
Burning of Rome July 64 Destruction of Jerus 70	MARK				James' death Flight to Pella 66	?

20
30
40
50
60
70

224

Year	Emperor							
	Vespasian 69—79							
	Titus 79—81	LUKE and ACTS	PASTORALS	MATTHEW →				
80								
	Domitian 81—96	HEBREWS ◄	John of Eph. and other Pal. disciples	JUDE ? →				Gospels of Heb.* Egypt.* Basilides
90								
	Nerva 96—98	I Clem. (96)	REVELATION. JOHN'S EPISTLES. JOHN	Menander Didache	Symeon's Death			
100								
	Trajan 98—117		Cerinth	Ignatius II PETER ??				
110		Ign. Rom.	Ignatius' Epistle Polycarp o Smyrna Papias o Hierapolis	Satornil	Book of Elchasa*			
	Pliny's Letters 111—113	Hermas	Phil.					
120								
	Hadrian 117—138	II Clem.					Barnabas' Epistle	
130		Valentinus Marcion			Gospel of Nazraean* and Ebionites* Keryg. Petr. ca. 60			Valentinus
	Bar Kokba Insurrection 132—135							
140								

BIBLIOGRAPHY

The following titles are frequently cited in an abbreviated form in the text and footnotes:

Baur, F. C., *Das Christentum und die christliche Kirche der ersten Jahrhunderte*, 1853, ³1863.

Bultmann, R., *Theology of the New Testament*, Eng. trans., 1951, of *Theologie des Neuen Testaments*, 1953, ³1959.

v. Campenhausen, H., *Kirchliches Amt und geistliche Vollmacht in den ersten drei Jahrhunderten*, 1953 (now in Eng. trans., 1969, *Ecclesiastical Authority and Spiritual Power in the Church of the firit three Centuries*).

Dibelius, M., *Aufsätze zur Apostelgeschichte*, 1951. Cf. Eng. trans., 1956, *Studies in the Acts of the Apostles*.

Foakes-Jackson, F. J., and K. Lake, *The Beginnings of Christianity: the Acts of the Apostles*, vols. I–IV, 1920–33.

Goppelt, L., *Jesus, Paul and Judaism*, Eng. trans., 1964, of *Christentum und Judentum im ersten und zweiten Jahrhundert*, 1954.

Haenchen, E., *Die Apostelgeschichte* (Meyer Kommentar, ¹⁰1956), ¹⁴1965.

v. Harnack, A., *History of Dogma*, Eng. trans., (rep. 1961), of *Lehrbuch der Dogmengeschichte*, ⁴1909.

v. Harnack, A., *The Mission and Expansion of Christianity in the First Three Centuries*, Eng. trans., 1908, of *Die Mission und Ausbreitung des Christentums in den ersten drei Jahrhunderten*, ⁴1924.

Jeremias, J., *Eucharistic Words of Jesus*, Eng. trans., ²1966, of *Die Abendmahlsworte Jesu*, ³1960.

Kümmel, W. G., *Kirchenbegriff und Geschichtsbewusstsein in der Urgemeinde und bei Jesus*, 1943.

Lietzmann, H., *The History of the Early Church: The Beginnings of the Christian Church*, vol. I, Eng. trans., 1963, of *Geschichte der alten Kirche*, vol. I, 1932.

Schweizer, E., *Erniedrigung und Erhöhung bei Jesus und seinen Nachfolgern*, 1955, ²1962. Cf. the revised and changed text in *Lordship and Discipleship*, 1960.

Weiss, J., *Earliest Christianity (A.D. 30–150)*, Eng. trans., 1937, of *Das Urchristentum*, 1917.

INDEX OF BIBLICAL REFERENCES

INDEX OF BIBLICAL REFERENCES